HAYEK, CO-ORDINATION AND EVOLUTION

'Many of the institutions on which human achievements rest have arisen and are functioning without a designing and directing mind . . . the spontaneous collaboration of free men often creates things which are greater than their individual minds can ever fully comprehend'.

(From the Preface to *Individualism and Economic Order*)

Recent years have witnessed a remarkable revival in Hayek's reputation as an economist, a political philosopher, and an intellectual historian. *Hayek, Co-ordination and Evolution* shows why this revival has taken place by demonstrating the continuing relevance and vitality of Hayek's ideas. A group of internationally known scholars critically assess his contribution to economics, political philosophy, legal theory, philosophy of science, cognitive psychology and the history of ideas.

Dealing with the development of Hayek's work chronologically, it begins with Hayek's economics, which is analytically the most rigorous of his career. The extension of Hayek's ideas into social and political philosophy produced the works for which he is most widely known, *The Road to Serfdom* and *The Constitution of Liberty*. However, this period is also notable for his work in cognitive psychology, legal philosophy and the philosophy of science. It was here that the evolutionary nature of his later work first became apparent.

Despite this apparently diverse subject matter the book reveals a fundamental unity in Hayek's thought. Its central and recurrent theme is the interrelated concern with the role of knowledge in society, the notion of spontaneous order and the problem of complexity.

Jack Birner is Associate Professor in the Department of Economics at the University of Maastricht. He teaches economics, the history of economics and philosophy of science. He has specialized in business cycle theory, the theory of economic policy and the theory of social amplifiers. **Rudy van Zijp** is a post-doctoral researcher in the Department of Economics and Econometrics at the Free University Amsterdam. His research interests include rational choice theory, business cycle theory and the theory of social evolution.

HAYEK, CO-ORDINATION AND EVOLUTION

His legacy in philosophy, politics, economics and the history of ideas

Edited by
Jack Birner and Rudy van Zijp

ROUTLEDGE
London and New York

First published in 1994
by Routledge
11 New Fetter Lane, London EC4P 4EE

Simultaneously published in the USA and Canada
by Routledge
29 West 35th Street, New York, NY 10001

Phototypeset in 10pt Garamond by Mews Photosetting, Beckenham, Kent
Printed and bound in Great Britain by
Mackays of Chatham PLC, Chatham, Kent

British Library Cataloguing in Publication Data

A catalogue record for this book is available from the British Library.

Library of Congress Cataloging in Publication Data
Hayek, co-ordination and evolution: his legacy in philosophy, politics, economics and the history of ideas / [edited by] Jack Birner and Rudy van Zijp.
p. cm.
Includes bibliographical references and index.
ISBN 0-415-09397-X
1. Hayek, Friedrich A. von (Friedrich August), 1899-
I. Birner, Jack, 1951- . II. Zijp, Rudy van, 1961-
HB101.H39H386 1993
330.1-dc20 93-10753
CIP

ISBN 0-415-09397-X

CONTENTS

Part II Incentives and the stability of spontaneous order

Part III Law and social order

Part IV Mind, knowledge and science

CONTRIBUTORS

Norman P. Barry, University of Buckingham.

Marina Bianchi, Dipartimento di Economia Pubblica, University of Rome "La Sapienza".

Jack Birner, Department of Economics, University of Limburg.

Meghnad Desai, Department of Economics, London School of Economics.

Frank van Dun, Faculty of Law, University of Limburg.

Harry Garretsen, Department of Economics, University of Groningen.

Roger W. Garrison, Department of Economics, Auburn University.

Willem Keizer, Department of Economics and Econometrics, Free University Amsterdam.

Inez Kotterman-van de Vosse, Department of Law, University of Leiden.

Karl Milford, Institut für Wirtschaftswissenschaften, University of Vienna.

D.P. O'Brien, Department of Economics, University of Durham.

Gerald P. O'Driscoll Jr, Research Department, Federal Reserve Bank of Dallas.

Raymond Plant, Department of Politics, University of Southampton.

Nikolas H.M. Roos, Faculty of Law, University of Limburg.

Peter Rosner, Institut für Wirtschaftswissenschaften, University of Vienna.

CONTRIBUTORS

Jeremy Shearmur, Department of Political Science, Australian National University

Hans Visser, Department of Economics and Econometrics, Free University Amsterdam.

Robert P. de Vries, Department of Health Sciences, University of Limburg.

Ulrich Witt, Department of Economics, University of Freiburg.

Rudy van Zijp, Department of Economics and Econometrics, Free University Amsterdam.

PREFACE

The initiative for this volume arose a few days after the death of Friedrich August Hayek on 23 March 1992. The original plan was to invite a number of scholars to Maastricht for a commemorative conference on what would have been Hayek's ninety-third birthday, on 8 May. But as was to be expected with the overfilled agendas of modern academe, a major conference was out of the question at such short notice, so it had to be kept very modest. Nevertheless, almost all who were approached but could not attend did not hesitate in promising a contribution to the present commemorative volume. We say almost all, because there was an exception the anecdote of which we will not withhold from you.

When we phoned Meghnad Desai at the LSE he replied that he was feeling far too depressed, let alone that he was inclined to think about Hayek. It took us a little while to realize that this was the day after the British elections, which were lost by Labour. However, Lord Desai, who is a Member of the House of Lords for Labour, told us to call back in ten days' time, and when we did he promptly promised to contribute an article. For many years, Desai has been unique in that he combined a left-progressive political preference with an active interest in Hayek's work. This independence of mind, all too rare, especially among economists, requires intellectual courage. One of us vividly remembers the difficulties he had when submitting a proposal for an MA thesis on Hayek's economics in the Netherlands at the end of the 1970s. It took quite some effort and persistence to get the subject accepted – grudgingly, because the only thing academics 'knew' about Hayek was that he was a reactionary.

Fortunately, this is no longer the case. Scholars in many different fields and of all political persuasions have rediscovered the work of the man who is, among many other things, one of the greatest philosophers of classical liberalism. This collection reflects that change in intellectual atmosphere. Apart from surprisingly including contributions from two Labour peers (Lord Plant being the other Labour

Member of the House of Lords), the contributions themselves are critical and creative rather than hagiographic ruminations. It also struck us how little effort it took to find authors covering almost all the aspects of Hayek's work, which ranges from business cycle theory, capital theory and monetary theory to cognitive psychology, the philosophy of social science, social and political philosophy, the philosophy of law, economic history, biography and the history of ideas. The result is a rather well-balanced volume, and the short time of about six months in which it was completed proves that nowadays there are many more intellectuals actively studying Hayek's work than the few noted Hayek scholars of long standing such as Meghnad Desai, Gerald O'Driscoll and Norman Barry.

Jack Birner, University of Limburg
Rudy van Zijp, Free University Amsterdam

INTRODUCTION

Hayek's grand research programme

Jack Birner

HAYEK'S TRAGEDY

Until recently, F.A. Hayek was very much an intellectual outcast. This position has its roots in his own independent attitude. Throughout his career, Hayek never chose the problems that were readily solvable, but rather the important and interesting problems. That meant that he had to tread beyond the boundaries of the state of contemporary research, and often Hayek had to construct his own instruments single-handedly. The prime example is his intertemporal general equilibrium theory. Though he built upon the foundations laid by Walras, Pareto and Böhm-Bawerk, he was the first to construct such a theory (in 1927 and 1928). Not as a sterile intellectual exercise, but as a theoretical instrument for explaining the dynamic disequilibrium phenomenon known as the business cycle. It was not until twenty-five years later, when the relevant mathematics had been sufficiently developed, that Arrow and Debreu started working on intertemporal general equilibrium models – without similar ulterior motives. These two authors, who were awarded the Nobel Prize for their work in this field, did not make use of Hayek's earlier work.

Thus it went time and again. De Vries shows in this volume that when Hayek developed his theory of cognitive psychology he took on the problems that, given the state of psychology, were virtually impossible to solve. It was the same with Hayek's theory of capital. By the time he had systematized the capital theory that underlies his theory of the business cycle, Keynes had become the dominant intellectual fashion for economists and Hayek's economics was rapidly sliding into almost complete oblivion (and capital theory disappeared from the agenda for at least a decade). The irony of this was that Hayek's main criticism of Keynes's work – namely that it lacked a theory of the long run (i.e. an analysis of the effects of changes in the capital structure of an economy) – was put forward independently by Joan Robinson, who clearly belonged to the Keynesian camp. Perhaps it came as a consolation to Hayek that her work, despite her being a left-wing Keynesian, did not gather a following either. When the economics profession discovered the need for a theory of growth, and still later came to consider business cycles as disequilibrium growth phenomena, no one remembered Hayek. No one, that is, except Robert Lucas, who says his New Classical Economics builds on Hayek's work of the 1930s. But this claim has to be taken with many critical *granibus salis*, as the chapters by van Zijp and Visser (Ch. 3) and Garretsen (Ch. 4) show convincingly.

So Hayek sailed a stable intellectual course throughout his life, unaffected by the changing tides of fads and fashions. After an initially comet-like ascendancy to the status of professor at the LSE, he was forgotten for a long time. When finally, in 1974, official recognition came when he was awarded the Nobel Prize for Economics, he told the baffled audience in his acceptance address that economics was not the sort of subject that deserved a Nobel Prize because this would lend credibility to a profession that had very few stable and reliable results to show for it. To this very day, Hayek's economics is almost completely unknown to his fellow-economists, and Hayek the economist remains a lone ranger. His social philosophy has fared only slightly better. Thus, most of Hayek's career is surrounded by a sense of tragedy. Personal tragedy in that he rarely found the recognition he deserves given the astounding width and depth of his thought which was so often so far ahead of developments in areas which he sometimes entered as a self-professed amateur.[1] There was tragedy, too, for those fields of intellectual endeavour that, usually out of ignorance, failed to use Hayek's insights to their advantage. What kept Hayek going despite his relative isolation was in large part the internal dynamics of his thought. With hindsight we can see that the thrust for the development of Hayek's work is provided by the evolution of the theme of co-ordination. In his later work, the evolution of co-ordination becomes an object of analysis in its own right.

HAYEK'S RESEARCH PROGRAMME IN ECONOMICS

What strikes even a casual reader of Hayek's work is that each time he starts working on a problem, he makes a systematic inventory. Hayek almost invariably gives an extensive historical account of the problem and the solutions that have been attempted to date. He analyses the strengths and weaknesses of previous theories, maps the lacunae that remain to be filled, and states the methodological constraints a prospective theory has to obey. In other words, Hayek very clearly sets himself a research agenda. This starts early in his career, with his economics. From the moment he starts publishing, he follows this pattern.[2]

What does Hayek's research programme in economics look like? In general, research programmes (RPs) are defined by problems and methodological principles. Hayek's global problem (or his original problem situation) in economics that defines the broad outlines of the programme, is how to explain the cyclical fluctuations in the level of production and employment, a dynamic disequilibrium phenomenon, in the framework of general equilibrium theory (GET). This choice reflects one of Hayek's methodological principles: the demand of *theoretical unification*. Previous attempts to explain cyclical fluctuations by means of a special theory that is unrelated to *the* basic theory of all of economics, GET (which is based on marginal value theory, which in its turn makes use of utility theory), are rejected because they violate this methodological constraint.

The global problem setting leads to two special problems. One derives from the tension that exists between the a-temporal static GET that was available on the one hand, and the time-dependent, dynamic phenomenon of the business cycle on the other. Either GET has to be adapted so as to incorporate the time element, or the business cycle has to be modelled as an a-temporal phenomenon. Hayek observes that the latter solution would deprive any resulting theory of the means to explain the inherently time-related business cycle. Therefore he chooses to incorporate time into the fundamental theory of economics. This means he has to develop an intertemporal general equilibrium theory (IGET). The way in which he goes about this is consistent with the second of his methodological principles: *methodological individualism* (MI). He develops his IGET in a consistently individualist way by taking a theory about the economic plans of individuals as his point of departure. Time is introduced with the concept of a plan, as planning involves a time horizon.

The second special problem that derives from the original problem situation involves explaining the disequilibria that characterize the business cycle. By definition, equilibrium theory does not provide these means, so the disequilibria must be attributed to an external factor. GET gives a model of a barter economy without money. Drawing on work by Wicksell and Mises, Hayek seeks the cause for disturbances of equilibrium in the monetary system of a modern economy, which is based on credit. The possibility of economic instability derives from the fact that credit loosens the rigid bond that links intertemporal relative prices in a barter economy.

IGET and credit money provide the ingredients for Hayek's theory of the business cycle. In a nutshell, it states that all disturbances, both of a monetary and a real origin, are amplified by the monetary system. This causes the system of intertemporal money prices to change in such a way that it no longer truthfully reflects relative scarcities. Because individual decision-makers react to the only prices they can perceive, namely money prices, they take the wrong decisions. The distinction between barter prices and money prices and its relation to individual decision-making reflects the third of Hayek's methodological principles, *subjectivism*. This states that what is relevant for explaining the behaviour of individuals are not the objective states of the world but the subjective perception by individuals of their environment.

An obvious objection to the use of IGET for explaining business cycles is that in the real world there hardly exist any of the futures markets that theory assumes. Hayek meets this objection in a roundabout way. A central element of his theory of fluctuations is that price changes may cause investors to change their investment behaviour and hence their productive apparatus. In the terms of the capital theory of Böhm-Bawerk, on which Hayek draws, this means that there is a change in the structure of production. Now, in equilibrium - the exact definition of which was one of the problems Hayek grappled with; see the contributions by Desai (Ch. 1) and Rosner (Ch. 2) - a particular structure of production corresponds to the way consumers distribute their income over time. Current spending goes into purchasing consumer goods, and what they do not spend now is put aside in the form of savings. The savings are lent to entrepreneurs to provide them with the means of investment in the current period. At the same time savings represent deferred consumption to the consumers. In equilibrium, the amount of savings and their distribution over time in the form of invested capital correspond exactly to the time preference of the consumers so that the amounts of consumer goods that are demanded at the various moments now and in the future are supplied by the productive apparatus at exactly the right moments. In this approach, which is typical of the Austrian School in economics, changes in the structure of production do what a full system of futures markets would do if it existed: to co-ordinate supply and demand of final goods and of means of production through time. The structure of production is a crucial element in this IGET-based business cycle theory.

When Hayek started to work out his business cycle theory, he thought Böhm-Bawerk's capital theory provided an adequate explanation of the changes in the structure of production. But he soon discovered its flaws. One was that it gave too restrictive an account of time preference, because it was based on a wrong version of utility theory. Another problem, which drew much more attention in the literature (and which re-emerged in the 1960s and 1970s)[3] was that it did not provide a satisfactory measure of the amount of capital. For one thing, Böhm-Bawerk's measure was an aggregate with the property that the same capital index might represent entirely different time structures of production. Therefore Hayek started to develop a capital theory of his own, a task which kept him occupied for most of the 1930s. This task amounted to carrying out a reductionist programme. In order to generalize the concept of time preference and construct a way of modelling the time structure of production adequately, capital theory had to be rewritten so as to be reducible to marginal value theory. This constitutes one sub-branch of Hayek's RP in economics. Its main defining problems have just been described, and the methodological principle by which it is co-determined is MI. The complexity and highly technical character of the task joined to Hayek's demand of theoretical unification led him to employ highly idealized models. These were subsequently developed systematically according to the so-called method of decreasing abstraction, and nowhere more systematically than in Hayek's capital-theoretic magnum opus, *The Pure Theory of Capital* (1941).[4] This method of ***idealization and factualization***[5] is the fourth methodological component of Hayek's RP in economics. It is in this branch of his RP that he reaches a standard of analytical rigour that is unequalled in his entire later work.[6] The ultimate goal Hayek wanted to achieve in his economic RP as a whole was the construction of a fully dynamic theory, which was to have filled a projected second volume of *The Pure Theory of Capital*. But this was never completed, and the economic programme remained unfinished.[7]

Gradually, as he was working his way towards a dynamic theory, a second sub-programme was gaining momentum, particularly after Hayek had contributed to the discussion of the feasibility of socialism halfway through the 1930s.[8] This part of Hayek's programme is defined by the problems of explaining the process of co-ordination of individual plans that brings about equilibrium and the existence and functioning of an economic order. Its defining methodological principle is subjectivism: the co-ordination of individual plans depends, *inter alia*, on the information sets of individuals. An explicit statement of this part of the programme is given in Hayek's 'Economics and Knowledge', published in 1937.[9] There he conjectures that the co-ordination problem is relevant to an understanding of all social institutions, not just markets. So he points to a generalization of the problem. At the same time he admits that he has reached the limits of what he can achieve in this sub-programme at that moment.

THE TRANSITION

In order to understand how Hayek's later work is related to his economics, a couple of lines must be devoted to a major controversy he was involved in: the debate with Keynes. Or perhaps I should say the absence of a debate, as the only time Keynes and Hayek were engaged in a direct and public exchange of views was when Hayek published his lengthy review of Keynes's *Treatise on Money* in 1931 and 1932 in the pages of *Economica*, to which Keynes replied. The controversy did not subside, but it was fought out openly by others. Until the publication of Keynes's *General Theory*, Hayek had quite a few followers, including some who were later to become prominent Keynesians, such as Nicholas Kaldor and Abba Lerner. But in or shortly after 1936 almost the whole of the profession converted to Keynes, and Hayek started on a course of rapid oblivion. This was one of the factors that contributed to his decision to give up his chair in economic science and statistics for another, in the social and moral sciences in Chicago in 1950.

This change of environment marks a redirection of Hayek's research activities. He increasingly started devoting himself to the philosophy of science and to problems of social and political philosophy. The first major result of this is *The Road to Serfdom*, which was published in 1944. Hayek's own account as to whether his reorientation was the result of a conscious decision, or that he more or less drifted into these fields spontaneously are somewhat contradictory. In 'The Campaign Against Keynesian Inflation', he writes:

> When it proved that . . . the *General Theory* of 1936 . . . conquered most of the professional opinion, and when in the end some of the colleagues I most respected supported the wholly Keynesian Bretton Woods agreement, I largely withdrew from the debate, since to proclaim my dissent from the near-unanimous views of the orthodox phalanx would merely have deprived me of a hearing on other matters about which I was more concerned at the time.
>
> (Hayek 1978: 219)

But the preface of the 1976 edition of *Road to Serfdom* suggests a stronger internal dynamics: 'though I tried hard to get back to economics proper, I could also not free myself of the feeling that the problems on which I had so undesignedly embarked were more challenging and important than those of economic theory' (Hayek 1976a: vii). But whether or not Hayek withdrew from economic theory for strategic reasons is of less importance than the question of how his later work is related to his RP in economics. There is no space for an extensive discussion, so I will sketch some of the most important connections.

In the Preface to *Individualism and Economic Order*, Hayek states that most of the essays collected there are united by 'the same central issue' (Hayek 1949: v), though he does not tell us what the issue is. It is the explanation of social institutions as co-ordinating the actions of individuals. But perhaps it is better to speak of a set of related principles instead of one issue. These turn out to be the methodological principles of MI, the method of idealization and factualization, subjectivism and unified theorizing that defined Hayek's RP in economics. This is perhaps clearest in 'Individualism True and False' (Hayek 1949), the argument of which can be summarized as follows. The true individualism of the Scottish moral philosophers is primarily the methodological principle of MI (and only in a derivative sense the political idea of individualism). The reductionist methodological programme of explaining social institutions in terms of the general principles underlying the behaviour of individuals (which amounts to the demand for theoretical unification) involves Carl Menger's 'compositive method', which Hayek had already applied in his capital theory in the form of the method of idealization and factualization. It leads us to the discovery that

> many of the institutions on which human achievements rest have arisen and are functioning without a designing and directing mind . . . and that the spontaneous collaboration of free men often creates things which are greater than their individual minds can ever fully comprehend.
>
> (Hayek 1949: 7)

There are two intermediary steps in the argument. One involves a variant of the principle of subjectivism, which probably owes its origin to the essays that were later collected as *Counter-Revolution of Science* (1955):

> the constitutional limitation of man's knowledge and interests, the fact that he *cannot* know more that a tiny part of the whole of society and that therefore all that can enter into his motives are the immediate effects which his actions will have in the sphere he knows.
>
> (Hayek 1949: 14)

The other step is the conception of social institutions as problem-solving mechanisms. The problem they solve is one that Hayek came to address explicitly and in general terms in his philosophy of science of the late 1950s and early 1960s, namely the problem of complexity. It has struck Hayek, following the philosophers of the Scottish Enlightenment, that institutions are capable of performing tasks that are far too complex for individual human minds. In a less general form the problem of complexity is addressed already in Hayek's 'Economics and Knowledge' of 1937 and 'The Use of Knowledge in Society' of 1945, which deal with the problem of co-ordination.

All these elements together lead to an explanation of social institutions as undesigned, spontaneously grown mechanisms that by discovering and co-ordinating dispersed knowledge reduce the complexity facing individuals with limited knowledge and thus allow their actions to be co-ordinated. So Hayek's transition from his economic RP to the field of social and political philosophy is the result of the application of the same methodological principles that defined his economic RP to different problems or rather to a problem situation that arose out of a generalization of the economic problem that defined the second branch of the economic RP, the problem of co-ordination. This answers those who claim that there was a fundamental discontinuity in the development of Hayek's thought in the second half of the 1930s.[10]

HAYEK'S GRAND RESEARCH PROGRAMME

From the time Hayek stopped working on the first, micro-reductionist branch of his RP in economics and generalized the theme of the second branch, the explanation of the co-ordination of individual actions in society becomes the central problem in his social philosophy. This is intimately related to the problems posed by the limits to human knowledge in social affairs, which can be seen as a variant of subjectivism. Hayek's work on the latter problem goes hand in hand with an analysis of the consequences the limitations of knowledge on the meta-level, that is, in his philosophy of the social sciences. As far as the problem of co-ordination in social affairs is concerned, this phase in the development of his thought is documented in the publications collected in *Individualism and Economic Order*. *Counter-Revolution of Science* is its counterpart in the field of the philosophy of science.

The next phase of Hayek's development is initiated with his starting to elaborate, probably from the late 1940s, the manuscript on psychology of his student days into what was published as *The Sensory Order* (SO) in 1952. I will sketch the theory it contains in a way that can necessarily only be extremely brief, and, indeed, sketchy. There are two 'orders' in which we arrange the objects in the world: the physical order, which classifies events as similar or different according to whether they produce similar or different other external events; and the sensory order, which classifies events according to their sensory properties. Contrary to what Mach taught, there is no simple one-to-one correspondence between the elements of the two orders. Events which appear to our senses to be of the same kind may be different in the physical order, and the other way around. The relation between the sensory order of the human mind (or the 'microscosm') and the physical order of external events (or 'macrocosm') is the central problem of SO.

The human mind works through a continuous process of classification and reclassification of sense impressions and of the classifications formed from them. This process takes place in the 'neural order' of the central nervous system, which is part of the physical order. The mind is continuously involved in a process of self-organization which consists of an evolutionary process that leads to an ever more complex set of classifications. The mind functions through this process of evolution.[11]

One of the central theses of the book, and one of the great differences with other psychological theories (mainly behaviourist theories, which at the time of publication of SO ruled supreme), is that

> the sensory (or other mental) qualities are not in some manner originally attached to, or an original attribute of, the individual physiological impulses, but that the whole of these qualities is determined by the system of connexions by which the impulses can be transmitted from neuron to neuron; that it is thus the position of the individual impulses or group of impulses in the whole system of such connexions which gives it its distinct quality; that this system of connexions is acquired in the course of the development of the species and the individual by a kind of 'experience' or 'learning'; and that it reproduces therefore at every stage of its development certain relationships existing in the physical environment between the stimuli evoking the impulses.
>
> (Hayek 1952: para. 2.49)

There are no pure sense data or facts, but all facts are embedded in a complex of relations to other facts, which we may call, in the terminology of SO, a 'map', or in more common language, a theory.

> Our task is . . . to show in what sense it is possible that within parts of the macrocosm a microcosm may be formed which reproduces certain aspects of the macrocosm and through this will enable the substructure of which it forms part to behave in a manner which will assist its continued existence.
>
> (ibid.: 5.78)

A corollary of the argument of SO is that something can only classify something else if it has a degree of complexity that is greater than that which is classified. Therefore the human mind can never fully comprehend itself. This forms a definite limit to human knowledge. That we can obtain knowledge of the world at all, is due to the accidental fact that the structure of the world is 'redundant', to use Herbert Simon's term.[12] In other words, the world obeys certain recurrent patterns or general, abstract rules.

For Hayek there is a close connection between his cognitive psychology and his philosophy of science. The book is concluded with a chapter called 'Philosophical consequences'. One of the conclusions Hayek draws is that all knowledge is necessarily theoretical. As the process of the acquisition of knowledge progresses, we are increasingly led away from the immediately given sensory qualities, and the more the elements described in terms of these qualities are replaced by new elements defined in terms of consciously experienced relations, the greater becomes the part of our knowledge which is embodied in the definitions of the elements, and which is therefore necessarily true. At the same time the part of our knowledge which is subject to control by experience becomes correspondingly smaller. As Bianchi puts it in this volume, the concrete is replaced by the abstract. The progressive growth of what we might call the tautological content of our knowledge is a consequence of the continuous readjustment of the classification system of the mind to make it correspond better to the physical order. One might say that from the Kantian premise that the mind obtains knowledge by actively imposing a system of classifications on sense experience Hayek derives the Aristotelian conclusion that the final state of knowledge is a system of tautologous definitions.

Obviously, as it stands this is not consistent with the view of Hayek's philosophy of science as belonging to the tradition of Popper's critical rationalism, a position that is taken by Milford in this volume. However, the place of the last chapter of SO in Hayek's philosophy of science as a whole is far from clear, and much more research is needed. Therefore I will not be detained by this, but turn to the connections between SO and Hayek's theory of society instead. That they are related is confirmed by Hayek:

> [T]he work on it [SO] has helped me greatly to clear my mind on much that is very relevant to social theory. My conception of evolution, of a spontaneous order and of the methods and limits of our endeavours to explain complex phenomena have been formed largely in the course of the work on that book.
>
> (Hayek 1979: 199 n. 26)

There are more connections than Hayek states here, but there is no space to go into them now. I will just correct the impression that may have arisen that all of Hayek's later philosophy of science and theory of society (and perhaps even his early work; after all, the manuscript of SO dates from 1920–1) was unidirectionally influenced by his cognitive psychology. Hayek's reminiscences point to a two-way influence:

> As I was using the work I had done in my student days on theoretical psychology in forming my views on the methodology of the social science, so the working out of my earlier ideas on

> psychology with the help of what I had learnt in the social science helped me greatly in all my later scientific development.
>
> (ibid.)

The historical details of what was influenced by what, and when, will in all likelihood be impossible to trace. But if we confine ourselves to the role played by one of Hayek's central methodological principles, subjectivism, what emerges both from Hayek's work and his observations on its development, is a picture that looks roughly as follows. Hayek's early subjectivism in economics may, in part at least, have been inspired by the early manuscript on cognitive psychology, the other influences being the work of Carl Menger and Hayek's study, during his stay in the United States in the early 1920s, of the statistical methods employed by the American Federal Reserve System. These gave much weight to non-aggregate factors such as relative prices instead of statistical constructs such as the general price level. Later, the early brand of subjectivism was elaborated and transformed into the theory of SO. There it became tainted with the evolutionary nature of that theory, and through it with the holistic aspects of the theory of the mind as a self-organizing *system*. But it took a while for holism to surface in Hayek's social theory.

EVOLUTION

How did the evolutionary approach emerge in Hayek's later work? Given the fact that the working of the human mind is described in such strongly evolutionary terms in SO, it seems reasonable to assume that here lie the roots of Hayek's later evolutionary theory of social institutions (including the legal system). Evolutionary arguments can already be found in *Constitution of Liberty* of 1960, Hayek's first systematic statement of a liberal social and political philosophy. But they are far less prominent than, for instance, in *Law, Legislation and Liberty*, which was published in 1973–9. In the former book, the evolutionary approach is still consistent with MI, while in the latter this is emphatically not the case (as several of the contributors to this volume remind us). In terms of the above reconstruction, it looks as if it took a long time for the individualistic thrust of Hayek's RP in economics to lose momentum and to be superseded by the evolutionary drive that had become nested in Hayek's subjectivism. I would lose myself in too much detail if I were to speculate at this point on the role the political ideal of freedom of the individual may have played in these developments.

Hayek is not unique in abandoning MI once evolutionary arguments enter the picture. That is also the case with such formerly unbending warriors in the battle against holism as Karl Popper and John Watkins.[13] All three agree in their later work that emergent properties may arise that cannot be explained in terms of the regularities governing the behaviour of individuals, and that these emergent properties may exert a direct causal influence, which Popper and Hayek, following Campbell, call 'downward causation'.[14] It seems to me that this surrender to holism is wholly unnecessary. It is the consequence of a failure to apply the deductive–nomological model consistently to collective effects. A two-stage version of the DN-model together with a causal–genetic explanation of social institutions seems entirely adequate to explain social institutions in terms that are consistent with MI. Institutions have to be included among the initial conditions from which, together with laws describing the behaviour of individuals, collective effects are explained.[15] Bianchi, in her contribution to this volume, seems to hold a similar view as she explains the evolution of co-ordination in individualistic terms.

THE UNITY OF HAYEK'S THOUGHT

In the above reconstruction, the continuity in the whole of Hayek's programme, from its beginning in the early 1920s till his last book of 1988, is provided by the methodological principles of subjectivism (in different variations), and theoretical unification. The latter expresses itself in Hayek's later work in his attempts to merge the various elements of his thought into one coherent system. The main defining problems are the problem of co-ordination and the closely related problems of complexity and the limitations of human knowledge. The theories with which Hayek tackles these problems never reach the heights of analytical rigour that characterize his early work in economics, when he dealt with the highly technical problems of reducing capital theory to marginal value theory. But although they are seldom beyond criticism, his ideas have great suggestive power, to Hayek himself, but also to others, as is demonstrated in this volume.

Of course, the account of Hayek's work as one encompassing research programme benefits from hindsight. Despite the fact that Hayek repeatedly made programmatic statements, he often discovered only gradually that the various parts of his thought were related in particular ways.[16] But once he had recognized the patterns in his own partly spontaneously evolved thought, he consciously attempted to co-ordinate the various elements of his thought into one system. This starts with *Road to Serfdom* and *Constitution of Liberty* (1960), but it is most apparent in *Law, Legislation and Liberty* (1973, 1976, 1979) and in *Fatal Conceit* (1988). Hayek wields his system as an instrument in the defence of liberalism through a scientific criticism of socialism, which he considers to be the main alternative to liberalism. This 'negative' road is part of Hayek's attempt to make the strongest possible case for a liberal society. But the advantages of his impressive attempt to construct a consistent system of ideas are not restricted to the possibility of criticizing rival philosophies. The systematic character of Hayek's work makes that work itself eminently criticizable, as the contributions to this volume clearly illustrate. No matter how one looks upon the content of Hayek's ideas, the systematic character of his thought offers an exemplar for all who want to develop a philosophy of any type of society.

ON THIS VOLUME

The structure of the present collection of essays follows to a large extent the order of development of Hayek's thought. The first section deals with several aspects of his economics. The next section addresses the central general theme of social co-ordination. This is taken up again in the context of Hayek's philosophy of law in the third section, which is followed by two discussions of what may be broadly defined as Hayek's theory of knowledge, which comprises cognitive psychology, epistemology and the philosophy of social science. The final section consists of a recapitulation of the whole of Hayek's work from the perspective of Hayek as a historian of ideas.

THEORY AND PRACTICE OF ECONOMIC CO-ORDINATION

The section starts with four contributions analysing theoretical issues. The idea that Hayek's economics constitutes a research programme is clearly stated in the first two essays. Desai (Ch. 1) shows how Hayek struggled in his technical economics to find an analytically satisfactory solution to the problem of equilibrium. In 1937 this quest culminated in the very promising characterization of the economic co-ordination problem as a problem of the division of knowledge. But what Hayek offered, eight years later, was a vision, be it a highly suggestive one, instead of an analytical solution. The vision is that of the price system as a mechanism of communication, which is an age-old truth of economics. By reviving it Hayek defuses the revolutionary potential of the knowledge problem, to Desai's disappointment. Rosner (Ch. 2) argues that Hayek's 1937 description of economic co-ordination as a problem of dispersed knowledge put the development of a theory of information processing and its integration into business cycle theory on the research agenda. However, this research programme was never completed because Hayek lacked the (mathematical) means to model information equilibria rigorously. That had to wait till the new-classical economics (NCE) constructed its theory of the business cycle, which, because of its mathematical rigour, constitutes a scientific advance over Hayek's theory. But at the same time Rosner weakens this claim by admitting that NCE's neglect of institutional factors narrowed the research agenda. Indeed, van Zijp and Visser (Ch. 3) argue that NCE's narrowing of the agenda is the reason why it *cannot* be considered an advance. The mathematical apparatus which provides the NCE's business cycle theory with rigour involves treating agents as homogeneous. This leads to the construction of aggregate models that have no room for distribution effects, which are the crux and the strength of Hayek's business cycle theory, which, however, lacks mathematical rigour.

Garretsen (Ch. 4) takes up the implicit challenge of the preceding paper. He argues that an integration of Austrian economics and mainstream, neo-classical economics is feasible. But this is not simply a matter of mixing the various ingredients because, contrary to what is sometimes thought, NCE is not a direct descendant of Hayek's economics. It is rather a microeconomic theory which is applied to macroeconomic aggregates that stand for representative agents. The assumption of representative agents removes the problem of co-ordination which is addressed by Hayek. A Hayekian element that emerges in modern Austrian economics is the substitution of 'pattern co-ordination' for the neoclassical concept of equilibrium: a spontaneous order resulting from individuals following rules and institutions inherited from the past. This implies, *inter alia*, path-dependence of the resulting states (and hence introduces 'historical time', which replaces 'logical time').[17] The integration of this idea into mainstream economics offers a perspective for progress.

The next two contributions show that Hayek's ideas are also a source of inspiration for solutions to current practical problems. Garrison (Ch. 5) argues that Hayekian macroeconomics contains a potential that may be used to remedy a situation that is presently a cause of concern. In a capital-theoretic context Hayek worked out the time aspect of the rate of interest. Much later, the Phillips-curve discussion in the Keynesian tradition focused on the inflation-premium element of the interest rate in a labour-market context. Yet a third component of the interest rate has hardly been analysed so far, namely the risk-premium element in the context of financial markets. A major current problem in the United States is that the risks of lending money are partially concealed to the lenders. This stimulates excessive risk-taking. As a remedy Garrison proposes, in a Hayekian spirit, to make credit markets more transparent by removing two factors that have encouraged the externalization of risk during the 1980s, namely the deregulation legislation which was introduced during this period, and the practice of deficit financing by the government. O'Driscoll (Ch. 6) advances a similar Hayek-inspired proposal. He argues in favour of allowing more competition into the US monetary system. The current restrictive banking regulations fail to take account of Carl Menger's theoretical lesson that the different evolutionary histories of the different federal states would, in the absence of such regulations, have led to different monetary systems which would have been more adapted to local circumstances. This seems to be corroborated by the recent experiences with the attempt to integrate the various monetary regimes of the member countries of the EEC into one European Monetary System. This gave rise to stormy developments, that were still to take place when this contribution was written. Yet they are anticipated by the author's doubts about the feasibility of a European Central Bank.

INCENTIVES AND THE STABILITY OF SPONTANEOUS ORDERS

Hayek's criticism of the role of reason and his emphasis on tradition in social affairs does not result in anti-rationalism but in a critical rationalism which stresses the limits of reason. This is argued in Barry's critical review of Hayek's social philosophy (Ch. 7). However, the elaboration of the role of tradition and the idea of a spontaneous order in Hayek's last book, *The Fatal Conceit*, is flawed. For one thing, Hayek measures the success of a social order by the number of people it can keep alive. This end-state criterion is inconsistent with his earlier insistence on process criteria, and it weakens his criticism of evaluating social systems in terms of redistributive criteria. There are other problems with Hayek's later evolutionary theory of society, such as its reliance on the holistic concept of group selection, and the underestimation of the disruptive forces of ethnicity, which weaken Hayek's earlier scientific criticism of socialism. Barry concludes that the *Constitution of Liberty* offers a more satisfactory defence of the liberal society than *Fatal Conceit*.

Plant (Ch. 8) considers Hayek's criticism of distributive justice the most important challenge to any theory of social democracy and he goes some way in meeting it. Thus he points to the fact that outcomes of the market process, though unintended, are not completely unpredictable and hence offer room for redistributive policies. Against Hayek's argument that such policies undermine the market order he argues that a market order without the possibility of redistribution is not likely to provide the incentives that are necessary for its continued existence.

According to Witt (Ch. 9) Hayek's theory of cultural and socioeconomic evolution fails to give an account of the transfer of rules and of learning in general, and more particularly of the role of scientific knowledge in the evolution of a social order. The argument that population growth enables a social order to withstand the pressure of evolutionary selection is refuted by empirical evidence, which suggests that good medical care and nutrition have far more survival value. Hayek's idea of group selection is inconsistent with methodological individualism, and it does not answer the question what incentives it would take to make individuals adopt rules that, though conflicting with their self-interest, have survival value for the social order as a whole. The important question of the relationship between incentives and the stability of spontaneous orders is also raised by Shearmur (Ch. 10). How can codes of conduct be maintained if their function in sustaining a social order is not understood and if their application harms the self-interest of rationally calculating individuals? This is closely related to the role of values in society, which Hayek fails to explain clearly. For social orders to be stable they must pass what Shearmur calls the 'test of disaggregation': the case for markets just like the case for social justice must be capable of being 'disaggregated so as to render it compelling at the level of individual action in the various situations of our day-to-day lives'. Keizer (Ch. 11) agrees that Hayek neglects the issues of motivation and rationality. What he concentrates on instead is the issue of informational efficiency. This was already the case with his contribution to the debate on socialism. Keizer discusses extensively Hayek's subsequent criticisms of centrally planned economies. They are based on the argument that such systems are inefficient in co-ordinating individual decisions. This is complementary to Mises's argument that a socialist system lacks the private property rights which provide incentives to managers. Without incentives there will be none of the rational economic calculation that makes the system of co-ordination work.

In a brilliant chapter Bianchi (Ch. 12) uses simple game-theoretic means to answer questions concerning the motivational structure underlying the creation of rules, the stability of social orders, and the evolutionary selection process that were raised by the preceding authors. She reformulates the problem of motivation as a paradox: when interests are opposed 'private interests cannot be generalized without losses, and what can be generalized (moral codes) does not obey private motivations'. Though Hayek never explains how opposing interests can be reconciled, his theory of competition as a dynamic discovery procedure contains the elements for an explanation of both the co-ordination and the incentive effects in a way that is consistent with methodological individualism. 'Hayek's game of catallaxy not only teaches the players how to transform the enemy into friend . . ., it also provides the incentive structure to discover and reward more social ways of "defection".' This makes Hayek a true intellectual descendant of Mandeville, whom he greatly admires. Bianchi improves on Hayek's theory of social evolution by giving an explanation of learning behaviour and by showing that there is no need for holistic elements such as group selection. It is the ability to learn rather than the number of people a social order can sustain that constitutes its selective evolutionary advantage. In this way she rehabilitates Hayek's 'knowledge problem', Hayek's original solution to which was such a cause of disappointment to Desai. Because it solves problems and answers criticisms that were raised by most of the preceding authors (and some of the following as well), this essay occupies a central place in the volume.

LAW AND SOCIAL ORDER

The exposition of Hayek's evolutionary ideas on the Rechtsstaat and the rule of law by Kotterman-van de Vosse (Ch. 13) links the previous contributions to the ones that follow and sets the tone for the section on Hayek's legal and political philosophy. The theme of Hayek's opposition to legal positivism, which she introduces, is taken up by van Dun (Ch. 14). His discussion of Hayek's ideas on social order includes a long digression on the differences between Hayek's and Mises's criticisms of centrally planned economies which comes to the same conclusions as Keizer. Despite his occasional references to Kant, it is Hume's philosophy of natural law that Hayek has incorporated into his own analysis of the co-ordination problem. Hume's philosophy, which is based on the notion of property rights, manifests itself in Hayek's emphasis on rules of justice as foundations of the institutions that are the necessary conditions for an efficient market order. Without a system of entitlements markets cannot fulfil their co-ordinating task. Hayek's Humean connection as highlighted by van Dun in effect reconciles the different (and, *pace* Keizer, complementary) elements in Hayek's and Mises's criticisms of socialism. Roos (Ch. 15) undertakes to develop the Kantian perspective of Hayek's legal and social philosophy. This results in a sketch of his own making of 'law as second-order morality', which takes epistemological considerations rather than the nature of man as the foundation of morality. This original transformation of Hayekian and Kantian ideas is applied to an analysis of the legitimacy of state action.

MIND, KNOWLEDGE AND SCIENCE

In the next contribution, de Vries (Ch. 16) provides a perceptive and illuminating account of a missing link in a crucial episode in Hayek's intellectual development: what defects in Mach's thought exactly prompted him to construct his theory of cognitive psychology? Though Hayek hints at the differences between Mach's psychology and his own, he never states them explicitly and clearly. De Vries's contribution is separated from the next by what (together with the theory of capital) is the only major gap in the coverage of Hayek's work in this volume: the content of Hayek's cognitive psychology and its link with his theories of knowledge and science. This reflects the fact that to date very little work has been done on these topics, which deserve more attention than could be given them in the brief remarks in this Introduction.

The strand running through Hayek's work is taken up again by Milford (Ch. 17), who discusses Hayek's philosophy of science in *Counter-Revolution of Science*. There Hayek reveals the pernicious political consequences of epistemological relativism. His philosophy of science amounts to a hypothecism that bears clear traces of Popper's critical rationalism. Using a surprisingly fruitful classification of possible different positions *vis-à-vis* the problem of induction, Milford demarcates Hayek's epistemological position from a number of others both within and outside the tradition of the Austrian School. Hayek is the only Austrian economist to come out of the analysis as an empirically orientated deductivist.

IDEAS OF THE PAST

The volume is concluded by O'Brien's thorough review of almost the whole of Hayek's work from the perspective of Hayek as an intellectual historian (Ch. 18). Because of his modesty, the originality of Hayek's contributions has often been underrated, and O'Brien rightly observes that Hayek's scholarliness and patience have perhaps been his own worst enemies. The great importance Hayek attaches to the history of ideas is consistent with his evolutionary view of the world as a whole. He is also keenly aware of the influence that ideas from and about the past may exert, which is why he goes to great lengths to discuss them and where needed reveal them as historical myths. In his turn Hayek is taken to task by the intellectual historian O'Brien for making some historical misjudgements of his own. This concludes the article in the same spirit that characterizes all the other contributions to this volume: a critical attitude that is the most convincing evidence that after Hayek's death his system of ideas is alive, perhaps even more so than it has ever been during his lifetime.

NOTES

1 The drama surrounding Hayek's career in economics has been documented by Hicks (see Hicks 1967a).
2 Cf., for instance, Hayek (1924: in particular 367, 370 and 378–9); Hayek (1925: 17, 20 and 25); and Hayek (1927: 68–9, n. 12).
3 This so-called Cambridge controversy in capital theory would not have taken place if Hayek's capital theory had become better known, or if Joan Robinson had understood her own 1953 contribution, which started the debate, better (and if she could have mustered enough support). Cf. Birner, (forthcoming 2).
4 A fuller description of the structure of Hayek's RP in economics is given in Birner (1993). An extensive analysis is given in Birner (forthcoming 1).
5 As it may be called following the methodological analysis of Wladislaw Krajewski and Leszek Nowak. The method is analysed in great detail in Birner (forthcoming 2).
6 I agree with Desai's judgement in his contribution to this volume.
7 Cf. also the contribution to this volume by Rosner (Ch. 2).
8 Cf. the contribution to this volume by Keizer (Ch. 11).
9 Cf. the chapters by Desai (Ch. 1) and Rosner (Ch. 2) in this volume. Hayek's article is now generally considered to be at the roots of the economics of information.
10 Defenders of the discontinuity thesis include Hutchison and Caldwell. See Caldwell (1988) and Hutchison (1981: 214 ff.). For a related but slightly different argument defending the continuity of Hayek's thought, cf. Birner (1993).
11 Notice that Hayek describes a system that is currently modelled by the theory of neural networks.
12 Cf. Simon (1968).
13 Cf., for instance, Popper and Eccles (1977, Part 1, para. 7), and Watkins (1976).
14 Cf. Popper (1978: 19 ff.); Hayek (1979); and Campbell (1974).
15 See Birner (forthcoming 1), where the argument is given in detail.
16 Cf., for instance, Hayek (1941: vi–vii) and Hayek (1965: 91–2).
17 So this would answer one of Joan Robinson's major complaints against neoclassical theory. For her distinction between logical and historical time, cf. for instance Robinson (1974).

REFERENCES

Ayala, F. and T. Dobzhansky (eds) (1974) *Studies in the Philosophy of Biology, Reduction and Related Problems*, London: Macmillan.

Birner, J. (1993), 'F.A. Hayek's Research Programme in Economics', in M. Colonna, H. Hagemann and O. Hamouda (eds) *The Economics of F.A. Hayek*, London: Edward Elgar.

—— (forthcoming 1) *The Development of Hayek's Research Programme in Economics*, London: Routledge.

—— (forthcoming 2) *Strategies and Programmes in Capital Theory, A Contribution to the Methodology of Theory Development*, London: Routledge.

Caldwell, B. (1988) 'Hayek's Transformation', *History of Political Economy*, 20(4): 513–41.

Campbell, D.T. (1974) '"Downward Causation" in Hierarchically Organised Biological Systems', in F. Ayala and T. Dobzhansky (eds) *Studies in the Philosophy of Biology, Reduction and Related Problems*, London: Macmillan.

Cohen, R.S., P.K. Feyerabend and M.F. Wartofsky (eds) (1976) *Essays in Memory of Imre Lakatos*, New York: Reidel.

Colonna, M., H. Hagemann and O. Hamouda (eds) (1993) *The Economics of F.A. Hayek*, London: Edward Elgar.

Hayek, F.A. (1924) 'Das Stabilisierungsproblem in Goldwährungsländern', *Z.f. Volksw.u.Soz.pol.*, 4: 366–90.

—— (1925) 'Die Währungspolitik der Vereinigten Staaten seit der Ueberwindung der Krise von 1920', I and II, *Z.f. Volksw.u.Soz.pol*, 5, Part I: 25–63; Part II: 254–317.

—— (1927) 'Zur Problemstellung der Zinstheorie', *Arch.f.Soz.w.u.Soz.pol.*, 58: 517–32.

—— (1928) 'Das interemporale Gleichgewichtssystem der Preise und die Bewegungen des "Geldwertes"', *Weltw. Arch.* XXVII: 33–76.

—— (1931) 'Reflections on the Pure Theory of Money of Mr. J.M. Keynes I', 11(33): 271–95 and 'A Rejoinder to Mr. Keynes', *Economica*, 11(34): 399–403.

—— (1932) 'Reflections on the Pure Theory of Money of Mr J.M. Keynes (continued)', *Economica*, 12(35): 23–44.

—— (1937) 'Economics and Knowledge', in F.A. Hayek, *Individualism and Economic Order*, London: Routledge & Kegan Paul, 1949, Ch. 2.

—— (1941) *The Pure Theory of Capital*, London: Routledge & Kegan Paul.

—— (1944) *The Road to Serfdom*, Routledge & Kegan Paul 1976.

—— (1945) 'The Use of Knowledge in Society', in F.A. Hayek, *Individualism and Economic Order*, London: Routledge & Kegan Paul, 1949, Ch. 4.

—— (1949) *Individualism and Economic Order*, London: Routledge & Kegan Paul.

—— (1952) *The Sensory Order: An Inquiry into the Foundations of Theoretical Psychology*, Chicago: University of Chicago Press.

—— (1955) *The Counter-Revolution of Science: Studies on the Abuse of Reason*, Glencoe, Ill.: Free Press.

—— (1960) *The Constitution of Liberty*, London: Routledge & Kegan Paul.

—— (1965) 'Kinds of Rationalism', in F.A. Hayek, *Studies in Philosophy, Politics and Economics*, Chicago: University of Chicago Press, 1967, Ch. 5.

—— (1967) *Studies in Philosophy, Politics and Economics*, Chicago: University of Chicago Press.

—— (1973) *Law, Legislation and Liberty: Volume 1, Rules and Order*, London: Routledge & Kegan Paul.

—— (1976a) *The Road to Serfdom*, London: Routledge & Kegan Paul; first published in 1944.

—— (1976b) *Law, Legislation and Liberty: Volume II, The Mirage of Social Justice*, London: Routledge & Kegan Paul.

—— (1978) *New Studies in Philosophy, Politics, Economics and the History*

of Ideas, London: Routledge & Kegan Paul.
—— (1979) *Law, Legislation and Liberty, Volume III, The Political Order of a Free People*, London: Routledge & Kegan Paul.
—— (1988) *The Fatal Conceit: The Errors of Socialism*, London: Routledge.
Hicks, J.R. (1967a) 'The Hayek Story', in J.R. Hicks, *Critical Essays in Monetary Theory*, Oxford: Oxford University Press.
—— (1967b) *Critical Essays in Monetary Theory*, Oxford: Oxford University Press.
Hutchison, T.W. (1981) *The Politics and Philosophy of Economics*, Oxford: Blackwell.
Popper, K.R. (1977) 'Natural Selection and Its Scientific Status', *Dialectica*.
Popper, K.R. and J.C. Eccles (1977) *The Self and Its Brain*, New York: Springer.
Robinson, J. (1974) 'History versus Equilibrium', in J. Robinson, *Collected Economic Papers*, Cambridge: Cambridge University Press, 1975, vol. 5.
Simon, H.A. (1968) *The Sciences of the Artificial*, Cambridge, Mass.: MIT Press.
Watkins, J.W.N. (1976) 'The Human Condition: Two Criticisms of Hobbes', in R.S. Cohen, P.K. Feyerabend and M.F. Wartofsky, (eds) *Essays in Memory of Imre Lakatos*, New York: Reidel.

Part I

THEORY AND PRACTICE OF ECONOMIC CO-ORDINATION

1

EQUILIBRIUM, EXPECTATIONS AND KNOWLEDGE

Meghnad Desai

The article 'Economics and Knowledge', published in 1937, constitutes a fundamental break with the Walrasian concept of equilibrium in Hayek's thinking. This led him similarly to break with the notion of competition as somehow a function of the homogeneity of product and the number of producers, Marshallian/Pigovian theories of perfect competition and monopoly along with the entire paraphernalia of duopoly, oligopoly, imperfect competition, and so on. (Remarkably in this connection Hayek does not refer to Sraffa's 1926 critique of Marshall as in some senses in his view it could be said to have led economic theory down the blind alley of imperfect competition.) From here on Hayek's break with mainstream microeconomics was decisive as was his disenchantment with what had become mainstream macroeconomics. Although his publication in economics continued for another few years, it lost that intense sense of engagement with filling the gaps in 'equilibrium theory', that is, Walrasian general equilibrium theory that he had in the late 1920s and early 1930s. As always it is possible to trace the origins of this change quite far back in Hayek's own work (see, however, Caldwell 1988).

In one sense the conflict is implicit as between the very different visions of Walras and Menger. Menger's opposition to historicism and to scientism, his passionate attempt to blend an organicist theory of the development of social relations with subjective rationalism, was the result of a long history of philosophical developments in Germany as a reaction to the French Revolution (Alter 1990). Menger has not been and could not be understood outside this tradition. While he got his place in the Marginalist Trinity, he had the least impact outside German economics. (His fundamental book was not even translated till 1950 and even this has several imperfections: Alter 1990.) He is also a very different kind of economic theorist. Thus Menger has a value-price duality unlike Jevons or Walras and hence a 'transformation problem' such as Marx does. While it is not possible at this stage to deal in detail with Menger's theory, it is necessary to adumbrate a little more on the philosophical background which gives rise to the very special theorizing of Menger which Hayek adopts in his 1937 paper. Menger is not merely a subjective utility theorist. He is also in the organicist tradition of German philosophy.

The organicist tradition believes that society grows not by overt, explicit direction, not by design, but as result of a cumulation of many acts undertaken in self-interest and without consciously seeking a higher good. The origins of this idea are traced variously in the English common-law tradition, among Spanish schoolmen of the sixteenth century but more articulately in the works of the Scottish philosophers of the eighteenth century – Hume, Ferguson and Smith. But while in English philosophy these beliefs were soon challenged by Bentham and the utilitarians, they had a profound impact on German (in the broader cultural sense including Austrian) philosophy. This was due to certain peculiarities of German history.

In the late eighteenth century, Germany was a collection of scores of small and middle-sized kingdoms. Only a few of them, such as Prussia, Bavaria or Saxony, were big enough to be called kingdoms. Juristically they all owed feudal allegiance to the Habsburg Emperor in Vienna. This was the Holy Roman Empire. Despite this political fragmentation, the humanities, and especially philosophy, flourished highly in Germany, producing Immanuel Kant's celebrated work. The French Revolution was a profoundly shocking event in this world as it raised basic questions about the nature of political obedience. Philosophers such as Schelling and Hegel began their philosophical work in this climate. But worse was to follow. The Napoleonic Wars destroyed the Holy Roman Empire in 1806 and many of the small feudal nobilities, untouched by events for centuries were shattered. In the areas ruled by the French, such as the right bank of the Rhine, modernizing reforms were put through changing a status-based society into one based on contract. Prussia, which had been a leader among these small kingdoms and an example looked up to, reacted to its defeat by pushing through a set of reforms (Stein-Hardberger reforms) to make it a modern, efficient bureaucratic Absolutist state. The old order gave way violently to the modern world in a sudden attack from above and from outside. The defeat of Napoleon at Waterloo and the restoration of the balance of power in the Metternich system at the Congress of Vienna in 1815 did not halt this tide of change. Positive legislation to forcibly reconstruct the society, to make it change its older ways faster than was natural to it, was imposed on rational grounds. This sparked off a long debate on the legitimacy of such legislation, on the nature of law itself, on the feasibility of imposing change from the outside.

In this Hegel played an influential but ambiguous role since both the constructionist and the organicist could claim him on their side, but finally the organicists came to reject him as a false prophet. Savigny, who pioneered studies in the history of jurisprudence, Herder and Roscher were the predecessors whose ideas influenced Menger (though he was to break with Roscher). The idea of a spontaneous, unguided but at the same time rational development of social relations guided by subjective perceptions rather than as instructed from above is thus basic to an organicist such as Menger. This notion fits in so well with the suggestive metaphor of the Invisible Hand that it is almost uncanny. But of course this is also because Smith can be claimed by the left radicals as by the right libertarians on their side. He comes to the organicist tradition in Germany via Burke and to the left radicals via Millar and Hegel. This comes from the richness of his work. Smith has a historical vision, a 'feel' for the gradual growth of relations, motivated by personal interest. But he also saw the shattering impact capitalism could have on old societies. For our present purposes it is sufficient to see that a Mengerian vision of the economy as a self-adjusting process is natural to Hayek. This was reinforced by Mises's writings. In this respect, it is Mises more than Böhm-Bawerk who is the true follower of Menger. In his works on monetary theory and the trade cycle, the influence of Mises on Hayek is combined with that of Böhm-Bawerk and Wicksell. Menger had little to say on such problems. But in the theory of expectations and market process, the line to be traced is Menger–Mises–Hayek.

HAYEK'S ESCAPE FROM WALRASIAN EQUILIBRIUM: A STEPWISE HISTORY

Intertemporal pricing and the entrepreneur's problem

In Hayek's work the first statement of the 1937 view of equilibrium occurs in the 1928 paper on intertemporal price equilibrium. After describing the static Walrasian equilibrium in the introductory paragraph, Hayek says:

> prices also fulfil a particularly significant role with respect to the distribution of the individual processes through time, as the guide and regulator of all economic activity in the exchange economy. It is precisely this function which hitherto has received only brief mention in economics.
>
> (Hayek 1984: 71)

This is the first mention of the guide and regulator function of prices. At this stage it could be thought innocuous and in no way denoting a departure from Walrasian theory. (Later on in the same paper Hayek explicitly mentions the value–price duality and says, 'A particularly close relationship thus exists between their [i.e. goods under discussion in the context of intertemporal pricing] value and their price, but their value and price do not always have to be the same' (ibid.: 82). Hayek was always aware that much of the entrepreneur's problem has to do with an uncertain future about which he has to hold expectations. Thus in *Monetary Theory and the Trade Cycle* (MTTC) he criticizes those business cycle theories which rely on the long gestation lag and the high accelerator coefficients as explaining the occurrence of overshooting (Hayek 1929: 51–98). He points out that the entrepreneur would be aware of these lags and, as one would say in today's language, incorporate them in computing his price expectations. These price expectations are unlikely to be incorrect in Hayek's view as a result of the considerations such as length of the gestation lag:

> [w]e have to assume that the price which entrepreneurs expect to result from a change in demand or from a change in the conditions of production will more or less coincide with the equilibrium price. For the entrepreneur, from his knowledge of the conditions of production and the market, will generally be in a position to estimate the price that will rule after the changes have taken place, as distinct from the quantitative changes in the total volume of demand. One can only say, as to this prospective price of the product concerned, that it is just as likely to be lower than the equilibrium price as to be higher and that, on the average, it should more or less coincide, since there is no reason to assume that deviations will take place only in one direction.
> (ibid.: 69–70)

In these few lines, it would be quite legitimate to read a rational-expectations mechanism. On the crucial question of whether complete information is assumed in this case (a question raised in the 1937 paper) one cannot be sure. The entrepreneur is supposed to know 'the conditions of production and of the market', but this may be only partial information. But later on in the same chapter, Hayek comes closer to expressing the basic notion that became the 1937 paper:

> At one point or another, all theories which start to explain cyclical fluctuations by miscalculations or ignorance as regards the economic situation fall into the same error as those naïve explanations which base themselves on the 'planlessness' of the economic system. They overlook the fact that, in the exchange

> economy, production is governed by prices, independently of any knowledge of the whole process on the part of individual producers, so that it is only when the pricing process is itself disturbed that a misdirection of production can occur. The 'wrong' prices, on the other hand, which lead to 'wrong' dispositions, cannot in turn be explained by a mistake. Within the framework of a system of explanation in which, as in all modern economic theory, prices are merely expressions of a necessary tendency towards a state of equilibrium.
>
> (ibid.: 84–5)

Again in the quotation above, while the unplanned co-ordination via prices is mentioned, it sits snugly within a Walrasian framework. Hayek at this stage is a staunch Walrasian. He continues to be Walrasian through Prices and Production (PP). It is only after PP that a subtle questioning of the compatibility of the expectations mechanism, and of the co-ordinating function of prices with the decentralized and scattered information within a Walrasian equilibrium notion occurs. (It is difficult in this respect to know whether Sraffa's critique of PP, especially his demonstration that the flexprice Walrasian system admitted no role for money and no possibility of cycles was influential. Hayek did abandon the flexprice assumption partly, but the broader influence is hard to pin down. It may have been sufficient however for Sraffa to have shown what a straight-jacket the Walrasian system was. (For references to this debate, see Desai 1982.))

Equilibrium versus dynamics

In a lecture given in December 1933 in Copenhagen which was published in German and French during 1935, Hayek came closer to the 1937 view. Indeed, by the time this article was translated into English and published as a chapter in *Profits, Interest and Investment* (PII) in 1939, he added a footnote to the effect that he had 'further elaborated and partly revised this discussion of the relationship between equilibrium and foresight in a paper on "Economics and Knowledge", published in Economica for February 1937' (PII: 140n). This then is the first specific earlier link and hence is worth examining in some detail.

In his paper 'Price Expectations, Monetary Disturbances and Malinvestments' (1935a), Hayek comes rapidly to the problem of constructing a theory for explaining dynamic phenomena, especially cycles. Such a theory, he once thought, could be 'organically superimposed upon the existing theory of equilibrium' (Hayek 1939: 137). But he now thinks that the equilibrium theory needs to be generalized.

This means 'elaboration of particular chapters of general theory, especially of the theory of capital and the theory of money' (ibid.: 138). But this sooner or later brings one 'back to the fundamental problem of all economic theory, that is to the question of the significance of the concept of equilibrium and its relevance to the explanation of a process which takes place in time' (ibid.). But then not only 'some of the formulations of the theory of equilibrium prove to be of little use but also the idea of equilibrium as such which they use will require a certain amount of revision' (ibid.). The Walrasian notion of 'a necessary equilibrium between the decisions which a person will make at a given moment' has meaning for a Robinson Crusoe economy or a centrally planned one,

> it is much less clear in what sense we can apply the same concept to the actions of a great number of persons, whose successive responses to the actions of their fellow-beings necessarily takes place in time, and which can be represented as a timeless equilibrium relationship only by means of unrealistic special constructions.
>
> (ibid.: 139)

This, however, did not take Hayek far enough. As one senses there are two interrelated issues here – the problem of a multi-person economy with people acting independently of each other and that of the element of time and uncertainty. The multi-person problem is the problem of co-ordination and, as such, is not difficult for Walrasian theory. It is uncertainty due to the imminence of the future and incompleteness of information that are more serious. Hayek senses the former but not yet the latter. The solution at this juncture is to state correctly the conditions for a perfect foresight equilibrium:

> It has become clear that, instead of completely disregarding the time element, we must make very definite assumptions about the attitude of persons towards the future. The assumptions of this kind which are implied in the concept of equilibrium are essentially that everybody foresees the future correctly and that this foresight includes not only the changes in the objective data, but also the behaviour of all the other people with whom he expects to perform economic transactions.
>
> (ibid.: 139–40)

(It is at this juncture that Hayek appends the footnote quoted above.)

But having stated these conditions, which he was to find unrealistic later, Hayek goes on in the same vein to sketch out the expectations equilibrium.

> It is evident that the various expectations on which different individuals base their decisions at a particular moment either will or will not be mutually compatible; and that if these expectations are not compatible those of some people at least must be disappointed. It is probably clear also that expectations existing at a particular moment will to a large extent be based on prices existing at that moment and that we can conceive of constellations of such prices which will create expectations inevitably doomed to disappointment, and of other constellations which do not bear the germ of such disappointments and which create expectations which – at least if there are no unforeseen changes in external circumstances – may be in harmony with the actual course of events.
>
> (ibid.: 140–1)

Equilibrium and expectations

There is in this later quotation a clear indication that Hayek was moving towards an *ex ante* equilibrium notion based on expectations which needed to be compatible but operating all the time on the set of prices. But he also had a perfect foresight version of such an equilibrium. Soon, however, he saw the absurd demands made by the notion of perfect foresight. In 'The Maintenance of Capital' (1935b), written soon after the Copenhagen lecture, he takes up the issue of perfect foresight. (The article itself is an extremely detailed technical consideration of the notion of permanent income – Hayek uses these words – in a world with fixed capital.) In discussing 'the action of the capitalist with perfect foresight', he says 'the next task, then, is to find out how the individual owner of capital goods will behave, if he wants to keep the income he derived from his possessions constant, and if he has complete foresight of all relevant changes'. Before specifying what such complete foresight would entail, Hayek adds a footnote to the quoted statement:

> It is, of course, not assumed that the capitalist under consideration has always possessed complete foresight, since in this case the problem of adaptation of his plans to anticipated change would not arise. . . . The difficulties which any such assumption of foresight of all relevant changes involves are well known. The only way in which such foresight, not only of the real changes, but of all prices during the relevant period, is conceivable is that all these prices are actually fixed simultaneously in advance on some single market, where not only present but also all future commodities that will become available during

> the relevant period are traded. This introduces the further difficulty that to fulfil the condition it would be necessary that the periods for which people foresee are the same for all individuals, and that the changes that will happen in the more distant future are disclosed periodically and simultaneously to all people. However, it is not necessary here to go further into all the difficulties raised by this assumption, . . . difficulties which are by no means exhausted by those mentioned. Attention has been drawn to them only to make us realise how unreal the assumption of perfect foresight is even for the limited periods relevant to our problem.
>
> (Hayek 1935b: 96n)

Those who are aware of the large number of simplifying assumptions which are required to establish the existence of equilibrium in an Arrow–Debreu economy, such as simultaneous market-clearing for all commodities, including contingent ones in all possible states of nature, will see that Hayek had seen that while such difficulties as perfect foresight could be overcome (by, in fact, assuming them away), the result is a very unreal theory. (Note that Hayek calls the assumption of perfect foresight not unrealistic but unreal.)

Thus some time after the publication of PP in 1931, Hayek had begun to find the Walrasian model a straight-jacket. The full objection to that model took, however, some time to mature. It also matured in the context of thinking of business cycle theory, that is disequilibrium dynamics, rather than in thinking about allocation problems as such. Thus it is remarkable that in the two longish pieces Hayek wrote at the beginning and the end of *Collectivist Economic Planning* (1935c), there is no mention of this problem at all. In those writings, the possibility of value calculus in planning is being compared with the same problem in a Walrasian competitive system. The issue of information which arises is one of detail, not of the essence. The question of expectations and their compatibility is not even hinted at. For Hayek, the nature of competitive equilibrium is a problem under capitalism; socialism is neither here nor there.

FROM WALRASIAN EQUILIBRIUM TO THE HAYEK PROBLEM

Economics and knowledge

It is against this background that we must see 'Economics and Knowledge'. In concluding his Presidential address to the London Economic Club, Hayek spoke of 'these rather desultory remarks on topics which would deserve much more careful examination' (1937: 54). One wonders though how many of his listeners were aware of the profoundly revolutionary nature of his remarks. It would take Hayek himself along a different path in economic theory, but even there, in my view, not far enough. It was in the 1960s and later that the full impact of his remarks began to be realized. Before discussing the nature of these remarks, something should be said about contemporary thinking on this issue. The key person here is Myrdal.

As a student of Gustav Cassel, Myrdal had started exploring the question of the dynamics of Walrasian equilibrium. But in 'Monetary Equilibrium' (Myrdal, 1939) he makes very disparaging remarks about the usefulness of the Walrasian model. His remarks stand in stark contrast to Hayek's fulsome tribute to the achievements of the Lausanne School in PP and MTTC. Myrdal chose instead Wicksell's dynamic method and destroyed Wicksell's model by immanent criticism. We are indebted to Myrdal's genius for having pointed out the importance of expectations. The distinction between *ex ante* and *ex post* which we owe to him, though routinely known today, is even now not fully appreciated. Myrdal did not however go into the compatibility of expectations. The Swedish economists on the whole did however see a macroeconomic equilibrium as requiring the compatibility of *ex ante* savings with *ex ante* investments. In this respect Hayek was drawing out the full microeconomic general-equilibrium implications of the Swedish theory. Keynes at the same time was also aware of the troublesome nature of expectations. Although less given to worrying about formal theory, he had picked up a Wicksellian dynamics via Robertson but somewhat critically in *The Treatise on Money*. It was in going away from the *Treatise* to the *General Theory* that expectations began to assume a major importance for Keynes. But again he finessed the problem by assuming that short-term expectations were fulfilled, the trouble arising from volatility of long-term expectations. But in Keynes the question of mutual compatibility of expectations only arises in the short term and is assured – the aggregate demand and supply curves intersect. The volatility of long-term expectations is the question of the validation of expectations of investors by outcomes, not of the compatibility of expectations of buyers and sellers. Thus, expectations were 'in the air' in the early 1930s. Scepticism about the Walrasian model had already been expressed by the Swedish School, which unlike the English was not hostile to general equilibrium *per se*. The compatibility of expectations for macroeconomic equilibrium was part of the Swedish theory. What Hayek brought to this debate was a much deeper critique of Walrasian competitive equilibrium from the viewpoint of an expectations-based world. But he did more than criticize Walras;

he offered the prospect of a complete alternative paradigm for equilibrium theorizing.

The Walrasian general equilibrium model sets out in full detail the optimizing problem of the consumers and the producers but in doing so makes considerable demands on the information assumed to be known to all the participants. Each consumer knows his or her utility function defined on all the available commodities and the prices of all the commodities exchanged, that is, what the consumer sells as well as what she or he buys. Every producer knows his or her production function, in general all the alternative processes available for production of the commodity/service supplied, plus all the prices of inputs and outputs. These prices emerge as solutions in equilibrium but all the actors are assumed to take them as given. As long as the utility functions and production functions are 'well behaved', an equilibrium can be shown to be established simultaneously, that is, in one gigantic transaction in which all markets are cleared.

There are technical problems in this story – problems internal to the logic of the model. Thus Walras had not provided a satisfactory proof of the existence of equilibrium, nor had Cassel. There has to be some allowance for the possibility that in some markets there may be excess supply at all prices and hence the price may be zero. Thus technically in equilibrium prices can only be non-negative not strictly positive. This problem was tackled in the 1930s by Abraham Wald in a paper given at the Menger seminar in Vienna. This, however, is not Hayek's major concern. He had arrived at yet another problem with Walrasian equilibrium which was not tackled till the 1950s when Arrow and Debreu and independently MacKenzie proposed their general solution (Arrow and Debreu 1954; MacKenzie 1954; for details, see Arrow and Hahn 1971).

It was the consideration of intertemporal equilibrium that creates a different class of problems. There is a problem of multiple periods over which plans have to be made and realized, and there is the problem of uncertainty, since all periods except the present for which plans must be made are in the future. Hayek had realized that the problem of multiple periods required an equilibrium gradient (term structure) of prices even for the same commodity as between the present and the future. Later developments allow for the fact that for each date in the future several outcomes are possible, only one of which will be actually realized. Thus to the set of actual commodities one must add contingent commodities which may exist in several possible states of nature. This is because once you see (as Hayek did in his 1928 paper) that the same physical commodity today and tomorrow are two different commodities, each possible scenario for 'what tomorrow may bring' makes for an additional commodity.

Now a Walrasian equilibrium would require that the markets not only for current 'actual' commodities and for all future realizations but also for all future contingencies be cleared. Also, since false trading is not allowed by assumption, no contracts can be made for contingent commodities which could involve false trading. Thus all future markets for actual and contingent commodities also have to clear in the same instant as the current market. What is more, individuals as consumers have to know about all these possible commodities and have well defined preferences over them. Similarly for producers.

This construction is at once elegant and breathtaking, but even as an abstraction it makes considerable demands on one's credulity. But the worst part of it is that all economic action has to be compressed in the initial instant (the Big Bang) when all markets have to be instantaneously cleared. There is not much scope for human action in the realm of economic choice and so on. There is no process, no activity in any sense even of a highly abstract variety which is needed. Once certain assumptions are guaranteed (e.g. convexity of production sets, risk aversion, etc.) the rest is ground out as a sheer mathematical exercise, albeit technically very demanding and, when properly executed, elegant.

The procedure for positing the commodity vector as containing actual, dated as well as contingent commodities differentiated by space, is a device for eliminating time as well as uncertainty (if they can at all be prised apart even conceptually). Thus the result is a timeless equilibrium concept. As Hayek correctly foresaw, '[M]any economists appear to have been unable to find a place for time in equilibrium analysis and consequently have suggested that equilibrium must be conceived as timeless. This seems to me to be a meaningless statement' (1937: 57). (For the sake of simplicity, in what follows, I shall acknowledge as quotations long quotations only: I use Hayek's phrases in many places without specific attribution.)

In his critique of the equilibrium concept, Hayek uses a framework that is an integral part of his economic thinking. Thus he proceeds by examining the equilibrium of an isolated person. Then, as Wieser did, he proceeds (though not so much in 'Economics and Knowledge') but more fully in *The Pure Theory of Capital* (1941, Ch. 2) with the analysis of a socialist economy with a single decision-maker. He finds that Walrasian theory, or what he calls the Pure Logic of Choice, is perfectly adequate in analysing these situations. Indeed, one could say that in these two situations Menger and Walras are in tandem. The key is that there is only a single individual whose subjective data are at issue and these data can be said to be known to the individual in an unproblematic way. (The objection that such an individual - a Robinson Crusoe - may not know how to optimize is not admissible according to Hayek. He quotes Ricardo's letter to Malthus (22 October 1811) in this connection:

> It would be no answer to me to say that men were ignorant of the best and cheapest mode of conducting their business and paying their debts, because that is a question of fact, not of science, and might be argued against almost every proposition in political economy.
>
> (cited in Hayek 1937: 48n)

The various actions of an individual have to stand in equilibrium relationships to each other and these must necessarily take place successively in time:

> Actions of a person can be said to be in equilibrium insofar as they can be understood as part of one plan. Only if this is the case, only if all these actions have been decided upon at one and the same moment, and in consideration of the same set of circumstances, have our statements about their interconnections, which we deduce from our assumptions about the knowledge and the preferences of the person, any application. It is important to remember that the so-called 'data' from which we set out in this sort of analysis, are (apart from his tastes) all facts given to the person in question, the things that are known to (or believed by) him to exist, and not, strictly speaking, objective facts.
>
> (ibid.: 36)

There are thus two important aspects. The content of knowledge and the way in which we can assume it is datum (i.e. given). But even then, since actions take time, an intertemporal plan has to be decided upon at one and the same moment. Such a plan may be revised if the exogenous factors on which it was conditioned change, but apart from that there is no other reason for the individual to be out of equilibrium as long as the plan he makes is feasible. But when we come to a society of many independent individuals, this procedure is no longer available. The interdependence of the different actions of a single individual over time is different from the relations between actions of different people.

Different individuals make their plans independently. They may face a common set of external events (exogenous variables), but their plans are conditional upon their expectations of what other people will do:

> This means that the plans of different individuals must in a special sense be compatible if it is to be even conceivable that they should be able to carry all of them out. . . . [s]ince some of the data on

> which any one person will base his plans will be the expectation that other people will act in a particular way, it is essential for the compatibility of the different plans that the plans of the one contain exactly those actions which form the data for the plans of the other.
>
> (ibid.: 38)

It is no good circumventing this problem by assuming that all demand schedules 'are equally given to all individuals and their acting on the same premises will somehow lead to their plans becoming adapted to each other'. This device used in traditional (or even modern) equilibrium theorizing involves a confusion about the notion of data. What can be assumed to be given (datum) and to whom?

> Economists appear subconsciously always to have been somewhat uneasy about this point and to have reassured themselves against the feeling that they did not quite know to whom the facts were given by underlining the fact that they were given - even by such pleonastic expressions as 'given data'. But this does not answer the question whether the facts referred to are supposed to be given to the observing economist, to the persons whose actions he wants to explain, and, if to the latter whether it is assumed that the same facts are known to all the different persons in the system or whether the 'data' for the different persons may be different.
>
> (ibid.: 39)

Having distinguished between objective real facts known to all, including the economist, and subjective data known to the persons whose behaviour is being studied, Hayek arrives at two senses in which equilibrium can be defined. First is the compatibility of the plans based on subjective data of different individuals. 'We may mean merely that these plans are mutually compatible and that there is consequently a conceivable set of external events which will allow all people to carry out their plans and not cause any disappointments' (ibid.: 40). The second sense is about the congruence of the subjective expectations with objective outcomes. This raises 'the other question of whether the individual sets of subjective data correspond to the objective data and whether, in consequence, the expectations on which plans were based are borne out by the facts' (ibid.: 40).

It will be obvious to the modern reader that these two notions of equilibrium are now very much part of the discourse of economists. There is a sense, however, in which (as I shall argue later) the habits of Walrasian equilibrium theorizing creep in here as well and too much knowledge is assumed on the part of the actors. But in the meantime, the two notions of interpersonal compatibility of plans and congruence of subjective expectations with objective facts have to be kept distinct but together. The recent upsurge in rational expectations does deal extensively with the congruence question, but the compatibility question also needs to be integrated with the congruence issue.

Of course, congruence can only be established *ex post* whereas compatibility is an *ex ante* notion. Hayek correctly sees that if there were any anticipated change in the exogenous variables then the *ex ante* equilibrium could fail to hold *ex post*. But in absence of an *ex ante* compatibility, any and all movement in exogenous variables will be contrary to someone's expectations.

But the next question is how are the two aspects related to each other - does congruence aid compatibility? What is the interplay between knowledge of facts and of their congruence with one's expectations and the clue that this gives one the key to other people's expectations? Can you 'read back' from objective outcomes into subjective expectations acting upon which brought the outcomes about? But this question is of interest in Hayek's view only if there exists a tendency towards equilibrium, that is, 'exists' out there in the real world not merely in pure theory: 'It is only by this assertion that such a tendency exists that economics ceases to be an exercise in pure logic and becomes an empirical science' (ibid.: 44).

We come, therefore, to the crucial consideration raised by this new notion of equilibrium. Given the duality of compatibility and convergence and their interrelationship, we ask about: '(a) the conditions under which this tendency (towards equilibrium) is supposed to exist, and (b) the nature of the process by which individual knowledge is changed' (ibid.: 45). Now it is clear that proofs of existence of equilibrium in an Arrow–Debreu (Walrasian) economy do not tackle these issues at all. Hayek correctly foresaw the stringent assumptions which would be required for such an equilibrium to be shown to exist:

> these apparent demonstrations (of existence of equilibrium) amount to no more than the apparent proof of what is already assumed. The device generally adopted for this purpose is the assumption of a perfect market where every event becomes known instantaneously to every member. It is necessary to remember here that the perfect market which is required to satisfy the assumptions of equilibrium analysis must not be confined to the particular markets of all the individual commodities: the whole economic system must be assumed to be one perfect market in which everybody knows everything. The assumption of a perfect market, then, means nothing less than that all

> the members of the community even if they are not supposed to be strictly omniscient, are at least supposed to know automatically all that is relevant for their decisions.
>
> (ibid.: 45–6)

Thus 'The assumption of a perfect market in this sense is just another way of saying that equilibrium exists but does not get us any nearer an explanation of when and how such a state will come about'. To do so 'we must explain by what process [people] will acquire the necessary knowledge' to bring equilibrium about. We must do so by making assumptions about causal connections as to 'how experience creates knowledge', but such assumptions must not only be possible but should also be likely to be true. In essence it is 'these apparently subsidiary hypotheses or assumptions that people do learn from experience, and about how they acquire knowledge, which constitute the empirical content of our propositions about what happens in the real word' (ibid.: 46).

This is the juncture at which Hayek arrives at what was then (and is even now not so far away from) the frontier of economic science, 'where it becomes exceedingly difficult to say what exactly are the assumptions on the basis of which we assert that there will be a tendency towards equilibrium and to claim that our analysis has an application to the real world' (ibid.: 48).

Hayek poses at this stage a question which fifty years later has come to attract much work of great ingenuity. This is the condition that the data are in some sense constant. He quite correctly interprets this to mean, not that nothing will ever happen, but 'that there must be some discernible regularity in the world which makes it possible to predict events correctly'. But while this is necessary, it is 'not sufficient to prove that people will learn to foresee events correctly'. The difficulty arises not as is now thought in the limitations of regression analysis (or any other econometric technique) as predictive tools but from the interpersonal dimensions. 'As all those other people will change their decision as they gain experience about the external facts and about other people's actions, there is no reason why these processes of successive changes should ever come to an end'. But Hayek does not pursue 'this question of the empirical probability that people will learn (that is, that their subjective data will come to correspond with each other and with the objective facts)' which is not 'lacking in unsolved and highly interesting problems'. He thinks however that he has 'another and more fruitful approach' (ibid.: 49–50).

It is at this stage that Hayek parts company even with the recent attempts by rational-expectations theorists to implement the congruence part of his dual conditions of equilibrium and to model how people learn from experience. Even in the rational-expectations literature, in one sense by interpreting experience as available statistical series and learning as predicting the conditional expectation with an orthogonal error, the modern-day followers of Hayek seem to have posed the question too narrowly. But we can take up those issues later. It is much more important to follow through Hayek's ingenious solution to this problem.

The solution proposed is to study the division of knowledge in the same way as the division of labour. There is specialization in knowledge and there consequently has to be a pooling of the specialized bits of knowledge. Hayek suddenly alights on a theme which has become the pillar of all his later work on the framework of the liberal order. At first it is proposed only tentatively:

> The problem which we pretend to solve is how the spontaneous interaction of a number of people, each possessing only bits of knowledge, brings about a state of affairs in which prices correspond to costs, etc., and which could be brought about by deliberate direction only by somebody who possessed the combined knowledge of all those individuals. Experience shows us that something of this sort does happen, since the empirical observation that prices do correspond to costs was the beginning of our science.
>
> (ibid.: 50–1)

But at this stage, this spontaneous interaction remains a puzzle to be explained rather than a truth to be asserted. What sort of knowledge is required on the part of individuals? It is not only the knowledge of prices, since 'price expectations and even the knowledge of current prices are only a very small section of the problem of knowledge as I see it' (ibid.). The problem is 'the knowledge of the basic fact of how the different commodities can be obtained and used, that is, the general question of why the subjective data to different persons correspond to the objective facts'. This problem of correspondence can be put as follows:

> why the propositions, which are necessarily true about the attitude of a person towards things which he believes to have certain properties, should come to be true of the action of society with regard to things which either do possess these properties, or which, for some reason which we shall have to explain, are commonly believed by the members of the society to possess these properties . . .
>
> (ibid.: 51–2)

Thus it is not only prices, current and forecast that are in the individual's 'information set' (to use a current expression). There is also some knowledge or belief about the 'opportunity set' - production and supply possibilities. But as the last quotation above shows, Hayek admits that the correspondence (congruence) between subjective beliefs and objective data may be of a 'bootstrap' equilibrium sort, that is, a thing may be so because everyone in a society believes it to be so.

Now a person need not know everything. But once he has formulated his plans he needs to be aware of all those things that in the course of carrying out his plans he should have known or else they will lead to a revision of plans, that is, 'the knowledge that he is bound to acquire in view of the position in which he originally is, and the plans which he then makes' (ibid.: 53). This 'local' knowledge requirement implies that any equilibrium is relative to this local knowledge and the position attained by the individual in such an equilibrium may be only locally but not globally optimal. To require as is asserted by the celebrated Theorem of Welfare Economics that a competitive equilibrium is Pareto optimum, 'further conditions must apparently be introduced' (ibid.).

This is, however, an extremely important point. The normative claims of a competitive equilibrium are a powerful support for the Invisible Hand story, however simplified the situation assumed. The Hayek equilibrium (if we may so call it) does not obviously have such properties, as he recognized. 'While such a position represents in one sense a position of equilibrium, it is clear that it is not an equilibrium in the special sense in which equilibrium is regarded as a sort of optimum position.' Indeed, one can go further. At this stage of the 1937 article, Hayek cannot be said to have established that such an equilibrium would exist or be unique if it did.

The only thing he does contribute towards this ultimate goal is that in addition to the (weak) requirement of local knowledge, he adds a very interesting condition which we can call 'connectedness'. Although each person only knows a part of the opportunity set, there is some overlap between different individuals' bits of knowledge to span the entire set:

> One condition would probably be that each of the alternative roles of any sort of resources is known to the owner of some such resources actually used for another purpose and that in this way all the different uses of these resources are connected directly or indirectly.
>
> (ibid.: 53)

Hayek elaborates this a little bit further in a long footnote attached to this sentence. In as much as this footnote makes an interesting conjecture about the way in which the connectedness condition operates, it is worth quoting it in full:

> This would be one, but probably not yet a sufficient condition to insure that, with a given state of demand, the marginal productivity of the different factors of production in their different uses should be equalized and that in this sense an equilibrium of production should be brought about. That it is not necessary, as one might think, that every possible alternative use of any kind of resources should be known to at least one among the owners of each group of such resources which are used for one particular purpose is due to the fact that the alternatives known to the owners of the resources in a particular use are reflected in the prices of these resources. In this way it may be a sufficient distribution of knowledge of the alternative uses, *m*, *n*, *o*, . . . *y*, *z* of a commodity, if *A*, who uses the quantity of these resources in his possession for *m*, knows of *n*, and *B*, who uses his for *n*, knows of *m*, while *C*, who uses his for *o*, knows of *n*, etc., until we get to *L*, who uses his for *z*, but knows only of *y*. I am not clear to what extent in addition to this a particular distribution of the knowledge of the different proportions is required in which different factors can be combined in the production of any one commodity. For complete equilibrium, additional assumptions will be required about the knowledge which consumers possess about the serviceability of commodities for the satisfaction of their wants.
>
> (ibid.: 53n)

Let us summarize the argument so far: (1) equilibrium involves compatibility of individual plans *ex ante* and the congruence (correspondence) of subjective expectations with objective data; (2) there is a causal connection between experience and knowledge and this is the avenue through which congruence helps to make compatibility possible; (3) knowledge is fragmented among individuals; the content of this specialized partial knowledge is not only prices but also some incomplete knowledge about the alternative use of resources (the opportunity set) owned by the individual concerned; (4) local knowledge may lead to equilibrium but such an equilibrium need not be optimal; (5) one sufficient condition (among others unspecified) for attaining optimality is connectedness of fragments of knowledge; connectedness requires that over all the individuals there is complete knowledge of, say, the opportunity set, though none possesses it individually.

This is clearly a substantial departure from Walrasian equilibrium, but also, at this stage there are many loose ends. One issue raised in the footnote quoted above is about the minimum requirements for the chain of connecting links to be complete. Is it necessary that all the uses of *m* to *z* form a closed chain through someone or other's knowledge? If so, what are the minimum overlaps required? What role do prices play in revealing the knowledge individuals have? This issue is the most important of all because if individuals act upon incomplete knowledge, they can reveal what they know only by entering into actual exchange, there being no mythical auctioneer here. But in that case some individuals must be trading out of equilibrium - that is, false trading (in a Walrasian sense) must occur. Does false trading eventually get eliminated as people learn from experience? If so, what are the conditions on the process of revising expectations which guarantee convergence?

FROM DIVISION OF KNOWLEDGE TO PRICES AS TELECOMMUNICATIONS

Hayek returns to this question in his AEA paper 'The Use of Knowledge in Society' (1945). (In between these two dates he repeats his concept of equilibrium in *The Pure Theory of Capital*. But here he fails to see the fundamental conflict between the view that spontaneous actions of individuals do bring about beneficial results and the persistence of cyclical fluctuations in an economy. Indeed after stating the new view of equilibrium, much of the book goes back to the Walrasian concerns of earlier books of which *The Pure Theory of Capital* forms the end link. This raises questions which I take up later.) This is a paper which brings together the concerns from the planning debate and the 1937 paper. After an introduction as to the nature of the economic problem - that is, not what the Walrasian theory addresses but 'the problem of utilization of knowledge which is not given to anyone in its totality' - he goes on to summarize the planning debate. This leads him to pose the relative merits of planning versus the market as follows:

> which of these systems is likely to be more efficient depends mainly on the question under which of them we can expect that fuller use will be made of the existing knowledge. This, in turn, depends on whether we are more likely to succeed in putting at the disposal of a single central authority all the knowledge which ought to be used but which is initially dispersed among many different individuals, or in conveying to the individuals

> such additional knowledge as they need in order to enable them to dovetail their plans with those of others.
>
> (Hayek 1945: 79)

It is obviously the last half of the statement that is the link with the 1937 paper. One possible interpretation is that it poses the problem of pooling of fragments of knowledge in a different way from the earlier paper. In that discussion, connectedness as one of the sufficient conditions was present because individuals were seen ensemble. In the 1945 paper, each individual can remain an island of fragmented knowledge as long as some additional knowledge is passed to him to enable him to make his plans compatible with others. The islands need not be linked together as in the connectedness argument. Unfortunately the paper does not proceed with the degree of analytical detail that the other one does, so we must leave that question open.

Hayek is more explicit about what these fragments of knowledge are that people are supposed to have. It is not 'scientific knowledge' so called, the preserve of experts, but 'the knowledge of the particular circumstances of time and place'. Each person has 'unique information of which beneficial use might be made, but of which use can be made only if the decisions depending on it are left to him or are made with his active cooperation' (ibid.: 80). Thus fragments of knowledge are here like 'named units of commodities' in direct contrast to the assumption of homogeneity of all units of a commodity in the competitive equilibrium story. This knowledge fragment is usable but only in a 'fixed coefficient' technology with the individual concerned. It cannot be alienated from him without his active co-operation. Only the individual can translate it in an alienable/exchangeable commodity/service. Indeed, 'the method by which such knowledge can be made as widely available as possible is precisely the problem to which we have found an answer' (ibid.: 81).

The method is of course decentralization: 'We need decentralization because only thus can we insure that the knowledge of the particular circumstances of time and place will be promptly used' (ibid.: 84). That much is clear; indeed, it is implicit in the notion of knowledge as a named commodity which cannot be alienated from the named individual without his active co-operation. There is, however, a difference between the autarky of totally isolated independent and self-sufficient islands and a decentralized economic system. This is where 'the additional knowledge' comes in:

> But the 'man on the spot' cannot decide solely on the basis of his limited but intimate knowledge of the facts of his immediate surroundings. There still remains the problem of communicating

> to him such further information as he needs to fit his decisions into the whole pattern of changes of the larger economic system.
>
> (ibid.)

The question as to how much knowledge does he need to do so (i.e. fit his decisions into the whole pattern of changes etc.) successfully, does not have to be answered in terms of the fragments of knowledge or the network of their possessors. The price system is assumed to have solved it:

> Fundamentally, in a system in which the knowledge of the relevant facts is dispersed among many people, prices can act to coordinate the separate actions of different people in the same way as subjective values help the individual to coordinate the parts of his plan.
>
> (ibid.)

It would seem that the answer to the question of how much knowledge is answered not in quantitative terms (number of fragments, their network forming a closed circle spanning the opportunity set), but in price terms. The price system provides the intermediate links required to close the circle of complete information. Thus, giving an example of the tin market in which an innovation has occurred, Hayek says,

> If only some of them know directly of the new demand, and switch resources over to it, and if the people who are aware of the new gap thus created in turn fill it from still other sources, the effect will rapidly spread through the whole economic system and influence not only all the uses of tin but also those of its substitutes and the substitutes of these substitutes, the supply of all things made of tin, and their substitutes, and so on; and all this without the great majority of those instrumental in bringing about these substitutions knowing anything at all about the original cause of these changes. The whole acts as one market, not because any of its members survey the whole field, but because their limited individual fields of vision sufficiently overlap so that through many intermediaries the relevant information is conveyed to all. The mere fact that there is one price for any commodity – or rather that local prices are connected in a manner determined by the cost of transport, etc. – brings about the solution which (it is just conceptually possible) might have been arrived at by one single mind possessing all the information which is in fact dispersed among all the people involved in the process.
>
> (ibid.: 86)

This long quotation strikes many chords of sympathy among economists. It has to be said, however, that it asserts what it was meant to demonstrate. How do people learn from prices and their movements? Do they need only to know the price of something else? What else? To say that one price exists is already to presume that an equilibrium exists, not to have shown that necessary and sufficient conditions are satisfied to bring it about. If one may quote Hayek against himself: 'Our problem of knowledge here is just the existence of this correspondence (between subjective expectations and objective facts/MD) which in much of the current equilibrium analysis is simply assumed to exist' (1937: 52). It seems that instead of assuming as the older theory did that 'everybody knows everything and so evade any real solution of the problem' (ibid.: 51) we now have to accept that 'the mere fact there is one price for any commodity' solves all the tricky problems of compatibility and congruence posed in the 1937 article.

In a sense, in the 1945 paper Hayek abandons the tough quest for a solution of the problem of equilibrium and substitutes a vision, highly suggestive but a vision rather than an analytical solution. The paper becomes a panegyric to the price system as

> a mechanism for communicating information . . . a kind of machinery for registering change, or a system of telecommunications which enables individual producers to watch merely the movement of a few pointers, as an engineer might watch the hands of a few dials in order to adjust their activities to changes of which they may never know more than is reflected in the price movement.
>
> (Hayek 1945: 86–7)

CONCLUSION: IS KNOWLEDGE A NON-PROBLEM?

But surely the questions raised earlier still remain. How do actual prices or their forecasts help shape *ex ante* plans, and how by acting upon these plans do individuals produce outcomes that sustain the initial plans? Uncertainty which played such a major role in the earlier paper disappears or is exorcized by the price system. Hayek even then does not claim that a full equilibrium is brought about by the 'marvel' of the price system, but only that there is a 'move in the right direction', that is, a tendency towards equilibrium. How do we know that it is a movement towards an equilibrium if we have no way of knowing that such an equilibrium exists? As we saw above, false trading is very likely, if not necessary, in a system like this since people operate on partial information. (Hayek's example of tin is interesting. Although all examples are arbitrary and not necessary to the argument, remember that the market for tin was international thanks to the investments by metropolitan capitalist countries Belgium, Netherlands and the United Kingdom in their colonies or a near dependency like Bolivia, that refineries were concentrated in these three countries in the 1930s and that in tin, like any other primary commodities, the London Metal Exchange was supplied by a network of field agents, postal and telegraph devices, regular trade bulletins and newspaper coverage. The 'price system' had a sophisticated material base in the case of tin which allowed such rapid transmission of information. That this would not be the case for, say, unemployed labour within a single country (e.g. the United Kingdom) had been shown in numerous reports, including the Beveridge investigation of 1907. Hayek merely invokes the magic words 'the price system' without examining its entrails. It is as if correctly sensing the importance of sunlight for life on earth, we were to merely worship the sun rather than study astronomy or photosynthesis.)

These issues are posed in these ways because they face any scenario of an equilibrium concept. One needs to know these questions in order to guarantee that the set of equilibria is non-empty: that at least one equilibrium exists. Then one can pursue questions of uniqueness, stability, convergence to equilibrium if displaced from it, and so on.

As of 1937, Hayek was probably one of the few people who could have pursued these questions. He had shown in his investigations of the theory of money and cycles that he took every question down to its fundamentals and undertook a rigorous analysis. In such an enterprise success is not guaranteed, but soon one gets the co-operation of others. The story of proving the existence of a Walrasian equilibrium is such a collective story. Starting from Cassel's proof and the objections of Zeuthen, Neisser and von Stackelberg, Wald was inspired to offer a solution. But it required the efforts of von Neumann and Morgenstern and a new generation of theorists till in the 1950s, twenty-five years after the initial question was raised, we had a satisfactory proof (see Arrow and Hahn 1971, Ch. 1).

Since the early 1970s, partly as a result of the rational-expectations revolution and partly as a conscious attempt to model the Hayek vision of 1937, many people have looked into these issues. The puzzle remains that Hayek himself abandoned any further work in this area. There is a conflict between his vision of the faultlessly working mechanism of the price system and the problem of cyclical fluctuations which were concerned with people getting false signals from the price movements which is never reconciled by him. Indeed, by the end of the 1930s in his 1937 paper and in *Profits, Interest and Investment* (PII), Hayek had dealt two severe blows to the complacency of equilibrium economics. The vision of PII is that equilibrium is hardly ever attained. PII promised 'an account of how . . . cyclical fluctuations, once started, tend to become self-generating, so that the economic system may never reach a position which could be described as equilibrium' (1939: 6). The 'Economics and Knowledge' paper posed a number of difficult questions about the notion of equilibrium, of it being exceedingly difficult to say what exactly are the assumptions on the basis of which we assert that there will be a tendency towards equilibrium and to claim that our analysis has an application to the real world.

But in the end Hayek's commitment to the price system overrides his analytical doubts. The search for a theory of fluctuations harmonized with a concept of equilibrium defined by compatibility and congruence, a search which is still the concern of PTC is abandoned. In the 1937 paper Hayek's celebration of the achievements of economics is still hemmed with a wish that it could do better. Thus 'to show that . . . the spontaneous action of individuals will, under conditions which we can define, bring about a distribution of resources which can be understood as if it were made according to a single plan, although nobody has planned it' is 'the central question of all social sciences' which 'economics has come nearer than any other social science to an answer'. However, Hayek adds, 'But we must not be surprised that such claims have usually been rejected, since we have not based them on the right grounds' (1937: 54).

The right grounds were to be sought in a theory of division of knowledge, a question the Pure Logic of Choice had neglected. By 1945, at the crucial stage where the question is posed of how much knowledge does an individual need to help better co-ordinate his plans, Hayek reverts back to the Pure Logic of Choice for answering it: 'It is in this connection that what I have called the "economic calculus" (or the Pure Logic of Choice) helps us, at least by analogy, to see how this problem can be solved' (ibid.: 84–5). It has done this by offering a theory of value, that is, 'by attaching to each kind of scenario resource or numerial index which cannot be derived from any property possessed by the particular thing but which reflects, or in which is condensed its significance in view of the whole means–end structure' (ibid.). (Note in this quotation that the requirement that the value (numerical index, etc.) of a particular thing is independent of any property it may possess is also common to Marx's discussion of value in the first three chapters of *Capital*, Vol. 1. Abstracting from physical specifications, Marx arrived at social labour as the substance of value, whereas Menger and the Austrian School arrived at the means–end structure as giving value. Value for the Austrians has no substance, but for Menger value and price were not the same for any commodity: see also Hayek, 1928: 82. However, in the 1945 paper Hayek passes over the value-price dichotomy and proceeds to celebrate the price system.)

But what one may ask happened to all the various objections to the Pure Logic of Choice as being not helpful in analysis of change or in explaining social processes (1937: 47–8)? Hayek has, however, decided by 1945 to stifle the doubts and abandon the hard search for answers. The tone is celebratory:

> The price system is just one of those formations which man has learned to use (though he is still very far from having learned to make the best use of it) after he had stumbled upon it without understanding it. Through it not only a division of labour but also a co-ordinated utilization of resources based on an equally divided knowledge has become possible.
>
> (1937: 50)

The division of knowledge was

> quite analogous to, and at least as important as, the problem of the division of labour. But while the latter has been one of the main subjects of investigation ever since the beginning of our science the former has been completely neglected, although it seems to me the really central problem of economics as a social science.
>
> (ibid.)

Having said this in 1937, Hayek discovered by 1945 that the problem was solved by the price system. So it was needless to have castigated economics as having neglected the problem. We had, like Monsieur Jourdain, been speaking prose all the time. The problem of knowledge is then a non-problem. Those economists like Schumpeter who cannot fathom the mystery of the price system are to be castigated. The price system and the elegance with which it solves the problem of fragmented knowledge becomes by repetition the whole content of Hayek's economics in the years following 1945.

REFERENCES

Alter, Max (1990) *Carl Menger and the Origins of Austrian Economics*, Boulder, Colo.: Westview Press.

Arrow, K.J. and G. Debren (1954) 'Existence of Equilibrium for a Competitive Economy', *Econometrica* 22: 265–90.

Arrow, K.J. and F.H. Hahn (1971) *General Competitive Analysis*, San Francisco: Holden-Day.

Caldwell, Bruce (1988) 'Hayek's Transformation', *HOPE* 20: 513–41.

Desai, Meghnad (1982) 'The Task of Monetary Theory: The Hayek–Sraffa Debate in a Modern Perspective', in M. Baranzini (ed.) *Advances in Economic Theory*, Oxford: Blackwell.

Hayek, F.A. (1928) 'Intertemporal Price Equilibrium and Movements in the Value of Money', F.A. Hayek, *Money, Capital and Fluctuations: Early Essays*, edited by R. McCloughy, Chicago: University of Chicago Press, 1984.

—— (1929) *Monetary Theory and the Trade Cycle*, London: Jonathan Cape, 1933.

—— (1931) *Prices and Production*, London: Routledge & Kegan Paul.

—— (1935a) 'Price Expectations, Monetary Disturbances and Malinvestments', in F.A. Hayek, *Profits, Interest and Investment*, London: Routledge & Kegan Paul, 1939.

—— (1935b) 'The Maintenance of Capital', *Economica* 2. Reprinted in F.A. von Hayek (1939): 83–134.

—— (1935c) *Collectivist Economic Planning*, London: Routledge & Kegan Paul.

—— (1937) 'Economics and Knowledge', *Economica* 4: 33–54. Reprinted in F.A. von Hayek (1949): 33–56.

—— (1939) *Profits,Interest and Investment*, London: Routledge & Kegan Paul.

—— (1941) *The Pure Theory of Capital*, London: Routledge & Kegan Paul.

—— (1945) 'The Use of Knowledge in Society', *American Economic Review* 35(4): 519–30.

—— (1984) *Money, Capital and Fluctuations: Early Essays*, edited by R. McCloughy, Chicago: University of Chicago Press.

Keynes, J.M. (1930) *A Treatise on Money*, London: MacMillan.

MacKenzie, L. (1954) 'On Equilibrium in Graham's Model of World Trade and Other Competitive Systems', *Econometrica* 22: 147–61.

Myrdal, G. (1939) 'Monetary Equilibrium', *Monetary Equilibrium*, London: William Hodge & Company.

2

IS HAYEK'S THEORY OF BUSINESS CYCLES AN AUSTRIAN THEORY?

Peter Rosner

The theory of New Classical Macroeconomics demonstrated that in order to study the ups and downs of economic activity one does not have to reject equilibrium analysis. This became possible by a change in the concept of equilibrium. The traditional concepts in which either flows and/or stocks had to be in equilibrium were challenged, because these concepts were suitable only for static situations or for economies with perfect foresight. Uncertainty, a basic feature of all business cycles, could not be dealt with properly.

Muth's path-breaking idea (1961), which was made fruitful for business cycle theory by Sargent and Lucas in the 1970s, integrated the formation of expectations into the concept of equilibrium by systematically linking objectively-given data to information the market participants have. As this is a topic which traditionally is at the centre of modern Austrian theory, the relation between New Classical Macroeconomics and Austrian theory has been examined (Butos 1985; Scheide 1986).[1] Butos's paper concentrates on Hayek, who insisted that business cycle theory has to be part of general equilibrium theory. He stated that the apparent similarities between these two theories are misleading, although Lucas (1977) himself wrote that Hayek put the problem of business cycles in the right perspective - namely that of equilibrium theory. Whereas New Classical Macroeconomics based its results on neoclassical microeconomic theory - that is, the logic of choice - it was Hayek's explicit purpose to distance himself from this approach and to analyse a society consisting of independent individuals. Scheide on the other hand evaluates the similarities and differences between the modern Austrians and the Lucas–Sargent approach. He concedes that basically the same tenets can be found in both schools of thought, particularly with regard to business cycle theory, but he claims that the modern Austrian theory is the more general of the two.

In this chapter a rather different question is put forward. It considers whether Hayek's theory of business cycles can really be seen as modern Austrian theory, in the sense that it is based on a theory of information-processing via markets.[2] It is shown in the sequel that, although Hayek began to pose the question of the working of the market already in his papers and books on trade-cycle theory, the arguments put forward to support the propositions of the theory were typical for static equilibrium theory. The question of information-processing is not really dealt with. This is not surprising as the path-breaking papers of Hayek on information were written after he had developed his theory of the business cycle. It is very likely that his research on business cycle theory furthered his insights concerning the importance of information-processing.

In the first section the problems of the working of the market and its relation to the concept of equilibrium as put forward by Hayek are shown. The consequences for a theory of trade cycles are formulated. In the second section the arguments that support Hayek's theory of trade cycles are examined.

I

Whereas in mainstream academic economics market equilibrium is the basic idea for organizing all theoretical deliberations, modern Austrian economists regard this idea as suspicious. The market is primarily seen as an institution in which information is processed by human agents. 'The market process is the outward manifestation of an unending stream of knowledge. This insight is fundamental to Austrian economics' (Lachmann 1976: 127). The importance of this idea lies in the emphasis Austrians put on the subjective interpretation of information via market agents. According to this idea one cannot assume that data are given to market agents and to outside observers alike, as is usually done in Walrasian economics. Data are not simply facts, but have to be interpreted by the agents of the economy. It is after all the decisive property of a market economy that the independent market agents use only the information they individually have. Thereby they can adapt easily to changing circumstances without having to rely on centrally aggregated data. Although there is nobody to safeguard that the decisions taken by the agents are mutually consistent, any inconsistency must manifest itself quickly through changing prices.[3] These changes of prices convey the information agents need. In a planned economy the planning agency has to have all the information beforehand, simply because in one plan all decisions for a given economy have to be made compatible.

Since the idea of economic equilibrium is only apt to mirror static situations, modern Austrians assert that elaborating equilibrium theory should not be the central task of theoretical economics, although they consider it to be of some use. What one can learn from the enquiry into the problems of the existence of equilibria is very limited, and therefore to capture the real working of a market society such an enquiry should rather serve as a preliminary exercise. However, in order to understand the working of the economic system, one has to look at the market as a process. This includes amongst other things the formation of expectations concerning future demand and supply. These expectations rest on beliefs concerning uncertain events.

The lack of precise knowledge of future events is not only a problem for the economist when predicting the future but, and this is the decisive point it is first of all a problem for the market participants. The uncertainty they face is an important aspect of a market society and cannot be handled properly by assuming the existence of contingent futures markets as is done in some versions of Arrow–Debreu economies. To become a theory of the actual process of the market, economic theory has to trace carefully the effects of this uncertainty on the decisions of the market actors. Thus the reaction of the agents to changes in the data play a prominent part in the analysis. The economic system is not to be equated with an automaton, which for given inputs produces an output, known in advance. Economic systems cannot be conceived as machines.

> The Social World consists not of facts but of our interpretation of the facts. Nothing will be achieved in the way of an inductive study of expectations until people's expectational responses to the facts of a situation are made *intelligible* to us, until we are able to understand *why* the acting and expecting individuals interpreted a set of facts in the way they actually did. From this point of view we need not deplore unduly the indeterminateness of expectations, for it is *intelligibility* and *determinateness* that social science should strive to achieve.
>
> (Lachmann 1943: 14)

Walrasian economics is accused of begging the real question of a market economy by assuming that data are given.

The authoritative text dealing with this problem which is mentioned and quoted again and again by the modern Austrians is, apart from Mises's *Human Action*, 'Economics and Knowledge' by Hayek. He distinguishes in this paper between data (objective data) known by the external spectator from the information (subjective data) known by the actors. The importance of this distinction lies in the fact that the market participants act according to the information they have and thus create new information for other market participants. It would be a mistake simply to assume definite reactions to given data and to draw macroeconomic conclusions from these reactions unless it is specified how decisions of agents influence the plans of other agents by changing their information set. The concept of equilibrium has to be changed accordingly:

> in order that all these plans can be carried out, it is necessary for them to be based on the expectation of the same set of external events, since, if different people were to base their plans on conflicting expectations, no set of external events could make the execution of all these plans possible. And, secondly, in a society based on exchange their plans will to a considerable extent refer to actions which require corresponding actions on the part of other individuals. This means that the plans of different individuals must in a special sense be compatible if it is to be even conceivable that they will be able to carry all of them out.
>
> (Hayek 1937: 38)[4]

Therefore, 'the question why the data in the subjective sense of the term should ever become to correspond to the objective data is one of the main problems we have to answer' (ibid.: 39).

In solving this problem economic theory will be able to include time in its analysis, because as expectations are related to the future they can provide the necessary link between different points of time. This link is activated by the market agents, since their expectations influence their decisions.

Hayek uses this idea to give the concept of equilibrium a wider application. The definition of an economic equilibrium has to include the fact that the plans of the actors are mutually consistent. However, it is not necessary that everything remains constant. If, for example, all agents expect the economy to grow, they will act accordingly and the economy can grow in equilibrium. If one compares this concept of equilibrium with Hayek's earlier one in 'Das intertemporale Gleichgewicht . . .' (1928) or with Hicks's attempt in 1933 to tackle this problem, one can see the importance of Hayek's contribution.

In Hayek (1928) equilibrium prices at different points of time are looked at. But this is done only in the (non-Austrian) spirit of a time which does not unfold. Hayek explicitly denies that a distinction has to be made between intertemporal price differences and interlocal ones. Just as marginal rates of transformation might differ at different localities at the same time, so they might be different at different points of time. Equilibrium prices might therefore be different. His favourite example is seasonal variations for agricultural products. However, such a type of variation of equilibrium prices can be perfectly foreseen. The problem of expectations concerning an unknown future, and whether these expectations are mutually consistent, cannot arise. Time does not really exist, as in an Arrow–Debreu economy, because all equilibrium prices, the current and the future ones, are known beforehand. In Hicks (1933) the problem is posed somewhat differently. Expectations concerning future prices are brought into the picture. His equilibrium condition is that prices evolve such as to equilibrate supply and demand at each and every point of time (Hicks 1933: 445).

The advantage of Hayek's 1937 concept is that, first, it dispenses with the idea that perfect foresight, in the sense that all agents know everything, is a prerequisite for equilibrium to prevail,[5] and second, it allows for changes in the economy to be considered not to upset an equilibrium. This is true not only for objectively given changes, like changing seasons, but for economically endogenous changes as well. Third, not only temporary-flow equilibria are to be considered, as Hicks's idea suggests, but stock equilibria as well. Hayek's idea is more general.

But of course Hayek was not primarily interested in equilibria. His question was whether there is a tendency in a market economy towards equilibrium in case it gets disturbed. If an economy is out of equilibrium, plans of different agents are not mutually consistent and therefore their plans will be disappointed if carried out. This in turn means that new facts are created, which in one way or another influence the decisions of other agents. The question then is not whether a new equilibrium exists which conforms to the new objectively given data – that is the way comparative static analysis proceeds – but how people react to the fact that their plans are not realized and how the information of the events is processed.

Unless economic theory can handle this problem, it cannot be called truly dynamic, since it cannot cover situations of a disturbed economy. Hayek has no answer to this problem, which looking back at all the attempts to provide one since is not surprising. An answer would be nothing short of a stability analysis of equilibrium. But he gives the expression 'tendency towards an equilibrium' a precise meaning:

> It can hardly mean anything but that under certain conditions the knowledge and intentions of the different members of society are supposed to come more and more into agreement, or . . . that the expectations of the people and particularly of the entrepreneurs will become more and more correct.
>
> (Hayek 1937: 44)

However, he discusses in which way the relevant questions have to be posed and gives some hints where to look for answers. The main point is that market actors do not have to have all information, nor do they have to evaluate the objectively given data uniformly, but they only need information which is relevant for their decisions – namely prices. They do not have to look into the underlying causes of a disequilibrium. To give answers, economics needs an understanding of learning.[6]

This problem remained a prominent one for Hayek (e.g. Hayek 1945) and it is at the centre of attention of modern Austrian economics. In their concept of entrepreneurial activity it is the entrepreneur who triggers the equilibrating process (e.g. Kirzner 1973). By searching for possibilities for arbitrage, prices are made uniform and all other actors are forced to economize resources according to prices which mirror real scarcities.

An Austrian theory of business cycles has, according to Hayek's research programme, to find an answer to the following question: if an equilibrium is upset by an external disturbance, how do people react to the disappointment of their plans which will necessarily arise, and in which way will they revise their plans? Will a new equilibrium thus be brought about, that is, will the change of plans result in expectations coming closer and closer to each other? In the second section of this chapter I shall question whether the Austrian theory of business cycles – namely the Mises–Hayek theory – is an Austrian theory in this respect.

II

In his first systematic approach to the theory of business cycles, *Monetary Theory and the Trade Cycle* (1933), the research agenda is put forward clearly:

> The simple fact that economic development does not go on quite uniformly, but that periods of relative rapid change alternate with periods of relative stagnation, does not in itself constitute a problem. It is sufficiently explained by the adjustment of the economic system to irregular changes in the data. . . . The real problem presented to economic theory is: Why does not this adjustment come about smoothly and continuously, just as a new equilibrium is formed after every change in the data? Why is there this temporary possibility of developments leading away from equilibrium and finally, without any changes in data, necessitating a change in the economic trend?
>
> (Hayek 1933: 55)
>
> For it is not the occurrence of a 'change of data' which is significant, but the fact that the economic system, instead of reacting to this change with an immediate 'adjustment' – i.e.

> the formation of a new equilibrium – begins a particular movement of 'boom' which contains, within itself, the seeds of the inevitable reaction.
>
> (ibid: 183)

The way the problem is set points already in the direction of the later concept of the market as a process. However, business cycle theory cannot simply be part of equilibrium theory, since it has to be elaborated why the tendencies towards equilibrium fail to be realized (ibid.: 70).

Hayek critically examines the then current theories to see whether they are able to give a coherent explanation of the trade cycle. These theories are classified into non-monetary and monetary theories, depending on the inclusion or exclusion of the price level into the realm of inquiry.

The non-monetary theories argue that the production structure is temporarily out of equilibrium due to the lumpiness of investment and the time necessary to bring forth capital goods. Capital-goods industries therefore advance for some time more than the future final demand for consumer goods requires. This growth of the capital-goods industries carries the seeds for its later decline. The fact that capital-goods industries are prone to big cyclical variations is not denied by Hayek. He admits that the statistical verification of this fact was a real success of business cycle research (ibid.: 54).

Hayek then goes on to question how this uneven development is brought about. How is it possible that entrepreneurs will supply too many capital goods? The arguments of the structural disequilibrium theory would be correct, according to Hayek, if the suppliers of capital goods would have to provide society with a given amount of these goods. This might be the task of a socialist investment agency, but not that of a capitalist firm (ibid.: 70). Such firms act only on the basis of given and expected prices. Since we cannot assume that expectations are systematically erroneous – otherwise we would need a theory to explain such expectations (ibid.: 84) – one needs a theory which can tell why prices can be wrong in the sense that they carry with them the seed of change.

The monetary theories which did not ignore prices concentrated on the price level and its change. A constant price level was seen as a necessary condition for equilibrium to prevail. But, as Hayek had already worked out before (Hayek 1928), only in a stationary state does an equilibrium require a constant price level. However, when real aggregates do change, a constant price level is a further cause for disturbance. Keeping the price level constant would necessitate a change in the amount of money. Such a change not only influences the price level, but relative intertemporal prices as well.

Neither the non-monetary theories nor the monetary ones were able to give a convincing answer to the problems of business cycles. This is due to posing the wrong questions. For Hayek the prime question is why firms expand the production of capital goods for some time so strongly that their expectations are not met and a contraction comes about although they react correctly to given prices. Some prices, even if correctly anticipated, must be wrong.

The villain is the process of credit expansion by the banks. The rate of interest charged for loans will fall below the natural rate of interest through deposit creation by the banking system. This in turn will bring about investment above the level which can be sustained by voluntary savings. The possibility for this process arises because the reserve ratio changes, since with a rising demand for capital goods it will be profitable for banks to lower their reserve ratio. A rising demand for loans at a given rate of interest can thus be satisfied.

> whereas previously, at the same rate of interest and with the same security, no new borrowers came forward, now, under the same conditions of borrowing, more loans can be placed. On the other hand, the cash holdings of the bank remain unchanged.
>
> (Hayek 1933: 171)

Once the process has started, the cumulative effects are clear. Further deposit creation allows more investment to be financed. A turning point will be reached as soon as the banks begin to curtail the expansion of credit. This may be due to an increased demand for cash, which reduces the liquidity of banks. The amount of money in circulation is thus positively correlated with real production. For Hayek credit expansion and contraction is a necessary process in a monetary economy with a banking system. Therefore a trade cycle prevails in such an economy.

In the light of Hayek's later insistence on information-processing via the market - and this remained the modern Austrian approach to markets as a process - some questions can be raised. How is it to be explained that bank managers are only guided by current interest rates when deciding on a loan? Although Hayek has shown that non-monetary theories of business cycle have to answer the question of why the decision to produce capital goods now is inelastic to future prices - and he accuses these theories of neglecting the basic features of a market economy - his own theory of the trade cycle put forward in *Monetary Theory and the Trade Cycle* assumes a complete inelasticity to the rate of interest of future demand and supply of capital.

This may be correct, but such an assumption requires, according to Hayek's later emphasis on the formation of expectations, a theory as to how this may emerge as a result of information-processing via the market. If credit expansion is a regular feature of a modern market economy, the credit cycle will be an objectively given fact, which everybody in business will be aware of and therefore will have to incorporate in his or her expectations.[7] Changing prices and the changing amount of money should not cause trade cycles to be seen as disequilibrium phenomena, just as seasonal variations in supply and demand for agricultural products or for heating materials are not signs of disequilibrium. A trade cycle which is purely endogenously caused and which therefore is a regular feature of a market economy should not pose any problem to equilibrium theory, as Hayek had worked out already in 1928.

In his second attempt to tackle the problem of business cycles, in *Prices and Production*, the main purpose is not any more to look for a cause of regular business cycles, but to explain more systematically, how a change in the amount of money will influence economic aggregates. First, it is shown in which way a change in the rate of (voluntary) saving affects the relation of the production of consumer goods to the production of capital goods. Such an increase in the rate of saving must result in more capitalist techniques being used, or, to express this in other terms, in capital deepening: in each period the public spends a smaller amount of income on consumer goods and therefore - given total output - a larger part is used for capital goods.

This is an exercise in comparative statics, as two different states which both are equilibria are compared. The important difference between these two states concerns the rate of saving. There is nothing in this exercise which suggests that problems of a market society are considered. Although the relation of capital goods to consumer goods has to be expressed in value terms, Hayek explicitly neglects prices. He will consider them in Chapter 3. In Chapter 2 he also does not take into account that the decisions to invest are made by a different group of agents from those who decide about saving: 'As a starting point, we may . . . suppose that consumers save and invest an amount of money equivalent to one fourth of their income of one period' (Hayek 1935: 50). To argue in this way is typical of equilibrium theory and has been a cause for many complaints by modern Austrian economics. After all one would expect a planning agency of a communist economy to follow this way of reasoning when considering the relation between the flow of savings and the stock of capital goods. Only such a planning agency has the power to decide on investment and savings in one instance. However, in that context Hayek uses this deliberation as a preliminary exercise to clarify certain points.

Then he goes on to discuss what will happen if the amount of money changes. For Hayek this is no longer a comparative static exercise, for such a change upsets any existing equilibrium. However, as the underlying fundamentals of the economy - such as preferences, techniques, rate of saving - have not changed, the situation is altogether different from the former one. In that case the old equilibrium did not correspond to the new fundamentals, namely the altered rate of saving. A change of economic aggregates is necessary and comparative static analysis is the appropriate way to look at the new equilibrium. In the latter case the final equilibrium cannot be different from the original one, since fundamentals have not changed. But, as it was precisely Hayek's intention to challenge the conclusion of traditional quantity theory - namely that a change in the quantity of money only influences the price level but has no effect on relative prices and therefore has no consequence for real aggregates - he could not simply compare two different equilibria when examining the effects of a change in the amount of money.

How the increase in the amount of money influences the real aggregates depends on who gets this money first - the consumers or the entrepreneurs. If it is the entrepreneurs who get hold of this money, perhaps by an easing of credit, they will, according to Hayek, react as if real savings had increased - they will alter the method of production and use more capitalist techniques. How this will come about - that is, why entrepreneurs act this way - is not argued in Chapter 2, but is postponed to Chapter 3, in which the working of the price mechanism is brought into the picture. However, the important point is that the capital structure thus created cannot be sustained, since the underlying fundamentals, the rate of voluntary saving, had not changed.

> In the same way [i.e. as in the case of increased voluntary savings PR] . . . the use of a larger proportion of the original means of production for the manufacture of intermediate products can only be brought about by a retrenchment of consumption. But now this sacrifice is not made voluntarily, and is not made by those who will reap the benefit from new investments. It is made by consumers. . . . It comes about not because they want to consume less, but because they get less goods for their money income. There can be no doubt that, if their receipts should rise again, they would immediately attempt to expand consumption to the usual proportion. . . . But if it does, then at once the money stream will be redistributed between consumptive and productive uses according to the wishes of the individual concerned, and the new artificial distribution, due to the injection of the new

> money, will . . . be reversed. . . . That is to say production will become less capitalistic, and that part of the new capital which was sunk in equipment adapted only to the more capitalistic processes will be lost.
>
> (ibid.: 58)

Factors of production will remain unemployed because a part of the capital goods can only be used in certain processes. The capital stock not only consists of putty but also of clay. The latter part will be lost when the processes, in which they were used, do not fit the changing price system.

If, on the other hand, consumption is enhanced by easing credit to consumers or by an increase of their income through other means, less capitalist methods of production will be introduced. As in the former case the result will not be a new equilibrium, since the rate of saving had not changed.

It is only after the problem has been examined so far that Hayek turns to the working of the price system:

> What we have to explain is why certain goods which have thus far been used in one stage of production can now be more profitably used in another stage of production. Now this will only be the case if there are changes in the proportions in which different producers' goods may be profitably used in any stage of production, and this in turn implies that there must be changes in the prices offered for them in different stages of production.
>
> (ibid.: 70)

The change in prices comes about, as the demand for some goods increases more than that for other goods - either because voluntary savings change or the amount of money does.

But in this deliberation Hayek lumps the two problems together, although, according to his own method, they have to be kept separate. One has only to look at the role of expectations to see the necessity to discriminate between these two cases. In the case of a changing rate of saving, the expectations of entrepreneurs are mutually consistent if they expect price relations to be in line with the final equilibrium and act according to these expectations. According to his later definition of equilibrium Hayek is justified when describing the process in the following way:

> I begin . . . with the supposition that consumers decide to save and invest a larger proportion of their income. The immediate effect of the increase in the demand for producers' goods and the decrease in demand for consumers' goods will be that there will be a relative rise in the prices of the former and a fall in the

> prices of the latter. But the prices of producers' goods will not rise equally, nor will they rise without exception. In the stage of production immediately preceding that in which the final touches are given to consumers' goods, the effect of the fall in the prices of consumers' goods will be felt more strongly than the effect of the increase of the funds available for the purchase of producers' goods of all kinds. The price of the product of this stage will, therefore, fall, but it will fall less than the prices of consumers' goods. This means a narrowing of the price margin between the last two stages. But this narrowing of the price margin will make the employment of funds in the last stage less profitable relatively to the earlier stages, and therefore some of the funds which had been used there will tend to be shifted to the earlier stages.
>
> (ibid.: 75)

If entrepreneurs expected this to happen, their expectations will be mutually consistent. There is a movement from one equilibrium to another, but no business cycle.

Then Hayek turns again to the problem of an increase in the amount of money and starts with the case that this extra amount is given to entrepreneurs:

> To secure borrowers for this additional amount of money, the rate of interest must be kept sufficiently below the equilibrium rate to make profitable the employment of just this sum and no more. Now the borrowers can only use the borrowed sums for buying producers' goods, and will only be able to obtain such goods by outbidding the entrepreneurs who used them before. At first sight it might seem improbable that these borrowers who were only put in a position to start longer processes by the lower rate of interest should be able to outbid those entrepreneurs who found the use of those means of production profitable when the rate of interest was still higher. But when it is remembered that the fall in the rate will also change the relative profitableness of the different factors of production for the existing concerns, it will be seen to be quite natural that it should give a relative advantage to those concerns which use proportionally more capital.
>
> (ibid.: 86)

For this line of thought to hold, two assumptions are essential. First, entrepreneurs can only increase their demand for capital goods, and second, the new structure of production only depends on the artificially lowered rate of interest.[8] Of course, both assumptions might be true, but Hayek does not give any reason why this must be so.

However, if entrepreneurs act in the way Hayek describes, their expectations will by necessity not be met, as they are not – *pace* Hayek – mutually consistent. But then again the question is open as to how the entrepreneurs will react. Hayek's entrepreneurs are extremely shortsighted, since they only act on current prices and interest rates and these prices do not reflect future scarcities. The entrepreneurs do not take into account that prices and the rate of interest must change, although they are not equilibrium prices. These entrepreneurs, unlike in modern Austrian economics, do not trigger the equilibrating process by discovering opportunities to make profit.

III

Apart from Mises, it is Hayek who has had the greatest impact on modern Austrian economics. This is not surprising, since with his scientific work he helped to turn the ideological belief in the prevalance of spontaneous order into a scientific theory. As far as economics was concerned there were two areas of research to which he returned again and again, one being the problems of trade cycles (in connection with capital theory), the other the problem of information-processing and the use of information.[9]

I have shown that Hayek could not integrate these two problems, although he clearly saw the necessity to do so. There is an inconsistency between Hayek's arguments concerning his theory of business cycles and the role prices have as signals. Entrepreneurs act as if the current prices were equilibrium prices. The inconsistency in his theory can be seen for example by mentioning the Austrian point of view – that is, that of modern Austrians: why is it that no entrepreneur is sufficiently alert to engage in profitable – and socially useful speculation, if, due to an increase in the amount of money, the economy is out of equilibrium? There are profits to be made since the expectations of prices are not mutually consistent, as the entrepreneurs base their decisions only on current prices and current interest rates.

This inconsistency in Hayek's theory is presumably due to the fact that his most important books on business cycle theory were written before he was able to formulate precisely the problem of expectations in relation to equilibria. We can assume that his research on business cycles made him aware of the problems of the consistency of expectations with regard to the existence of an equilibrium. This inconsistency is therefore not a failure of Hayek, but rather the result of a development of his ideas. The fact that he did not work out a new version of his business cycle theory in the light of his approach to information equilibrium is not surprising as he lacked the means to pursue the idea of such an equilibrium rigorously. They were not developed until the 1960s and the 1970s.

The models of New Classical Macroeconomics can therefore be seen to be in line with basic ideas of Hayek. It is argued anew that business cycle theory has to be based firmly on equilibrium theory. The processing of information and its influence on expectations is carefully worked out. The two problems of Hayek's economic theory are brought together. Lucas (1972), basing himself on Phelps's island parable (1969), has shown in which way a changing amount of money which is not foreseen and which is not detected immediately, changes economic aggregates by changing relative prices and expectations.[10] Problems which were important for Hayek and are still important for the Austrians are eliminated, and the institutional setting of Lucas's paper is too simple to provide an answer to all the problems of business cycles. However, it provides a big step forward. Perhaps some of the neo-Austrians are not happy with it, but I would call this theory scientifically more advanced than Hayek's theory: with new instruments based on an old idea, first put forward by Hayek, an old scientific problem is examined. It would be a bad symptom for the science of economics if the leading theoreticians in the 1970s did not know more than one of the leading theoreticians in the 1930s. But one should not forget that the clear answers the New Classical Economics is able to give rest on a narrowing of the research agenda.

NOTES

Karl Milford helped with his persistent criticism to get this chapter finished. I also thank the editors for their critical remarks.

1 Naturally, the aversion against discretionary stabilization policy, which is typical for both schools, furthered the interest in a comparison of these two schools.
2 O'Driscoll (1977) and Moss and Vaughn (1986) pursue a similar question.
3 Rizzo (1989) argues that Hayek assumed 'near equilibrium prices' to support the tendency toward equilibrium.
4 External events cannot be regarded as objective data as they must be perceived by the actors.
5 It therefore does not make sense to include into the defining conditions of a Hayekian equilibrium a complete dissemination of knowledge, as Rizzo has done (Rizzo 1989: 9)
6 In Rizzo's work strong and weak analytical tendencies towards equilibrium learning from disappointment play a prominent role.
7 I do not suggest that the rational expectations hypothesis is the only sensible assumption, but the point is that Hayek in this theory did not pose the problem of the formation of expectations. This may be due to the fact that a solution to the problem of integrating the formation of

expectations into the concept of equilibrium did not seem to be viable (Morgenstern 1935).

8 The same problems arise in the elaboration of the Ricardo effect in Hayek (1939), where the emphasis is laid on the immobility of labour (O'Driscoll 1977: 92 ff.).

9 The problem of information-processing was important in the discussion about planning.

10 It is therefore not correct to say that the new classical macroeconomists assumed the economy to be on the 'full-information' path (Scheide 1986: 577).

REFERENCES

Butos, William N. (1985) 'Hayek and General Equilibrium Analysis', *Southern Economic Journal* 52: 332–42.

Hayek, Friedrich A. (1928) 'Das intertemporale Gleichgewichtssystem der Preise und die Bewegungen des "Geldwertes"', *Weltwirtschaftliches Archiv* 28: 33–76.

—— (1933) *Monetary Theory and the Trade Cycle*, London: Jonathan Cape (first published in 1929).

—— (1935) *Prices and Production*, 2nd edn, London: Routledge & Kegan Paul.

—— (1937) 'Economics and Knowledge', *Economica* 4: 33–54.

—— (1939) *Profits, Interest and Investment*, London: Routledge & Kegan Paul.

—— (1945) 'The Use of Knowledge in Society', *American Economic Review* 35: 519–30.

Hicks, J.R. (1933) 'Gleichgewicht und Konjunktur', *Zeitschrift für Nationalökonomie* 4: 441–55.

Kirzner, Isreal M. (1973) *Competition and Entrepreneurship*, Chicago: University of Chicago Press.

Lachmann, Ludwig M. (1943) 'The Role of Expectations in Economics as a Social Science', *Economica* 10: 12–23.

—— (1976) 'On the central concept of Austrian economics: Market Process', in E.G. Dolan (ed.) *The Foundations of Austrian Economics*, Kansas City: Sheed & Ward.

Lucas, Robert E. (1972) 'Expectations and the Neutrality of Money', *Journal of Economic Theory* 4: 103–24.

—— (1977) 'Understanding business cycles', *Journal of Monetary Economics*, supplement, 7–30.

Morgenstern, Oskar (1935) 'Vollkommenes Voraussicht und wirtschaftliches Gleichgewicht', *Zeitschrift für Nationalökonomie* 6: 337–57.

Moss, Laurence, S. and Vaughn, Karen I. (1986) 'Hayek's Ricardo Effect: A Second Look', *History of Political Economy* 18: 545–65.

Muth, John F. (1961) 'Rational Expectations and the Theory of Price Movements', *Econometrica* 29: 315–35.

O'Driscoll, Gerald P. (1977) *Economics as a Coordination Problem*, Kansas City: Sheed Andrews & McMeel.

Phelps, Edmund S. (1969) 'Introduction' in E.S. Phelps *et al.*, *Microeconomic Foundations of Employment and Inflation Theory*, New York: Norton.

Rizzo, Mario J. (1989) 'Hayek's Four Tendencies Toward Equilibrium', C.V. Starr Center for Applied Economics, New York University.

Scheide, Joachim (1986) 'New Classical and Austrian Business Cycle Theory: Is There a Difference?' *Weltwirtschaftliches Archiv* 122: 575–98.

3

MATHEMATICAL FORMALIZATION AND THE DOMAIN OF ECONOMICS

The case of Hayek and New Classical Economics

Rudy van Zijp and Hans Visser

The 1970s and 1980s saw a revival of interest in economic research traditions which were highly critical of the then prevalent Keynesian orthodoxy. The main reason for this revival may be found in the fact that Keynesianism could not provide a satisfactory explanation of the phenomenon of stagflation, and hence could not suggest policy measures that would alleviate its undesirable consequences. Quite naturally, the Keynesian failure to deal with stagflation gave rival approaches the opportunity to come to the forefront. The main rival approach in this regard has been monetarism, as propounded by the Chicago School. This research tradition did provide an explanation of stagflation, thereby stressing the rationality of economic agents and the allocative efficiency of the price system. Deviations of the full-information 'natural-rate equilibrium' were considered to be caused by expectational errors on the part of the economic agents. Consequently, monetarists argued that economic, or rather monetary, policy should be as predictable as possible in order to prevent these errors. New Classical Economics (NCE) continued to pursue this line of reasoning. It also stressed the rationality of economic agents, and argued that such agents will take changes in economic policy into account. It even developed a formal model in which it 'demonstrated' the ineffectiveness of anticipated economic policy in stabilizing economic activity. Deviations of the natural-rate equilibrium, and hence business cycles, were caused by unanticipated changes in the money supply. Following Friedman, New Classicals concluded that the monetary authorities should refrain from active stabilization policy and instead should adopt a fixed-percentage money growth rule. Under such a rule, it was claimed, economic agents could easily determine whether changes in prices were caused by real or by monetary factors, and act accordingly.

A second rival to the Keynesian approach, the Austrian School, is a rather old one. Its rivalry with Keynesianism, and particularly Hayek's controversy with Keynes and Sraffa, dates back to the early

1930s. The Keynesian revolution of the late 1930s dealt a serious blow to Austrian economics, which had given one of the most prominent and promising explanations of cyclical fluctuations.By the late 1970s, the Austrian School had recovered from this blow, although it has never regained the prominent position it occupied almost half a century before. The Austrian revival can be decomposed into two developments. First, in the early 1970s it criticized mainstream (neoclassical) economics for completely eliminating entrepreneurship from the domain of economics. Without a theory of entrepreneurship, mainstream economics could not make clear that market economies differ fundamentally from centrally planned economic systems. The second development that reflects the Austrian revival consists of an increase in the attention given to the business cycle theories of Mises and particularly Hayek. These theorists argued that cyclical fluctuations result from price distortions that are brought about by disturbances of monetary equilibrium. These disturbances affect relative prices and market rates of interest. The resulting investments are not in accordance with real (rates of) productivity and time preferences. Mises and Hayek suggested that the monetary authorities should refrain from active stabilization policies, because these would only prolong the inevitable depression, thus hampering the adjustment process during which unprofitable investment projects are eliminated.

Austrians and New Classicals thus both explain cyclical fluctuations in terms of price distortions. Furthermore, they both play down the effectiveness of active monetary stabilization policy. This has led several economists to adopt the so-called common-roots claim, which holds that New Classicals not only stand in the monetarist tradition, but also share common roots with the Austrian School, with the communicative function of the price system as the underlying and unifying theme.[1] However, the similarities between Hayekian and New Classical business cycle theories hide fundamental methodological and economic-theoretical differences.[2] The present chapter is concerned with one of these differences, namely the role to be played in economics by mathematical formalization. It argues that this difference leads to analytical differences. In the case of Austrian and New Classical Economics, the heuristic prescription of mathematical formalization thus affects the domain of economics.

The paper starts from the common-roots claim, as expounded above. The analysis is restricted to monetary business-cycle theories, which use the notion of monetary neutrality as a benchmark. However, this notion is somewhat ambiguous, in the sense that two concepts of monetary neutrality can be discerned. Both are discussed in section 1. Section 2 subsequently covers Hayek's business cycle theory, which can be seen as a comlex synthesis of Menger's structure of production, Wicksell's distinction between the natural and the market rate of interest, Mises's monetary theory, Cantillon's distribution effects and Hayek's own views on the dispersion of knowledge. Section 3 discusses New Classical monetary business-cycle theory in general, and its modelling strategies in particular. Section 4 lists the simplifying assumptions introduced by the NCE, and discusses the way in which they preclude the analysis of distribution effects.

1. MONETARY (NON-)NEUTRALITY

In the discussion of the neutrality of money two strands can be discerned. First of all we have the quantity theory proposition that *ceteris paribus* a change in the money supply only influences the price level. Neutrality in this case means that changes in the money supply in a comparative-statics analysis leave relative prices and real magnitudes unaffected.[3] However, during the adjustment process from one equilibrium state to another money is seen as affecting relative prices and quantities. Second, attempts have been made to identify the conditions under which money would not affect relative prices and quantities at all (not even in the short term). Neutrality in this case means that monetary equilibrium is maintained at all times.[4] We shall first discuss neutrality of money in the second (monetary equilibrium) sense and then dwell somewhat longer on neutrality in the first (comparative-static) sense.

The idea of neutrality of money in the sense of uninterrupted monetary equilibrium is commonly traced back to Wicksell's *Geldzins und Güterpreise* (1898 (1962): 102), even if Wicksell did not use the term *neutral money*.[5] However, his definition of *neutral interest* was tantamount to neutrality of money in the second sense.[6] Wicksell maintained that neutrality implied a stable price level. His Swedish colleague Davidson was quick to point out that in an economy with increasing factor productivity monetary equilibrium, or neutral money, implied a falling price level.[7] Hayek refined Wicksell's analysis, first seeing a constant money supply and later a constant money flow per unit of time as the criterion for the neutrality of money, until Koopmans finally showed that no empirical yardstick can be found for monetary equilibrium.[8]

The aim of the monetary equilibrium theorists was to find the conditions under which a monetary economy would function as if money did not exist and relative prices consequently were only determined in the real sector.[9] A monetary economy was thus compared with a barter economy. However, this comparison was based on the assumption that markets function without frictions.[10] This amounts to a wild goose chase, because if markets function without frictions, no reason can be found why people would ever decide to use money in the first place. Money that is no more than a veil will be blown away and if it is indeed the 'oil which renders the motion of the wheels [of trade] more smooth and easy', as Hume (1752: 33) put it, the wheels of trade will run much faster and further with money than without. In other words, a monetary economy has a different transactions technology than a barter economy. Now, the likes of Koopmans realized full well that money is used just because barter exchange is *not* frictionless and their construct of a frictionless barter economy was only a thought experiment.[11] Lutz (1969: 105) sees this as an attempt to express the idea that, if a general depression is to be avoided in a monetary economy, it should behave like a barter economy because in a barter economy Say's Law applies.[12] Still, this could not disguise the futility of the whole operation. Leaving on one side the question whether there is much sense in analysing money in a general equilibrium model where all goods exchange against all goods, the analysis of neutral money in the sense of monetary equilibrium at all times can better remain confined to the model of a monetary economy. There is no need to make a comparison with a barter economy.[13] Incidentally, if barter trade is not frictionless, even Say's Law would not suffice to prevent depressions. With frictions, in particular imperfect information on other agents' supply and demand functions, some goods offered in the market may fail to find a taker and economic activity declines, even if all excess demands neatly sum up to zero. In a general equilibrium model with money, the conditions under which monetary equilibrium is maintained can be analysed with exactly the results which Wicksell, Davidson, Hayek and Koopmans came up with. If monetary equilibrium is maintained at all times, Say's Equality holds true, that is, there is no excess demand or excess supply on all goods markets combined (if we neglect the markets for other financial assets than money). Still, equilibrium relative prices in goods markets are also dependent on monetary factors, as has been made clear by the discussion of the classical dichotomy.[14] If the monetary and real sectors are completely separate, the price level is indeterminate and the quantity theory cannot hold good.

The discussion on the neutrality of money in the monetary equilibrium sense focused on the conditions necessary for maintaining monetary equilibrium in the face of specific changes in the real sector of the economy. The excess demand functions in the real sector of the economy and with it the demand functions for real cash balances were assumed to change. By contrast, the quantity-theory comparative-statics approach to the neutrality of money can be said to study the effects of changes in the money supply with constant excess demand functions in the real sectors of the economy and consequently a constant demand function for real cash balances. The interesting question here is whether, and if so to what extent, developments in the monetary sphere can have lasting effects on relative prices and hence quantities in the real sector.[15] The conditions for neutrality in the comparative-statics sense have been shown to be quite strict. First of all, money should be intrinsically valueless paper money or bank money. A change in the volume of full-blooded silver or gold money would not only have an impact on the general price level, but would also change relative prices of goods produced from silver or gold and other goods. Aschheim and Hsieh (1969: 213–15) formulate six further conditions for neutrality of money in the comparative-statics sense: (1) price flexibility, (2) absence of money illusion, (3) absence of distribution effects, (4) static price-expectations, (5) absence of a combination of internal and external money, or credit money and base money and (6) absence of government debt and open-market policies.[16] Aschheim (1973: 78) even goes so far as to claim that the conditions for neutrality of money imply, again, the absence of money (as a unit of account). Static price-expectations are in his view incompatible with perfectly flexible prices, freedom from money illusion and the absence of uncompensated distribution effects of price level changes.[17] The condition of static price-expectations may, however, be too strict.[18] Conditions 5 and 6 are based on the idea that changes in the money supply alter the composition of asset holders' wealth portfolios and with it the rate of interest.[19] These conditions could be reformulated in the sense that portfolio composition should not change, so that if the money supply changes, the volume of nominal debt changes proportionally. Likewise, condition 3 could be broadened to include the neutrality of distribution effects, as Aschheim in fact did in his 1973 article. Finally, the long-term inflation rate in the economy should be constant, as both the Mundell–Tobin effect and non-neutral tax effects preclude superneutrality.[20] Neutrality in the comparative-statics sense therefore can only be restricted to stepwise changes in the money supply, not to changes in the growth rate of money. This case could be subsumed under the condition of the neutrality of distribution effects.

The distribution effects call for further comment. As will be discussed more extensively below, Hayek's analysis follows Cantillon and emphasizes that money enters into circulation in specific ways, affecting the structure of spending and consequently relative prices, including the rate of interest, and quantities. It follows that money, especially if created through credit but also from an international payments balance, changes demand and supply functions in the real sector.[21] Cantillon explained that money that enters into circulation through money-lenders brings with it a lowering of the rate of interest, while money that enters into circulation through consumptive expenditure by the rich makes the rate of interest rise, because the producers of consumption goods face an increase in demand and have to borrow money in order to increase production (Cantillon 1955, Part 2, Ch. 10). One expression of distribution effects is the phenomenon of *forced savings*. This follows if the expenditure of entrepreneurs who borrow money to increase production makes prices rise and in that way brings about a reduction in real consumption.[22] Another case of distribution effects is the redistribution of real wealth between debtors and creditors in the case of (unforeseen) price level changes, a redistribution that according to Fisher (1933) and Keynes (1936: 264) could seriously worsen a depression, once started. A special kind of distribution effect, which has only recently received serious attention (Bikker 1991a, 1991b), concerns the redistribution of interest income when the rate of interest changes.

New developments in growth theory serve to underline the likelihood of non-neutrality of money supply changes. In general-equilibrium models, demand and supply functions usually are well-behaved linear functions and the system is stable or assumed to be stable: after the business cycle has run its course everybody is back on his or her unchanged demand or supply curve. With nonlinearities, as emphasized by the new growth theory, any temporary expansion in an industry may perpetuate itself because relative prices between goods are changed in the process. The new growth economics thus holds that investment may recreate investment opportunities, and that success breeds success.[23] Distribution effects are then even more likely to result in lasting changes in the real sectors. More generally it is acknowledged that deviations from an equilibrium growth path through their impact on investments and technology, may change the equilibrium growth path itself if technological growth is endogenous.[24] This ties in with chaos theory, which shows that in nonlinear systems a small change in initial conditions will lead to significant changes in the time path of a function.[25] The result is hysteresis, or the phenomenon that deviations from an equilibrium path change the equilibrium path itself. New developments in economic theory thus tend to emphasize the deviation-amplifying tendencies of shocks rather than the stability of any growth path.

The above indicates that recently economists have increasingly recognized the importance of forces that affect the comparative-statics neutrality of money. In the 1930s Hayek already focused on a subset of these forces. As was stated above, his business cycle theory interprets cyclical fluctuations in output and investment in terms of non-neutral monetary injections in a specific market. The ensuing Cantillon effects distort the so-called 'structure of production'.[26] The next section will discuss this theory in more detail.

2. THE ANALYSIS OF CANTILLON EFFECTS: HAYEKIAN BUSINESS CYCLE THEORY

Hayek's business cycle theory starts from an intertemporal perfect-information general equilibrium, which he defined as a series of situations in which economic agents have complete information and perfect foresight about preferences and the means of production at every point of time during the planning period (Hayek 1982: 76). Such an equilibrium is maintained if the agents do not make expectational errors (ibid.: 85). However, Hayek (1933c) recognized that in reality agents do not have complete information, and hence cannot avoid making such errors. In fact, he claimed that 'Every explanation of economic crisis [and, more generally, of business cycles] must include the assumption that entrepreneurs have committed errors' (ibid.: 141). He added that cycles will only arise when these economic agents make *similar* expectational errors, suggesting that this similarity follows from the fact that the agents base their actions on signals which as a rule prove reliable (ibid., 141). The most important signals in this regard are provided by the price system.

Disregarding the fact that Hayek's business cycle theory has been formulated in several versions, it can be reconstructed as follows. The theory concentrates on the variable which figures most prominently in investment decisions, namely the interest rate. Hayek adopted Wicksell's distinction between the natural and the market rate of interest.[27] The former is defined as the long-run equilibrium rate of interest, which reflects the time-preferences of the economic agents. The 'market' (or money) rate of interest is the rate at which the supply of loanable funds equals the demand for loans. It need not equal the natural rate, and thus need not reflect the agents' time-preferences. The difference results from either a change in the natural rate, or a change in the market rate. Hayek argued that the process resulting from the former change must be interpreted as a mere adjustment process to a new equilibrium situation instead of a business cycle. In his view, business cycles thus follow from changes in the market rate of interest which (initially) do not affect the natural rate. This means that they are by definition caused by monetary expansion, that is, by the absence of monetary neutrality in a monetary-equilibrium sense. The expansion may result from (1) changes in the volume of cash, caused by the in- and outflow of gold, (2) changes in the volume of money, as regulated by the monetary authorities (i.e. the government and the central bank), and/or (3) the creation of credit by private banks.[28] As Hayek shifted emphasis in time, we shall discuss monetary expansion in general, disregarding its source.[29] Hayekian business cycle theory assumes that such an expansion enters the economy on the loan market. The market rate of interest then falls below the natural rate, which raises the present value of all investment projects. As O'Driscoll and Rizzo (1985: 205) showed, this rise in present value is a result of three effects: (1) a discount rate effect, (2) cost effects, and (3) derived-demand (or relative-price) effects. The third effect is most characteristic for Hayek's business cycle theory. But before discussing it, we briefly discuss the other two effects.

The discount rate effect starts from the fact that the market rate of interest is used as a discount rate, so that the present value of the expected future returns of investment projects increases. The cost effect reflects that the market rate is also the price to be paid for loans. A fall in this rate reduces the costs of investment projects, and therefore increases their net present value. Both the discount rate and cost effect thus result in general *over*investment, which will exist as long as entrepreneurs find it worthwhile to invest (i.e. as long as they expect that the process of monetary expansion continues).[30] The ensuing gap between planned investment and planned savings is filled by forced savings. As noted in the previous section, this phenomenon results from redistributions in income.[31] It presupposes that some individuals will experience a rise in income earlier than others, because their productive activities are more in demand. This can only be the case if their (productive) activities differ from those of others. Furthermore, the non-simultaneity of the rise in their respective incomes also reflects Hayek's assumption that money does not spread immediately throughout the economy. Instead, production is a time-consuming activity, in the sense that it takes place in successive stages of production (see below).

The discount-rate and cost effects work in the same direction, namely by increasing the present value of all investment projects, thus explaining the emergence of a boom. However, they do not suffice to explain the upper turning-point of the business cycle. Hayek distinguished two reasons why this turn is inevitable. First, he argued that the boom would come to an end when the additional money stops flowing into the economy. Entrepreneurs will then recognize that they have made expectational errors about the profitability of their overinvestments. Consequently, these overinvestments will be eliminated. This leads to a fall in the demand for producer goods, which will spread throughout the economy, reducing economic activity. As Wilson (1940) pointed out, though, this recession is by no means inevitable, because it can be postponed by continuing to increase the money supply.[32] Hayek's second explanation of the upper turning-point was less easy to refute. It builds on the derived-demand effect, which holds that the initial fall in the market rate of interest does not only affect the volume of investment but also its composition. Before discussing this effect, we must first discuss the framework in which it takes place.

Following Menger (1871: 8–10), Hayek adopted the structure of production as his framework of analysis. Menger had classified capital goods according to the functions they perform in the process of production, using their 'remoteness' from consumption as a criterion for classification. Consumer goods are called 'goods of the first order', capital goods which are used in the production of these first-order goods are called second-order goods, capital goods which produce second-order goods are called third-order goods, and so forth. Hence there is a vertical relationship between heterogeneous capital goods. It is then possible to distinguish stages of production which can be classified in a manner similar to that of capital goods. Taken together, these stages form a structure of production. This structure is vertical, in the sense that production takes place in successive stages: production in a given stage depends on production in a higher-order stage.

The derived-demand effect can now be explained as follows. The fall in the market rate of interest does not affect all investment projects to the same degree, or even in the same manner. Different orders of goods, and hence different stages of production, are affected differently. If entrepreneurs mistakenly interpret the fall in the market rate of interest as reflecting a fall in the natural rate, they will conclude that the agents' time-preferences have decreased. This means that they expect current consumption demand to fall and future consumption demand to rise. It will then appear to be more profitable to invest in productive activities which yield consumption output in the more distant future. In other words, the present value of investment projects which involve higher order goods has increased, whereas that of others has decreased. This induces entrepreneurs to reallocate capital from the lower to the higher stages of production. In Austrian language, the structure of production is 'lengthened' (or has become more 'roundabout'). However, eventually this process of lengthening will be checked by a shortage of resources. Hayek argued that during the later stages of the boom 'the prices of consumer goods do as a rule rise and real wages fall' (Hayek 1939: 11).[33] The rise in consumer prices increases the profit margins on these goods, and hence induces entrepreneurs to reallocate capital from the production of capital goods to that of consumer goods. The fall in real wages makes 'shorter' methods of production more profitable, so that there will be a tendency to use more labour with the existing machinery (by working overtime, double shifts, etc.), and to invest in less expensive, less labour-saving or less durable machinery. Hayek argued that the implied decrease in the demand for capital goods will become so strong as to turn the boom into a recession. This effect is called the Ricardo effect.[34] During the recession entrepreneurs will correct their investment errors by reallocating their capital from higher- to lower-order goods.[35] The recession ends either because of an increase in the supply of money or because of the reverse operation of the Ricardo effect.

The above suggests that Hayek's business cycle theory contains at least two unique features. First, it adopts the Mengerian framework of the structure of production. This means that capital goods are heterogeneous, and that they stand in a vertical, time-consuming relationship to each other. Second, the theory incorporates Cantillon effects, in the sense that an increase in the supply of money leads to redistributions between the owners of different factors of production and between the entrepreneurs in different stages of production. As Foss pointed out, 'Hayek's argument is . . . dependent . . . on the time path of real factor incomes relative to the linear representation of productive activities [i.e. the vertical structure of production] and the lags *this* implies' (Foss 1990: 6, original emphasis). It takes time before the additional money is spread out evenly throughout the economy.[36] The ensuing distortion of the structure of relative prices follows from the fact that economic agents differ from each other. These differences may concern: (1) their utility functions, (2) their abilities to gather information (and hence their information sets), (3) their expectations formation functions, and/or (4) their productive activities (i.e. the order of goods which they produce). In his work on business cycles, Hayek did not explicitly discuss the heterogeneity of the first three issues, but merely stressed the fourth. The heterogeneity of production goods and productive activities accounts for the *mal*investments and the ensuing distortion of the structure of production. In his later work, Hayek increasingly recognized the importance of the dispersion of knowledge, which implies heterogeneity of information as well as expectations.

3. THE ROLE OF MATHEMATICAL FORMALIZATION IN HAYEKIAN AND NEW CLASSICAL ECONOMICS

The above exposition of Hayek's business cycle theory indicates that business cycles are highly complex phenomena. According to Hayek (1952), this complexity reduces the scope of mathematical formalization. He argued that mathematics is the appropriate language for those sciences which adopt the so-called analytic method. This method derives the unobservable behaviour of the elements of a system from the observable behaviour of the system as a whole. For instance, the unobservable behaviour of atoms in some substance is derived from the observable behaviour of that substance. According to Hayek, the usefulness of mathematics for explanatory purposes in the natural sciences follows from the fact that it is 'the discipline developed to describe complexes of relationships between elements which have no attributes except these relations' (ibid.: 33). The relationships and hence the system as a whole implicitly define the elements.[37] If transposed to the social sciences, the analytic method would mean that the behaviour of the elements is explained in terms of inductively obtained developmental laws for the social system as a whole. Hayek rejected this transposition, and instead proposed that the social sciences should adopt the compositive method (ibid.: 43). This method holds that the behaviour of the system as a whole should be composed from the behaviour of the elements, whereby knowledge about the latter is derived from introspection. Consequently, unlike the natural scientist, the social scientist reconstructs social phenomena from the known properties of the elements (ibid.: 67). However, it should be noted that this reconstruction is confronted with the inevitable imperfection of the human mind. According to Hayek, 'The number of separate variables which in any particular social phenomenon will determine the result of a given change will as a rule be far too large for any human mind to master and manipulate effectively' (ibid.: 73). Instead, he claimed that mathematical models show merely the principle of coherence between the composing elements of the system, and cannot yield precise predictions without knowledge of the numerical values of all its constants. Quoting similar observations by Cournot and Pareto, he concluded that this would practically exceed the power of algebraic analysis. Stated differently, he opposed the heuristic prescription of building mathematical models which can be solved analytically (ibid.: 75, n. 8), because this prescription could only be adhered to by imposing restrictions on economic theory that exclude relevant aspects of economic reality from analysis. This is not to say that Hayek rejected abstraction and simplification. After all, all theorizing implies the introduction of simplifying assumptions.

Instead, Hayek argued that such mathematical models *over*simplify social reality. Consequently, they affect the domain of economic analysis, eliminating those problems from that domain that cannot be formalized in analytically solvable models.

Hayek thus downplayed the appropriateness and usefulness of mathematical formalization. Nevertheless, in recent years some attempts have been undertaken to formalize his views mathematically. For instance, Thalenhorst and Wenig offer such a formalization of Hayek's *Prices and Production* (1931), but they assume that the rate of profit is identical for each stage of production (Thalenhorst and Wenig 1984: 217). This absence of inter-stage profit opportunities means that there are no distortions of the structure of production and hence that there cannot have been malinvestments. As Thalenhorst and Wenig acknowledge, their analysis cannot discuss Hayekian monetary dynamics (ibid.: 215). It should be noted, though, that their mathematical model may serve as a starting-point for a mathematical analysis. Relaxation of some of its assumptions may render the analysis of Hayekian monetary dynamics possible. Nevertheless, until now Hayek's business cycle theory has never been formalized as a mathematical model.

In contrast, New Classicals adopt the heuristic prescription that economics should build analogue models which mimic the behaviour of (the time series as generated by) actual economies. One of its main proponents, Robert E. Lucas, defined a theory as 'an explicit set of instructions for building a parallel or analogue system – a mechanical, imitation economy' (Lucas 1980: 272). This 'fully articulated artificial economy [should] behave through time so as to imitate closely the time series behavior of actual economies' (Lucas 1977: 219). Arguing that advances in mathematical problem-solving techniques constitute a main source of scientific progress, Lucas implied that such models should be analytically solvable (1980: 272). This led Butos to conclude that 'new classical economists limit their conceptualization by the techniques available, while for Hayek the conceptualization of a problem points to the limitations of the available techniques' (Butos 1986: 337). The limitations of these techniques force New Classicals to introduce additional simplifying assumptions. More particularly, they lead to the elimination of Cantillon effects.

4. THE ELIMINATION OF CANTILLON EFFECTS: NEW CLASSICAL BUSINESS CYCLE THEORY

New Classical Economics (NCE) started as an attempt to formalize Friedman's (1968) and Phelps's (1967) explanation of the relationship between the rate of inflation and (the rate of change of) the unemployment rate, the so-called Phillips curve.[38] This explanation adopts the Natural Rate Hypothesis (NRH), according to which the economy will tend towards its 'natural rate of output' or 'natural rate of unemployment'.[39] The resulting full-information general equilibrium is called the Natural Rate Equilibrium (NRE). Given the absence of money illusion on the part of the economic agents, it implies that there is no relationship between real and purely monetary variables, so that money is neutral in the comparative-static sense.[40] However, this clearly conflicts with the Phillips curve, which does reflect such a relationship. Friedman and Phelps had argued that deviations of the NRE reflect expectational errors, due to incomplete information. Phelps (1970) additionally suggested that this incompleteness of information could be explained in a general-equilibrium framework in which local markets are spatially and informationally separated. The NCE would elaborate this suggestion.

New Classicals adopt at least four crucial assumptions. First, economic agents are considered to be price-takers. A Walrasian *tâtonnement* process is assumed to ensure perfect price flexibility and hence continuous market-clearing. As a corollary, New Classical business cycle theory is also called equilibrium business cycle theory. Second, aggregate real output is formulated as the 'Lucas supply function'. This function holds that deviations from the NRE can only result from unanticipated nominal price changes and hence from expectational errors. However, these errors are rational in the sense that they only differ randomly from actual realizations of economic variables. This Rational Expectations Hypothesis (REH) is the third assumption. The fourth assumption is that economic agents have incomplete information about relevant economic variables.

The NCE explains expectational errors in terms of exogenous shocks, which are either real or monetary in nature. The shocks are reflected in the prices which agents observe. Given the fourth (informational) assumption, agents must act on the basis of incomplete information. This means that they will make expectational errors. According to the REH, rational economic agents do not make systematic expectational errors, because such errors are easily detectable. The problem then arises how unsystematic, serially uncorrelated, shocks can account for the persistence which characterizes the economic data over the business cycle. The NCE solves this problem by adopting a solution which had already been given in the 1930s. Slutzky (1937) and Frisch (1933) had already shown that random shocks could lead to serially correlated movements of the variables in the system under consideration, due to some propagation mechanism. Thus, the crucial distinction, as Lucas and Sargent (1978: 313) noted, is that between sources of impulses and propagation mechanisms. The latter ensure that serially uncorrelated disturbances will have serially correlated effects. Instances of such mechanisms have been provided by Lucas (1975), Blinder and Fischer (1981) and Kydland and Prescott (1980), among others.[41] These mechanisms are instances of what Barro called 'adjustment-costs explanations' of persistence (Barrow 1981b: 48). They explain persistence by introducing friction into the economic system.

The above description of New Classical business cycle theory already reflects that New Classicals formulate their views as mathematical models. However, mathematical formalization usually involves the introduction of additional simplifying assumptions. These assumptions will depend on the modelling strategy followed. New Classicals use two such strategies, namely the representative-agent approach and the islands approach.

The representative-agent approach

Early New Classical models were so-called 'representative-agent models'. The concept of the representative agent was first explicitly introduced by Marshall (1890), whose 'representative firm' is some sort of non-mathematical, fictituous average entity.[42] In contrast, the NCE defines the representative agent (individual, household, firm) as the mathematical mean of the (sub)system as a whole.[43] This means that the concept is used as a hypostatization of this system.[44] As Hoover (1988: 242) observed, New Classicals treat aggregates and index numbers as if they obey the principles of microeconomics. They restrict their analyses to the mathematical mean, accounting for deviations from this mean by adding a probability distribution. As stated above, the NCE uses Friedman's (1968) natural rate of output (unemployment) as its benchmark. The Lucas supply function can therefore be formulated as follows:

$$y_t = z + \alpha(1 - \beta)(p_t - p_t^e) \qquad (4.1)$$

in which y is the actual aggregated level of real output, z is the 'natural rate of output, p_t is the actual general price level, p_t^e is the expected general price level, α is a parameter indicating the extent to which a deviation of p_t^e from p_t influences y_t, and β is a parameter indicating that the higher the volatility of changes in p_t the less output differs from its natural rate.

The Lucas supply function shows that an unanticipated change in the general price level will induce the representative agent to change his output. Given the New Classical assumption of comparative-static neutrality of money, this indicates that unanticipated changes in the money supply can raise actual output above its natural rate (and equivalently actual unemployment below its natural rate). In this case, the incompleteness of information ensures that the representative agent makes an expectational error about the nature of the change in the actual general price level, believing that it reflects real instead of monetary changes in the economy. However, the agent will adjust his actions as soon as the correct information becomes available. This does not mean, though, that the economy immediately returns to its new NRE, because propagation mechanisms may hamper this adjustment by transmitting the effects of the random expectational errors to subsequent periods. This transmission yields a business cycle.

Incomplete information may thus explain why monetary changes have real effects. The representative agent's information set therefore plays a crucial role in the New Classical approach under consideration.[45] Given this set, the representative agent by definition forms rational expectations which equal the mathematical mean of the aggregate expectations, albeit in a probabilistic sense. That is, the 'representative agent approach' assumes away systematic differences between economic agents. This may be based on the argument that the expectational deviations will cancel out, presumably due to the 'Law of Large Numbers'.[46] This 'law' is a statistical regularity which applies only if the elements of the population under consideration belong to the same 'class', that is, if they do not differ from each other in any relevant aspect. The assumption that the agents are identical will be called the homogeneity postulate. This postulate is adopted in the New Classical representative-agent models, so that these models concentrate on the magnitude of aggregates, disregarding (changes in) their composition. This implies that redistributions between economic agents are considered to be irrelevant in the explanation of industrial fluctuations. This restriction of the domain of New Classical Economics could be circumvented by introducing several 'representative agents'. This strategy is adopted in the 'islands approach', which can be regarded as a more sophisticated version of the representative-agent approach.

The islands approach

The 'islands approach' uses Phelps's (1970) suggestion that markets can be seen as islands. In particular, it was adopted by Lucas (1972, 1975), Lucas and Prescott (1974) and Barro (1976, 1980). These models consider an economy in which a single output is produced, which must be divided between private consumption, government consumption, and next period's capital. The population consists of identical households, so that their utility functions do not differ. The conjunction of these two assumptions implies that economic agents are also identical with respect to their productive activities. However, this does not mean that there are no differences at all between them. As Lucas stated, the 'islands' or markets are 'imperfectly linked both physically and informationally' (1975: 180), so that information is assumed to be homogeneous across agents in a given market, but heterogeneous across markets.[47] The 'islands approach' thus assumes that economic agents only differ from each other as regards their information sets. Hence, it disregards 'intra-market' distributional effects. The study of such effects *between* markets, however, appears to remain possible.

As was stated above, New Classical business cycle theory explains industrial fluctuations in terms of expectational errors. These errors are caused by discrepancies between changes in the relative prices and in the general price level. That is, the economic agents must determine how much of a given change in their respective local prices must be attributed to a change in the general price level, and how much of the change in local prices reflects changes in real factors. Agents must therefore form expectations about the difference between their local price level and the general (global) price level. Given the assumption of complete local and incomplete global information, the agents' information sets include $p_t(z)$ but not p_t. They must then form expectations about the latter, so that their output decision can be described as follows:

$$y_t(z) = z + \alpha (1 - \beta) (p_t(z) - p_t^e) \quad (4.2)$$

where the subscripts denote the time period under consideration, and z is an index of location. Since expectations are rational, agents are assumed to know the 'true' probability distribution of p_t^e and hence the difference between $p_t(z)$ and p_t^e.[48] According to Pesaran (1989: 57), this means that the problem of heterogeneity of information across markets is circumvented. After all, the relevant decision variable is $d_t(z) = p_t(z) - p_t$, and all agents are assumed to know its 'true' distribution. As there can only be one 'true' distribution, this means that their respective information sets do not differ in any relevant (i.e. systematic) manner.[49] Information about the relevant decision variable turns out to be homogeneous across markets. The problem of the heterogeneity of information across markets in the 'islands models' is thus circumvented by assuming that all economic agents know the 'true' probability distribution of $d_t(z)$.[50]

In conclusion, the islands approach and the representative-agent approach assume that economic agents do not differ with respect to their utility functions, their abilities to gather information (and hence their relevant information sets), their expectations formation functions (and, given the information sets, their expectations) and their productive activities. This means that distribution effects, such as

Cantillon effects, cannot be analysed. Their elimination from the domain of economics is the price to be paid by New Classicals for their particular version of the heuristic prescription of mathematical formalization.

5. CONCLUSIONS

According to Blaug 'the Cantillon effect . . . denies "the homogeneity postulate" by asserting that changes in prices produced by cash injections vary with the nature of the injection and, moreover, that changes in absolute prices are almost always associated with alterations in relative prices' (Blaug 1962: 155). Our analysis allows for a more explicit formulation of this homogeneity postulate. In particular, the NCE assumes that agents are homogeneous with respect to:

1 the utility functions,
2 the abilities to gather information (and hence the information sets),
3 the expectations formation processes (and, given (2), the expectations), and
4 their productive activities (i.e. the order of goods they produce).

These assumptions reflect that New Classical business cycle theory explains cyclical fluctuations in terms of aggregate variables, thereby implying that distributional effects do not play an important role. In contrast, Hayekian business cycle theory also incorporates changes in the composition of aggregate variables. It stresses the complexity of social reality, but in doing so it completely surrenders to the impossibility of modelling the economy in full.[51] Hayek's business cycle theory allows for the inclusion of Cantillon effects and the ensuing (comparative-static) non-neutrality of money, but it does so at the cost of mathematical rigour. In contrast, the NCE attempts to build analytically solvable models that mimic the behaviour of actual economies. In doing so it introduces simplifying assumptions which eliminate Cantillon and other distribution effects from this domain. In this sense the New Classical heuristic prescription of mathematical formalization adversely affects the domain of economic explanation as compared with Hayek's analysis.

NOTES

The authors wish to thank Jack Birner, Ben Elzas, Harry Garretsen, Maarten Janssen and Emiel Wubben for their useful comments on an earlier version of this paper. Of course, the authors remain responsible for any errors.

1 For example, see Kantor (1979), Colander and Guthrie (1980), Laidler (1982) and Scheide (1986).

2 Cf. Butos (1986) and van Zijp (1990). For an analysis of the respective developments in and differences between Austrian and New Classical Economics, see van Zijp (1993).

3 Some writers see this as the more recent definition of neutral money, cf. Lutz (1969: 112) and Klausinger (1989: 177). But it was implied in the quantity theory all along and thus predates the other connotation of neutral money by a couple of centuries.

4 Monetary equilibrium is defined as the situation in which the money supply at any moment in time equals the volume of money demanded. In Dutch discussions of the 1950s the term was also used within the framework of period analysis, in the sense that income earned in one period and available in the next period is equal to income earned in the next period. In other words, national income is constant. This connotation of the term is not applied here. See for references Visser (1971: 404).

5 The term 'neutral money' appears to have been introduced by L. von Bortkiewicz in 1919; see de Jong (1973: 8n) and Patinkin and Steiger (1989: 135).

6 Wicksell (1898: 102) defines the natural rate of interest as 'the rate of interest which would be determined by supply and demand if no use were made of money and all lending were effected in the form of real capital goods'.

7 Cf. Myrdal (1933: 436) and Thomas (1935: 37–40).

8 The discussion has been admirably summarized by de Jong (1973). See also Visser (1971).

9 Cf. Hayek (1967: 31; 1933b: 159) and Koopmans (1933: 228).

10 In a letter to Robertson (reprinted in Fase 1983: 322–8) Koopmans explained that his frame of reference was an *ideal* equilibrium economy where, in his words, no stocks of goods had to be held for mere liquidity purposes, i.e. a frictionless barter economy.

11 Koopmans (1933: 230) talks about an hypothetical situation that could not exist in reality, a '*hypothetische*, in der Realität wohl überhaupt nicht denkbare Zustand'.

12 Hayek defined the problem as 'one of isolating the one-sided effects of money . . . which will appear when, after the division of the barter transaction into two separate transactions, one of these takes place without the other complementary transaction' (Hayek 1967: 130). This supports Lutz's view.

13 Patinkin attempted to 'conceive of a barter economy as the limiting position of a money economy whose nominal quantity of money is made smaller and smaller' (Patinkin 1965: 75). He could not but concede that the price level falls in the process, leaving the real quantity of money unchanged, but still maintained, then and also a quarter of a century later that 'This drawback notwithstanding, there does not seem to be any other meaningful way of comparing the respective equilibrium positions of a barter and money economy' (Patinkin and Steiger 1989: 138). We would suggest that there is no meaningful way at all to compare these equilibrium positions.

14 See Becker and Baumol (1962) and Patinkin (1965: 75, 175).

15 Few, if any, quantity theorists denied that money is non-neutral in the short period, see Visser (1974: 135–6) and Humphrey (1991).

16 Cf. the seminal article by Metzler (1951).

17 Conditions 5 and 6 are not mentioned in Aschheim's 1973 article and condition 3 is reformulated as the absence of *uncompensated* distribution effects. Presumably he subsumed conditions 5 and 6 under 3.
18 See Visser (1971: 423–5; 1974: 176–7).
19 See on this Patinkin (1965: 288–94), who notes that neutrality is retained if government bonds are not seen as net wealth. See also Patinkin (1989).
20 Cf. Tobin (1965).
21 Post-Keynesian analysis also emphasizes distribution effects, but it tends to play down the impact of money on other economic variables, stressing instead the residual character of money. None the less, money is considered far from neutral, as its creation is dependent on the borrowing needs of all kinds of economic actors and borrowing is influenced by the central bank's interest rate policies. See Arestis (1988).
22 The phenomenon of 'forced savings' was already discerned by Ricardo, who considered it relevant for the short run only. Other economists have acknowledged that forced savings could also change the natural rate of interest. For a history of this phenomenon, see Hayek (1932), Viner (1964: 187–97) and Humphrey (1991: 9–11).
23 See FitzGerald Scott (1989, in particular p. 159), Lucas (1988), and Romer (1986).
24 Cf. Solow (1988, in particular pp. 311–12).
25 See, for example, Butler (1990) and Kelsey (1990).
26 It appears that Blaug (1962: 21) was the first to use the term 'Cantillon effect'.
27 Wicksell (1898) was not the first to use the concept of a natural rate. As Haberler (1946: 36, n. 1) observed, this concept (and even the term) can be found in earlier English economic writings. For instance, Smith (1776, I. vii, p. 65) argued that 'The natural price . . . is, as it were, the central price, to which the prices of all commodities are continually gravitating'. More importantly, Thornton (1802: 253–5) already explicated the so-called indirect mechanism, which holds that an increase in the supply of money is translated in a rise in the general price level through a fall in the market rate of interest and the ensuing increase in investment. He thereby identified an equilibrium rate of interest, using the adjective 'natural' as early as 1811. However, as Wicksell's student Carl Uhr (1960: 200) pointed out, Wicksell had not been directly exposed to Thornton's ideas, and the influence has been merely indirect, through Ricardo.
28 This process of credit creation will result in a process of 'credit multiplication' if the initial credit expansion is (partly) deposited at another private bank, which in turn increases its loans. This process of 'credit multiplication' presupposes that banks adhere to a fractional reserve ratio, and it can go on as long as the additional credit is not used in a way which leads quickly to the market for consumer goods.
29 Contrary to his Austrian forerunner Mises, Hayek (1933a: 150) considered the first influence empirically less important and the second a rather special case. Mises had criticized the monetary policy of the 1920s, which were highly inflationist, thus explaining cyclical fluctuations as the result of exogenous disturbances. In contrast, Hayek attempted to elaborate an *endogenous* business cycle theory, thereby concentrating on the third influence. However, in the 1970s he considered the second influence

to be the most important. He then proposed to denationalize money which would render it impossible for the monetary authorities to pursue inflationary policy. This changed his explanation of business cycles from an endogenous into an exogenous one.

30 Note that this result not only applies to unanticipated but also to anticipated monetary expansion.

31 Note that when preferences and patterns of expenditure differ between economic agents, the redistributions of income also imply shifts in the relevant general equilibrium, and hence changes in the natural rate of interest. Moreover, the effects of the redistributions depend on the route according to which the additional money spreads throughout the economy. It seems therefore correct to infer that the relevant general equilibrium changes continuously: 'the target is moving'.

32 Hayek (1933d: 180) considered this possibility very unlikely.

33 He defined the real wage rate as the ratio of the money wage rate and the prices of the consumer goods produced by the labour under consideration (p. 8).

34 This effect derives its name from Ricardo's statement that 'with every rise in the price of labour, new temptations are offered to the use of machinery' (1817, Ch. I, Section V, pp. 26 ff.). It is designed to show that the boom will come to an end even if the market rate of interest were to remain constant. Hayek (1931) had already shown that the boom would cease in a situation in which the market rate of interest was perfectly flexible.

35 It should be noted that the Ricardo effect assumes that entrepreneurs expect the relatively higher prices of consumer goods and the relatively lower real wages to persist for a period of time that is long enough to make it worthwhile to change their methods of production. Hayek, (1939: 16–18) acknowledged this. Moreover, he also addressed the case in which entrepreneurs expect that the prices of consumer goods continue to rise. This will merely reinforce the effect, due to the continuing fall in real wages.

36 In order to clarify his views Hayek compared a situation of continuous credit creation to a situation in which a viscous liquid, such as honey (read: money), is poured into a vessel (the economy): 'if the stream hits the surface at one point, a little mound will form there from which the additional matter will slowly spread outward' (Hayek 1969: 281). This analogy reflects that there is no such thing as 'helicopter money'. It leaves the question unanswered why the liquid is viscous (i.e. why it takes so long for the additional money to spread throughout the economy).

37 In this sense, the natural sciences create a 'new world', consisting of implicitly defined elements which cannot be perceived by man's senses. According to Hayek, the significance of the theories of these sciences 'is due to the fact that we possess rules, a "key", which enables us to translate them into statements about perceptible phenomena' (Hayek 1952: 34).

38 The main New Classical proponents are Robert Lucas, Jr, Thomas Sargent, Neil Wallace, Robert Barro, Edward Prescott and Finn Kydland.

39 As Maddock observed, 'It is quite common in this [i.e. New Classical] literature to switch back and forth between income and unemployment by replacing log unemployment for log income minus log trend income'

(Maddock 1979; 158, n. 4). Therefore the natural rate of output (NRO) and the natural rate of unemployment (NRU) are considered to be reciprocal.

40 For instance, see Sargent and Wallace (1975: 221–4).

41 Lucas (1975) accounted for persistence effects by incorporating physical capital, which is affected by random changes in the growth rate of money and the ensuing Mundell–Tobin effect. Once installed, the physical capital stock can only be adjusted at the rate of depreciation. Blinder and Fischer (1981) used the gradual adjustment of inventory stocks of finished goods as a mechanism to ensure serial correlation. Kydland and Prescott explain persistence by arguing that 'there are long lags from the time when changes in its determinants call for an increase in the capital stock until the time when the new capital starts yielding services' (Kydland and Prescott 1980: 175).

42 In Marshall's view, 'a Representative firm is that particular average sort of firm, at which we need to look in order to see how far the economies, *internal and external*, of production on a large scale have extended generally in the industry and country in question' (Marshall 1890: 317–18, original emphasis.,

43 For instance, Lucas and Rapping (1969: 25) deflate the aggregate labour supply function by an index of the number of households, Lucas (1972: 68) assumes that each period N identical individuals are born who each supply n units of labour which yield n units of output. Sargent (1972, 1973, 1976) uses aggregates only. His work builds on the microfoundations as provided by Lucas.

44 This was already stressed by Runde and Torr (1985: 217), who argued that the rational expectations approach (i.e. the NCE) does not analyse individual, but rather the market's behaviour. In a general-equilibrium analysis this means that the representative individual is merely another way of depicting the system as a whole.

45 Lucas emphasized this property of the NCE when discussing the (New-) Keynesian assumption that nominal prices are rigid because of some form of collective bargaining. He objected that 'The central issue for a theory of nominal price rigidity . . . is not the nature of the game agents are assumed to be engaged in, but rather the *information* agents are assumed to have about the state of the system at each date' (Lucas 1987: 94).

46 Haltiwanger and Waldman (1989) argue that this will only hold under very special circumstances which concern the nature and intensity of the interrelations between the actions of the individuals. They distinguish two types of interrelations, namely *congestion* and *synergism*. The former applies when the incentive for agent i to engage in an activity will be lower if the number of participants is higher. In the case of synergism the reverse holds. Agent i's costs and benefits of participating in an activity can therefore be modelled as a function of the number of participants. Their analysis comes to the conclusion that 'Only under very special conditions do standard [i.e. micro-type] rational expectations and aggregate rational expectations yield equivalent results' (ibid.: 631). It turns out that 'The size of the difference [between the two equilibria] will be larger (i) the larger is the divergence in expectations under aggregate rational expectations, and (ii) the more synergistic is the environment' (ibid.). This means that New Classicals implicitly assume

that there is no congestion or synergism. The number of participants does not influence the individuals' cost–benefit analysis.

47 According to Pesaran, this feature follows from the New Classical assumption that 'All firms [or individuals] observe current equilibrium prices in their local markets' (Pesaran 1989: 57). Such prices clear the market under consideration, thus conveying all information on that market. As on a given market individuals derive their information from observing the same equilibrium price, they will have identical information. That is, information will be homogeneous on that market, but heterogeneous across markets.

48 The fact that the agents know the 'true' probability distributions of changes in the money supply, and in the distribution of individuals over both markets is merely another way of stating that expectations are formed rationally in the sense of Muth (1961). Muth's REH holds that 'expectations of firms (or, more generally, the subjective probability distribution of outcomes) tend to be distributed, for the same information set, about the prediction of the theory (or the "objective" probability distributions of outcomes)' (ibid.: 316).

49 For instance, Barro explicitly assumed that 'all markets have the same *ex ante* distribution of price (Barro 1976: 85).

50 McCallum (1979) and Machlup (1983) have criticized the New Classical assumption that economic agents know the 'true' probability distributions, because it implies that they also know the 'correct' structure ('model') of the economy. It is not even clear why all agents would use the same (New Classical) 'model', and hence why expectations would be Muth-rational. Frydman concluded that 'the assumption that agents form rational expectations appears to conflict with the fact that the economy is decentralized' (Frydman 1983: 115).

51 This emphasis is consistent with the Austrian view that economic agents differ from each other in relevant aspects. These differences may even concern the 'models' which agents use.

REFERENCES

Arestis, Ph. (ed.) (1988) *Post-Keynesian Monetary Economics*, Aldershot: Edward Elgar.

Aschheim, J. (1973) 'Neutral money reconsidered', *Banca Nazionale del Lavoro Quarterly Review* 105: 75–83.

Aschheim, J., and C.-Y. Hsieh (1969) *Macroeconomics, Income and Monetary Theory*, Columbus, Ohio: Charles E. Merrill.

Barro, R.J. (1976) 'Rational expectations and the role of monetary policy', *Journal of Monetary Economics* 2: 1–32. Reprinted in R.J. Barro (1981), pp. 79–110.

—— (1980) 'A capital market in an equilibrium business cycle model', *Econometrica* 48: 1393–417. Reprinted in R.J. Barro (1981a) pp. 111–36.

—— (1981a) *Money, Expectations, and Business Cycles*, New York: Academic Press.

—— (1981b) 'The equilibrium approach to business cycles', in R.J. Barro *Money, Expectations, and Business Cycles*, New York: Academic Press, 1981, pp. 41–78.

Becker, G.S. and W.J. Baumol (1962) 'The Classical monetary theory: the outcome of the discussion', in J.J. Spengler and W.R. Allen (eds), *Essays in*

Economic Thought, 2nd edn, Chicago: Rand McNally.

Bikker, J.A. (1991a) 'Rente- en dividendstromen tussen sectoren', *Maandschrift Economie* 55(3): 207–25.

—— (1991b) 'Reële rente en sectorale verdeling van inkomen en vermogen', in A. Knoester and H. Visser (eds) *De hoge rëele rente en de Nederlandse economie*, Leiden-Antwerpen: Stenfert Kroese.

Blaug, M.(1962) *Economic Theory in Retrospect*, Cambridge: Cambridge University Press, 1990.

Blinder, A.S., and S. Fischer (1981) 'Inventories, rational expectations, and the business cycle', *Journal of Monetary Economics* 8: 277–304.

Butler, A. (1990) 'A Methodological approach to chaos: are economists missing the point?', *Review*, Federal Reserve Bank of St Louis, 72: 36–48.

Butos, W. (1986) 'Hayek and general equilibrium analysis', *Southern Economic Journal* 52: 332–43.

Cantillon, R. (1755) *Essai sur la nature du commerce en général* (edited and translated into English by H. Higgs), New York: A.M. Kelley, 1964. Reprint of a 1931 edition. Originally written between 1730 and 1734.

Colander, D. and Guthrie, R. (1980) 'Great expectations: What the Dickens do rational expectations mean?', *Journal of Post-Keynesian Economics* 3: 219–34.

Fase, M.M.G. (1983) 'The 1930 correspondence between Koopmans, Robertson and Gregory', *De Economist*, 131(3): 305–43.

Fisher, I. (1933) 'The debt-deflation theory of great depressions', *Econometrica* 1: 337–57.

FitzGerald Scott, M. (1989) *A New View of Economic Growth*, Oxford: Oxford University Press.

Foss, N.J. (1990) 'A note on the lag-structure in Austrian business cycle theory', unpublished paper, Copenhagen: Center for Educational Research.

Friedman, M. (1968) 'The role of monetary policy', *American Economic Review* 58: 1–17.

Frisch, R.A. (1933) 'Propagation problems and impulses problems in dynamic economics', in *Economic Essays in Honour of Gustav Cassel*, London: Allen & Unwin, pp. 171–205.

Frydman, R. (1983) 'Individual rationality, decentralization, and the rational expectations hypothesis', in R. Frydman and E.S. Phelps (eds) *Individual Forecasting and Aggregate Outcomes*, Cambridge: Cambridge University Press.

Haberler, G. (1946) *Prosperity and Depression*, New York: United Nations, Lake Success.

Haltiwanger, J.C., and M. Waldman (1989) 'Rational expectations in the aggregate', *Economic Inquiry* 27: 619–36.

Hayek, F.A. (1928) 'Intertemporal price equilibrium and movements in the value of money', in F.A. Hayek *Money, Capital and Fluctuations*, ed. R. McCloughry, London: Routledge, 1984, pp. 71–117.

—— (1931) *Prices and Production*, London: Routledge & Kegan Paul, 1935.

—— (1932) 'A note on the development of the doctrine of "forced saving"', *Quarterly Journal of Economics* 47(3). Reprinted in F.A. von Hayek (1939) 183–98.

—— (1933a) *Monetary Theory and the Trade Cycle*, New York: August Kelley, 1966. First published in German as *Geldtheorie und Konjunkturtheorie*, Wien: Hölder-Pichler-Tempski (reprint Salzburg: Wolfgang Neugebauer, 1976).

—— (1933b) 'Über "neutrales Geld"', *Zeitschrift für Nationalökonomie* 4. Reprinted as 'On "neutral money"', in F.A. Hayek *Money, Capital and Fluctuations*, ed. R. McCloughry, London: Routledge, 1984.

—— (1933c) 'Price expectations, monetary disturbances and malinvestments', in F.A. Hayek (1939), pp. 135–56.

—— (1933d) 'The present state and immediate prospects of the study of industrial fluctuations', in F.A. Hayek (1939), pp. 171–82.

—— (1939) *Profits, Interest and Investment*, London: Routledge & Kegan Paul, 1950.

—— (1942) 'The Ricardo effect', *Economica* IX, 127–52. Reprinted in F.A. Hayek (1949) *Individualism and Economic Order*, London: Routledge & Kegan Paul, 1976.

—— (1952) *The Counter-Revolution of Science*, Part I, Indianapolis, Liberty Press, 1979. First published in *Economica* IX: 267–91, and *Economica* X: 34–63.

—— (1967) 'The theory of complex phenomena', in F.A. Hayek *Studies in Philosophy, Politics and Economics*, Chicago: University of Chicago Press.

—— (1969) 'Three elucidations of the Ricardo effect', *Journal of Political Economy* 77: 274–85. Reprinted in F.A. Hayek *New Studies in Philosophy, Politics, Economics and the History of Ideas*, London: Routledge & Kegan Paul, 1978, pp. 165–78.

Hoover, K.D. (1988) *The New Classical Macroeconomics*, Oxford: Blackwell.

Hume, D. (1752) 'Of money', in *Political Discourses*, Edinburgh. Reprinted in D. Hume, *Writings in Economics*, ed. E. Rotwein, Edinburgh: Nelson, 1955.

Humphrey, T.M. (1991) 'Nonneutrality of money in Classical monetary thought', *Economic Review*, Federal Reserve Bank of Richmond, 77(2) 3–15.

de Jong, F.J. (1973) *Developments of Monetary Theory in the Netherlands*, Rotterdam: Rotterdam University Press.

Kantor, B. (1979) 'Rational expectations and economic thought', *Journal of Economic Literature* 17: 1422–41.

Kelsey, D. (1990) 'An introduction to nonlinear dynamics and its application to economics', in F. Hahn (ed.) *The Economics of Missing Markets, Information, and Games*, Oxford: Oxford University Press.

Keynes, J.M. (1936) *The General Theory of Employment, Interest and Money*, London: Macmillan, 1961.

Klausinger, H. (1989) 'On the history of neutral money', in D.A. Walker (ed.) *Perspectives on the History of Economic Thought; Volume II: Twentieth-Century Economic Thought*, Aldershot: Edward Elgar.

Koopmans, J.G. (1933) 'Zum Problem des "neutralen" Geldes', in F.A. von Hayek (ed.) *Beiträge zur Geldtheorie*, Vienna: Springer.

Kydland, F.E., and E.C. Prescott (1980) 'A competitive theory of fluctuations and the feasibility and desirability of stabilization policy', in S. Fisher (ed.) *Rational Expectations and Economic Policy*, Chicago: University of Chicago Press.

Laidler, D. (1982) *Monetarist Perspectives*, Oxford: Philip Allan.

Lucas, R.E., Jr (1972) 'Expectations and the neutrality of money', *Journal of Political Economy* 83: 1113–44. Reprinted in R.E. Lucas, Jr (1981), pp. 66–89.

—— (1975) 'An equilibrium model of the business cycle, *Journal of Political*

Economy 83: 1113–44. Reprinted in R.E. Lucas, Jr (1981), pp. 179–214.

—— (1977) 'Understanding business cycles', in R.E. Lucas, Jr (1981), pp. 215–39.

—— (1980) 'Methods and problems in business cycle theory', *Journal of Money, Credit and Banking* 12: 696–715. Reprinted in R.E. Lucas, Jr (1981), pp. 271–96.

—— (1981) *Studies in Business-Cycle Theory*, Oxford: Blackwell.

—— (1987) *Models of Business Cycles*, Oxford: Blackwell.

—— (1988) 'On the mechanism of economic development', *Journal of Monetary Economics* 22(1) 3–42.

Lucas, R.E., Jr and E.C. Prescott (1974) 'Equilibrium search and unemployment', *Journal of Economic Theory* 7, 188–209. Reprinted in Lucas (1981), pp. 156–78.

Lucas, R.E., Jr and L.E. Rapping (1969) 'Real wages, employment, and inflation', *Journal of Political Economy* 77: 721–54. Reprinted in Lucas (1981), pp. 19–58.

Lucas, R.E., Jr and T.J. Sargent (1978) 'After Keynesian macroeconomics', *After the Phillips Curve: Persistence of High Inflation and High Unemployment*, Boston: Federal Reserve Bank of Boston. Reprinted in Lucas and Sargent (1981), pp. 295–319.

Lucas, R.E., Jr and T.J. Sargent (eds) (1981) *Rational Expectations and Econometric Practice*, London: Allen & Unwin.

Lutz, F.A. (1969) 'On neutral money', in E. Streissler *et al.*, *Roads to Freedom: Essays in Honour of Friedrich A. von Hayek*, London: Routledge & Kegan Paul.

Machlup, F. (1983) 'The rationality of "rational expectations"', *Kredit und Kapital* 16: 72–83.

Maddock, R. (1979) 'Rational Expectations, Political Business Cycles and the Course of Macroeconomic Theory', unpublished Ph.D. dissertation, Duke University, Durham (NC).

Marshall, A. (1890) *Principles of Economics*, London: Macmillan, 1947.

McCallum, B. (1979) 'The current state of the policy-ineffectiveness debate', *American Economic Review* 69: 240–5.

Menger, C. (1871) *Grundsätze der Volkswirtschaftslehre*, Gesammelte Werke, Band I, Tübingen: J.C.B. Mohr (Paul Siebeck), 1968.

Metzler, L.A. (1951) 'Wealth, saving, and the rate of interest', *Journal of Political Economy* 59(2): 93–116.

Muth, J. (1961) 'Rational expectations and the theory of price movements', *Econometrica* 29: 315–35.

Myrdal, G. (1933) 'Der Gleichgewichtsbegriff als Instrument der geldtheoretischen Analyse', in F.A. von Hayek (ed.) (1933) *Beiträge zur Geldtheorie*, Vienna: Springer.

O'Driscoll, G.P., Jr and M. Rizzo (1985) *The Economics of Time and Ignorance*, Oxford: Blackwell.

Patinkin, D. (1965) *Money, Interest, and Prices*, 2nd edn, New York: Harper & Row.

—— (1989) 'Neutrality of money', in J. Eatwell, M. Milgate and P. Newman (eds) *Money (The New Palgrave)*, London: Macmillan.

Patinkin, D. and O. Steiger (1989) 'In search of the "veil of money" and the "neutrality of money": a note on the origin of terms', *Scandinavian Journal of Economics* 91: 131–46.

Pesaran, M.H. (1989) *The Limits of Rational Expectations*, Oxford: Blackwell, 2nd revised printing.

Phelps, E.S. (1967) 'Phillips curves, expectations of inflation and optimal unemployment over time', *Economica* 34: 254–81.

—— (1970) 'The new microeconomics in employment and inflation theory', in E.S. Phelps (ed.) *Microeconomic Foundations of Employment and Inflation Theory*, New York: Norton.

Ricardo, D. (1817) *The Principles of Political Economy and Taxation*, London: Everyman's Library, 1978.

Romer, P.M. (1986) 'Increasing returns and long-run growth', *Journal of Political Economy* 94(5): 1002–37.

Runde, J. and C. Torr (1985) 'Divergent expectations and rational expectations', *South African Journal of Economics* 53: 217–25.

Sargent, T.J. (1972) 'Anticipated inflation and the nominal rate of interest', *Quarterly Journal of Economics* 86: 212–25.

—— (1973) 'Rational expectations, the real rate of interest, and the natural rate of unemployment', *Brookings Papers on Economic Activity* 2: 429–72. Reprinted in Lucas and Sargent (1981), pp. 159–98.

—— (1976) 'A classical macroeconometric model for the United States', *Journal of Political Economy* 84: 207–38. Reprinted in Lucas and Sargent (1981), pp. 521–51.

Sargent, T.J. and N. Wallace (1975) '"Rational" expectations, the optimal monetary instrument and the optimal money supply rule', *Journal of Political Economy* 83: 241–54. Reprinted in Lucas and Sargent (1981), pp. 215–28.

Scheide, J. (1986) 'New Classical and Austrian business cycle theory: is there a difference?', *Weltwirtschaftliches Archiv* 122: 575–98.

Slutzky, E. (1937) 'The summation of random causes as the source of cyclical processes', *Econometrica* 5: 105–46.

Smith, A. (1776) *An Inquiry into the Nature and Causes of the Wealth of Nations*, 2 vols, Chicago: University of Chicago Press, 1976.

Solow, R.M. (198) 'Growth theory and after', *American Economic Review* 78(3): 307–17.

Thalenhorst, J. and A. Wenig (1984) 'F.A. Hayek's "Prices and Production" re-analyzed', *Jahrbücher für Nationalökonomie und Statistik* 199: 213–36.

Thomas, B. (1935) 'The monetary doctrines of Professor Davidson', *Economic Journal* 45: 36–50.

Thornton, H. (1802) *An Enquiry into the Nature and Effects of the Paper Credit of Great Britain*, London: J. Hatchard and F. and C. Rivington. Reprinted 1939 by Allen & Unwin, London, and 1978 by A.M. Kelley, Fairfield, NJ.

Tobin, J. (1965) 'Money and economic growth', *Econometrica* 33: 671–84.

Uhr, C.G. (1960) *Economic Doctrines of Knut Wicksell*, Berkeley: University of California Press.

Viner, J. (1964) *Studies in the Theory of International Trade*, London: George Allen & Unwin.

Visser, H. (1971) 'Neutraal geld, een overzicht', *De Economist* 119: 169–79.

—— (1974) *The Quantity of Money*, London: Martin Robertson.

Wicksell, K. (1898) *Geldzins und Güterpreise*, Jena: Gustav Fischer. Translated in English as *Interest and Prices* (1936). Reprinted 1962 by A.M. Kelley, New York.

Wilson, T. (1940) 'Capital theory and the trade cycle', *Review of Economic Studies* 7: 169–79.

Zijp, R.W. van (1990) 'Hayek en Lucas: een vergelijking', *Maandschrift Economie* 54: 128–39.

—(1993) *Austrian and New Classical Business Cycle Theories*, Aldershot: Edward Elgar.

4

THE RELEVANCE OF HAYEK FOR MAINSTREAM ECONOMICS

Harry Garretsen

Within mainstream economics or neoclassical economics the influence of Austrian economics is rather limited. In microeconomic textbooks the work of early Austrians like Menger is recognized as one of the main influences in the development of the neoclassical theory of value. The reliance on a subjective theory of value in neoclassical economics can be traced back to Menger. In their discussion of the allocative properties of a decentralized economy as compared to those of a centrally guided economy, mainstream economists sometimes also refer to the Austrian contribution to the so-called calculation debate. In macroeconomic theory the Austrian monetary business-cycle theory as developed by Hayek is sometimes thought to be an important predecessor of the new-classical monetary and real equilibrium business-cycle theories. This representation of the relevance of Austrian economics in the mainstream literature is, however, seriously incomplete and incorrect in our view. It is incorrect to the extent that it rests upon an erroneous interpretation of Austrian subjectivism. It is incomplete because it neglects important developments in Austrian economics that were particularly initiated by Hayek's seminal paper 'Economics and Knowledge' (Hayek 1937).

The main goal of this chapter is to argue that the relevance of Austrian economics in general and Hayek's work in particular for the development of mainstream economic theory increases once the defects in the mainstream representation of Austrian economics are accounted for. This is especially true for those developments in neoclassical economics that try to deal with the co-ordination problem in decentralized economies. It turns out that in their analysis of the co-ordination problem neoclassical economics eventually has to face analytical questions (e.g. as to information dissemination, expectations formation and the role of conventions and institutions) that are central to Austrian economics.

It should be emphasized from the outset that our discussion of Austrian economics builds strongly on the theoretical insights as developed by Hayek. As will become clear in the remainder of this chapter this 'Hayekian' point of view implies that the Austrian ideas that build on Mises's approach to subjectivism (Mises 1949) are not considered to offer a fruitful starting-point for an analysis of the relevance of Austrian economics for neoclassical economics.

1. THE MISUSE OF AUSTRIAN IDEAS IN MAINSTREAM ECONOMICS

Austrian Economics and Neoclassical Microeconomics

The core concept of Austrian economics is subjectivism. The Austrian interpretation of subjectivism is rather different from its meaning in the neoclassical theory of value. In the latter the analysis focuses primarily upon the objective consequences of individual choices in terms of (changes in) relative prices on the aggregated level of the market. The individual agent is only used as a starting-point for the analysis whereas the individual agent is the focal point in the Austrian approach. This Austrian view of subjectivism has important implications for economic theorizing which are markedly different from those that arise out of the neoclassical version of subjectivism.

First of all, the uniqueness of individual choice means that the concept of equilibrium has a well-defined meaning on the level of the individual agent. Given the assumption of rational behaviour each agent is always in individual equilibrium. Note that this does not imply that each agent is also in expectational equilibrium. Individual equilibrium does not exclude that expectations are disappointed. In fact, the possibility that actual market prices do *not* meet agents' expectations must be looked upon as one of the driving forces of a market economy. In the neoclassical theory of value market prices are by definition equilibrium prices, and the use of these prices by individual agents combined with the equilibrium assumptions of perfect foresight or rational expectations precludes that expectations are disappointed. Hence, individual equilibrium, expectational equilibrium and market equilibrium coincide.

Second, one of the main criticisms by Austrians of neoclassical economics is precisely that the latter somehow assumes that the transition of individual equilibrium to a market equilibrium poses no analytical difficulties. According to this criticism the analytical difficulties are either directly assumed away (the Walrasian auctioneer, the representative agent assumption) or assumed away indirectly (the use of the rational expectations hypothesis).

Thirdly, the autonomy of individual choice implies that for every agent the knowledge about the (planned) actions of other agents is necessarily incomplete or simply non-existent and the amount of existing knowledge changes as time unfolds. This points to the importance of uncertainty and of historical time in Austrian economics. In mainstream economics uncertainty (as opposed to risk) is excluded from the analysis basically because it is thought to foreclose the analysis of wholly determinate outcomes, which are, of course, characteristic for neoclassical economics. For the same reason mainstream economists adhere to the concept of logical time instead of historical time.

These brief remarks on the different use of subjectivism already reveal that the Austrian analysis of a market economy differs sharply from the neoclassical analysis. In Austrian economics the concept of market process substitutes for the neoclassical concept of market equilibrium. What does the focus upon market process (which is by definition indeterminate) imply for the analysis of the actions of individual agents? Given the assumption of rational behaviour agents use (imperfect) price signals as a guide in their attempt to improve their position. Knoweldge of present and future market conditions is inevitably dispersed. Past individual decisions can always be improved upon in the present period either by changing your own actions or by alert behaviour by other agents. The actual realization of this opportunity implies a tendency towards a market equilibrium, but a particular market equilibrium will never be established, for as time goes by new information will become available and circumstances may change, creating scope for additional improvements, and so on.

The role of prices as transmitters of information is essential in the market process. Given the dispersion of knowledge, prices (imperfectly) disseminate information and provide incentives which may improve economic performance. In mainstream economics prices are also conceived of as transmitters of information but the transmission merely consists of agents deciding upon their actions *given* the existence of equilibrium prices. Prices co-ordinate the decisions of economic agents by assumption. The problem of dispersed knowledge that is the central co-ordination problem in Hayek's analysis does not exist in mainstream economics either because individual agents have full knowledge or because some external agency like the Walrasian auctioneer has the relevant knowledge that leads to the establishment of equilibrium prices. This implies that the reference by mainstream economists to the Austrian contribution to the calculation debate is misguided. The Austrian (and notably Hayek's) well-known criticism of a centrally guided economy also applies to the neoclassical analysis of a decentralized economy. By assuming that equilibrium always prevails it becomes difficult to discriminate between a decentralized economy and a centrally guided economy. The auctioneer in the former becomes the central planner in the latter and there is no fundamental difference between the two systems (see also O'Driscoll 1977: 24 and Hahn 1984: 128). Neoclassical economists sometimes refer to Hayek's contribution to the calculation debate when asked for the allocative advantages of Western market economies as compared to the former centrally guided economies of Eastern Europe. This reference is hard to reconcile with the fact that in advising the newly established market economies in Eastern Europe these same economists make use of a theoretical framework that is incapable of discriminating between a market and a centrally guided economy. As far as the theory of value and hence the role of prices in a market economy are concerned it must therefore be concluded that the mainstream assessment of the (limited) relevance of Austrian ideas is based on an erroneous interpretation of Austrian economics. Next we turn to the alleged relevance of Austrian ideas in mainstream macroeconomics.

Austrian Economics and Neoclassical Macroeconomics

The consequences of changes in monetary variables for the functioning of the market process in terms of changes in relative prices are, of course, at the heart of Hayek's monetary business-cycle theory. It is here that Lucas (1981) for instance concludes that his monetary equilibrium business-cycle theory is similar to Hayek's. The more recent off-spring of new-classical business-cycle theory, the so-called real business-cycle theory, is also conceived of as a 'modernized' version of Hayek (1931) by some of its proponents (see, for instance, Correia, Neves and Rebelo 1991). The main similarities are thought to be the insistence on explaining business cycles in terms of equilibrium behaviour on the one hand and the need to cast the analysis in terms of individual decision-making on the other. The mutual conclusions as to the effectiveness of monetary policy are thought to reinforce the similarity. Such an interpretation of Austrian monetary business-cycle theory overlooks at least two crucial features of Austrian economics.[1] First of all, Austrian monetary theory deals with the origin and relevance of money. In new-classical theory the existence and relevance of money is merely assumed as in the monetary business-cycle approach (Lucas 1973) or monetary variables are even nonexistent (the real business cycle approach). Second, and probably more importantly, the idea of a similarity between new-classical and Austrian theory underrates the importance of subsquent developments in Hayek's own work, which amount to an amendment of the equilibrium concept.

To begin with the first issue, the analysis of money as a medium of exchange has a longstanding tradition in Austrian economics which goes back to Menger (1892) (but see also Mises 1953). The establishment of monetary exchange is thought to be the outcome of a process in which self-interested agents somehow recognize that their well-being can be improved upon by the introduction of a commonly accepted medium of exchange. It is probably the best example of a naturally evolved institutional solution to a particular co-ordination problem, the double coincidence of wants problem. In our view, this important Austrian contribution to the analysis of monetary exchange is fundamentally different from the analysis of money in Lucas (1973). In a general equilibrium framework on which new-classical economics is explictly founded the Walrasian auctioneer is assumed to take care of this co-ordination problem and money is superfluous. This leads us to the second important difference between new-classical and Austrian theory, the use of the equilibrium concept.

We will illustrate our argument with Hayek (1937). The aim of Hayek (1937) is to analyse 'the role which assumptions and propositions about knowledge possessed by the different members of society plays in economic analysis' (Hayek 1937: 33). It is here that the aforementioned distinction between individual and market equilibrium arises. According to Hayek it is in the transition from an individual equilibrium to a general equilibrium that it is assumed that every agent somehow knows the objective facts that correspond to a state of general equilibrium, whereas for individual equilibrium ***subjective*** knowledge of the facts is relevant. Hence, the essential question arises how this knowledge on the level of the individual agent, subjective knowledge, is transformed into a situation of general equilibrium in which each agent must have the same, objective knowledge. In equilibrium theory, Hayek continues, the need to analyse this fundamental co-ordination problem is avoided by assuming that each agent possesses the necessary amount of objective knowledge. In other words, the problem is avoided by assuming perfect foresight.

> The statement that, if people know everything, they are in equilibrium is true simply because that is how we define equilibrium. The assumption of a perfect market in this sense is just another way of saying that equilibrium exists but does not get us any nearer an explanation of when and how such a state will come about. It is clear that, if we want to make the assertion that, under certain conditions, people will approach that state, we must explain by what process they will acquire the necessary knowledge.
>
> (Hayek 1937: 46)

Hayek's analysis of the equilibrium assumption and hence of the perfect foresight assumption also applies to the two core new-classical assumptions of general market-clearing and rational expectations. As far as the assumption of general market clearing is concerned our remarks on subjectivism in the previous section and Hayek's emphasis on the crucial difference between objective facts and subjective knowledge make clear why this assumption can never be at home in Austrian economics as Lucas *et al.* are inclined to think.

The assumption of rational expectations that underlies new-classical economics turns out to be an equilibrium assumption too (see also O'Driscoll and Rizzo 1985: 213–26). This ultimately means that the rational expectations hypothesis is not solely based on individual behaviour as new classicals claim but also on the fact that the economy is always in a state of expectational equilibrium. The same point was raised by Hayek (1937) in his criticism of the perfect foresight assumption as is illustrated by the above quotation. The new-classical assumption that the rational expectations hypothesis is a *behavioural* hypothesis is thus incorrect since it turns out that it tells nothing about individual behaviour apart from the fact that agents are supposed to behave rationally. The assumption that agents are always in expectational equilibrium is warranted in order to avoid the necessity of analysing higher-order expectations.

From the two core new-classical assumptions the new-classical analysis of the role of prices as transmitters of information follows directly. Some new-classical economists see this role as further enhancing the similarity with Austrian theory (see also Hoover 1988: 235–6). It should be clear by now that in new-classical economics this transmission solely concerns equilibrium prices whereas in Austrian economics this transmission is linked with the dispersion of knowledge and deals with the role of prices in situations of disequilibrium (see Hayek 1946: 105–6).

With respect to our example of the use of Austrian ideas in mainstream macroeconomics we are therefore led to the same conclusion as with the use of Austrian ideas in the neoclassical theory of value. Basically the use of these ideas turns out to be a misuse because of the failure of neoclassical economics to understand that so-called Austrian concepts cannot be separated from the fundamental question in Austrian economics as to how a decentralized economy is capable of dealing with the co-ordination problem arising out of the fact that knowledge is dispersed. Once this failure is recognized it becomes clear that Austrian concepts are incompatible with neoclassical economics, in which this co-ordination problem is directly or indirectly assumed away. In the next section we will briefly investigate whether there are theoretical developments in mainstream economics in which the co-ordination problem is somehow not (completely) assumed away.

2. THE CO-ORDINATION PROBLEM AND MAINSTREAM ECONOMICS

Dismissal of the Uniqueness of the General Equilibrium

As our discussion in the previous section showed, any analysis based upon a standard Walrasian general-equilibrium framework is incapable of dealing with the co-ordination problem that is at the heart of Austrian economics.[2] The Walrasian auctioneer (in his dual role as the establisher of unique equilibrium prices and of exchange arrangements) is assumed to take care of the co-ordination of individual decisions in a world in which by assumption the future is indistinguishable from the present. It is not very surprising that in order to be able to deal with aspects of the co-ordination problem in neoclassical theories one has to change the main assumptions on which the Walrasian general equilibrium theory is based. Some recent theoretical developments in the microfoundations literature analyse the implications of the dismissal of the assumption of a unique, stable Pareto-efficient equilibrium.[3] The details of these developments need not concern us here since we are primarily interested in the implications of these developments for the relevance of the Austrian analysis of the co-ordination problem for neoclassical economics.

A first example is the approach in which the auctioneer is no longer assumed to be able to establish a unique equilibrium. In the so-called co-ordination failures approach (see especially Cooper and John 1988) multiple equilibria may arise because, in the absence of an auctioneer, agents need to make expectations of other agents' behaviour in deciding upon the level of their own activity. Due to imperfect information, agents are assumed to take the decisions of other agents on prices or quantities as given. Co-ordination failures basically result because the mutual interdependencies cannot be communicated through the market mechanism. The assumption of non-co-operative behaviour implies that the resulting equilibria are of a bootstrap nature because for every state of (rational) expectations a different equilibrium may result. The bootstrap nature of equilibria is also at the heart of the second example. The search-equilibrium framework as originally developed by Diamond (1982) takes as its starting-point that the Walrasian auctioneer is no longer around to establish exchange arrangements. Trade externalities and (given some additional assumptions) multiple equilibria arise if agents have to make up their own exchange arrangements. The self-fulfilling nature of equilibria is a consequence of the fact that the optimal level of activity of agent i depends positively on the level of activity of agent j, but as in our first example, this positive interdependence cannot be communicated.

Since the search-equilibrium framework as opposed to a standard general-equilibrium framework deals explicitly with the question of decentralized *exchange* this framework is also used to arrive at an endogenization of the medium of exchange function of money (see, for instance, Warneryd 1990). Money as a commonly accepted medium of exchange is conceived of as an institutional solution to a co-ordination problem in much the same way as in Menger (1892). In fact, in virtually all the contributions to this literature Menger (1892) is the starting-point for the analysis.

A third example of introducing aspects of the co-ordination problem is the dismissal of the assumption that the economy should have a definite beginning and end. Once one allows for the fact that the economic system is an open system it can be shown that indeterminacy reigns. Self-fulfilling expectations are of particular relevance in these kinds of models as the theory of sunspots shows. This theory extends the indeterminacy result of overlapping generations models through the incorporation of the idea that a random variable (sunspot) can affect the equilibrium conditions of the economy with the result that multiple stochastic equilibria may exist. What drives the sunspot result is the composition of the information set on which each agent bases his rational expectations. If every agent believes that a random variable influences the equilibrium conditions because every agent believes that other agents believe so, the equilibrium condition will indeed be changed. Sunspots may arise in a world in which agents must act upon their beliefs concerning the expectations of other agents. It is an excellent illustration of the kind of analytical problems neo-classical theory encounters once the problem of analysing higher-order expectations arises. One of the uses of overlapping generation models is to show how the stability-properties of a general equilibrium change if one allows for non-linear dynamics. Very small changes in the initial conditions of the key variables may produce a very different time-path for the economy. In the theory of deterministic chaos this implies that the economy never converges to a steady state.

How to Proceed Beyond the Result of Multiple Equilibria?

This (non-exhaustive) list of examples is meant to illustrate that once the above-mentioned core assumptions of the general-equilibrium framework are somewhat relaxed, mainstream theorists are confronted with an economy which is characterized by the possibility of many (bootstrap) equilibria or of complete instability of the economy. Pareto-inefficiencies may result because individual agents simply lack the information on the actions and expectations of other agents. Full-price flexibility is not a solution to this co-ordination problem because prices are by definition equilibrium prices and hence the way prices are assumed to transmit information in neoclassical theory forecloses a solution to this co-ordination problem. A similar observation can be made with respect to the way expectations (both perfect foresight and rational expectations) enter into the analysis. As we have already argued in the previous section it can be observed, following Hayek (1937), that both forms of expectations are ultimately equilibrium assumptions. If the economy is no longer characterized by a unique equilibrium, the rational-expectations or perfect-foresight assumption are of no use in eliminating the resulting co-ordination problem since these assumptions sustain any equilibrium. Hence, in case indeterminacy or multiplicity of equilibria prevails, the equilibrium nature of the expectations assumption becomes troublesome because it clearly shows that perfect foresight or rational expectations do not represent a *theory* of expectations formation.

One important question thus becomes how to model expectations when perfect foresight and rational expectations are dismissed. One approach followed in recent literature on this subject within a general-equilibrium framework is to fall back on the assumption of adaptive expectations. The assumption of adaptive expectations is supplemented with a particular learning rule. It is assumed that agents are able to learn that their forecasts are not correct and that they may revise their expectations accordingly. Given the appropriate assumptions on the parameters of the reduced-form estimation of the underlying structural model, this process of expectations revision, or in other words, this learning rule, may eventually lead to convergence to a rational-expectations equilibrium. While it is no longer assumed that agents know the structural model, agents are still supposed to be able to distil the reduced-form equations of the structural model. This is somewhat less demanding in terms of information dissemination but it is still based on a number of very restrictive assumptions.[4] First of all, the specific learning rule(s) is (are) assumed to be given to each agent and also to be the same for all agents. Second, agents are somehow supposed to know that (all agents know that) the specific learning rule used by all agents leads to convergence to a rational expectations equilibrium. Finally, it is typically assumed that there are no costs of information gathering and processing.

The first two assumptions imply that the recent work on learning within a general-equilibrium framework presupposes individual agents to possess a substantial amount of common knowledge. In the absence of these two assumptions, problems of infinite regress arise because of the existence of higher-order expectations. The third assumption, information is costless, is important because in the presence of information costs 'it is less likely that learning will ever be complete.

Given agents' subjective beliefs it may not be worthwhile to learn the true model even if it were in fact possible' (Pesaran 1987: 45). Furthermore, following our discussion of knowledge and the role of markets in the previous section, costless information is difficult to reconcile with learning in a market economy.

It is clear that given these restrictive assumptions the introduction of a learning rule is a short-cut for re-establishing the existence of a unique equilibrium and hence for dismissing the co-ordination problem from the outset. In our view any useful analysis of learning has to take into account that learning is an outstanding example of a process and that the introduction of a learning process necessariy contradicts a fully deterministic outcome. It is also clear that these neoclassical attempts to model learning behaviour are prone to Hayek's critique of constructivism (Hayek 1978: 13), according to which the neoclassical attempts to reconcile learning behaviour and a unique, fully determinate outcome are at odds with the very existence of the co-ordination problem.

A second typical example of dealing with the non-uniqueness of equilibria can for instance be found in Cooper (1987). The aim of the analysis is to show that in the case of multiple equilibria the Pareto-dominant equilibrium is not a natural focal point (in the sense of Schelling 1960). It is obvious that Pareto dominance cannot be reconciled with the co-ordination failures approach. Cooper (1987) therefore develops an equilibrium selection criterion in which equilibria are history-dependent or path-dependent. In our view, however, the use of path-dependency in an equilibrium framework is beset with analytical difficulties because the question why a particular equilibrium in period t has been established is merely 'explained' by assuming the existence of an equilibrium in $t-i$. In fact, as in our first example, the basic difficulty is that the incorporation of a concept (like learning or path-dependency) that has its origin in the process nature of economics cannot be reconciled with an analytical framework which focuses on wholly determinate outcomes.

This brief discussion of two examples which try to cope with endogenous expectations formation and equilibrium selection, respectively, indicates that, given the unchanged rationality and equilibrium assumption, these examples do not yield any insights into the implications of the co-ordination problem for individual behaviour.

3. THE USEFULNESS OF A HAYEKIAN PERSPECTIVE

Changing the Basic Concepts of Neoclassical Economics

In order to illustrate the usefulness of an Austrian perspective we will take the Hayekian concept of pattern co-ordination as our starting-point. We will illustrate our argument by means of the two examples (learning and equilibrium selection) of the previous section.

In the example of a learning rule the common knowledge assumption with respect to the optimal learning rule and the existence of a rational expectations equilibrium beg the question of how such a rule and a particular rational expectations equilibrium get established. A way out of these kinds of infinite-regress problems is to broaden the rather narrow interpretations of rationality (maximizing under a given set of constraints) and equilibrium. In that case, learning behaviour can be conceived of as at least partially determined by conventional behaviour and as being (necessarily) partly indeterminate,[5] which implies that the need to explain the optimality of a learning rule disappears. If learning behaviour is governed by uncertainty and by past experience, the question of convergence to a rational expectations equilibrium loses its relevance.

A similar observation can be made with respect to the issue of information costs. Not only is the assumption of costless information difficult to reconcile with the existence of markets, it also forecloses the analysis of other institutions. If information costs are not negligible or more far reaching if uncertainty (lack of information) prevails, the degree of indeterminateness may very well diminish since agents may be reluctant to change their actions in case information gathering and-processing is costly. Lack of knowledge may increase predictable behaviour, as Heiner (1983) showed. The existence of information costs or lack of information may also explain the existence of various non-market institutions. This notion lies at the heart of the so-called new-institutional economics, in which various forms of economic organization are seen as resulting from the necessary incompleteness of markets. Incomplete markets basically exist in this approach either because the use of the price system is not without its costs (the transaction costs approach) or because the prevalence of uncertainty induces agents to adhere to all kinds of conventions and institutions. These conventions and institutions are thus conceived of as substitutes for missing markets. A survey of this approach is beyond the scope of this chapter, but as these three themes and the various chapters in Langlois (1986) reveal, this approach is clearly influenced by the ideas of Austrian economists on this subject.

With respect to the second example mentioned in the previous section, the analysis of equilibrium selection in case of multiple equilibria, the following remarks are in order. In, for instance, a game-theoretic framework like Cooper and John (1988), the analysis of the implications of the co-ordination problem can be improved in our view once it is recognized that the standard notion of rationality in game theory (the behaviour of each player completely determined by knowledge of pay-offs and strategies) hinders instead of helps the attempts to solve the problem of (too) many equilibria. Particular equilibria may act as a focal point merely because a particular convention, however established, to act in a certain way exists, or even because agents think they ought to stick to a certain convention. Sugden (1989) explicitly refers to Hayek's concept of spontaneous order in his analysis of co-ordination problems in a game-theoretic framework and accordingly argues that 'the belief that one ought to follow a certain convention is the product of the same process of evolution as the convention itself' (Sugden 1989: 87). Though the explanation of the origin of a particular convention or institution is therefore probably not very useful, the idea of a convention or institution can be analysed for co-ordination problems in a game-theoretic framework as is shown by Schotter (1981), who also builds on Austrian insights, as he showed in the introduction to his book. The basic idea is that in the context of repeated games it may be rational for individual agents to restrict their strategies because of the possibility of a higher equilibrium pay-off for each player. This deliberate restraint on the part of the players can be looked upon as the adherence to a certain rule.

The main point of an extension along the above-mentioned lines of the examples to model learning behaviour and history-dependency of equilibria is that the analysis of the co-ordination problem calls for important deviations from the standard notions of rationality and equilibrium behaviour upon which general equilibrium theory and hence neoclassical economics is based.[6] In our view, less demanding assumptions as to both notions in terms of knowledge and information dissemination will enlarge our understanding of the implications of the co-ordination problem. Austrian economic theory illustrates how a change in these assumptions brings the co-ordination problem and its implications for the behaviour of individual agents to the fore.

Pattern Co-ordination[7]

The modern Austrian alternative is to dismiss the traditional notion of equilibrium and to substitute the concept of pattern co-ordination for this neoclassical equilibrium concept. In this concept the behaviour of individual agents is thought to be governed by rules and institutions which are inherited from the past. These rules and institutions co-ordinate economic activity in the sense that they influence (but do not wholly determine) individual decision-making. The resulting order is spontaneous to the extent that these rules and institutions are not a product of rational design and the history-dependency of this order ensures that certain rules that somehow came into existence in the past are carried over to the present. The idea that these rules and institutions (laws, property rights and a system of markets) influence but do not fully determine decision-making is important, for it illustrates that analysing the co-ordination issue in terms of arriving at a unique equilibrium is at odds with the subjectivistic principles of Austrian economics as discussed in section 2.[8] Rules and institutions constitute a pattern for the economy as a whole that serves as a guideline for (unique) individual decisions.

We must conclude that once neoclassical economics starts to develop theories in which the co-ordination problem is not taken care of by some external agency (like the Walrasian auctioneer) or is not an issue at all (like in representative agent models), the basic neoclassical assumptions must be fundamentally changed. In the end this may very well lead to theories of decentralized co-ordination that have a clear resemblance to the concept of pattern co-ordination as developed by Hayek. To begin with, neoclassical economists might start by taking Austrian economics seriously.

NOTES

Department of Economics, University of Groningen, P.O. Box 800, 9700 AV Groningen, the Netherlands. A first version of this chapter was presented at the European Conference on Austrian Economics 1992 in Maastricht, the Netherlands. I would like to thank Jack Birner, Lex Hoogduin, Simon Kuipers and Rudy van Zijp for their comments on an earlier version of this paper. Of course, the usual disclaimer applies.

1 See, for instance, Laidler (1982) who argues that new-classicals are indeed better described as neo-Austrians. Our analysis of the similarity between new-classical and Austrian business-cycle theory can also be found in Hoover (1988, Ch. 10). See also Garrison (1986).

2 It must be emphasized that in this chapter we do not deal with the important question as to how the price mechanism influences the acquisition of knowledge. See Snippe (1987) for a rather critical assessment. We also abstract from the relation between Keynes's and the post-Keynesian analysis of the co-ordination problem on the one hand and the Austrian analysis on this subject on the other. Both the acquisition of knowledge and the (dis)similarities with post-Keynesian theory are beyond the scope of this paper.

3 For a detailed discussion of these attempts see Garretsen (1991, 1992).

4 The following discussion of learning behaviour is largely based on Pesaran (1987).

5 Following Sugden (1989) a convention can be defined as an established pattern of behaviour in case there are several other solutions to a co-ordination problem. The indeterminateness of learning is connected with the existence of uncertainty. See, for instance, O'Driscoll and Rizzo (1986) for an analysis of the interrelation between conventional

or rule-following behaviour on the one hand and uncertainty on the other.

6 Note that these standard notions are after all nothing but mere conventions themselves; they are devoid of any analytical superiority.

7 Pattern co-ordination or pattern equilibrium can be defined as follows: 'plans are in a pattern equilibrium if they are coordinated with respect to their typical features, even if their unique aspects fail to mesh' (O'Driscoll and Rizzo 1985: 85).

8 See, for instance, Hayek (1967, Ch. 3); Hayek (1973, Ch. 2) and Hayek (1978, Ch. 1).

REFERENCES

Caldwell, B. (1988) 'Hayek's Transformation', *History of Political Economy* 20: 513–43.

Correia, I.H., J.L. Neves, and S. Rebelo (1991) 'Business Cycles from 1850 to 1950: New Facts about Old Data', paper presented at the Sixth Annual Convention of the European Economic Association, Cambridge, August.

Cooper, R. (1987) 'Dynamic Behavior of Imperfectly Competitive Economies with Multiple Equilibria', *NBER Working Paper*, no. 2388.

Cooper, R. and A. John (1988) 'Coordinating Coordination Failures in Keynesian Models', *Quarterly Journal of Economics* 103: 441–65.

Diamond, P. (1982) 'Aggregate Demand Management in Search Equilibrium', *Journal of Political Economy*, 51: 881–94.

Frydman, R. and E. Phelps (eds) (1983) *Individual Forecasting and Individual Outcomes*, Cambridge: Cambridge University Press.

Garretsen, H. (1991) 'Some Remarks on Determinate Solutions and the Foreclosure of Process', *Journal of Post-Keynesian Economics* 13: 414–24.

—— (1992) *Keynes, Coordination and Beyond*, Aldershot: Edward Elgar.

Garrison, R.W. (1986) 'From Lachmann to Lucas: On Institutions, Expectations and Equilibrating Tendencies', in I.M. Kirzner (ed.) *Subjectivism, Intelligibility and Economic Understanding*, New York: New York University Press.

Hahn, F.H. (1984) 'Keynesian Economics and Equilibrium Theory: Reflections on Some Current Debates', in F.H. Hahn, *Equilibrium and Macroeconomics*, Oxford: Blackwell.

Hayek, F.A. (1931) *Prices and Production*, London: Routledge & Kegan Paul, 1935.

—— (1937) 'Economics and Knowledge', reprinted in F.A. Hayek, *Individualism and Economic Order*, London: Routledge & Kegan Paul, 1949.

—— (1945) 'The Use of Knowledge in Society', *American Economic Review* 35: 519–30.

—— (1946) 'The Meaning of Competition', in F.A. Hayek, *Individualism and Economic Order*, London: Routledge & Kegan Paul, 1949.

—— (1967) *Studies in Philosophy, Politics and Economics*, London: Routledge & Kegan Paul.

—— (1973) *Law, Legislation and Liberty*, London: Routledge & Kegan Paul, vol. 1.

—— (1978) *New Studies in Philosophy, Politics, Economics and the History of Ideas*, London: Routledge & Kegan Paul.

Heiner, R.H. (1983) 'The Origin of Predictable Behavior', *American Economic Review* 73: 560–96.

Hoover, K.D. (1988) *The New Classical Macroeconomics*, Oxford: Blackwell.

Laidler, D. (1982) *Monetarist Perspectives*, Oxford: Philip Allan.

Langlois, R.N. (ed.) (1986) *Economics as a Process: Essays in the New Institutional Economics*, Cambridge: Cambridge University Press.

Lucas, R.E. (1973) 'Some International Evidence on Output-Inflation Trade-offs', *American Economic Review* 63: 326–34.

—— (1981) *Studies in Business-Cycle Theory*, Oxford: Blackwell.

Menger, K. (1892) 'On the Origin of Money', reprinted in R.M. Starr (ed.) *General Equilibrium Models of Monetary Economics: Studies in the Static Foundations of Monetary Theory*, San Diego: Academic Press, 1989.

Mises, L. von (1949) *Human Action: A Treatise on Economics*, New Haven, Conn.: Yale University Press.

—— (1953) *The Theory of Money and Credit*, Indianapolis: Liberty Classics, 1981.

O'Driscoll, G.P. (1977) *Economics as a Coordination Problem: The Contributions of Friedrich A. Hayek*, Kansas City: Sheed Andrews and McMeel.

O'Driscoll, G.P. and M.J. Rizzo (1985) *The Economics of Time and Ignorance*, Oxford: Blackwell.

O'Driscoll, G.P. and M.J. Rizzo (1986) 'Subjectivism, Uncertainty and Rules', in I.M. Kirzner (ed.) *Subjectivism, Intelligibility and Economic Understanding*, New York: New York University Press.

Pesaran, H. (1987) *The Limits of Rational Expectations*, Oxford: Blackwell.

Schelling, T. (1960) *The Strategy of Conflict*, Cambridge MA: Harvard University Press.

Schotter, A. (1981) *The Economic Theory of Social Institutions*, Cambridge: Cambridge University Press.

Snippe, J. (1987) 'An Invisible Hand without Foresight and Hindsight: Comment on Garrison', *History of Political Economy*, 19: 329–34.

Sugden, R. (1989) 'Spontaneous Order', *Journal of Economic Perspectives*, 3: 85–97.

Warneryd, K. (1990) 'Legal Restrictions and Monetary Evolution', *Journal of Economic Behavior and Organization* 13: 117–24.

5

HAYEKIAN TRIANGLES AND BEYOND

Roger W. Garrison

The lectures that F.A. Hayek delivered at the London School of Economics in the early 1930s were punctuated with triangles - triangles of a sort his audience had never before seen. Now, more than sixty years after those lectures were published as *Prices and Production* (1931), the triangles still hold the key to understanding Hayekian macroeconomics. What exactly did Hayek see in them? Why could most of his audience see nothing at all in them? Satisfying answers to these two questions can go a long way towards identifying the core differences between Austrian and Anglo-American macroeconomics.

Considering a third question can add significance to our answers. What relevance do the ideas that Hayek hung on those triangles have today? The lectures were written at a time when Hayek and the rest of the profession were contemplating the dramatic economic boom of the 1920s and the subsequent depression that had yet to find its bottom. The early 1990s find the profession in similar circumstances - contemplating the dramatic bull market of the 1980s and wondering if and how the current recession is related. It would be a mistake to assume that Hayek's triangulation as applied to the earlier episode applies in some wholesale fashion to the current one, but it would be a greater mistake to assume that Hayek's insights have no current application at all.

Hayek's theory of boom and bust can be generalized so as to increase its plausibility as an account of the 1920s and 1930s and give it new life in accounting for the 1980s and 1990s. After making the appropriate conceptual and institutional adjustments, the story in *Prices and Production* can be retold in a way that sheds light on contemporary macroeconomic problems. Also, reconsidering the triangles as Hayek employed them then and as present-day Hayekians might employ them now, helps to put in perspective the macroeconomics of the intervening years which grew out of the Keynesian revolution.

THE MACROECONOMIC SIGNIFICANCE OF THE TRIANGLES

The Hayekian triangle, as described in Hayek's second lecture (Hayek 1967: 36–47), is a heuristic device that gives analytical legs to a theory of business cycles first offered by Ludwig von Mises (1953: 339–66). A right triangle depicts the macroeconomy as having a value dimension and a time dimension. It represents at the highest level of abstraction the economy's production process and the consumer goods that flow from it. One leg of the triangle represents dollar-denominated spending on consumer goods; the other leg represents the time dimension that characterizes the production process (Figure 5.1). In a fundamental sense, the Hayekian triangles in their various configurations illustrate a trade-off recognized by Carl Menger and emphasized by Eugen von Böhm-Bawerk. At a given point in time and in the absence of resource idleness, investment is made at the expense of consumption. Investment, which entails the commitment of resources to a time-consuming production process, adds to the time dimension of the economy's structure of production. To allow for investment, consumption must fall initially in both nominal and real terms. Once capital restructuring is complete, the corresponding level of consumption is higher in real terms than its initial level. The nominal level of consumption spending, however, is lower than its initial level because a greater proportion of total spending is devoted to the maintenance of a more time-consuming production structure.

The relative lengths of the triangle's two legs, then, represent the inverse relationship between nominal consumption spending and nominal non-consumption spending – the latter as reflected by the

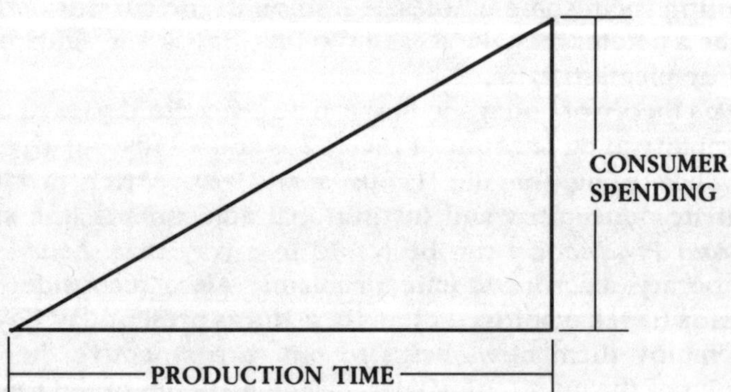

Figure 5.1 Hayekian triangle

time dimension of the economy's capital structure. Hayek makes use of several heuristic assumptions that cause production time and non-consumption spending to be more tightly linked in his graphics than in reality. He assumes, for instance, that the production process consists of stages of production such that output of one stage sells as input for the next and that the number of stages varies directly with production time. For the purpose of defining the triangles, the quantity of money and the velocity of circulation - and hence the product *MV* - are assumed constant. (Episodes of monetary expansion, however, provide the most interesting and relevant circumstances for application of the graphics.)

The Hayekian triangles can change in shape in circumstances of a constant *MV* - and hence a constant *PQ*, where *Q* is understood to include the sum of the outputs of each stage of production including the final stage whose output is consumption goods. The Hayekian *Q*, then, lies somewhere between the Fisherian *T*, which stands for total transactions and the Friedmanian *Y*, which stands for income or final output (consumption plus net investment); the corresponding *V* lies somewhere between the transactions velocity and the income velocity.

The basis for a change in the shape of the triangle is a hypothetical preference change *within* the output aggregate. Suppose that consumers become more future orientated. Their time-preferences - to use the Austrian term - are lower than before. In the first instance, this preference change means a decrease in demand for current consumption and an increase in saving. In the Austrian formulation, saving means more than simply not consuming. Income earners do not just save; they save-up-for-something. Saving-up-for-something is another terminological in-betweener lying somewhere between the conventional polar concepts of saving as a flow and saving*s* as a stock. Increased saving in the Austrian formulation gets translated through market mechanisms and entrepreneurial foresight into higher demands for inputs in the relative early stages of production. The demand for output as a whole, then, is neither higher nor lower than before the preference change. Rather, the pattern of demand has changed in a way that is conveniently depicted by a Hayekian triangle whose consumer-spending leg has become shorter and whose production-time leg has become longer (Figure 5.2).

The height of the hypotenuse of the reconfigured triangle measured at each stage of production along the production-time leg shows (1) that the demand for input is reduced in the final and late stages of production, (2) that the extent of the reduction diminishes as stages further removed from consumption are considered, (3) that stages remote from consumption experience an increased demand for input and (4) that stages of production more remote than had existed

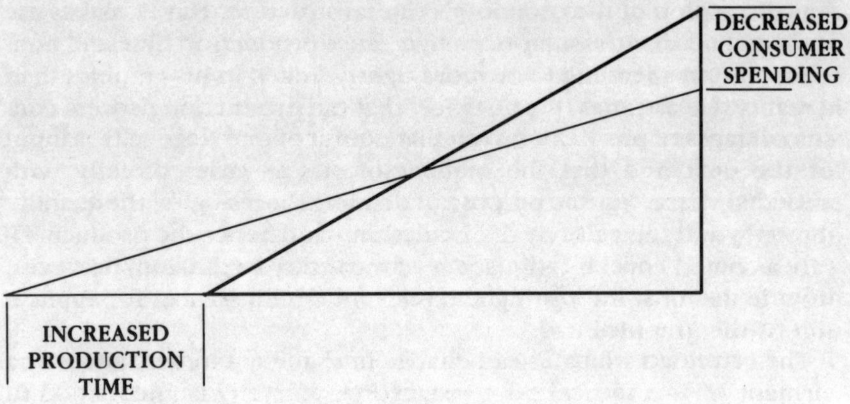

Figure 5.2 Lengthening of production structure

before have been created anew. The slope of the hypotenuse, now less steep than before, reflects a lower rate of interest corresponding to the reduced time-preference.

Reduced time-preference means a smaller time-discount on future consumption. Consumers are more willing to sacrifice consumption goods available now and in the immediate future for consumption goods available in the relatively remote future. Tailoring production plans to consumption preferences requires that the structure of production be modified in precisely the way depicted by the change in the Hayekian triangle just described. Hayek went beyond determining what changes in the structure of production were required by the preference change, to identifying, in his third lecture, the market mechanisms that could allocate resources among the stages of production in conformity with the time-preferences of consumers. Lower time-preferences mean increased saving and hence a lower rate of interest. The lower interest rate drives down the competitive gross profit margin in each stage of production. That is, for each stage input prices are bid up in relationship to output prices. The cumulative effect of this relative-price adjustment increases with increased remoteness from the final stage. Accordingly, resources are shifted out of late stages and into early stages in response to the lower time-preferences.

It is easy to fault Hayek and his triangles for sins of omission. What about durable capital and consumer durables? What about changes in the degree of vertical integration? What about instances of input-output circularity such as coal as an input in the production of steel and steel as an input in the production of coal? The realization that there are many aspects of a modern decentralized capitalist economy not captured by a triangle should come as no surprise. What is surprising is how much the triangles do depict or imply. Implicit, for instance, is the notion that the structure of production is characterized by some - but not complete - specificity: if all capital goods were wholly nonspecific, then no structure could be defined; if every capital good were completely specific, then no modifications could be made. The notion of stage-specific capital implies a certain intertemporal complementarity that characterizes the structure of production. Complementarity through time gives special significance to the time element in the production process, which was so emphasized by Menger and Böhm-Bawerk.

Treating the problem of intertemporal allocation of resources in terms of the economy's capital structure keeps the entrepreneurial element of the argument in perspective. In the alternative Anglo-American formulations, capital theory is suppressed. Hence, the concept of investment, which is defined as the rate of change in the capital stock, is not well anchored, and doubts that saving will get translated into investment dominate in discussions of both theory and policy. The Hayekian triangles are a constant reminder that a certain amount of entrepreneurial foresight governing the intertemporal allocation of resources is essential to the functioning of a capitalist economy whether or not there are any net additions to the economy's capital stock. If market mechanisms governing intertemporal allocation are working properly, saving and investment pose no special problems. Changes in saving propensities have a direct impact on the rate of interest. Market mechanisms together with entrepreneurial foresight continue to operate as before - only now under different credit conditions - to allocate capital and other resources among the stages of production.

The ultimate effect of a change in the rate of interest on the capital structure is seen as a difference in shape between the initial and subsequent Hayekian triangle. In *Prices and Production*, Hayek did not treat in any detail the issues of the traverse, as John Hicks (1965: 183–97) was later to call it. The intertemporal profile of output *during* the capital restructuring - the traverse - is dependent on a myriad of details involving the specifics of technology and the intertemporal complementarities and substitutabilities that characterized the existing capital structure. Implicit in Hayek's application of the triangles, however, is one critical distinction. Depending upon what caused the interest rate to fall, the traverse may or may not be consistent with an actual completion of the capital restructuring. In summary terms, we can say that if the lower interest rate is attributable to new economic realities, particularly if it reflects lower time-preferences of consumers, then the traverse will be consistent with completing the process of capital restructuring. If, instead, the lower interest rate is attributable to new economic policies, particularly if it reflects credit expansion by the central bank, then the traverse will be inconsistent with completing the process of capital restructuring. The preference-induced process is one of economic growth; the policy-induced process is one of boom and bust (Hayek 1967: 50–60).

HAYEKIAN SHAPES AND KEYNESIAN SIZES

Capital theory in which value is played off against time should not have been totally foreign to Hayek's English audience. A half-century before Hayek molded his lectures around those triangles, an essentially equivalent construction, not then known by Hayek (1967: 38), had been offered by William Stanley Jevons. The Jevonian investment figures, which were the core of Jevons's chapter on capital (Jevons 1970: 225–53), showed capital value rising linearly with time as production proceeded from inception to completion. What was foreign to the English audience was the use of the triangular construction as the basis for macroeconomic theorizing and for theorizing, in particular, about boom and bust.

Capital theory is complex in its own right as are most theories of cyclical variation. Hayek's attempt to present a capital-based theory of cyclical variation in an early stage of development involved the compounding of complexity with complexity. It is not at all surprising, then, that these ideas would seem foreign to most and bewildering to many. Reflecting years later on *Prices and Production*, Hicks remarked that the book 'was in English, but it was not English economics' (Hicks 1967: 204). Joan Robinson, who had heard Hayek lecture at Cambridge on his way to the London School, referred to Hayek's theory as a 'pitiful state of confusion', and believed that his whole argument 'consisted in confusing the current rate of investment with the total stock of capital goods' (Robinson 1972: 2).

John Maynard Keynes (1931) reviewed Hayek's book in what was purportedly a reply to Hayek's critique of Keynes's *Treatise on Money*; Piero Sraffa (1932) defended his own views on production and distribution theory in what was purportedly a review of Hayek's book. Both Keynes and Sraffa were unreceptive and even hostile to the ideas in *Prices and Production*. After reporting his own early fascination with Hayekian theory, Nicholas Kaldor (1942) reassessed *Prices and Production* in the light of subsequent application of the theory. He concluded that the basic ideas in that book must be wrong and referred jeeringly to Hayek's capital-based theory of boom and bust as the 'Concertina Effect'.

Some English economists, notably Lionel Robbins (1934) and to a lesser extent John Hicks and Abba Lerner, were persuaded, at least temporarily, of the merit of Hayek's theory. But the general direction the economics profession was taking at the time was not conducive to the acceptance of a capital-based macroeconomics. The very complexity of a capital structure in macroeconomic disequilibrium seemed to be grounds for sending value and capital theory in one direction and macroeconomics in another. The breaking away of macroeconomics from considerations of capital structure became complete with the publication in 1936 of Keynes's *General Theory* (Keynes 1964).

If the assumptions Hayek invoked to make his theory tractable seem severe, the ones Keynes invoked in Chapter 4 of his *General Theory* should seem more so. Keynes's assumption of a fixed structure of industry effectively took the triangles out of play. So long as fixity characterizes the relationship among the stages of production, questions about the intertemporal allocation of resources are moot, and scope for intertemporal discoordination is nil. With a given ratio of the value leg and time leg of the Hayekian triangle, the issue of the triangle's shape, so emphasized by Hayek, gave way in Keynes's own theorizing to the issue of the triangle's size. Scope for variation in size is simply the mirror image of scope for variation in resource idleness.

The capital-based Hayekian vision and the capital-free Keynesian vision can be put into perspective with the aid of a simple production-possibilities frontier in which investment is traded off against consumption. So long as investment is positive, the frontier itself moves outwards from one period to the next enabling higher levels of both investment and consumption. The two visions differ fundamentally in terms of the assumed initial conditions, or starting-point, underlying the theory and in terms of acknowledged market forces that propel or constrain movement from those initial conditions.

Hayek took some point on the frontier as his starting-point and concerned himself with market processes and central bank policies that move the economy along the frontier in the direction of more investment. He argued, in effect, that if lower time-preferences - and hence a reduction in the natural rate of interest - underlie the shift of resources away from consumption and towards investment, the intertemporal market process governed largely by the interest rate would move the economy along the frontier facilitating a more rapid expansion of the frontier itself. If, however, credit expansion - and hence a suppression of the interest rate below its natural level - underlies the shift of resources in the direction of more investment, then the market process, forced in the direction of more investment, would create internal tensions within the capital structure which ultimately would throw the economy off the production possibilities curve in the direction of resource idleness.

Keynes took some point interior to the frontier as his starting-point and concerned himself with fiscal and monetary policies as well as institutional and social reforms that may facilitate movement back to the frontier. Prospects for a market-driven mobilization of idle resources were ruled out in his preliminary chapters. With capital theory suppressed, concerns about which particular point on the frontier to aim at were secondary - if that - to the basic concern of eliminating resource idleness. The idea of a natural rate of interest and implied mix of investment and consumption spending held no significance for Keynes (1964: 373). He held, in effect, that there are as many natural rates as there are combinations of demands that put the economy on its production possibilities frontier. Market forces within the capital structure that may favour one point on the frontier over another on the basis of intertemporal consumption preferences were no part of his theory. In sum, Hayek offered a capital-based explanation of how the economy got into a depression; Keynes offered a capital-free prescription for getting out.

THE ECONOMICS OF CREDIT CONTROLS AND CREDIT EXPANSION

Abstract as the Hayekian triangles are, their application has strong counterparts in basic microeconomic theory. The macroeconomic flavour can be retained by virtue of the explicit accounting of the time element in the production process which may involve scope for economy-wide intertemporal discoordination. Alternative credit-market interventions can be considered in the context of basic supply-and-demand analysis. The particular intervention, conceived in microeconomic terms, may or may not have significant macro-economic consequences depending upon whether or not there is scope for a systematic discoordination within the structure of production.

First, consider the economics of credit control in the form of an interest-rate ceiling. So long as the legal maximum is below the market-clearing rate of interest, the credit market will be cut short. The supply of credit becomes the binding constraint. Savers who would have been willing to supply funds at interest rates between the legal-maximum rate and the market-clearing rate will now find additional consumption more attractive. The credit shortage reflects the many would-be borrowers eager to take advantage of investment opportunities made attractive by a low interest rate - which is to say, opportunities in the relative early stages of production. The incentives created by credit control, then, push in opposite directions: erstwhile savers prefer to increase their current rate of consumption while investors become - or at least would like to become - more future orientated.

By the very nature of price ceilings, however, the constrained preferences do not get translated into realities. There is no scope even for the beginnings of a process of capital restructuring as would be guided by a low market-clearing rate of interest. In fact, to the extent that black markets or grey markets, which flout or skirt the legal restriction, come into being, the corresponding rate of interest will be demand-determined. Some demanders of credit who would have been shut out by the legislated ceiling are accommodated but at an interest rate above the old market-clearing rate. This high rate of interest puts a premium on time and channels resources into the relative late stages of production. The ultimate result is that both the time pattern of production and the time pattern of consumption are less future orientated than before the imposition of the interest-rate ceiling.

Second, consider the imposition of an interest-rate ceiling accompanied with a further intervention to prevent the credit-shortage from materializing immediately. Suppose that the difference between credit supplied and credit demanded at the legal maximum is made up for by credit creation. The creating and lending of money to fill the gap between supply and demand has the effect of papering over the shortage. It keeps the discrepancy in incentives between the two sides of the market from showing itself immediately.

If borrowers were to respond to the combination of a ceiling rate and abundant credit in the same way they would respond to a low market rate, resources would be allocated away from late stages of production and into the early stages. As this capital restructuring is underway, income earners would be turning from saving to consumption in the face of the interest-rate ceiling. The market linkages through which the production process is tailored to consumption preferences, however, are not so tight as to curtail the capital restructuring in its incipiency. The time element inherent in the production process translates directly into scope for capital restructuring even in the absence of any change in consumption preferences. But the discrepancy in incentives means that the capital restructuring is necessarily ill-fated. Unavoidably, there will be a clash between producers and consumers as the restructuring process goes forward. Misallocations revealed in the clash will require liquidation and reallocations more consistent with consumer preferences and the interest-rate ceiling.

It is doubtful that investors would actually respond to a ceiling rate - even with the would-be credit shortage papered over with credit creation - in the same way they would respond to a low market rate. The very enactment of the interest-rate ceiling would have a certain announcement effect that would warn borrowers away from business-as-usual investment strategies. The credit creation, however, initially described as 'further intervention' aimed at concealing temporarily the effects of the interest-rate ceiling, actually makes the interest-rate ceiling largely redundant. That is, the expansion of credit by itself has the effect of reducing the interest rate as it adds to the supply of loanable funds. The allocational consequences, somewhat implausible in the face of a legislated interest-rate ceiling, gain in plausibility – and historical relevance – when attributable to credit expansion alone.

Finally, then, consider the economics of credit expansion. The differences to be highlighted by considering this particular sequence of interventions are differences in announcement effects and in expectations about future credit-market conditions. Unlike an interest-rate ceiling as might be imposed by the legislature, credit expansion orchestrated by the central bank can be initiated without public debate and without any strong announcement effect. Borrowers are likely to respond to favourable credit conditions attributable to central-bank policy in about the same way they would have responded to favourable credit conditions attributable to increased saving. In fact, many borrowers would not bother to find answers or even to ask questions about the basis for the lower interest rate. Yet, the policy-induced lower rate creates the same discrepancy of incentives as does an interest-rate ceiling. Savers save less, and borrowers borrow more, with the difference between saving and borrowing being made up by credit expansion.

Business-as-usual investment decisions under favourable credit conditions are the makings of an economic boom. Increased funds in the hands of investors and the increased profit prospects in long-term projects allow for increased employment opportunities as resources are drawn away from late stages of production and into earlier stages. The multi-stage production process as depicted by the Hayekian triangles provides scope for extensive capital restructuring in the direction of a more time-consuming production process despite the actual reduction in saving. The tug-of-war between producers and consumers implicit in the policy-induced economic expansion does not produce a victor in a timely manner. It is a tug-of-war with an expandable rope.

If the business community continues to respond to the credit expansion as if favourable credit conditions will last indefinitely, then the duration of the boom will be limited by the time element in the production process itself. Outputs of earlier stages feed successively into subsequent stages. At some stage in this process, the viability of the policy-induced capital restructuring comes into question. Capital and labour resources complementary to those already committed to earlier stages are in short supply (Hayek 1967: 85–91). The bidding up of input prices in the late stages of production impinges on credit markets as well. So-called desperation borrowing puts an upward pressure on interest rates wholly separate from any inflation premium attributable to the credit expansion.

In the final throes of a policy-induced boom, the role of the central bank becomes more evident and more visible. Will the central bank supply additional credit, which will more fully satisfy each demand in nominal terms but will translate generally into higher resource prices rather than more successful bidding? Or, will the central bank curtail credit to avoid still further misallocation of resources and a general price inflation? The tug-of-war between producers and consumers becomes, from the perspective of the central bank, a tiger by the tail. Both bulls and bears engage in speculative transactions on the basis of their guesses about how long the central bank will hang on and just when it will let go.

Economists who do not theorize in terms of a capital structure and who question the meaning or significance of the natural rate of interest, tend to see little harm – and may see great benefit – in credit expansion. Most of those same economists would see as foolish, wasteful and counter-productive any attempt to impose a price ceiling on any market and especially an attempt to impose an interest-rate ceiling on credit markets. Yet, the key difference emphasized above between an interest-rate ceiling and credit expansion in the context of a multi-stage capital structure is that the perversities of the interest-rate ceiling manifest themselves more directly and more quickly and, although disruptive, are less so than the alternative policy of credit expansion. The perversities of a credit-induced boom are obscured by the initial positive effects of credit expansion, the time element that separates credit expansion from its negative effects, and the complexity of the capital theory needed to make the theoretical connection between expansion and crisis.

THREE COMPONENTS OF THE INTEREST RATE

Attention to the time element in the capital structure allows the message in Hayek's *Prices and Production* to be generalized and then adapted so as to apply in contexts other than the one that inspired his London lectures. Production time inherent in the multi-stage production process can put a lag between intervention in credit markets and the ultimate consequences of that intervention. The particular intervention of concern to Hayek, credit expansion, affected the capital structure's intertemporal orientation. The cheap credit favoured a reallocation of resources among the stages of production that was inconsistent with intertemporal consumer preference. More specifically, the artificially low rate of interest caused production plans to become more future orientated and consumption plans to become less so.

Other sorts of intervention that might have lagged consequences on an economy-wide scale can be identified by taking the interest rate to be the key market signal that translates cause into lagged effect and considering the individual components of the market rate of interest. To this end, it is convenient to conceive of the market rate as consisting of three components: an underlying time discount, an inflation premium, and a risk premium. Hayek's triangulation in the early 1930s was based squarely on the first component.

By the 1960s, the focus of macroeconomists had shifted from the first component to the second. Practised use of monetary tools as economic stimulants - however temporary the actual effects - gave increasing importance to the role of expectations. Scope for a significant discrepancy between expected and actual inflation rates resulted in macroeconomic constructions that featured the inflation premium. Arguably, the most interesting consequences of imperfectly anticipated inflation are those that manifest themselves as the misallocation of capital and labour among the stages of production as might be depicted by Hayekian triangles. But by the time the problem of inflation had captured the attention of modern macroeconomists, capital theory had been in eclipse for more than two decades.

The Keynesian revolution had so weakened the perceived link between capital and interest that it became commonplace to theorize in terms of the level of employment in the context of a given capital structure. Monetary expansion, which has most direct effects on credit markets and interest rates, came to be analysed in terms of labour markets and wage rates. This shift in focus was seen as a glaring incongruity to economists who learnt their macroeconomics from Hayek but was second nature to economists who had long since left capital theory behind.

The nature and significance of the inverse relationship between inflation rate and the level of employment as depicted by the Phillips curve was derived from differences in the abilities of employers and employees in forming relevant expectations and on differences in the way market participants, broadly conceived, adjust their expectations about inflation (Friedman 1976). The first difference governed the strength of the short-run trade-off between inflation and unemployment; the second difference governed the length of the short run. What came to be the conventional account of the consequences of monetary expansion traces the movement along a short-run Phillips curve, which reflects given expectations, followed by a shifting of the curve to reflect a change in expectations. The adjustment process involves a temporary decrease in the unemployment rate as wage adjustments lag behind price adjustments followed by a permanent increase in the inflation rate as the general level of prices catches up to the expanding money supply. Except for occasional references to temporary and wholly incidental disturbances affecting stock–flow relationships in markets for financial and real assets, business-cycle theory based upon short-run/long-run Phillips curve dynamics takes no account of capital misallocation. The critical time element, which was a fundamental aspect of the capital-based theory of Hayek's theory, was retained in the tenuous form of time-consuming adjustments - accomplished differentially by employers and employees - of perceptions to realities.

The general focus of macroeconomic discussion changed dramatically between the 1930s and the 1960s as the focus changed from the time-discount component of the interest rate to the inflation premium and from capital markets to labour markets. In summary terms, Hayek's *Prices and Production* provided a capital-based account of policy-induced distortions in time discounts, while the macroeconomics of the 1960s provided a labour-based account of policy-induced changes in the inflation premium. The purpose here in making the contrast in this way is not to pit one macroeconomic framework against the other (as is done in Bellante and Garrison 1988) but rather to point in the direction of a third framework that may prove more applicable to the 1990s.

The third component of the market rate of interest, the risk premium, has played a significant role neither in Hayekian constructions nor in more modern ones. Typically, risk premiums get mentioned only in introductory throat-clearing paragraphs in which considerations of risks along with administrative charges and other workaday matters are assumed away. At most, the perceived riskiness of holding non-monetary assets helps in some formulations to explain the demand for money. But there has been no macroeconomic theory attempting to explain any episode of boom and bust in terms of the market's allocation of risk-bearing or policy-induced distortions of risk-related market mechanisms. Until recently, such a theoretical formulation would have little if any application. But the macroeconomic experience of the 1980s and 1990s might best be accounted for by just such a formulation.

The risk-based formulation parallels Hayek's original triangulation and, to a lesser extent, the more modern theorizing about short-run and long-run Phillips curves. In summary terms, we can say that the market allocates risk-bearing among market participants in accordance with the willingness of each to bear risk. Policies can create a discrepancy between risk willingly born and risk actually born. Because of a critical time element embedded in risk-bearing, such policies can have cause-and-effect relationships that manifest themselves macroeconomically as boom and bust.

THE ECONOMICS OF RISK CONTROL AND RISK EXTERNALIZATION

Not all conceivable policies that would interfere with the market's allocation of risk-bearing would have significant macroeconomic effects. Suppose, for example, that the legislature, which might take all market rates of interest more than, say, 5 per cent above the Treasury-bill rate to reflect excessive riskiness, were to declare all payment for such risk-bearing politically incorrect. A legislated Treasury-plus-five cap on interest rates would have a direct and immediate effect on credit markets. Entrepreneurs interested in relatively risky undertakings would face a credit shortage. The effects of this partial prohibition against risk-taking would differ little from effects of a simple interest-rate cap. Black and grey credit markets would emerge to partially offset the effect of legislation, and the trade-off between debt and equity financing would be biased in favour of equity. Apart from these effects, which are wholly predictable on the basis of conventional microeconomics, there is no basis for predicting that any macroeconomically significant consequences would follow from such risk-control legislation.

The effects of this hypothetical risk-control legislation are set out here in order to provide a basis for contrasting those distortions of market mechanisms for allocating risk-bearing that do have macroeconomically significant effects and those that do not. The exposition also allows us to identify links between the economics of risk allocation and the economics of credit allocation. We can anticipate the argument by saying that, in terms of the macroeconomic significance of the effects of intervention, credit control is to risk control what credit expansion is to risk externalization. Legislative actions and policy innovations may allow borrowers to take risks that are systematically out of line with the risks perceived or actually born by lenders. So long as risk is effectively concealed from lenders or actually shifted to others, risk-taking will be excessive. The initial phase of excessive risk-taking will manifest itself as an economic boom, but eventually, when actual losses begin to change the perception of lenders and begin to impinge upon unsuspecting others, the boom will give way to a bust.

Adding substance to this summary account of boom and bust attributable to distortions of risk premium requires the identification of legislative action and policy innovation that create a discrepancy between risk-taking and (perceived) risk-bearing. The market process set in motion by the discrepancy can then be shown to play itself out in the context of actual markets that embody risk-taking. In this way, a capital-based account of legislative and policy-based distortions in risk premiums can point to specific interventions that underlay the boom of the 1980s and sowed the seeds for the bust in the 1990s.

The single piece of US legislation most relevant to risk allocation in the 1980s' boom was the Depository Institutions Deregulation and Monetary Control Act of 1980 (DIDMCA), which dramatically changed the banking industry's ability and willingness to finance risky undertakings. Increased competition within the banking industry and from non-bank financial institutions drove commercial banks to alter their lending policy so as to accept greater risks in order to achieve higher yields. The deregulation gave new significance to the Federal Deposit Insurance Corporation (FDIC), which continued to absolve the banks' depositors of all worries about illiquidity and even about bankruptcy, while the Federal Reserve in its long-established capacity of lender of last resort diminished the banks' own concerns about such problems. The risks in the private sector, then, were only partially reflected in higher borrowing costs and lower share prices. In substantial measure, private-sector risks were transformed into risks of inflation in the event of excessive last-resort lending by the Federal Reserve and risks of a large and unbudgeted liability in the event of excessive last-resort closings by the FDIC. But these risks are born unknowingly and hence unwillingly by market participants and taxpayers throughout the economy. During the 1980s, then, the increased riskiness in the private sector was effectively externalized and diffused so that the private-sector activity, spurred on by correspondingly increased yields, was largely unattenuated by considerations of risk.

The policy innovation most relevant to risk allocation in the 1980s' boom was the federal government's dramatically increased reliance on deficit finance. The Federal Reserve in its capacity to monetize government debt keeps the default-risk premium off Treasury bills. This is not to say that the risk that would otherwise attach itself to government securities is actually eliminated. The burden of bearing risk is simply shifted from the holders of Treasury securities to others. Borrowing and investing in the private sector is more risky than it otherwise would be. Holders of private debt and equity shares must concern themselves with all the usual risks and uncertainties of the marketplace plus the risks and uncertainties attributable to potential changes in the way the federal deficit is accommodated. The massive selling of debt by the Treasury in foreign credit-markets, in domestic credit-markets or to the Federal Reserve can have major effects on the strength of export markets, on domestic interest rates and on the inflation rate. Inability of market participants to anticipate the Treasury's borrowing strategy translates into unanticipated changes in the value of private securities and the real assets they represent. Speculative lending in the private sector such as for commercial real-estate development or for highly leveraged financial reorganizations are risky in large part because of possible changes in such things as the inflation rate, interest rate, trade flows and tax rates – the very things that can undergo substantial and unpredictable change when the federal budget is dramatically out of balance (Garrison 1993).

In circumstances where considerations of risk figure importantly in accounting for the performance of the economy, capital markets become the natural focus of attention. The focus on capital is what makes the macroeconomics of the 1980s and 1990s more closely related to Hayekian triangulation than to the labour-based short-run/long-run Phillips curve analysis of the 1960s. Long-term, or capital-intensive, undertakings are inherently more risky than short-term undertakings precisely because more time must elapse before such undertakings can prove their profitability – more time that increases the likelihood of some major change in deficit accommodation or some attempt at deficit reduction that can turn expected profits into losses.

The temporal segregation of stages of production that make up the economy's capital structure puts a dimension in the analysis that is absent in labour-based theorizing. There is scope for profit-taking in early stages of production in cases where ultimately the entire project – all stages considered – yields a substantial loss. The possibility for short-term commitments in the early stages of long-term projects coupled with the many imperfections in contingency markets that allow for some hedging against changes in the federal government's fiscal and monetary strategy warn against too literal an application of the so-called efficient-market hypothesis. Ordinarily, markets allocate both capital and labour efficiently – or at least more efficiently than any alternative allocation mechanism. But a market system whose credit markets involve risks that are partially concealed from the lender and partially shifted to others will be biased in the direction of excessive risk-taking. Excessive risks are converted in time into excessive losses.

HAYEKIAN TRIANGLES FOR THE 1990s

Frequent but vague references in the financial and popular press to the 'excesses of the 1980s', can be taken to mean excess riskiness in comparison to wealth holders' willingness to bear risk. The 1980s may best be understood, then, as a decade in which risk externalization attributable to legislative action and policy innovation gave rise to a substantial but ultimately unsustainable economic boom.

This diagnosis of the macroeconomic ills of the 1990s is more suggestive than conclusive. The purpose here is to demonstrate the versatility of Hayekian theory rather than render a final verdict on the most recent episode of boom and bust. Hayek gave us a good start on a capital-based macroeconomics. The insights wrapped up in those triangles and the prospects for development and application are yet to be fully developed or fully appreciated.

REFERENCES

Bellante, D. and Garrison, R.W. (1988) 'Phillips Curves and Hayekian Triangles: Two Perspectives on Monetary Dynamics', *History of Political Economy* 20(2): 207–34.

Friedman, M. (1976) 'Wage Determination and Unemployment', in M. Friedman, *Price Theory*, Chicago: Aldine.

Garrison, R.W. (1992) 'Public-Sector Deficits and Private-Sector Performance', in L. White (ed.) *The Crisis in the Banking Industry*, New York: New York University Press.

Hayek, F.A. (1967) *Prices and Production*, 2nd edn, New York: Augustus M. Kelly (first published in 1931, 2nd edn published in 1935, reprinted in 1967).

Hicks, J.R. (1965) *Capital and Growth*, Oxford: Oxford University Press.

—— (1967) 'The Hayek Story', in J.R. Hicks, *Critical Essays in Monetary Theory*, Oxford: Oxford University Press.

Jevons, W.S. (1970) *The Theory of Political Economy*, Harmondsworth: Penguin Books (first published in 1871).

Kaldor, N. (1942) 'Professor Hayek and the Concertina Effect', *Economica* n.s. 9: 359–82.

Keynes, J.M. (1931) 'A Reply to Dr Hayek', *Economica* 11: 387–97.

—— (1964) *The General Theory of Employment, Interest, and Money*, New York: Harcourt, Brace & World (first published in 1936).

Mises, L. von (1953) *The Theory of Money and Credit*, New Haven, Conn: Yale University Press (first published in 1912).

Robbins, L. (1934) *The Great Depression*, London: Macmillan.

Robinson, J. (1972) 'The Second Crisis in Economic Theory', *American Economic Review* 62, 2: 1–10.

Sraffa, P. (1932) 'Dr Hayek on Money and Capital', *Economic Journal* 42: 42–53.

6

AN EVOLUTIONARY APPROACH TO BANKING AND MONEY

Gerald P. O'Driscoll, Jr

> The past instability of the market economy is the consequence of the exclusion of the most important regulator of the market mechanism, money, from itself being regulated by the market process.
>
> (Hayek 1976: 79)

In this chapter I offer an approach to analysing banking and monetary institutions that is Hayekian in spirit. While Hayek wrote a great deal on monetary economics, only in later years did he really specify the kind of monetary institutions that would not be a source of instability in the economy. Hayek (1967) offered neutrality as the conceptual standard against which to assess monetary policy, but did not tell the reader what a neutral money would look like or what monetary institutions would be associated with neutral money. Mises rejected the concept of neutral money entirely: 'Money without a driving force of its own would not, as people assume, be a perfect money; it would not be money at all' (Mises 1966: 1418).[1]

Hayek (1976) sketched features of a competitive monetary system, as well as dealing with some of the specifics of a transition process towards a competitive monetary system. Hayek did not so much predict as speculate how private money could be introduced (Hayek 1976: 39).

The chief difficulty with specifying the Hayekian theory of money is that Hayek changed his own views fundamentally towards the end of his career. For instance, Hayek (1966) is written in the vein of offering advice to a central bank on what monetary policy would avoid generating cyclical fluctuations. By contrast, in 1976 Hayek announced that 'the central banking system, which only 50 years ago was regarded as the crowning achievement of financial wisdom, has largely discredited itself' (Hayek 1976: 78). Hayek's later work, however, though informed by a lifetime of monetary research, was more polemical than theoretical.

…ve an impressionistic Hayekian portrait
…t comes to the banking system, however,
…t brush was applied to palette. I would
…is no Austrian theory of banking, at least
…nks were discussed chiefly in their role
…ne business cycle. Banks are causal links
…y are never viewed as interesting in their
…economic analysis of banking and finance,
… Hayekian approach to banking. In what
I do my best to be Hayekian in spirit.

AN EVOLUTIONARY ANALYSIS OF BANKING AND MONEY

One of the Austrian School's most important contributions was the development of an evolutionary theory of money (O'Driscoll 1986). Menger viewed money as an 'organic' institution, that is, one that is 'not the result of socially teleological causes, but the unintended result of innumerable efforts of economic subjects pursuing *individual* interests' (Menger 1963: 158–9). Among modern Austrians, Hayek was the most Mengerian in his evolutionary analysis of complex social institutions. He viewed money as one of the complex social institutions that is 'the result of human action but not of human design' (Hayek 1967: 96). The evolutionary approach is a species of Smithian invisible-hand reasoning.

In sketching the emergence of a common medium of exchange, Menger anticipated the modern transaction-cost literature. That literature starts with the observation that the spread between buying and selling prices persists for commodities even in competitive markets (Menger 1963: 243). The magnitude of the bid-asked spread varies for different commodities. Commodities with comparatively small bid-asked spreads are more marketable than those with larger spreads. Self-interested individuals will be more willing to invest their wealth in the more marketable commodities. Over time, individuals will come to accept commodities in exchange simply because they are highly marketable. This self-interested behaviour is self-reinforcing: as more traders willingly accept highly marketable goods, their acceptability and marketability are enhanced. As the marketability of these goods increases, the bid-asked spread declines further. What evolves into money is the most commonly accepted good.

For Menger, his conjectural history explains the evolution of a medium of exchange, that is, the good most commonly accepted in exchange. Gold and silver have historically often been those goods. The evolutionary process did not cease with the development of commodity money, of course, but continued with the development of cash and deposit substitutes. Indeed, the process is unending, and today we see the development of more and more deposit and deposit-like instruments.

The proliferation of deposit types has blurred the distinction between money and other financial instruments, and led to confusion over what magnitudes to include in the definition of money. In the United States, we presently follow M1, M2 and M3, with variations such as M1A, and even broader magnitudes (of which 'liquidity' is the broadest). As one moves to higher-order definitions, more and more draftable deposits are included. Next, deposits on which drafts or checks cannot be drawn, but which are viewed as relatively close substitutes for checkable accounts, are added.

What is an Hayekian to make of the debate over money's definition? We know what Hayek himself thought:

> Although we usually assume there is a sharp line of distinction between what is money and what is not - and the law generally tries to make such a distinction - so far as the causal effects of monetary events are concerned, there is no such clear difference. What we find is rather a continuum in which objects of various degrees of liquidity, or with values which can fluctuate independently of each other, shade into each other in the degree to which they function as money.
>
> (Hayek 1976: 47)

Hayek went on to say it is a 'misfortune' that 'money' is a noun rather than an adjective. If it were an adjective, the word would reinforce the view that moneyness is present in different degrees in different assets.

Hayek's view is well founded in a tradition that emphasizes methodological individualism. Substitutability is inherently an individualistic concept. If an economic agent perceives a financial asset as a close substitute for money, then for him that asset may be nearly as good as an equal sum of more narrowly defined money. What is true for an individual, however, is surely not always true in the aggregate. One need only consider the classic case of a bank run, when large numbers of individuals attempt to convert deposits into cash. What had been a perfect substitute for cash for any individual becomes a very imperfect and undesired substitute.[2]

There is an undeniable element of truth in Hayek's belief that there is no sharp distinction between money and other assets. In the ordinary course of business of a developed economy, Hayek's position is sound. In times of market stress, however, the difference in liquidity of assets that are otherwise close substitutes for each other can become

Similarly, in order to successfully achieve [illegible] goals, [illegible] to obey the basic rules (the law) of society.[4] Language and law are, then, social constructions. So, also, is money.

Of course, one can stretch an analogy too far. There are clear and relevant differences between language, law and money. To cite but one, there are arbiters of law. Courts exist to settle legal disputes. There are no similar arbiters of language, though the French have been accused of trying to create them. Grammarians have expertise in good usage but lack the social authority of judges. This situation is both the reflection and cause of language's flexibility and openness to change. In language, as in law, custom is important, but there is no *stare decisis* in language. Is money more like language or law in this regard?

One is tempted to bring in the doctrine of legal tender at this point. To do so, however, would be to do violence to the Mengerian or evolutionary theory of money. In that theory, money is not the creation of the state. Legal tender is a state imposition that, at best, hastens the evolutionary process, and, at worst, hobbles it. The issue is whether, in the absence of state intervention, market forces would produce a single medium of exchange. Menger answered yes, despite the fact that competition ordinarily produces a multiplicity of goods and producers. Money is different, however, because what makes an asset money is its ready acceptability in virtually all transactions.

Is not, then, the argument for money equally an argument for one world money? The logic of the evolutionary theory might lead one to respond affirmatively. Economists often invoke monetary sovereignty as a justification for the continued existence of national monies. This argument suggests, however, that a nation's monetary system is a choice variable. This suggestion clashes with an evolutionary approach. Upon reflection, one can invoke Mengerian analysis itself to justify the continued existence of distinct national monies.

Evolutionary outcomes are inherently path-dependent (Langlois 1986: 21, 241–7). The end-state is not independent of the path taken. This point is obvious when applied to language, but equally applicable to law and legal institutions. Could not the same be said of money and monetary institutions? Each of these evolved social institutions – language, law and money – are complex orders whose evolutionary outcome is part of no one's intention.

As Langlois observes, institutions are 'bounds to and definitions of the agent's situation' (Langlois 1986: 252). It is through institutions that the present and future are bound up with the past. Institutions help explain the individual's present situation and circumscribe his future choices. For example, language sets limits on what individuals speaking that language can say or even conceptualize. A particular legal system constrains the range of possible civil relationships in a society. In countless ways, a nation's monetary and banking systems set boundaries on the transactions structure of an economy. Each of these major social institutions influences in a myriad of ways the evolution of other economic institutions and organizations. At any moment, then, a society's economic organization is adapted to its evolved monetary and banking systems. This insight suggests limits to monetary convergence (i.e. the movement to one world money).

Each society is a prisoner of its past, especially of its evolutionary path. Paths converge, but may also diverge. There is no compelling logical reason why multiple monetary systems will necessarily converge to one monetary unit. There are compelling external reasons for an individual country to adopt a different monetary unit that is dominant internationally. There are also compelling reasons internal to its own evolutionary logic, however, that may move in the opposite direction.

One can make an analogy with language. Tremendous savings could be captured were all nations to speak one language. There are, however, staggering costs of effecting such a situation. Certainly at this moment in human history, forces leading to convergence in language are weak at best. One can see contrary forces (with the resurgence of regional languages, like Catalan).

Among other things, language and law are symbolic of nationhood. Invaders seeking to subjugate a nation will sometimes attempt to forcibly destroy that nation's language and legal system. We thus learn how bound up with a culture and national identity are language and law. I suspect this is less true for money. In the past and today, we see more examples of a nation's willingness to adapt its monetary system to that of larger, more successful neighbours than we see convergence of language and law.[5] None the less, as a complex, evolved order, different monetary systems may continue to co-exist side by side in the world, just as legal systems and languages do.

These considerations suggest that Hayek's later concept of competing currencies embodies an important insight. An evolutionary a Hayekian. Other critics of the Maastricht Accord, however, invoke considerations congenial to my analysis. The Germans do appear to have an approach to money and inflation that is different from, say, the British. Surely the histories of the two countries matter in this regard. Histories can neither be merged nor forgotten. My personal guess (and that is all it can be) is that the European Community may be close, but is not yet at the point where the benefits demonstrably outweigh the costs. If not one money for Europe, surely not one for the world - certainly not in our lifetime.

Beyond these considerations, the proposed method of effecting monetary union is not congruent with Hayek's own suggestion. Hayek (1976: 17) preferred a permissive rule that would guarantee to each citizen of the European Community (and preferably other countries, including North America) the right to transact in any currency of the Community (plus other participating countries). He would then let market forces dictate the outcome. He argued that competition would compel all monetary authorities to improve their performance. It would be an interesting experiment if the Community tried this route instead of that currently being followed.

BANKING

Banking systems reveal at least as much variation as monetary systems. The banking systems of English-speaking countries, like the United Kingdom, Canada, the United States, Australia and New Zealand evidence significant institutional variation. All differ as a group, however, from Germany's system of universal banks with their close ties to non-financial corporations. In most English-speaking countries, banks have gradually gained more powers. They may even superficially come to resemble their German counterparts. It is not likely, however, that banks in the United Kingdom will ever become so intertwined with their large corporate customers as is true of German banks. Anglo-Saxon political and legal institutions are not fertile grounds upon which to sow Germany's banking and financial system (Lewis 1990).

Any discussion of banking must acknowledge the role of regulation. Many of the differences between national banking systems reflect political choice as much as economic decisions. Consider again the differing legal treatment of joining banking and commerce. In Germany, there is now a long tradition of mixing the two. According to Lewis, the separation of banking and commerce in the United Kingdom only arose with the chartering of the Bank of England, which was forbidden to 'deal or trade . . . in the buying and selling of any goods, wares or merchandise whatsoever' (Lewis 1990: 355). The Bank of England was provided with both a monopoly and a public-policy role. Being able to engage directly in commercial pursuits was viewed as inconsistent with both grants. Well after the Bank's charter, however, English merchant banks arose to bridge banking and commerce (Chapman 1984).

The case of the United States is equally if not more complex. Many believe that there is a long tradition against mixing banking and commerce in the United States, but the opposite is more nearly the case historically. Huertas (1988: 743–5) shows that not until the Bank Holding Company Act of 1956 was the principle of separating banking and commerce established. This Act only forbids non-financial corporations from owning two or more commercial banks. It always was and still is legal for an individual to own and control a bank as well as commercial or industrial firms:

> In practice, corporate affiliation between banks and commercial firms has a long tradition in the United States, dating back to at least 1799 when the Bank of the Manhattan Company was formed as a subsidiary of a company chartered to supply New York City with fresh water. Since then, commercial banks have at various times been affiliated with or owned by insurance companies, shipping companies, department stores, and manufacturers. Thrift institutions have been affiliated with or owned by retailers, insurance companies, securities firms, real estate developers, and electric utilities. And so-called nonbank banks are currently owned by a wide variety of commercial enterprises, including securities firms, insurance companies, and retailers.
>
> (Huertas 1988: 745)

In making international comparisons of regulation, one must first separate fact and fiction. The issue of mixing banking and commerce illustrates, first, that regulatory principles and regulatory practice often diverge. Second, the issue shows the complexity of apparently simple principles. Once one embarks on separating banking from commerce (or any other activity), the simple act of defining what constitutes a bank becomes a task not unlike that facing Sisyphus.

banks failed in Texas (454) than existed in France, West Germany or the United Kingdom (Clair and O'Driscoll 1992: 2).

Figures for the whole of the United States are equally striking. As of 31 March 1992, there were 11,786 commercial banks in the United States with median asset size of $50 million. Branches are still relatively rare, with banks averaging only five each. There were 4,869 unit or single-office banks in the United States (Clair and O'Driscoll 1992: 3).

These figures reflect longstanding antipathy to large banks and widespread state restrictions on branching. The branching restrictions are being relaxed, and mergers and consolidations are occurring rapidly. Antipathy towards large banks remains, however, and will always constrain the size of US banks. For these and other reasons, the number of US banks will probably always number in the thousands.

Banks in the United States are also severely restricted in the range of assets they can purchase. Commercial and investment banking were separated by the Banking Act of 1933.[7] As a practical matter, commercial banks were barred from underwriting corporate securities. In recent years, these restrictions have been eased administratively but basically remain in force. Banks are also restricted in marketing or providing insurance products. Despite all the change and upheaval in financial markets, these and other restrictions on bank powers remain. With non-bank financial firms, like Merrill Lynch, or even commercial firms, like Sears, General Electric and General Motors, now providing traditional banking services, commercial banks have been put at a competitive disadvantage.

The US regulatory system hobbles banks. The system, often called the dual banking system, shares regulatory responsibility between the states and the federal government. (Three major regulatory agencies share responsibility for what falls to the federal government.) The activities even of banks with a charter from the federal government are subject to a great deal of state regulation.[8] Most important among these is the right of each state to set the rules under which a bank may enter from another state. This feature of US banking regulation differs sharply from that adopted in the European Community.

In the United States, *host* states determine the rules under which banks operate. For instance, a bank domiciled in California (even if it possesses a federal or national charter) can enter Texas only if Texas law permits that. At the beginning of this century, a few organizations established banks across state lines. The McFadden Act of 1927 gave states the right to ban interstate banking. Those interstate banks already in existence were permitted to continue operating but could not expand further across state lines.

In 1978, Maine became the first state to pass permissive legislation. Banks could establish a presence in Maine by the use of a multi-bank holding company. Since then, forty-six states and the District of Columbia have enacted some form of interstate banking. Despite the proliferation of legislation, interstate banking is more dream than reality. The typical interstate bank holding company operates in only two states. More than 80 per cent of the 163 interstate bank holding companies operate in no more than three states. First Interstate Bancorp, one of the original, pre-1927 interstate banks, operates in the largest number of states – fourteen. Even Citicorp, the nation's largest banking organization, has banking operations in only ten states (Clair, Tucker and Siems 1991).

Even with the liberalization that has taken place in the United States, interstate *branching* is still forbidden. To move across state lines, a holding company must establish a new banking subsidiary. If this were true in Germany, for instance, then the banking organizations in each federal state would be legally separate from those in all other states. They could be combined in a holding company, but no one bank could branch into another federal state. The US system creates needless inefficiencies in the form of duplicate boards of directors, corporate officers, reporting, and so on.

As I have already suggested, what drives the US system is the fact that regulation is at the host-state level. This system runs contrary to the general rule in the United States, embodied in the Commerce Clause of the US Constitution, which guarantees the right of firms to compete across state lines.[9] As history has amply demonstrated, host-state rules stifle competition. In formulating the single-market initiative, the European Community understood this and set forth *home* state regulation in banking and elsewhere. Consider the difference this would make for the United States.

Under home state regulation, any bank legally chartered in one state could operate in another state. Moreover, the bank would operate under the charter and regulatory structure of the home state. This change, which, again, is more consistent with the US Constitution than is the current system, would resolve both the problem of interstate branching and the competitive disadvantage of banks. The home-state

Many observers fear that [illegible] lead to lax regulation. Once again, the European Community has addressed the problem by setting minimum standards that all national banking acts must meet. This could be done in the United States (and is already done for some bank regulatory issues).

Alternatively, Congress could mandate interstate branching, a solution that many prefer. It is unlikely to occur, however, because of entrenched interests. Not only do small banks traditionally oppose any policy that facilitates merger and consolidation (though less so than formerly), but state regulators oppose the federal government's moving in on their regulatory turf. Congress heeds both groups and, so, banking reform is gridlocked. If the locus of state regulation could merely be shifted from the host to the home state, perhaps at least one lobby - state regulators - could be mollified. Moreover, that change would require less explicit advance agreement on outcomes. No balancing of special interest need take place to effect change in bank powers. The regulatory competition among states would take care of that.

COMPETITION

As I indicated at the beginning of this chapter, I am only able to provide analysis that is Hayekian in spirit. This is especially so for banking, on which Hayek wrote surprisingly little. I have focused on banking regulation, because it influences the structure and performance of an economy's banking system in many ways. My analysis indicates that the locus of regulatory responsibility can greatly affect the operation of competitive forces.

Hayek maintained that competition is a dynamic process. No policy can determine the outcome of a competitive process. But public policy can inhibit or facilitate the operation of competitive market forces. Much about the current US regulatory structure impedes innovation, as well as adaptation to market forces. My analysis indicates a way of lowering the barriers against competitive innovation.

It is in this latter sense that, whatever its merits, the argument is Hayekian.

NOTES

The author is Vice-President and Economic Advisor at the US Federal Reserve Bank of Dallas. The views contained in this chapter are the author's alone and do not represent the official position of any part of the US Federal Reserve System.

1 Compare Hayek 'I have long since come to the conclusion that no real money can ever be neutral in this sense, and that we must be content with a system that rapidly corrects the inevitable errors' (1976: 69).

2 Permitting the relative price between cash and deposits to fluctuate temporarily can clear the market. In effect, this is what occurred when convertibility was suspended at the 'official' exchange rate of one dollar of cash per dollar of deposit.

3 Hayek (1973) distinguishes between the common or private law in a legal system, and legislation. It is the former that he argues is largely an evolved order.

4 Lawless behaviour clearly exists. Even bandits, however, adapt to common or civil law when engaging in ordinary transactions. Moreover, the criminal class is notorious for having its own code of behaviour, a breach of which is often accompanied by penalties more severe than in civil society.

5 In the European Community, the Benelux countries have virtually adopted the mark standard. Likewise, Argentina has all but adopted the dollar standard. I see no indication, however, that Belgium, the Netherlands and Luxembourg will adopt German as their national language or incorporate their legal system into Germany's. I also doubt that, no matter how successful its current monetary experiment, English will become the native tongue in Argentina.

6 The analysis here is obviously related to the literature on optimal currency areas. The latter comes to the question from a different perspective. It would be interesting – but beyond the scope of this chapter – to reconcile the two approaches.

7 Again, however, banking and commerce were not separated by this act.

8 Banks with a federal charter are known as 'national banks'. They are not 'national', however,in the sense of operating nation-wide. Nation-wide banking is only slowly emerging and still faces many impediments.

9 Once again, reality is more complex than principle. There are many examples of barriers to interstate trade, of which banking is only the most conspicuous. See O'Driscoll and Sigalla (1992).

REFERENCES

Chapman, Stanley (1984) *The Rise of Merchant Banking*, London: Allen & Unwin.

Clair, Robert T. and Gerald P. O'Driscoll, Jr (1992) 'Learning from One Another: The U.S. and European Banking Experience', *Journal of Multinational Financial Management*, forthcoming.

7(3): 743–62.

Langlois, Richard N. (1986) *Economics as a Process: Essays in the New Institutional Economics*, New York: Cambridge University Press.

Lewis, Mervyn K. (1990) 'Banking, Securities, and Commerce: A European Perspective', *Cato Journal* 10(2): 347–56.

Menger, Carl (1892) 'On the Origin of Money', trans. Caroline A. Foley, *Economic Journal* 2: 238–55.

—— (1963) Problems of Economics and Sociology, trans. F.J. Nock in Louis Schneider (ed.) Urbana Ill.: University of Illinois Press.

Mises, Ludwig von (1966) *Human Action*, 3rd edn, Chicago: Henry Regnery.

O'Driscoll, Jr, Gerald P. (1986) 'Money: Menger's Evolutionary Theory', *History of Political Economy* 18(4); 601–16.

O'Driscoll, Jr, Gerald P. and Fiona Sigalla (1992) 'Interstate Barriers to Trade', *Regulation*, forthcoming.

White, L.H. (1984) *Free Banking in Britain*, Cambridge: Cambridge University Press.

Clair, Robert T., Paula K. Tucker and Thomas F. Siems (1990) 'Removing the Remaining Barriers to Interstate Banking', *The Bankers Magazine* 173(1) 11–17.

Hayek, F.A. (1966) *Monetary Theory and the Trade Cycle*, London: Routledge & Kegan Paul.

—— (1967) 'The results of human action but not of human design', in F.A. von Hayek (1967) *Studies in Philosophy, Politics and Economics*, Chicago: University of Chicago Press.

—— (1976) *Denationalisation of Money*, Hobart Paper 70, London: Institute of Economic Affairs.

STABILITY OF SPONTANEOUS ORDER

In an era when academics are narrow specialists, scarcely venturing outside the narrow confines of a sub-section of their own subjects let alone mastering other disciplines, the breadth and range of Friedrich von Hayek's work is remarkable. Although originally a pure economic theorist (he was awarded the Nobel Prize for Economic Science in 1974), he has mastered several other equally daunting subjects: epistemology and philosophy, jurisprudence, the methodology of science, political theory and ethics, the history of ideas and theoretical psychology.[1] Whatever differences there are between Hayek and, say, John Stuart Mill in substantive political philosophy (and there are many) the structures of their ideas display similar architectonic qualities. In fact, Hayek has suggested that an economist who knows only economics is more likely to be a hindrance than a help in the understanding of social phenomena.

Yet Hayek's career has not been entirely that of the dry, detached scholar; he was involved in some of the most important intellectual and policy debates of the twentieth century. In the 1930s he was engaged in an important controversy with Keynes over monetary theory and the limitations of government's anti-depression policy (ironically this dispute preceded publication of Keynes's *General Theory* in 1936); in 1944 Hayek achieved some notoriety with his *The Road to Serfdom*,[2] and its grim prognosis that totalitarianism and the destruction of freedom were the likely consequences of even mild interferences with liberty under the rule of law; during the period of the 'social democratic' consensus which ruled post-war Western democracies, he elaborated and modified his philosophy of classical liberalism with a stream of learned treatises and articles which eventually found favour with Western political leaders, including Mrs Thatcher: if the world is ruled by ideas, which Hayek believed was the case (as did Keynes) then Western society may be about to be engulfed by a 'tide' of Hayekian ideas just as it was once swamped by Keynesianism.[3] Though one suspects that they are likely to find a more favourable reception in former communist regimes than in the West.

Despite the diversity of Hayek's intellectual endeavours, they are united by their concentration on one big idea: the explanation of that spontaneous order of events called, misleadingly, 'society', or more accurately, the 'extended order', and the scientific investigation of its aspects – economic, legal, political and moral. It is only through an understanding of the complexity of these interrelated phenomena can we expect our normative conclusions, our recommendations for public policy, to have any permanent hold on our intellects. Thus, although Hayek is publicly associated with the defence of the market, private property, the rule of law and the 'minimum' state, this is not mere ideology, or even justified in straightforward utilitarian terms (as it is with Milton Friedman) but is deeply embedded in a philosophy of man. However, this philosophy was fully articulated after Hayek's economic and social views had become widely known. So the task is to reconstruct Hayek's thought by, in a sense, working backwards from the epistemology and philosophy to the more familiar policy statements. The recent publication of Hayek's *The Fatal Conceit* (1988)[4] has been welcomed by Hayekian scholars precisely because it blends abstract philosophy with percipient observations on more immediate policy issues.

A proper understanding of the Hayekian project of restating the conditions for the emergence and maintenance of the liberal order must take account of a number of important criticisms that have been made of his political philosophy and his justification of it. Such a consideration is necessary not only for the purposes of scholarship but also for the continued intellectual replenishment of the liberal tradition. I shall identify a number of areas of controversy and explore them in a reconstruction of Hayek's thought.

Most important is the apparent confusion, or at least tension, between Hayek the social scientist and Hayek the normative theorist of liberalism. This is illustrated in his last work, *The Fatal Conceit*, which purports to demonstrate that socialists are 'mistaken about the facts' and not the victims of some kind of moral error or inadequacy. Allied to this is the complaint often made that Hayek's rejection of an *active* reason in the understanding of human affairs has, in the development of his thought, become too identified with a tame acceptance of the natural process of evolution, whatever that may be. Indeed, there seems to be an implicit acknowledgement in *The Fatal Conceit* that those social institutions and practices that have survived an evolutionary struggle ought to be valued for that reason alone. The question has been asked, then, whether the stress on spontaneous evolution has contributed to the corrosion of our critical accordance with their ability to sustain large populations? [illegible] different from Hayek's much more persuasive claim that it is illegitimate to evaluate social and economic systems in accordance with some redistributive criteria?

REASON AND SOCIETY

At the foundational level of Hayek's critical philosophy is a complex and subtle appreciation of the roles of reason and tradition in human affairs. Since Descartes the Western intellectual tradition has presented a false dichotomy between reason and tradition; as if a rejection of the idea that an active human reason capable of determining the course of events and restructuring the world according to abstract principles irrespective of experience, meant that man's behaviour was governed by mere instincts, that our critical faculties are powerless. On the contrary our reason is itself dependent on tradition and the development of mind is an evolutionary process, just as social and economic institutions themselves must be so understood. Indeed, in Hayek's view, freedom itself necessitates a willingness to submit to traditional rules 'so long as one has no definite reason to the contrary'.[5]

The following of a tradition is contrasted with obedience to the personalized orders of a political superior. This argument has been expressed more forcibly in later writings where the following of traditional rules and practices is specifically linked to progress: 'Tradition is not something constant but the product of a process guided not by reason but success'.[6] Further, the fragility and limitations of the human mind imply that 'all progress must be based on tradition'.[7]

Thus, instead of the hubristic rationalist model of society in which mind is deemed capable of restructuring the social world according to principles of its own making (constructivist rationalism), Hayek has attempted to restate that scepticism associated with David Hume and the Scottish Enlightenment. In this, the rejection of rationalism does not imply irrationalism, or blind faith, but entails the proposition that the proper use of reason is to 'whittle down the claims of reason'. This philosophy is concretized in Hayek's, ultimately epistemological, objection to the presumptions of the economic planner: for the ideal of a 'rational organization' of an economy does presuppose that the human mind can construct some measure of 'efficiency' and, furthermore, that it can have access to that dispersed knowledge which is required to make the realization of that ideal possible. Yet, as Hayek has been at pains to show, economic knowledge (i.e. information about prices, costs, the state of technology, consumer preferences, and so on) does not exist in a centralized form precisely because a human society is inhabited by acting, choosing individuals who face a world of uncertainty.[8] For reason to be of use in the evaluation of social affairs it must be a critical reason and informed by that limited knowledge which we have of social and economic processes.

The fundamental difference between social science and physical science, which Hayek has constantly stressed, is that knowledge of the latter is objective and measurable, it is knowledge of stable, replicable systems. The former is subjective, and relates to the actions of decentralized agents. Thus the social scientist is limited to a reconstruction of the general features of social systems and his predictions are confined to the formation of 'patterned' phenomena, such as the price system itself and not the particular movement of its parts.[9] Such orders are logically reconstructed out of the actions of individuals. This doctrine of methodological individualism is to be contrasted with 'conceptual realism', the theory that aggregative concepts, such as 'class' and 'state' can be given an existence independently of human agents.

In Hayek's later work, however, we can detect subtle departures from this subjectivist and individualist model of explanation. In *The Fatal Conceit*, the idea of progress is specifically identified with the success that particular societies have had in coping with a niggardly nature and with the exploitation of natural resources. There would appear to be no external standards by which we can appraise societies, such as their contribution to moral freedom, because that would be to impose (illegitimately) a standard on societies which have their own ordering principles. The limits of a society's progress are set by the structure of rules and practices of that society itself. Of course, Hayek tries to hide the Social Darwinist implications of this position by drawing a distinction between biological or genetic evolution and cultural evolution. Social evolution proceeds by the gradual acquisition of learnt rules and practices rather than through biologically determined traits. This avoids the possibility of any link with race (the possibilities of the adoption of successful norms and practices is insensitive to race) but it nevertheless does not completely counter the charge that Hayek's position requires us to accept as culturally definitive (in moral and efficiency terms) the stage at which a given society has reached.

ing processes of discrete (although hypothetical) individuals. Indeed, the normative appeal of market institutions is that they permit the breaking down of culturally determined impediments to individual achievement. Yet Hayek's sociology presupposes that individuals are identified in terms of group membership: with the concomitant implication that group rules should prescribe the limits of individuality. Thus, the presence of collectively determined rules which are favourable to the market turns out to be a product of, if not quite chance, certainly a somewhat mysterious process. Indeed, the actions of individuals who wish to break out of the constraints of a received order to enjoy the benefits of freedom would be condemnable by Hayek's strict evolutionary criteria.

Hayek would deny that his evolutionary hypothesis had anything to do with an ethical evaluative method that identified the 'right' with the most evolved,[11] yet it is not surprising that commentators have suggested that it has that implication. His argument that societies that do not choose the evolutionary path towards market capitalism are condemned to misery is simply not compelling. Historically, many societies have happily lived below their potential productivity, but it is surely plausible to suggest that Hayek's most extreme flights of anti-rationalism preclude him from critical comment on them. Indeed, Hume's cautious utilitarianism, with its commitment to more or less universal rules of justice as the mainsprings of progress, is surely a more satisfactory account of the process of evaluation. Certainly in *The Fatal Conceit*, Hayek's attempt to make social evolution consistent with Humean ethics is less than wholly convincing.

One is driven to the conclusion that the Hayek of *The Constitution of Liberty* is a more cogent apologist of the liberal order than the Hayek of *The Fatal Conceit*. No doubt he was tempted by a more strident evolutionary doctrine in the latter work in order to provide a 'scientific' refutation of socialism. But in so doing did he not reduce the effectiveness of those intellectual weapons which he had used so expertly in his earlier work? No doubt it is possible to argue that evolution was always present in his philosophy, but towards the end of his life it seems to have displaced other, more conventional, normative arguments.

MORALITY AND FREEDOM

In a logically not dissimilar way, the principles of morality on which a free order rests have a non-rationalist foundation. They are neither a product of an unaided reason nor of instinct but constitute a learnt tradition. Again, like Hume, Hayek regards moral rules as restraints which, although they are in a sense 'artificial' in that they are devices which men have stumbled upon to cope with those more or less permanent features of the human condition such as scarcity, self-interest and the propensity to violence and so on, they may just as well be called natural because of their congruence with man's needs and purposes. The rules of private property (which Hayek now prefers to call 'several property' in order to highlight its individualist and diverse form)[12] are, for example, the only forms of ownership which are harmonious with the natural, though not precisely measurable, regularities of the market.

The identification of moral rules with necessary restraints on human conduct, restraints which make *ordered* liberty possible, is essential to Hayek's dissociation of morality from both an unaided reason and instinct.[13] The rationalist expresses his permanent dissatisfaction with those learnt rules either because they have no justification in meeting with immediate demands (as a Benthamite utilitarian would maintain that they ought to have) or because they fail to satisfy the criteria of 'natural rights' validated by something other than tradition. A particular problem of the modern world is that the abstract rules that make ordered liberty possible seem to run counter to a morality that derives from certain communal instincts. A pertinent example is the distribution of income that is determined by the impersonal forces of the market. Its apparent randomness and detachment from the emotionally more appealing but primordial principles of social justice and equality, is sufficient to condemn it in the eyes of modern intellecutals.

Again, those who interpret freedom as a liberation from all forms of restraint, a malign mutation of the liberal tradition that begins with Rousseau and continues through to those anarchic protests against rules and which were such a feature of the 1960s and 1970s, similarly represent a reversion to, ultimately, irrational and instinctive forms of behaviour. Those who would mistakenly define freedom as merely the absence of restraint neglect the fact that some sorts of rules are necessary for the emergence of civilization; a process which involves the mastery of nature rather than desperately seeking some infallible source of morality in a 'nature' uncontaminated by conventional rules.

of natural rights grounds, in addition to Hayek's argument that they coagulate the sources of innovation and hence disrupt the flow and co-ordination of dispersed knowledge. In theory, however, Hayek's definition should also preclude conscription and, indeed, direct taxation. Naturally, Hayek regards these as unavoidable, but the impression he gives is that these are *ad hoc* exceptions to a general principle rather than conclusions of a fully-worked-out theory that authoritatively determines the respective roles of the individual and the state in a modern society.

What is more disturbing is Hayek's claim that general rules of justice, both criminal and civil, which do not compel action but merely forbid certain forms of conduct, are somehow not coercive. He accounts for coercion in the following way: 'Provided that I know beforehand that if I place myself in a particular position, I shall be coerced and provided that I can avoid putting myself in such a situation, I need never be coerced'.[14] This has the alarming implication that almost any amount of conduct-forbidding laws would not be coercive merely because the individual could always abstain from the prohibited course of action. Yet that proposed conduct could be essential to a person's well-being, and not damaging to other people's interest in the sense described by John Stuart Mill. In *Rules and Order* Hayek does talk of the need for the preservation of a 'protected domain',[15] in which, presumably self-regarding actions would not be forbidden, but the moral justification for this requires a rather different rationale for law than the simple demand that it be perfectly general and non-compulsory. It would indeed require a certain element of rationalism in its account of the proper relationship between individual liberty and law.

Again, to the disappointment of many, Hayek appears to justify liberty in almost exclusively instrumental terms, as an essential mechanism for the conquest of ignorance in the co-ordination of decentralized knowledge. He writes that 'if there were omniscient men, if we could know not only all that affects the attainment of our present wishes, but also our future wants and desires, there would be little case for liberty'.[16] It is undoubtedly true that in the modern world the debate about liberty has been dominated by those who value freedom for its contribution to personal development and the fulfilment of essentially non-economic goals, and those who have discounted its contribution to economic progress, but Hayek surely attenuates the liberal case by his reluctance to engage in argument about the morality of freedom. Of course, in much of his writing Hayek does make the conceptual link between economic and personal liberty, never more so than in *The Road to Serfdom*,[17] but in his later work there is a tendency for straightforward utilitarian arguments about freedom to predominate. Not only is this hard to square with his professed anti-utilitarianism (at least his anti-Benthamism) but it also seriously underestimates important elements of human well-being. Surely, Hayek cannot mean that the only objection to *dirigiste* economic planning is that it failed dismally in economic terms?

EVOLUTION AND SOCIAL PROGRESS

One further point is crucially relevant to Hayek's understanding of nature and reason and their roles in the control of those instinctive impulses which are potentially destructive of civilization. It is that societies progress through an evolutionary process of natural selection of rules and institutions: that prosperity is a result of the 'imitation'[18] of the more successful ones rather than the product of an unaided reason determining alleged laws of cause and effect.

A rather commonplace example of this process of imitation might be the contemporary phenomenon of (hitherto) collectivized economic regimes avidly following the practices and conventions of market societies precisely because the latter have been more successful in coping with those seemingly ineradicable features of the human condition – scarcity and the infinite and diverse nature of human wants.

The particular criterion of success in this process that is identified by Hayek is the capacity for a social system to sustain large populations, a claim elaborated in some detail in *The Fatal Conceit*.[19] It is by this criterion he maintains that capitalism is to be judged. However, it is subject to many difficulties. At the theoretical level it seems to introduce an idea that is alien to the main structure of his liberal thought. It is the notion that a social system, and its validating theory, can be appraised in accordance with the achievement of some particular end-state or outcome. It was his original, and fundamental, claim that ineradicable human ignorance prevented us from specifying goals for any human activity. Spontaneous orders develop in unpredictable ways and cannot be attributed purposes. The justification for the liberal order lies in the fact it protects individuals in whatever purposes they choose. There may be a convoluted notion non-market societies, including the former Soviet bloc, [illegible] large populations, albeit at a low level of welfare. For a utilitarian, of course, there are serious questions as to whether the principle of utility requires that the highest overall level of welfare in aggregate should be aimed at or whether some average level should be the object of policy irrespective of the effect on total utility. What is chosen, of course, has serious implications for questions of population control. Hayek denies that he is a utilitarian in the conventional sense, but his sudden invocation of the population principle invites the very same questions that have vexed the followers of that traditional doctrine.

THE EXTENDED ORDER

Thus it is by a process of evolution, not conscious reason, that mankind has developed what Hayek has called the extended order, or civilization. The substantive features of this can easily be adumbrated. It is a notion that derives from the ideas of Adam Smith, David Hume and other writers of the Scottish Enlightenment who first noted, through their description of the market and the division of labour, how the actions of decentralized agents (individuals), can be co-ordinated without the invocation of a central designer or planner. Darwin, of course, later showed how explanation of order in the natural world was possible without the necessity for a Creator but the germ of the idea was discovered by social scientists long before it became a feature of the biological sciences.

Not only was it a revolutionary idea at the time it was first formulated but even today many eminent social theorists find it difficult to accept. The more prevalent view of social order is that it is a product of agreement between people about a set of common purposes and that political participation and communal action are necessary to create and sustain that order. It is a conception that derives from ancient Greek political philosophy, and in English political thought it is known as 'republicanism' or 'civic humanism'. The assumption is that the legal order and social rules should embody common purposes; and that in their absence a society is unsustainable and individuals would become anomic and alienated from any structure of rules.

However, the peculiar genius of liberal individualist social theory lies in its explanation of how it is that individuals are held together by common rules rather than common purposes. Thus individualism is not merely the methodological doctrine that the only genuine propositions about aggregate social phenomena are those that can be (logically) reduced to propositions about the actions, intentions and volitions of individual agents, but the more ambitious project of explaining how such essentially anonymous persons can produce a co-ordinated order of great complexity (in economic terms, efficiency). Its rules are necessarily 'abstract' in the sense that they embody no particular purpose but constitute a structure which permits anonymous individuals to pursue their subjective purposes with some security and predictability. In Michael Oakeshott's instructive phrase they are 'adverbial rules',[20] that is, they tell us how to do things rather than dictate, instruct, or command individuals to perform actions on behalf of a (fictitious) common end or public good.

Hayek likes to describe the emergence of this order in evolutionary terms, although it might be just as plausible to explain it in terms of chance, or serendipity. For the liberal it is perhaps less important to enquire into its genesis than it is to understand its structural features and to indicate ways in which it might be preserved (if that is not too rationalist a demand). The best short description Hayek gives of the extended order, or *cosmos*, and its emergence, is as follows: 'Under the enforcement of universal rules of just conduct, protecting a recognizable private domain of individuals, a spontaneous order of human activities of much greater complexity will form itself than could ever be produced by deliberate arrangement.'[21]

In *The Fatal Conceit* he makes an illuminating contrast between the spontaneous order of the *cosmos* and that of the 'troop':[22] a troop of soldiers cannot be an extended order precisely because it exists only to sustain the particular purpose appropriate to it. The family, the small group and the face-to-face intimate organization of the tribe are analysable in precisely the same way. Furthermore Hayek does not deny that within the extended order there will remain such essential associations which would be crushed if they were organized under the same principles as those of the extended order. However, the main danger to civilization is the obverse of this: it is that modern socialism involves an atavistic attempt to replace the anonymity and the abstract nature of the extended order with the intimacy of the closed society.

However, it has to be said that Hayek underestimates the pull of ethnicity and communal affiliations which is clearly present in though the latter is a more overtly conservative philosopher. Both these understandings of society are at odds with the prevailing tendency of modern communitarian politics, which is to attribute concrete functions (or 'end-states') to government and to evaluate governmental activity in accordance with how it fulfils them; and not for its achievements in sustaining the framework of abstract rules. Thus it is that politics comes to dominate men's lives since politics necessarily involves the pursuit of preordained goals and rational schemes – 'economic growth', the welfare state, a 'fair distribution of incomes' and so on – which can only be realized, if at all, through public action. Public law then replaces private law in the organization of society. It is through the idea of law, then, that we can gain a full understanding of the notion of the extended order.

THE THEORY OF LAW

The maintenance of the extended order requires a specific structure of rules. The difficulty here is that spontaneity and evolution only explain part of the legal order, for Hayek himself concedes that there is a place for two types of law in a liberal society: *nomos* (the rules of a spontaneous order) and *thesis*, the law appropriate to an order with a specific purpose (the rules of government itself).[23] The former is clearly more explicable in evolutionary terms than the latter.

The English common law is the most obvious candidate for explanation in Hayekian concepts. The principles of the law of contract, and of tort, developed in a case by case manner without the aid of statute (or 'legislation'). Indeed, Hayek is quite correct in his claim that statutory or 'made' law is a comparative latecomer in judicial history. Furthermore, judicial activity is a kind of puzzle-solving where a judge, in difficult cases, tries to find a rule to settle disputes between individual parties. In this sense law is 'discovered' rather than created. Furthermore, *the* law (*nomos*) is not concerned with public policy but only with the rights and wrongs of a particular case. Although there is no reason why codified legal systems could not be couched in the form of purpose-independent abstract rules – indeed, many classical liberals have argued that liberty under the law is better protected by them than the common law, the record of which in sustaining freedom is by no means flawless – Hayek has his own epistemological reasons for favouring an evolutionary jurisprudence.[24] These relate to the impossibility of a 'legislative' mind having the knowledge of human circumstances which would be necessary to devise a code of rules for an extended order. He has argued that since many of these cannot be fully articulated, any attempt to encapsulate them in a precise code will almost certainly mean that some traditional rules will be lost to the legal order.

It is undoubtedly true that Hayek's jurisprudence is one of the most impressive features of Hayek's work. Yet even here one feels that he has placed far too much emphasis on the virtues of the common law and neglected the vices to which it is prone. Vices which may be serious enough to threaten the serviceability of the common law as a mechanism for the market order.

I refer here to the work of Ronald Dworkin, whose jurisprudence bears an uncanny resemblance to Hayek's. Yet Dworkin is able to impose on a common law system a kind of 'liberal' (in the American sense) social agenda which would be anathema to Hayek. Dworkin makes a distinction between rules and principles:[25] rules can be precisely articulated and applied uncontroversially to routine cases while principles have to be invoked by judges to settle hard cases (where the law is in dispute or unclear). Principles are locked in the interstices of a community's tradition, but when they are revealed by the judge they are part of the law and not some deduction from natural law or a conclusion of abstract reason. For example, when a New York court invoked the principle that 'no man shall profit from his own wrongs' in the famous case of ***Riggs*** v ***Palmer*** it was in effect performing a Hayekian exercise of 'discovering' the law that is implicitly contained in previously non-articulated rules.

However, Dworkin has proceeded to discover highly controversial 'liberal' principles to do with affirmative action, the 'rights' of pornographers, justified civil disobedience and other matters which have little to do with the written statutes of American law, or indeed, much connection with American public opinion. Also, Dworkin would exclude, for example, property and contract from special protection. For him, economic matters are aspects of public policy in which judges are forbidden to intrude (unless a fundamental moral right is at stake). Yet the creative activity of Dworkinian judges is not, conceptually at least, unlike that which Hayek expects of his. When Hayek writes that new rules should be 'compatible with the rest of the system from the angle of their effectiveness in contributing to the same kind of affairs traditionally [illegible] been a consequence of that hubristic rationalism that has infected politics since the Enlightenment, or even the all-pervading presence of *power* in the modern political world. It is also to do with the fact that the source of that power in Britain, the absolute sovereignty of Parliament, is itself an undesigned and unplanned rule of the common law. It just happened spontaneously that judges accorded to Parliament the authority of unlimited legislative power.[27]

The devastating effect this would have on the structure of *nomos* was not realized until the legislature in a democratic society began to be organized on party lines, mainly as a consequence of the extension of the franchise. Under these conditions 'legislation' (*thesis*) has gradually superseded private law, and the implementation of public plans has become the object of government policy. As Hayek and other classical liberals have been at pains to point out, those plans do not represent a genuine public interest but only the interests of groups necessarily smaller than the public.[28] Hayek was very impressed by the 'economic theory of democracy': it has demonstrated that political competition, powered by the 'vote motive', produces very different results from economic competition, spurred by a benign self-interest. The extended order, because its benefits are widely dispersed (and also because it has no immediate appeal to our instincts) is itself a kind of public good which it is in no one's interest to promote.

It is here that a certain kind of constructivist rationalism enters even Hayek's social philosophy. He recognizes that the gradual disintegration of *nomos*, or traditional rules of just conduct, has come about through sovereign legislatures possessing the power to make not only law for those public activities which Hayek readily admits are necessary for the extended order, but also the power to make the abstract, purposeless law of *nomos* (hence, for example, legislative interference with the traditional law of contract). His solution to this problem is an elaborate constitutional rearrangement, or reconstruction, of legislative authority so that those two law-making powers are in separate institutional hands.[29] This does suggest that there are limits to spontaneity, even though the reform proposals clearly do not of abstract rules for a more effective servicing of the extended order. Even Hayek, then, cannot avoid the use of reason in the approach to constitutional reform.

THE RULE OF LAW

Those classical liberals who find Hayek's constitutional reforms somewhat arcane and impracticable nevertheless value highly the doctrine of the *rule of law* that lies behind them; this ideal constituted Hayek's earlier theoretical argument for the limits on a *taxis* (or government).[30] Hayek has never favoured absolute and immutable limitations on government activity, either by the invocation of a rationalistic set of 'natural' rights or by reference to some aggregate welfare function derived from orthodox public-good theory: both of these techniques would be examples of constructivism. In an uncertain world it is impossible to specify in advance what is, or is not, the appropriate sphere of government activity. The point Hayek stresses is that the appropriate sphere of government should depend on its lawfulness rather than its consistency with some rationalistic criteria. Its rules should therefore be universal, non-discriminatory, non-retrospective and applied impartially. Most important of all, coercion should only be applied to prevent a greater coercion (by private agents). It follows from this that freedom can be preserved in the context of government as long as the state does not claim a monopoly in any activity (except in defence).

Yet critics of Hayek have not been entirely happy with the idea that the purely formal criteria of the rule of law can function satisfactorily as the touchstone of legislation. As Ronald Hamowy has pointed out,[31] it would not take too much imagination for a legislature to construct a law in such a way that it picked out people for special treatment. A simple example might be a law that banned all sport on a Sunday: it does not specifically name Catholics but it obviously harms them. Again, it would be possible to make massive inroads into the private economy while still keeping with Hayek's definition of law. The only direct moral and intellectual protection would be to appeal directly to rights or utility in the evaluation. But this does not sit easily with his pronounced anti-rationalism, and Hayek, in fact, rejects these approaches.

Hayek's rather more prosaic recommendations on government policy have much more power than his appeals to an abstract doctrine of the rule of law. Of particular importance is his simple but persuasive claim that government should not be permitted a monopoly in any activity (except in such things as national defence).

intervention of government. The latter is costly and necessarily based on inadequate knowledge.

ECONOMICS

The extended order is not merely the order of the market but a complex arrangement of rules and institutions which provide a framework of predictability for individuals with diverse ends and purposes. Nevertheless, it was in economics that Hayek established the first of his intellectual reputations and it is undoubtedly the case that the logic of the extended social order is structured out of the logic of the market order.

Hayek's economics is rooted firmly in the Austrian tradition which began with Carl Menger's *Principles of Economics* (1870). Although the latter's work is conventionally bracketed with that of Walras and Jevons in that all three economists almost simultaneously discovered (or rediscovered) the idea of marginal utility as the ordering principle of resource allocation in a market system, it differed considerably from what was to become the neoclassical orthodoxy. It was those differences that Hayek was to develop in economic theory and philosophy.

The most important is the critique of the emphasis on equilibrium, that is, the perfect co-ordination of economic activities in which prices clear all markets, every factor of production is paid its marginal product, there are no supra-normal profits and no possibility of further improvement.[33] Orthodox neoclassical economists became obsessed with the problem of proving mathematically the existence of such an exquisite organization of economic phenomena; at the cost of neglecting those features of human action that characterize genuine economic decision-making. Furthermore, within the equilibrium model there lurks an implicit normative judgement: that the state ought to intervene to correct those inefficiencies, monopoly, excess profits, and so on, that were visible in existing imperfect capitalist economies. Indeed, the original model of 'market socialism'[34] was, in effect, the attempt to replicate artificially (by bureaucratic commands rather than price signals) an equilibrium, on the assumption that spontaneous processes would generate waste, monopoly 'rents' and unproductive inequality.

The equilibrium model, however, is a rationalist delusion, for it presupposes that an omniscient economic legislator can know what a perfect allocation of resources would be in advance of the trial-and-error process of the market itself. More specifically, he would have to know what costs are in order to satisfy efficiency criteria. However the cost of anything is always an alternative use of the same resources; yet this must be a subjective phenomenon, indeed, it is the opinion of the economic transactor. Thus it is the case that economics deals with the mental phenomena rather than objective facts. Whatever 'facts' there are in economic life are dispersed across transactors and are only 'revealed' through a process of exchange in an uncertain and ever-changing world.[35]

In fact, Hayek's theory of the market departs considerably from the standard 'allocational' model used by orthodox neoclassical economists. There are no 'given' resources to be allocated according to some scientistic criterion of social 'efficiency', but only individuals using their bits of decentralized knowledge to realise their subjective plans. Hence his rejection of the rationalist's use of the word 'economy' (which does imply the existence of an end-state, the achievement of which requires a mechanical allocation of resources) and its replacement by the word *catallaxy*.[36] Modern economic society (the catallaxy) consists of a myriad of individual economies (firms, organizations and so on) each with their purposes, while it has no overall purpose. Catallactics, or exchange, is simply the process by which an agent improves his well-being, and in so doing produces, unintentionally, an overall co-ordination of activities. The market is then a 'discovery procedure' through which individuals, guided by the information transmitted by prices, adjust to the flux and uncertainty of economic life.[37] It is important to note here that it is not only the information that is transmitted by prices that has economic value but also the opportunities for economic improvement that they indicate.

Although Hayek rightly rejects the 'engineering' notion of efficiency (or, indeed any aggregate welfare function) as a normative criterion for the success of the market, catallactics is not a mindless playing of a game for its own sake: it does produce social benefits of an *indirect* utilitarian kind. The achievement of such benefits depends primarily on government inactivity in the economic sphere; for it is by its non-involvement in a catallaxy that the state can retain its legitimate role as the neutral enforcer of the rules of just conduct; and in so doing it permits individuals to exploit dispersed knowledge points out in *The Fatal Conceit*, it is historically [illegible] that the development of commerce depended upon government. Exchange between individuals, held together by only 'vulgar' economic relations, preceded the creation of political institutions: 'Governments have more often hindered than initiated the development of long-distance trade'.[38]

Part of the rationalist's *animus* against the market stems from a misunderstanding of the nature of commerce; especially the role of the entrepreneur in the co-ordinating process. Again the errors here derive from the influence of equilibrium theory. For theoretically, in a perfectly competitive market there is no entrepreneurial profit: each factor of production is paid that income just sufficient to keep it in operation. In market socialism, managers are paid a salary. A major achievement of Hayek's political economy is its emphasis on the necessity for profit, even monopoly profit, if the dispersed knowledge is to be co-ordinated; for it is that alertness to the distinction between factor cost and product price (which constitutes profit) that powers a catallaxy.[39] While rationalists may resent the fact that economic success should depend on the alleged baser motives (in Keynes's phrase, 'animal spirits'), it should be remembered that this resentment is itself an instinctive rather than an intellectual response.

It is an emotional reaction to the apparent dominance of 'selfishness' rather than a reasoned consideration of the all-pervading problems of ignorance and uncertainty; problems which have been shown to be insoluble whenever and wherever the profit motive has been suppressed.

It is not, of course, only socialism that is predicated upon the hubris of reason; there are many other social and economic doctrines which, in the twentieth century especially, have similarly depended on the alleged ability of a presumptuous rational faculty to improve upon spontaneity. It is not implausible to argue that the major threat to the extended order in Western democracies has not come from overt socialism but from the (ultimately) enervating effects of the pursuit of full-employment policies by Keynesian macroeconomic methods and from the enervating effects of welfarism.

Keynesian economics depends almost entirely on the rejection of the idea that an extended market order is self-correcting (except in the very, very long run, at which time, said Keynes, most damagingly, 'we are all dead') and required government to secure an equilibrium of full employment of all resources. Hence, the post-war history of 'demand management' policies achieved through budget deficits and monetary profligacy. Quite apart from demonstrating the ruinous effects that inflation has on a catallaxy, Hayek has been as much concerned to show the epistemological errors that underlie the attempts to cure unemployment by this method. He writes, in his Nobel Lecture, 'The Pretence of Knowledge':

> when we are asked for quantitative evidence for the particular structure of prices and wages that would be required in order to assure a smooth and continuous sale of the products and services offered, we must admit that we have no such information. We know . . . the general conditions in which what we call, somewhat misleadingly, an equilibrium will establish itself: but we never know what the particular prices or wages are which would exist if the market were to bring about such an equilibrium.[40]

The cure for unemployment is to be found in the correction of those institutional impediments (which are mainly of government origin) to the smooth functioning of the catallaxy. Especially damaging are the actions of sectional groups embedded in the interstices of political society (trade unions are the major example) which are able to prevent the emergence of market clearing prices, especially that of labour. Furthermore, inflation, by distorting the structure of relative prices, misleads transactors into investing in activities which are ultimately unsustainable. It is the liquidation of such investments that causes widespread and persistent unemployment.

However, there is one implication of subjectivism that Hayek did not consider. This is the possibility, recognized in the work of Shackle[41] and Lachmann,[42] that the market process may not always show co-ordinating tendencies. This is accounted for by a consideration of the discoordinating effects that (necessarily subjective) expectations have on the market. If all economic activity really consists in guesses about the future then there would appear to be no necessity for the price system to co-ordinate activity, except in the very long run. Lachmann makes an important distinction between ordinary product prices and asset prices.[43] We would expect the market to do its co-ordinating role with regard to the former (after all, individuals will only hold products for a short length of time), but with respect to the latter, the future yield of an asset depends

None of this is meant to imply that government [illegible] economic conditions: such distressing phenomena may indeed be ineradicable features of the human and social condition. It merely indicates that basic Hayekian economic ideas are capable of further exploration.

However, it is in the field of monetary policy that Hayek's imagination has been at its most active. In fact, the implication of the theory of the extended order is that we do not need monetary policy at all. As Menger demonstrated[44], the money good (based normally on a precious commodity) would emerge spontaneously in a barter economy and its value would be a function of the self-interested actions of transactors rather than of the imprimatur of the state. Despite the excellent historical record of the traditional monetary device, the gold standard, the modern rationalist regards it as absurd that a society should depend for its money good on 'wasting' resources in digging gold out of the ground; especially as this can (allegedly) lead to 'shortages'. Yet, the tradition of 'metal' contained a hidden wisdom which was scarcely articulated until monetary stability had been virtually destroyed by the rise of 'fiat' money: it imposed a constraint on government.

The problem of money, that one 'loose joint'[45] in an otherwise self-correcting catallaxy, has been a major concern of Hayek's career both as an economist and philosopher. As recently as 1976 he surprised liberal economists with his radical solution to the problem of inflation caused by 'nationalized' money.[46] Instead of recommending a return to gold, or some surrogate for this such as a fixed (constitutional) monetary rule, he argued for a free market in currencies so that natural economic forces would deter governments from debasing their currency (since nobody would use a money good that failed to keep its value). Whatever the technical merits of this particular scheme, it is a superb example of Hayek's fertile anti-rationalism, for although it looks like a revolutionary proposal, it is in fact quite consonant with those traditional customs and practices which Hayek, as a social scientist, has spent a lifetime explicating.

CONCLUSION

There is a central problem in Hayek's social thought and it turns on the place of reason in social analysis. In earlier work, especially *The Constitution of Liberty* (1960), he appears to be a cricial rationalist in the Popperian tradition. Thus, although this book showed a familiar caution about an over-extended use of reason in social affairs (indeed, it includes several passages that indicate Hayek's reverence for Burke), it nevertheless pursued arguments to their logical conclusion. Some of these were quite iconoclastic and actually disruptive of prevailing social arrangements. The analysis of the existing welfare state practices and institutions is conducted on impeccably classical liberal grounds and the normative conclusions that are drawn follow inexorably from these premises. The same could be said of Hayek's monetary reforms and his constitutional proposals. All of them, given the prevailing social and political mores of Western liberal democracies, were quite radical.

The difficulty is that these social practices, which might be said to wilt in the face of radical individualist economics (and, indeed, ethics) could be validated by reference to the more extreme version of social evolution that Hayek presents in his later work. Many of them developed not as the result of specific rational design but out of a kind of gradual process of accumulated responses to specific problems. This is especially true of the institutions, practices and policies of the welfare state. Given that Hayek sets much store by epistemological uncertainty, that is, that we can never have sufficient knowledge of social and economic affairs to predict exactly the consequences of particular interventions, it is not implausible to suggest that similar uncertainty should restrain us from interfering too radically with received institutional arrangements. Many of these have achieved 'success' in the Hayekian way; they have survived an evolutionary process and their existence cannot be attributed to a single designing mind.

A persistence, however, with this attitude may well induce a certain kind of fatalism, that we must wait for evolution to pronounce its verdict on social events. This is, however, a predisposition that is precluded by Hayek's earlier critical rationalism but validated perhaps by *The Fatal Conceit*. It seems that we need another principle to distinguish between false rationalism and critical rationalism. All Hayek's criticisms of false rationalism are derived from an application of the doctrine of evolution but that idea cannot help us in determining the limits of critical reason, of indicating when and under what circumstances the latter disintegrates into a socially malevolent version of post-Enlightenment, *a priori* rationalism. It is hard to see what that principle might be.

(some of the features of which resemble Hayek's description of the closed or tribal society). Would it not be an example of constructivist rationalism to impose a Hayekian type of anonymous market society on societies which have little or no experience of its legal and moral subtleties? Can we ever know the proper limits of radical social change?

I mention these points only to suggest pointers of further development of classical liberal thought. The fact that they spring from an examination of Hayek's thought is indicative of its richness. The road to freedom which he has recommended does not follow a straight and uncontroversial route but is complex and sometimes difficult to describe with any sort of precision. But that is the nature of enquiry into social affairs: the elusive qualities of the subject matter makes definitive solutions to abiding problems impossible to achieve. The real long-term danger of rationalism is that the sense of certainty which it generates tends to obliterate, either through politics or by a kind of intellectual osmosis, competing and rival research programmes. That indeed looked to be the fate of classical liberalism throughout much of the twentieth century, and it might well have turned out that way but for the work of Hayek.

NOTES

1 Hayek's major philosophical writings are *The Sensory Order*, London: Routledge & Kegan Paul, 1952; *The Counter-Revolution of Science*, Glencoe: The Free Press, 1952; *The Constitution of Liberty*, London: Routledge & Kegan Paul, 1960; *Studies in Philosophy, Politics and Economics*, London: Routledge & Kegan Paul, 1967; *Law, Legislation and Liberty*; vol. 1, *Rules and Order* (1973); vol. 2, *The Mirage of Social Justice* (1976), vol. 3, *The Political Order of a Free People; New Studies in Philosophy, Politics, Economics, and the History of Ideas* London: Routledge & Kegan Paul, 1978; *The Fatal Conceit*, London: Routledge, 1988. For commentaries, see Norman Barry, *Hayek's Social and Economic Philosophy*, London: Macmillan, 1979; John Gray, *Hayek on Liberty*, Oxford; Blackwell, 1984; Chandran Kukathas, *Hayek and Modern Liberalism*, Oxford: Clarendon Press, 1989.

2 F.A. Hayek, *The Road to Serfdom*, London: Routledge & Kegan Paul, 1944.

3 For a discussion of the role of ideas in politics, see Norman Barry, 'Ideas versus Interests: the Classical Liberal Dilemma', in N.P. Barry, J. Burton, H.H. Gissurarson, J. Grey, J. Shearmur and K.I. Vaughn, *Hayek's Serfdom Revisited*, London: Institute of Economic Affairs, 1984.
4 It constitutes the first volume of what will be Hayek's collected works, edited by W. W. Bartley III and to be published by Routledge.
5 F.A. Hayek, 'Individualism: True and False', in Hayek, *Individualism and Economic Order*, London: Routledge & Kegan Paul, 1948, p. 23.
6 F.A. Hayek, 'Three Sources of Human Values', in Hayek, *The Political Order of a Free People*, p. 166.
7 Ibid., p. 167.
8 Hayek, *The Constitution of Liberty*, Ch. 2.
9 See Hayek, *Philosophy, Politics and Economics*, Chs 1 and 2.
10 Hayek, *The Fatal Conceit*, p. 25.
11 Ibid., p. 27.
12 Ibid., Ch. 2.
13 Ibid., Ch. 1.
14 Hayek, *The Constitution of Liberty*, p. 142.
15 Hayek, *Rules and Order*, pp. 106–10.
16 Hayek, *The Constitution of Liberty*, p. 142.
17 Especially Ch. 1.
18 Hayek, *The Fatal Conceit*, pp. 21–3.
19 Ibid., Ch. 8.
20 See his essay, 'The Rule of Law', in *On History*, Oxford: Blackwell, 1983.
21 F.A. Hayek, 'The Principles of a Liberal Social Order', in *Philosophy, Politics and Economics*, p. 162.
22 Hayek, *The Fatal Conceit*, p. 18.
23 See Hayek, *Rules and Order*, *passim*.
24 See ibid., Ch. 6.
25 Ronald Dworkin, *Taking Rights Seriously*, London: Duckworth, 1977, Chs 1 and 2. Also, Dworkin, *Law's Empire*, London: Fontana, 1986.
26 Hayek, *Mirage of Social Justice*, p. 167.
27 See Norman Barry, *The Crisis in Law*, Sydney: Centre for Independent Studies, 1989.
28 Hayek, *The Political Economy of a Free People*, Ch. 16.
29 Ibid., Ch. 17.
30 Hayek, *The Constitution of Liberty*, pp. 222–4.
31 R. Hamowy, 'Hayek's Concept of Freedom: A Critique', in *New Individualist Review* 1 (1961): 28–31.
32 F.A. Hayek, 'The Problem of Social Cost', *Journal of Law and Economics*, 3 (1960): 1–44.
33 See Norman Barry, *The Invisible Hand in Economics and Politics*, London: Institute of Economic Affairs, 1988.
34 See Don Lavoie, *Rivalry and Central Planning: The Calculation Debate Revisited*, Cambridge: Cambridge University Press, 1985.
35 F.A. Hayek, 'The Meaning of Competition', in Hayek, *Individualism and Economic Order*, London: Routledge & Kegan Paul, 1948, p. 100.
36 Hayek, *The Mirage of Social Justice*, Ch. 10.
37 F.A. Hayek, 'Competition as a Discovery Procedure', in Hayek, *New Studies in Philosophy, Politics, Economics and the History of Ideas*, pp. 179–90.

54–62.

44 Carl Menger, ***Problems of Economics and Sociology***, Urbana: University of Illinois Press, Urbana, 1963, pp. 154–5. First published as ***Untersuchungen über die Methode der Sozialwissenschaften und der politischen Ökonomie insbesondere*** in 1883.

45 F.A. Hayek, ***The Pure Theory of Capital***, London: Routledge & Kegan Paul, 1941, p. 408.

46 F.A. Hayek, ***The Denationalisation of Money***, 2nd edn, London: Institute of Economic Affairs, 1978.

8

HAYEK ON SOCIAL JUSTICE

A critique

Raymond Plant

The aim of this chapter is to subject Hayek's account of social justice to a sustained critical anlaysis. I shall conclude that his grounds for rejecting the idea of social or distributive justice as an illusion or a mirage are insubstantial. Nevertheless they do constitute the most searching criticism of the much-invoked idea of social justice, and it is one to which the socialist or social democrat must respond if this fundamental value is to retain any cogency. I believe that Hayek is right in thinking that the idea of social justice is central to both democratic socialism and social democracy: both believe in the just distribution of resources in society. The difference between the two, as Hayek argues, is largely about means: the socialist believing that socially just economic outcomes can only arise out of the common ownership of the means of production; the social democrat believing that within a mixed economy, with substantial private ownership, a just distribution can be secured by political means. The end or goal is the same; the means differ, and it is for this reason that Hayek's critique of social justice, as the most cogent on offer, has to be answered by the Left if this central value in their political philosophy is to have any meaning. Hence the argument about social justice, although conducted at a fairly high level of philosophical abstraction, is of the first importance for political practice. Despite the fact that my response to Hayek will be critical, I should say at the outset that I believe that Hayek is an outstandingly important social and political thinker and that when we met for the one and only time as fellow symposiasts at a conference in Oxford in 1979 I found the occasion to be one of the most stimulating in my academic life.

My strategy is as follows: first of all I shall try to set out as clearly as I can the substance of Hayek's critique before moving on to a critical assessment in the second part of the chapter.

The initial point of Hayek's critique is an argument about the nature of intention in relation to justice and injustice generally. Hayek argues that an injustice only occurs when one person intentionally interferes that I happen to have contracted and having that bacterium injected into me by someone who knew what he was doing. Injustice is the result of intentional action; misfortune is not. There is a political rub to this distinction which should already be clear. We rightly look to the state for protection against injustice and for a remedy when it occurs; however, the appeal arising out of bad luck or misfortune is to the charity, benevolence, humanity or altruism of our fellow human beings. If poverty and the lack of resources is to be seen as a misfortune rather than an injustice, then there is no clear reason why the state should be involved in remedying that condition. Hayek argues that being at the bottom of the distribution of income and wealth is a misfortune rather than an injustice because there is no intentional distribution of resources in a free-market economy. The core of this argument depends upon his characterization of markets as producing unintended outcomes. In so far as they are unintended, these outcomes cannot be regarded as unjust precisely because of the relationship between injustice and intentional interference. In a free market millions of individuals buy and sell goods and services. While of course each of these acts is intentional, nevertheless in so far as these acts of economic exchange are uncoerced (on which more later) their outcomes in terms of the pattern of holdings of income and wealth are not unjust, since this overall outcome is not intended by anyone. The so-called distribution of income and wealth is an unintended outcome of millions of individual intentional acts of exchange. Of course, an individual act of exchange can be coercive and produce injustice and there is a role for the state in preventing such acts of coercion. However, if the rules of law are in place to secure free exchange then the outcomes of such exchanges are not unjust, however disastrous they may be for particular individuals and groups. Hence in a free economy there is no moral basis for a critique of economic exchanges in terms of their supposed injustice.

Hayek also has a clear view about the nature of coercion which both relates to the points already made and leads on to a further element in his critique of social justice. For Hayek, freedom is essentially negative, it is freedom from the intentional coercion of another. I am only coerced when another identifiable individual prevents me from doing something that I would otherwise have done. The fact that, for example, I lack the resources to do something that I would otherwise have done is not coercive unless my resources have been removed by the intentional acts of another. Hence, the poor person who is in this position is not coerced by his or her lack of resources, unless, as I have said, these have been intentionally removed from that person. Except in these circumstances a poor person is not coerced by an economic exchange that is disadvantageous to him or her. So the first conclusion from this is that an individual is not constrained or coerced by a lack of resources, and this means that the nature of free exchange in a market economy is only limited by such intentional coercion. Where such coercion does not occur, the outcomes of such free exchange are not unjust.

The core idea here is that being free to do *x* must be regarded as being categorically different from being able to do *x*. Hayek believes that it has been central to the spurious moral case for social justice that freedom and ability, and the resources that go along with having the ability to do something, have been confused. It has been assumed by socialists and social democrats that being free to do *x* is the same as being able to do *x* and that therefore the ideal of a free society must involve the redistribution of resources to equalize people's abilities to a far greater degree than would be the case in a free-market system. Hayek makes it clear in the chapter on coercion in *The Constitution of Liberty* (1960) that this assimilation of freedom and ability lies at the heart of the demand for social justice and for the redistribution of resources in the name of freedom.

Hayek, however, decisively rejects this assimilation. I am free to do everything that I am not prevented by the intentional action of another person or persons from doing; whether I am able to do what I am free to do is quite a separate question. No human is able to do all that he or she is free to do because the list of what I am not prevented from doing is indefinitely large and I am able to do only a relatively small number of the things that I am free to do – however rich or poor, clever or stupid I am. The commitment to social justice in the distribution of resources as a necessary means to liberty is a delusion which rests on this false assimilation of freedom and ability. Hence the argument of socialists, social democrats and social liberals since the 1880s that freedom implies the possession of resources to make more equal the ability to do what we are free to do rests upon this false assimilation of freedom and liberty. More than that for Hayek, it undermines the possibility of a liberal society based upon the idea of equal liberty. It makes sense to talk about equal liberty in terms of being equally free from coercion under a set of universal and abstract clear criteria of distributive justice which would then provide clear rules to guide policy. There are many possible criteria of distribution: merit and desert, need, equality (of what?), marginal product of labour, and so on. Adopting one or other of these distributive rules would lead to quite different forms of distribution and thus to quite different distributive shares. In a morally diverse and pluralistic society there is no way in which we can overcome this pluralism to engender agreement over the criteria of just distribution.

The failure to do this leads to baleful political consequences. First of all, to try to achieve distributive justice in a situation of moral diversity will lead to a zero-sum type of politics in which different groups and individuals attempt to secure what they believe from their subjective point of view to be their just share of social resources. This is clearly shown in attempts to operate incomes policies which attempt to define just or fair rewards for labour when this is different from the market price that labour can demand in a free-market economy. Far from social justice being a noble kind of ideal, it becomes a kind of fig leaf to disguise severe interest-group competition for resources which governments committed to just distribution have to distribute. Government will fall victim to coalitions of the strongest interest groups in such circumstances. This in turn breeds resentment on the part of those individuals and groups which fail to secure what they believe, from their own interpretation of social justice, they are entitled to. Distributive governments therefore tend to become captives of coalitions of strong interest groups while at the same time creating resentment among losers.

There is a second political problem that arises from the attempt to secure social justice in a morally pluralistic society in which we lack clear criteria for distribution. Because we lack a clear moral framework for distribution, it will become impossible to write rules of law to govern the allocation of resources. This is partly because of intractable disputes about the nature of social justice on which rules would have to be based, and partly because social justice would confer social rights such as to health care and education. The latter are however, scarce resources and there can be no rule of law of a universalizable nature which could confer entitlements to scarce resources. This means in effect that a very great deal of discretion would be given to those with the bureaucratic responsibility of allocating scarce resources and the claim that this discretion is endemic and cannot be made responsive to the rule of law, for reasons already given. Hence, the distributive state entrenches at its heart a degree of arbitrary and discretionary power within those bureaucratic bodies charged with the allocation of necessarily scarce resources.

Finally, Hayek argues that the impossibility of securing social justice in a situation in which people have diverse individual attitudes to what is just is likely to lead to a government committed to social justice becoming an object of resentment on the part of those individuals and groups who have not received what they regard as their legitimate distributive share of social resources. Because there can be no general agreement on the criteria of social justice, expectations are always likely to be frustrated and this will breed resentment against the government and envy of those groups who have done well, perhaps because they have been a part of the distributive coalitions mentioned earlier.

It is in these respects that the theoretical and moral critique of social justice in Hayek implies a clear political critique of distributive governments. Distributive politics cannot mobilize overall legitimacy behind the distributive project because it is being pursued in a situation in which there is little or no distributive consensus. The Hayekian project in contrast is to mobilize consent around a market as an arena of free exchange, in which the outcomes of uncoerced exchange are regarded as legitimate and which, through the echelon-advance or trickle-down effect, is likely to make the worst-off groups in society better off at least in their own terms, if not relative to the rich, more effectively than attempts to secure social justice will. The outcomes of markets have to be accepted as in principle unprincipled in Fred Hirsch's words, and the legitimacy of markets lies in the fact that they do not serve any overall distributive ends but rather combine the securing of individual negative liberty and progressive material enrichment.

This does not mean that Hayek rejects the welfare state but it is very clear from *The Constitution of Liberty* that he wants to distinguish between a welfare state which tries to secure a minimum level of provision to protect those who are unsuccessful in the market from destitution and one which, as for example in social-democratic politics, acts as an instrument of distributive justice through securing greater social and economic equality. It is, for example, important here to contrast Hayek's whole approach with that of the typical social-democratic thinker such as Anthony Crosland. Crosland argued in rich and the poor to grow if this is what free exchange in the market leads to, while arguing that the position of the worst off will be improved in absolute terms by a market economy in the sense that the poorest groups will, through the trickle-down effect of the market, be better off on a year-by-year basis even though the gap between rich and poor will grow. As we have seen, this growing gap between the rich and the poor cannot be criticized on grounds of social justice. For those unable to make their way in the market, a safety-net welfare state to prevent destitution, seemingly defined in terms of some sort of basic needs, will be provided. The important point, however, is that for Hayek the welfare state is separated from spurious questions of distributive justice and the social democratic project is reversed.

All of this adds up to a very formidable critique of the idea of social justice and the political practice of socialism and social democracy. Any reflective social democrat will have to face the force of these criticisms and try to respond to them. In my view, whatever the surface plausibility of the Hayekian case, most of the arguments critical of the idea of social justice are in fact deeply flawed, and in the remainder of this chapter I shall attempt to explain why.

The first argument, it will be recalled, is that questions of justice and injustice arise only where there is the identifiable intention of a specific individual. Market outcomes are not intentional in the requisite sense. Their outcomes are the unintended consequence of millions of individual economic exchanges. The aggregate effect of all these individual acts is itself unintended and therefore cannot create an injustice. There are two responses that can be made to this. The first is that while it may be true that in a free market without monopolies the outcomes of markets are unintended, they can nevertheless be foreseen in broad terms. This must be so because were it not the case market defenders would in fact deny themselves the opportunity of explaining why markets should be extended. It is only because they produce results that can be broadly foreseen that there can be arguments to the effect that these results will be beneficial and therefore that markets should be extended because of these beneficial consequences. In everyday life when we are assessing the degree of responsibility for our actions we are usually held to be responsible not just for the intended but also for the reasonably foreseeable results of actions. If this were not the case then there would be no such crime as manslaughter for example. If this is so then it can be argued that in the case of markets, while their results may be unintended, this does not absolve us from the moral responsibility for the outcome if those outcomes were in fact reasonably foreseeable. The social democrat will argue therefore, first of all, that the broad foreseeability of market outcomes gives moral categories such as justice some purchase of the critique of market outcomes, and he or she will also argue that against a background of antecedent inequalities in property rights an extension of markets is likely to mean that those who enter the market with least are likely to leave it with least (there are of course individual exceptions) and that if this is a foreseeable outcome of markets then we bear moral responsibility for those outcomes even though they were not intended. The Hayekian is therefore mistaken in assuming that the argument about intention blocks any critique of market outcomes in terms of some end-state principle such as social justice. The only response to this for Hayek would be to claim two things: first that market outcomes are not in fact foreseeable and, second, that what matters is whether they are foreseeable for individuals. The first claim must be implausible for reasons that I have suggested, namely that if markets produced general unforeseeable outcomes there would be very little basis to any argument about the importance of extending markets. The second part of the response is philosophically more difficult. Hayek might well claim that we can only be morally responsible for the foreseeable outcomes of our actions if the consequences are foreseeable in respect of identifiable individuals rather than groups such as the worst-off 10 per cent in society. However, this would be more or less a definitional way of avoiding the problem (it does connect up with Hayek's commitment to methodological individualism), but there is no obvious reason why moral responsibility for outcomes has to be confined to predicting the consequences of action for specified individuals.

The second reason why this argument seems to be defective is that it means that questions of justice and injustice cannot arise when we are confronted with the result of unintended processes or an impersonal force. However, this seems to be counter-intuitive, for the question of justice or injustice seems not to be settled only by determining how a situation arose but also by our response to that situation. Take the following example which might make the counter-intuitive nature of Hayek's proposal clearer. Imagine that I am walking down a street on a wet and windy day. A very frail elderly person is walking in front of me and is blown over by the wind (an resolved merely by drawing attention to the fact that it arose as a result of impersonal action. Rather the question of justice and injustice has to do with our response as much as it has to do with the sequence of events that led to the position in the first place. If the analogy is cashed on a social level it would mean that questions of justice do arise when some are made poor and destitute by the impersonal operation of the market and in which there are courses of action open to government which it refuses to take to rectify their position. For Hayek this is not unjust; the force of the analogy suggested that it is.

As we saw, the argument about the nature of freedom is central to Hayek's attempt to combat the case for social justice. If freedom has to do with resources, opportunities and abilities then there will be a demand for a just allocation of those resources and opportunities which bear most closely on our abilities which, in turn, are part of liberty. It is central to Hayek's project, therefore, that this assimilation of freedom and ability is rejected and a very purist account of negative freedom adopted. However, I believe that his account of freedom can be faulted on several grounds.

The first has to do with the assimilation of freedom and ability. I think that it is difficult to suggest, as Hayek does, that there is a categorical distinction between them and this is so for three reasons:

1 If freedom and ability are separated then it is very difficult for the defender of negative liberty to explain why liberty is valuable to us. On Hayek's view, liberty in the negative sense is valuable because it helps us to cope with dispersed knowledge and the unpredictable nature of human existence. However, this justification for negative liberty refers, at least implicitly, to ability. To be free in a negative sense secures to us an ability which we would not have without it, namely the ability to cope effectively with the limitations of human knowledge. If freedom were to be seen as categorically distinct from ability and some conception of human powers, this argument which explains why liberty should be important to us would lose its purchase.

2 This point can be further developed. It is at least arguable that the issue of whether one is free or unfree to do x is logically dependent on there being a general ability to do x. If I were to ask whether people in the eleventh century were free or unfree to fly aeroplanes, most would be inclined to say that the question of being free or unfree did not arise, since there was no generalized ability to do this. It could then be argued that a general capacity among people to be able to do x is logically necessary for the question of whether people are free or unfree to do x to make sense. If this is so, then it is impossible to draw a categorical distinction between freedom and ability since a generalized ability to do x is a necessary condition for being able to determine whether a particular individual is free or unfree to do it. Hence the identification of a limitation on freedom is dependent on there being a generalized ability in the group in question to do x. While this may seem very abstract, there is a direct political point at stake. Hayek wants to argue that a poor person is not rendered unfree by his or her poverty. This is crucial to his account of the legitimacy of markets as the arena of free exchange. The inequality of income and wealth between a rich and a poor person does not mean that they cannot contract freely, since poverty is not a restriction of freedom as freedom has nothing to do with ability and resources. However, if the force of the counter-argument is that if there is a general set of abilities and opportunities in society which poverty prevents an individual from realizing, then this can be regarded at least as a potential restriction on liberty. Of course, Hayek will then argue that it is only if that person's poverty is a result of the intentional action of others that this argument would go through. I will confront this argument below.

3 The third reason why liberty and ability cannot be separated in the way Hayek suggests is because of the implicitly quantitative approach to the judgement of whether one society is freer than another on the pure negative-liberty approach. On this view liberty is defined by the absence of intentional interference with the actions of another. It has nothing to do with an account of what people can do with the freedom that they have when they are not being coerced. So the judgement of whether society A is freer than society B is to be settled by a quantitative account of the number of rules there are in each society and the limits which these impose on action; it has nothing to do with the kinds of actions which people can perform since this would involve an illicit positive conception of freedom. This is, however, implausible. Take an example that is due to Charles Taylor. Say that in the mid-1980s we wanted to know how we would ground the

cut the link between freedom and an account of those human abilities which stand at the heart of freedom, it would then be possible to argue that Albania was a freer society than the United Kingdom. Very few negative libertarians would find this a remotely plausible judgement, but in order to resist it some conception of human abilities would be invoked, such as the claim that we are able to do more important things in Britain than in Albania, for example criticize the government or emigrate. This is a much more plausible response, but it is one which is fatal to the view that there is a categorical distinction between freedom and ability, since it is a particular set of abilities which is now being invoked as a basis for the judgement that the United Kingdom is a freer society than Albania.

Thus I believe that it can be argued, *contra* Hayek, that not only is it implausible to maintain that there is a categorical distinction between freedom and ability, but that some account of human abilities is either invoked, as in (1) and (3) above,or is presupposed in making the judgement that a person is unfree to do x as in (2) above. I think Hayek is right to say that freedom and ability cannot be regarded as being synonymous, but equally they cannot be distinct in the sharp way that Hayek presumes. If, however, his argument is flawed then I think the way is open to the social democrat or socialist to provide an account of those abilities which stand close to the heart of freedom. These will typically be an account of the basic needs or the primary goods which have to be satisfied before a person can in fact exercise freedom. These will typically involve freedom from interference, but will also include resources and opportunities. If there are needs the satisfaction of which stand at the centre of being free to act, then the state, which on the liberal view should seek to protect a fair value for negative freedom, should also be involved in securing a fair distribution of those resources and opportunities which relate to those abilities which are necessary conditions of free action.

I want now to return to the second argument cited above which left one issue unresolved. Even if an Hayekian came to admit that a general ability to do x is a necessary condition of being free or unfree to do it, it could still be objected that poverty, for example, which might prevent *A* from doing *x*, is not a restriction of freedom since in order for freedom to be infringed it is not only necessary that someone should be unable to do *x* but also that this inability is the result of the intentional action of another. In a free-market economy if someone ends up in poverty this may prevent him from doing *x* but this is not a restriction on freedom because poverty in a free market is not an intentional result of market processes. Poverty is not therefore a limitation on liberty unless that poverty is caused by the intentional action of another, and this is not so in regard to the overall distribution of income and wealth in a free-market economy for the reasons set out earlier.

The response to this is to draw attention again to the issue of foreseeability. It may well be true as I have said that the outcomes of markets are unintended, but at the group level they can be foreseeable. If it is a foreseeable result of market transactions that some people will not be able to do what they were able to do before because they lack the resources which, let us surmise, were earlier secured to them by government, then this can be regarded as a limitation on liberty. Take a simple example at the level of individual interaction. Imagine that I live next door to a keen gardener who wants to enter his prize vegetables in an agricultural show. I want to kill weeds in my garden and I use a powerful pesticide without looking at all the instructions on the label which show that it can permeate the soil over a wide area. My intention is to kill my weeds; the effect which was reasonably foreseeable is that the other person's vegetables are killed. My action has prevented him from doing what he would otherwise have done. I would argue that while this was not part of my intention, it was nevertheless a foreseeable consequence of my action and as such is an infringement of the other person's freedom. If this is so then it is at least arguable that if the extension of a market in some area is likely to lead to individuals and groups of people being unable to do what they were able to do before the extension of the market, then this can be regarded as an infringement of liberty even though this was not intended.

I want to turn now to other aspects of Hayek's critique of social justice. As we saw earlier, one criticism is that under the rules of just distribution individuals would be given rights and entitlements to scarce resources such as health care and education and that from a Hayekian point of view this is objectionable in a number of ways. The principle is that this confers illusory rights to scarce resources and, as such rights to scarce resources cannot be enforced, this entrenches discretion in the allocation of resources to meet such rights and thus is incompatible with the idea of the rule of law.

or manager has to use discretion about how to deploy scarce resources in response to needs and claims arising out of those needs. Exactly the same is true in respect of the role of a chief constable or chief of police in terms of deploying resources to protect what Hayek would call the rule of law. A national health service or educational service has a generalized duty to provide health care or education, but exactly how and to whom this is delivered, in what quantity and to what standard, is bound to involve discretion because resources are scarce in relation to demand. The same is true of the way the law is enforced. This severely weakens Hayek's claim that there is as it were on the one side the pure rule of law realized ideally in a *Rechtsstaat*; on the other the welfare state which is corrupting because it cannot be brought within the rule of law because in allocating scarce resources it involves discretion. However, if one looks closely at enforcement, which is not some kind of optional extra within the rule of law (for how could we characterize law at all if it did not involve the idea of legitimate enforcement?), then exactly the same questions of resource allocation arise and along with that the role of discretion. It is the conviction of those who defend social justice that this exercise of discretion must be guided by a conception of fairness; Hayek, in rejecting social justice, has nothing to say about the allocation of resources which are necessary to protect the rule of law.

Finally I want to turn to the idea of social justice and moral pluralism where Hayek has identified a genuine problem for social justice, but where also I believe that Hayek's own views are embedded in exactly the same type of difficulties. There are two issues I want to take up here. First of all he claims that in a pluralistic society there can be no overall moral foundation for distributive politics, and that, second, ideas about human needs which seem to be central to the social-democratic/socialist project in relation to social justice are vague and open-ended and could not serve as a genuine distributive principle. In response to these two claims I want us to notice first of all that Hayek does believe in the legitimacy of a basic welfare state which is there to prevent destitution, but he wishes to distinguish this very clearly from a welfare state which seeks to create social justice between individuals and groups. I think that Hayek's strictures on social justice sit very badly with this claim about what is a defensible welfare state. First of all, he assumes that it is possible to define a level of basic need which will be equivalent to avoiding destitution. If this is so then he is operating with an idea of need as a distributive principle, namely that even in a free-market order individuals have a justified claim to have access to these basic resources to meet their basic needs when they cannot satisfy them via the market and this will involve some redistribution from those who in a free market have acquired their resources through a process of free exchange.

Second, he assumes that there is a range of basic needs which seemingly are satiable by a minimal welfare state, but he does not tell us how these needs are to be identified or distinguished from those objectionable ideas about needs which enter social democratic and socialist theories of social justice. It is part of the Hayekian case against these sorts of needs that they can be bid up by interest-group pressures and thus lead to an ever-expanding public sector geared to meeting needs which expand as the result of the political pressures of interest groups. However, once Hayek has conceded the case for a minimal welfare state, as he does, he fails to explain how this welfare state and the conception of needs implicit within it will be immune to precisely the same interest-group pressures which in his view pose a fatal political objection to social-democratic ideas of distributive justice. Presumably the only way such interest-group pressures could be regarded as irrelevant for the kind of welfare safety net that he has in mind is because he assumes that the needs in question concerned with destitution are satiable. However, he has given us no clue as to how to define the class of acceptable satiable basic needs and those that are not so satiable. Until this is done it is not clear that Hayek has at all a consistent position.

I want to conclude with a general point about legitimacy. Because Hayek does not want to see the market constrained by any outcome criteria of just distribution, he has to assume that the legitimacy of markets will rest presumably on two things: one is the perceived legitimacy of free exchange; the other is that markets will increase prosperity more effectively than any other alternative. In Hayek's view poverty is not a restriction of freedom and therefore unequal individuals can still exchange freely. We have, however, seen good reasons to doubt this. The second argument depends a good deal on empirical judgements about the effect of the trickle-down effect or the echelon-advance effect of markets: that the worst-off groups will be better off in absolute terms under markets because of trickle-down compared with what would happen under social justice. However, I am not convinced that this argument is likely to mobilize the in its outcomes and detached from serving moral outcomes. Hayek is brutally honest with himself at this point. I am sure that he is right, and that is why I have been so critical of his attempts to detach the market from determinate moral outcomes.

REFERENCES

Crosland, A. (1976) *Social Democracy in Europe*,

Hayek, F.A. (1960) *The Constitution of Liberty*, London: Routledge & Kegan Paul.

—— (1976) *Law Legislation and Liberty*, vol. 2, *The Mirage of Social Justice*, London: Routledge & Kegan Paul.

9

THE THEORY OF SOCIETAL EVOLUTION

Hayek's unfinished legacy

Ulrich Witt

Friedrich August von Hayek was one of this century's most productive economists. His many publications span more than sixty years. Initially his interest was primarily on economics in the narrower sense and his early works show a consistent emphasis on price-theoretic questions, for example in business cycle theory (Hayek 1933) and capital theory (Hayek 1941). The focus of his writings shifted significantly as a result of the political turmoil and the increasing influence of totalitarian ideas that characterized the 1920s and 1930s. This is nowhere more evident than in his dramatic warning in 1944 of the dangers inherent in embarking on the road to serfdom (Hayek 1944). From the 1950s onwards Hayek elaborated on what may be considered this century's most significant contribution to social philosophy. The key element in this contribution is a theory of civilization which, in turn, builds on an economic foundation: the theory of the spontaneous order of the markets as it emerged under conditions of freedom and the rule of law.

In Hayek's social philosophy, hypotheses on cultural and socio-economic evolution are of central importance. He developed and repeatedly discussed these hypotheses in numerous places in his *oeuvre* from the 1960s onwards. (By contrast, the idea of evolution is totally absent in his earlier work on economic theory, and Hayek never made an effort to reconsider his approach to economics in evolutionary terms.) A thorough exegesis and a discussion of all these sources has only begun in the literature (see Radnitzky 1984; Gray 1986; Vanberg 1986; Hodgson 1991). A conclusive appraisal of Hayek's theory of societal evolution is therefore beyond what is possible here. Rather, a brief outline of the basic assumptions and concepts in Hayek's theory of societal evolution will be given in the next two sections of this chapter. Thereafter follow some remarks which try to highlight the major problems involved. The final section offers some tentative conclusions.

EPISTEMOLOGICAL BACKGROUND: THE INCOMPLETENESS OF INDIVIDUAL KNOWLEDGE

To understand the basic view that underlies Hayek's theory of cultural and socioeconomic evolution it is important to recognize the epistemological background. For Hayek the limitations of individual knowledge, its incomplete, imperfect and hypothetical nature, are basic facts. In this respect he continues an Austrian tradition established by Menger (1871: 94). However, in his highly original, and for an economist certainly unusual theory of a sensory order in human perception, Hayek (1952) extends the theoretical foundation of the premise way beyond what was common thought in Vienna in his time and he makes it a point of departure for his social philosophy (Streit 1992).

In the domain of societal and economic interactions the incompleteness of individual knowledge implies that people do not fully recognize the influence which their own action has on the scope for, and the limits on, decision-making by other people. To a certain extent these effects are transmitted, in an impersonal form, through the price mechanism (Hayek 1945: 519–30), as is well-known to economists. However, on a more basic level, the effects are also reflected by the emergence of an impersonal system of rules of conduct (Hayek 1967a). Since the complexity of the price mechanism as well as systems of rules of conduct make it extremely difficult for the human mind to comprehend them, they cannot be the result of deliberate design and choice. Rather these forms of coherent behaviour, the 'spontaneous order', must have emerged from the interactions of all members of society as a largely unintended and unplanned outcome (Hayek 1969). Thus, spontaneous order in the interactions of the members of society is something to which everyone contributes, from which everyone benefits, which everyone normally takes for granted, but which individuals rarely understand.

The lack of understanding of how mutually expected attendance to rules of conduct results in the emergence of order applies not only to complex modern societies with a highly developed division of labour and huge markets. It is already found in less complex societies characterized by self-sufficient household production where it is language, tradition, morality, custom and law which have emerged as impersonal regularities but whose ways of functioning have not been (fully) discerned. Hayek thus interprets the co-ordination of economic behaviour by way of multilateral exchange and the division of labour as a phenomenon similar to the inter-individual co-ordination turning up in, and brought about by, language, tradition, morality, custom and law. The basic idea is not new. Since the times of

Adam Smith and the Scottish moral philosophers, for example David Hume and Adam Ferguson, several attempts have been made to identify a spontaneous order in economic market interactions.

The foundations (see Hayek 1967b) had already been laid by Bernard Mandeville who, in his *Fable of the Bees* of 1705, for the edification of the public put in verses like: 'The Worst of all the Multitude/Did something for the Common Good'. This is meant to say that neither overt nor covert motives for human action can explain the consequences of these actions taken as a whole. Just the contrary, the limits imposed by every agent following his own interest on other agents' behaviour produce a spontaneous order, an outcome which is 'the result of human action but not of human design' (Ferguson) where, as if guided by an 'invisible hand' (Smith) everyone may fare better. Later on, Menger (1963, first published 1883) elaborated the same point in an apparently independent approach. Propagating his 'causal-genetic' method he explicitly referred to language, custom and law as other examples of unintended collective outcomes, that is, spontaneous order.

There can be no doubt that the spontaneous development of such structures has made possible a vast improvement in human standards of living. This is particularly true of the order that results from the operation of modern specialized markets which depend on the exercise of private autonomy (rule of law, property rights, freedom of contract; see Hayek 1973). Many people take the fruits of this development process for granted. At the same time, however, in social and political discussion, the spontaneous order in which this prosperity has its origin frequently appears to be out of favour. The 'public opinion' in many prosperous market economies shows little sympathy for the free market, that is, undiluted private autonomy, as a problem-solving and co-ordinating mechanism. For Hayek, this is simply a clear indication of the incompleteness of individual knowledge and the difficulties involved in trying to understand the complex way spontaneous order emerges.

Hayek (1988) identifies this lack of understanding in two kinds of opposition against the extended order of the markets which have long since been launched with varying success. One kind of opposition is motivated by an overrated appraisal of the power of human reason, the other is motivated by the frustration of human instinct. The first, Hayek claims, has its origins in Aristotelian philosophy. It sees order only where it is a planned product of human intelligence. The second is based on a rather irrational desire to re-establish the relationships and values of the small groups that have played a decisive role in human phylogeny. The abstract, impersonal form of human relationships in the extended order of the market seems, to this form of opposition, to be inferior to the often romanticized and glorified relationships of the small group, and the reinstatement of the latter is seen as highly desirable.

To Hayek, both kinds of opposition are involved in the rationalist revolution of the Enlightenment. He argues that Descartes, Rousseau, and later Marx, grossly overestimate the power of human reason on the one hand, and on the other exhibit a romantic propensity to make erroneous judgements about the instinctive small-group values such as solidarity and nostalgia for a 'natural' way of life. This combination of ideas, Hayek submits, has been causal to the formation of the false synthesis of constructivist illusions and socialist ideals that dominated the intellectual climate of the nineteenth and twentieth centuries. The proponents of this synthesis fail to appreciate that it is impossible for rationally constructed systems of social and economic interaction to achieve the complexity characteristic of spontaneously emerging orders. This is particularly true where attempts are made to restore the forms of interaction found in the early stages of human history (Hayek 1970).

EVOLUTION AS THE EXPANSION OF SPONTANEOUS ORDER

Hayek takes pains to give his argument a foundation by a theory of socio-economic and cultural evolution. Many people today regard the concept of evolution as synonymous with the neo-Darwinian theory of biological evolution. However, the concept of evolution, as an autonomous development of increasingly complex structures, is in fact older than Darwin's theory. It had already been formulated, and even terms like 'genetic' been created, by the beginning of the nineteenth century with the school of thought in the humanities and social sciences associated with names like Herder, Savigny and Wilhelm von Humboldt (see Hayek 1967b, 1983). Since it is not clear to what extent cultural and socio-economic evolution have something in common with Darwinian theory, Hayek's concern is to develop and make precise an independent approach which is built on the 'twin ideas of spontaneous order and evolution'.

In his set-up, he distinguishes between the different levels on which the development of human society takes place (Hayek 1979: 153–76). The first level is that of biological evolution during human phylogeny. At this level, primitive forms of social behaviour, values and attitudes became genetically fixed as a result of selection processes. The criterion that led this genetic adaptation was survival fitness relative to the particular environment. As a result an observable order of social interactions emerged for which socio-biology provides the explanatory model (see Witt 1985). Once they were genetically established, these attitudes and values have continued to be part of the natural inheritance of modern humans, even though biological selection pressure has now been largely relaxed. For Hayek, they explain the instinctive preferences, mentioned above, for values and ideals that are no longer appropriate to the much more complex forms of social life in large societies.

A second level of evolution is that of human intelligence and its products, that is knowledge and the numerous ways of recording, transmitting and processing it. Superficially, development here occurs in a manner similar to that of biological evolution - variation as the source of new ideas; selection or pursuit of new ideas according to the current state of preferences and in the light of existing knowledge; replication and diffusion of successful ideas. The systematic propagation, elaboration and storing of knowledge, which is independent of the existence of any individual human brain, has made possible an enormously accelerated scientific and technological progress and a mastery of nature as no other species has ever achieved it. Although individual human intelligence is a crucial input to the undisputed scientific and technological progress, it is certainly not the only success factor and, Hayek argues, cannot serve as a justification for scientism and constructivism. The extended order of human interactions in advanced civilizations is a no less important prerequisite for the growth of the sciences, and this order is not a product of deliberate design. This order is in itself a manifestation of an impersonal, or perhaps better, collective intelligence.

This brings Hayek to the third, frequently overlooked, level of evolution, which he therefore deems the most important point in his own contribution. It is the cultural and socio-economic evolution located between instinct and reason (Hayek 1979: 153–76, and 1988, Ch. 1). Focus here is on the emergence of rules of conduct, morals and traditions that govern human interactions and that induce an order in culture, society and economy likewise. Extending the ideas of the Scottish moral philosophers, Hayek sees these rules of conduct - and thus the spontaneous order - as the product of a development process, taking place over thousands of years, during which those patterns of behaviour have been learnt without much reflection on their meaning. It was presumably already in the small groups characteristic of early human history that such rules of conduct developed into cultural norms and were being learnt and passed on in cultural, non-genetic, transmission.

The establishment of, and changes in, such norms is 'blind', in the sense that they are not deliberately planned or controlled. To Hayek, historical accidents determine which new forms of rule-following behaviour arise within the group, but which of these survive and are successful is not a matter of chance but of a selection process. However groups come to adopt rules, provided these rules make a superior form of social and economic life feasible, the groups are capable of growing due to more successful procreation and integration of outsiders. A growing population fosters specialization and division of labour which favour, in turn, groups with superior rules. By the same logic, groups not adopting appropriate rules, whether inventing or imitating them, will decline. (The same is claimed for those groups that are unable to counteract destructive influences on their spontaneous order, especially the influence of misguided constructivism.) Through this selection process, the rules of conduct, norms and morals which eventually prevail are suited for the survival of more and more members of the group (Hayek 1983).

Obviously, what is claimed to govern the third level of evolution is a group selection process. Hayek interprets natural selection to choose not only between competing species but also between competing groups of humans defined by common cultural norms. The cultural learning process, in which a kind of collective intelligence is accumulated in a population in the form of rules of behaviour, never comes to a halt. However, as the thus induced spontaneous order grows and extends its scope, the rules themselves become more and more differentiated, abstract and inaccessible to rational reconstruction by the individual mind. In comparison to the process of genetic variation that occurs through generational change, rules of conduct and cultural norms can be acquired and transmitted much faster. Following Hayek's group selection hypothesis it should not be surprising, therefore, that in the long history of human culture the exceptionally rich and diversified spontaneous orders characteristic of modern times could develop. Probably the most important order, the one that has made possible prosperity and civilization, is the market (Hayek 1988, Ch. 3).

SOME PROBLEMS AND OPEN QUESTIONS

Despite its abstractness, Hayek's theory of spontaneous order and its emergence has several practical implications with respect to economic policy issues.[1] However, the thrust of this theory of societal evolution clearly relates to more basic issues and should therefore be discussed here on that level. The central point Hayek wants to make is that the knowledge incorporated in the extended spontaneous order must not be sacrificed to constructivist illusions, for example in economic and social policy, which are based on a rationalistic, supposedly 'progressive' intellectual attitude. The recent insights into the consequences of actual socialist planned economies, especially their inherent tendency to totalitarianism, seem to confirm Hayek's plea. Yet, on a closer look it turns out that the theory of societal evolution appears rather unfinished and leaves several questions open.

First, the group-selection hypothesis, the very core of the theory, is in many respects sketchy and vulnerable to criticism. In this modified version of 'Social Darwinism', as Gray (1986: 140–5) has called it, the differential growth of competing groups plays a decisive role. It is attributed to comparative advantages in producing descendants and the groups' differing capacity to attract and assimilate outsiders, abilities which Hayek relates to the rules of conduct which the groups follow. In view of the fact that in present times selection pressure on humans, even on relatively less-developed human sub-populations, is weak or almost absent the asserted relationship between rules of conduct and the number of descendants is difficult to see. The capacity to survive is primarily dependent on adequate medical care and a minimum intake of calories. Today, at least, both these requirements can be met even under poor economic conditions.

Indeed, a comparison of the geographical distribution of groups with the highest population growth rates with the distribution of groups with the best-developed and most-extended orders in Hayek's sense, casts serious doubts on the validity of the group-selection argument. Even when the population-increasing effect of development aid is taken into account, the huge differences in population growth rates between the less-developed countries and those countries with the most-productive and most-diversified market systems do not seem to be compatible with Hayek's conjecture. It appears that it is not so much a difference in the efficiency of the rules of conduct, that is population-bound intelligence, that determines differential population growth rates, but rather something like individual preferences or habits. A highly developed and economically most successful order is just as compatible with a preference of its members for a small number of children as are less-developed orders with a preference of their members for large numbers of children.

Hayek has not made an attempt to work out the details of his theory of societal evolution or even to present it in more rigorous form. It may well be that the intricacies of any such theory have escaped his attention. For instance, evolution presupposes some kind of continuity. In societal evolution this should be established by the way in which learnt rules of conduct are transmitted between the generations. How does the transmission process work and how much continuity does it produce? Hayek just assumes that the mechanisms of transmission are imitation, often unconscious, and learning, but this view may be too simple. New studies of the process of cultural evolution show that imitation and learning are very complex processes (Cavalli-Sforza and Feldman 1981; Lumsden and Wilson 1981; Boyd and Richerson 1985). In these studies formal analogies with genetic transmission mechanisms have been developed, but the range of application of the models is narrowly confined to rather primitive societies and concrete objects such as the handing-down of particular artifacts and ways of using them. Nevertheless, even on this elementary level the often puzzling and anti-intuitive implications of occupancy and status-quo effects of selection, well-known from biology, turn up. Compared to these, Hayek's notion of group selection appears somewhat naïve.

A second set of problems is related to the fact that relying on the impersonal forces of group selection (i.e. a population bound criterion) as a crucial argument implies a unit of analysis which is not easily brought in line with an individualistic approach. Vanberg (1986) rightly points to the tensions between Hayek's eloquent creed for methodological individualism (Hayek 1948), in which he followed the tradition of the Austrian School, and the position he assumes in his later theory of societal evolution. From an individualistic point of view little is explained by referring to the conjecture that differential growth among groups determines what rules of conduct are best suited for developing an extended order. What would have to be explained is how the individuals whose behaviour is concerned are induced to adopt and adhere to those rules especially where individual self-interest may be opposed to their adoption and adherence. This may be the case where following the rules of conduct may imply contributing to the provision of a public good (namely the group success): 'free-riding' incentives would then prevent the adoption of the rules. Well-known social dilemmas and rationality traps may be hidden here which Hayek does not seem to notice.[2] These problems vanish if, in terms of an individualistic approach, rule-bound behaviour is assumed instead of discretionary opportunistic decision-making and if - quite in a Hayekian spirit - social learning and imitation hypotheses are introduced (see Witt 1986).

Related to the missing link between the population-orientated perspective and the individualistic approach is the question of what role scientific reasoning and insight can play in societal evolution: what do economists and social scientists contribute to the further development of the spontaneous order? Is there room, or even a need, for a policy that designs social and economic interactions - for example, in the choice of a constitution - on the basis of human reason and experience? Hayek correctly presumes that cultural evolution is Lamarckian rather than Darwinian. This means that the evolving unit is able to pass on attributes that have been acquired, rather than inherited, to the next generation. In the present context this implies that the group, or better the set of rules of conduct practised within the group, is able to change under the influence of experience and learning. The members can invent new rules or modify old ones. Of course this may be the result of reasoning about current rules and their efficiency, deliberate action, and even consciously planned modifications. If the notion of group selection is taken seriously, what matters is only whether or not the modifications lead to superior adaptation to the current state of the environment. Hence, deliberate change founded on reason and reflection cannot be rejected *per se*.

Thus there is a problem in determining the boundary between constructivist presumptiousness on the one hand and reflection on existing rules and suggestions for improving them that can usefully inform policy action on the other. Since Hayek did not address the problem, the borderline can only be determined indirectly on the basis of his theory. A point of departure is provided by the insight which he gained in his study of the price mechanism and the use of knowledge in society (Hayek 1937, 1945). In these contributions Hayek had argued that the knowledge necessary for the daily operating of, and co-ordination in, modern economies is highly dispersed among the members of society. Only by the efficient, decentralized information-processing of the market system – the extended order that has in Hayek's perspective emerged from societal evolution – is it possible to utilize all this knowledge. He therefore submits that any suggested modification and deliberate plan that presumes knowledge and co-ordinating power which is not actually feasible would amount to a 'pretence of knowledge' (Hayek 1978b). It would be doomed to fail because of the lack of co-ordination that it induces.

Unfortunately, failure and abortion of such proposals may take a long time to become apparent if one had to rely on group selection pressure alone. In an environment in which competing groups are equally weak or weakened, poor rules and inefficient policies can survive for hundreds and thousands of years even though they entail economic decline and starvation for some or even all group members. History has seen many such incidents and Hayek himself sometimes refers to several of them. It is precisely at this point that the above mentioned social dilemmas and rationality traps acquire a sad significance. All the more important do rationally reflected proposals and pleas for change appear, suggested for whatever motives, in order to save society from the potentially harmful hard test of group selection. The theoretical understanding of social dilemmas has made considerable progress in recent years, thanks to the individualistic economic approach to collective action, democracy and politics. This knowledge can be made instrumental in avoiding negative developments and improving human interactions (see Witt 1992 for a model of such an intervention). Indeed, it would be difficult to justify Hayek's own example in his crusading for a free society (Hayek 1944, 1988), his suggestions for a constitutional reform (Hayek 1979, Ch. 17), and his recommendation for the denationalization of money (Hayek 1978c) if this conclusion were not drawn.

CONCLUSIONS

The hypotheses concerning cultural and socioeconomic evolution form a central part of Hayek's social philosophy. His theory, which follows in the tradition of the Scottish moral philosophers, explains the complex interactions in modern society exhibited in language, law and the market system, as a manifestation of a spontaneous, unplanned order. For Hayek this order is based on rules that are neither instinctive, that is, genetically determined, nor the product of individual human reason. Rather, the rules have developed over thousands of years in a process of innovation, imitation and learning. In this process, a group-selection principle causes those groups to prosper and grow which have succeeded in developing rules of conduct which are well adapted to their environment. Hayek submits that the complexity and problem-solving capacity of such rules of conduct far exceeds that of planning carried out by the exercise of individual reason. He therefore warns against overrating the power of reason as in the Cartesian view of rationality. The latter amounts to a pretence of knowledge and encourages misunderstanding of the spontaneous order, in particular the extended order of the markets, that has grown without plan or deliberate design during human history.

However, as briefly pointed out here the actual analysis of socioeconomic evolution in Hayek's work appears sketchy and unfinished. The nature and significance of collective rule learning, transmission and selection processes are still unclear. Unclear, too, is the extent to which the spontaneous development of rules can avoid the emergence of social dilemmas. Where such dilemmas occur it may be incumbent upon economists and social scientists, or individual intelligence generally, to help avoid, or escape from, such development traps. Unfortunately, the role of the individual in the group selection principle has not been defined by Hayek. All these issues, it may be concluded, deserve and, in fact, necessitate deeper reflection by anyone interested in an evolutionary theory of society and economy.

NOTES

The present chapter draws on material that has been published under the title 'Bemerkungen zu Hayeks Theorie sozioökonomischer Evolution',

Wirtschaftspolitische Blätter, no. 2, 1989, in honour of F.A. von Hayek's ninetieth birthday. I wish to thank J. Irving-Lessmann for translating the material and E. Blocher for research assistance.

1 An example is antitrust policy especially in view of the concept of 'competition as a discovery procedure' which Hayek (1978a) derived from his basic epistemological position. Through the influential work of Erich Hoppmann, his successor to the chair at the University of Freiburg, Hayek's ideas had a significant impact on policy-making and antitrust court ruling in Germany; see Hoppmann (1988, Part II).

2 It is noteworthy that in sociobiology precisely the problem of explaining altruism in face of these free-riding incentives has given rise to substituting the elder notion of group selection for the concept of inclusive fitness; see Witt (1985).

REFERENCES

Boyd, R. and Richerson, P.J. (1985) *Culture and the Evolutionary Process*, Chicago: University of Chicago Press.

Cavalli-Sforza, L. and Feldman, M. (1981) *Cultural Transmission and Evolution: A Quantative Approach*, Princeton, NJ: Princeton University Press.

Gray, J. (1986) *Hayek on Liberty*, 2nd edn, New York: Blackwell.

Hayek, F.A. (1933) *Monetary Theory and the Trade Cycle*, London: Routledge & Kegan Paul.

—— (1937) 'Economics and Knowledge', *Economica* 4: 33–54.

—— (1941) *The Pure Theory of Capital*, London: Routledge & Kegan Paul.

—— (1944) *The Road to Serfdom*, London: Routledge & Kegan Paul.

—— (1945) 'The Use of Knowledge in Society', *American Economic Review* 35: 519–30.

—— (1948) *Individualism and Economic Order*, London: Routledge & Kegan Paul.

—— (1952) *The Sensory Order*, London: Routledge & Kegan Paul.

—— (1967a) 'Notes on the Evolution of Systems of Rules of Conduct', in F.A. Hayek, *Studies in Philosophy, Politics and Economics*, London: Routledge & Kegan Paul, pp. 66–81.

—— (1967b) 'Dr Bernard Mandeville', *Proceedings of the British Academy* 12, Oxford: Oxford University Press.

—— (1969) 'Rechtsordnung und Handelnsordnung', in F.A. Hayek, *Freiburger Studien*, Tübingen: Mohr (Siebeck).

—— (1973) *Law, Legislation and Liberty*: 1, *Rules and Order*, London: Routledge & Kegan Paul.

—— (1975) *Die Irrtümer des Konstruktivismus und die Grundlagen legitimer Kritik gesellschaftlicher Gebilde*, Tübingen: J.C.B. Mohr.

—— (1978a) 'Competition as a Discovery Procedure', in F.A. Hayek, *New Studies in Philosophy, Politics, Economics and the History of Ideas*, London: Routledge & Kegan Paul, pp. 179–90.

—— (1978b) 'The Pretence of Knowledge', in F.A. Hayek, *New Studies in Philosophy, Politics, Economics and the History of Ideas*, London: Routledge & Kegan Paul, pp. 23–34.

—— (1978c) *Denationalization of Money*, 2nd edn, London: Routledge & Kegan Paul.

—— (1979) *Law, Legislation and Liberty*: 3, *The Political Order of a Free People*, London: Routledge & Kegan Paul.

—— (1983) *Evolution und spontane Ordnung*, Private Edition, Zürich: Bank Hoffmann.

—— (1988) *The Fatal Conceit*, London: Routledge.

Hodgson, G.M. (1991) 'Hayek's Theory of Cultural Evolution: An Evaluation in the Light of Vanberg's Critique', *Economics and Philosophy* 7: 67–82.

Hoppman, E. (1988) *Wirtschaftsordnung und Wettbewerb*, Baden-Baden: Nomos.

Lumsden, C.J. and Wilson, E.O. (1981) *Genes, Mind, and Culture: The Coevolutionary Process*, Cambridge, Mass: Harvard University Press.

Menger, C. (1871) *Grundsätze der Volkswirtschaftslehre*, Wien: Braumüller.

—— (1963) *Problems of Economics and Sociology*, Urbana: University of Illinois Press.

Radnitzky, G. (1984) 'Die ungeplante Gesellschaft: Friedrich von Hayeks Theorie spontaner Ordnungen und selbst organisierender Systeme', *Hamburger Jahrbuch für Wirtschaft und Gesellschaft*, pp. 9–33.

Streit, M.E. (1992) 'Cognition, Competition and Catallaxy: In Memory of Friedrich August von Hayek', *Papers on Economics and Evolution*, no. 9204, edited by the European Study Group for Evolutionary Economics.

Vanberg, V. (1986) 'Spontaneous Market Order and Social Rules: A Critical Examination of F.A. von Hayek's Theory of Cultural Evolution', *Economics and Philosophy* 2: 75–100.

Witt, U. (1985) 'Economic Behavior and Biological Evolution: Some Remarks on the Sociobiology Debate', *Zeitschrift für die gesamte Staatswissenschaft* 141: 365–89.

—— (1986) 'Evolution and Stability of Cooperation Without Enforceable Contracts', *Kyklos* 38: 245–65.

—— (1992) 'The Endogenous Public Choice Theorist', *Public Choice* 73: 117–29.

10

HAYEK AND THE CASE FOR MARKETS

Jeremy Shearmur

HAYEK'S PROGRESS

Hayek is well known as an advocate of markets. But in what terms does he argue for them? As I have suggested elsewhere,[1] his earliest concern seems to have been with the relief of the kind of suffering that he encountered in Vienna after the First World War. In the face of this, he became a socialist, a perspective from which he departed as a result of his contacts with the work and the person of Ludwig von Mises. As is evidenced by his 'Inaugural Address' at the London School of Economics, Hayek accepted the conclusion of Mises's argument about socialist calculation. He was further influenced by Mises and, it would seem, by his reading of the work of Carl Menger,[2] to take the view that one must understand markets as systems, the functioning of which may depend upon things which, when considered in isolation, may be thought undesirable. All this led Hayek to the belief that a concern for human well-being should not only lead one to espouse markets rather than socialism, but also that the broad requirements for the effective functioning of markets may limit our ability to remedy other social ills. For Hayek, economics became important as something that told us about the cake that we could not both have and eat: it informed us as to what aspects of our normative aspirations could not be realized together.[3]

Hayek subsequently contributed to the debate about economic calculation under socialism. This work was important not only because of the criticisms that he made of socialism during the course of that debate, but also because of positive theses of his own concerning human knowledge which emerged during his participation in that debate. Two issues are of especial importance. The first is subjectivism.[4] This is a topic upon which I have written elsewhere at greater length,[5] so I will mention here only briefly that Hayek emphasized several themes, notably that each individual possesses knowledge which may be tacit in its character and which cannot be centralized, and that individuals act on the basis of their own plans, concerns and orderings of the world, some of which may not be accessible to others. Some of these ideas were developed in tandem with his ideas about perception; for example, as set out in *The Sensory Order* (1952).

The second issue, which complements the former, is of prices as conveying information and thus allowing for the co-ordination of the behaviour of individuals who are not in face-to-face relationships. (Hayek is also concerned with the idea of markets as vehicles for discovery, a theme to which I will return later.) If people act in a market, their preferences affect the prices of goods, and these prices then convey information to other actors. People are thus able to bring their actions into better co-ordination with those of other people, even when they have no idea at all what the preferences and specific goals of those other people may be. For such activity to take place, however, Hayek has argued that it is necessary that these people share a legal order appropriate to such a society. He has also placed emphasis upon the benefits (to the co-ordination of behaviour) that follow through the sharing of more substantive moral codes, too.

Hayek is here involved in an attempt to hold the middle ground, against problems that face his views from two different directions. On the one side, Hayek criticizes moral codes that place duties on the individual that Hayek thinks will be deleterious to the successful functioning of a wider market order. His special concern is that such duties may cut across the incentives required for the functioning of a properly-working market-based society. Such problems may arise on a private level: Hayek is concerned that charitable demands upon an individual may lead him to give away seed corn to a beggar rather than planting it. But his major concern is if such matters spill over into the public realm and become the basis for a redistributive agenda for governmental action. He is worried both by the economic consequences that may follow from the adoption of such measures, and because he thinks that we lack both the knowledge and the mechanisms to pursue such matters effectively. He is also concerned that the direct consequences of the pursuit of such measures will be undesirable. Rather than assistance going to those who need it, plunder will go to the powerful and the astute. He is also concerned with the indirect consequences of the acceptance of such goals as legitimate: that damage may be done to the effective functioning of a market-based society if measures are introduced which make no sense within such a regime. Further, frustration at the lack of success in the pursuit of such goals may lead to demands for the political transformation of a market-based society into something different and – in Hayek's view – much less morally desirable.[6]

Hayek, however, is also concerned with the problem of how a social order of the kind which he considers to be morally desirable, and of specific patterns of social interaction, may be maintained in the face of what he fears to be too radical an individualism. Hayek faces a particular problem here, in that he sees the codes of conduct that sustain the social order that he favours as depending neither upon a perception on the part of the members of the societies in question, of their utility, nor as being sustained on the basis of individual self-interest. Rather, they are, in Hayek's view, 'evolutionary' products: practices which exist because they have happened to be successful in the past. Such products may consist, variously, of codes of behaviour which happen to have been adopted and persisted in, or - as in the case of his analysis of common law - something which (on his account) has reformed itself over time largely on the basis of criteria internal to itself.

HAYEK'S VALUES

My account initially referred to the young Hayek's concern about the relief of suffering. As his work develops, however, this concern is transformed. To it, he adds explicitly a concern for the minimization of coercion. Thereafter, one is offered various formulations of Hayek's values. They might best be described as combining a concern for (negative) liberty with something close to a preference utilitarianism, in which the individual's tastes are understood as in part shaped by the social and cultural system within which he is living. All this adds up to a view which is interesting - and distinctive - but which is in some respects also rather odd.

First, it should be noted that how Hayek appraises a social system differs from the approach that would be taken by many other economists - both with respect to the moral basis for his appraisal and how the appraisal is itself undertaken. The moral basis of the appraisal may seem a slightly unusual issue to raise, just because this is an issue seldom explicitly discussed by economists. (They often, to the outsider, seem more interested in solving technical problems within welfare economics than in asking what it is that they are doing when working on such problems.) At one level, Hayek's approach is distinctive because it is aggregative rather than individualistic. Hayek is concerned, typically, with the minimization of coercion of individuals in a society; with the well-being of an individual picked at random, and with the general ability of individuals to co-ordinate their plans. All of these things, it should be noted, are characteristics of societies as a whole, rather than things that are themselves enjoyed by each individual within such a society. This has the consequence that what Hayek favours, how he argues for it and the problems that his views encounter, differ significantly from the approaches of those economists and philosophers who argue from a rational-choice perspective. (Or, indeed, from within an individualistic, rights-based approach.)

It is simply not the case that for Hayek a condition of a situation's adequacy is its being in the interest of each of its members, as compared, say, with the situation that preceded it. That this is the case follows in part from the non-individualistic basis upon which Hayek evaluates societies. But it also stems in large part from what it is about markets that seems to him of most importance. For *if* their merits pertain especially to the utilization of dispersed knowledge, to the co-ordination of action in conditions of ignorance and to processes of discovery, then to concentrate upon that which betters the condition of each individual is beside the point. For much that happens within such a market-based society will not be to the advantage - or even not to the disadvantage - of *each* individual.

The distinctiveness of Hayek's view, I would suggest, is in part the result of the fact that he is explicitly concerned with the meta-level evaluation of different forms of social order. If one compares his approach to that of the rational-choice theorist, it might at first seem as if Hayek's approach is strange, because he is not operating with a Pareto criterion, or even with the idea that what is desirable must be constructed from the activities of self-interested individuals. Hayek, however, is concerned with the meta-level question: what form of social order is itself desirable? This issue is vital, but is one which it seems to me, many economists do not address, even in circumstances where they clearly need to do so.

The issue is vital just because the constitutional economist (when playing his role as a theorist) is not an actor within a market but someone who is (in my view, properly) concerned with discussing with us, and recommending - as desirable or otherwise - various kinds of social arrangements. Thus, if he wishes to commend to us some social order on the ground, say, that it is compatible with some version of the Pareto criterion, it is not enough that he shows this to be the case. He also has to explain why it is that the meeting of the Pareto criterion is itself of moral importance. It simply is not *self-evidently* true that the Pareto criterion is one that is desirable that a social order should meet. It seems to involve the moral assumption that everyone (but presumably just people, not animals) should count, and that a transformation of social arrangements is acceptable if someone gains without any individual being left with a lower degree of the satisfaction of his preferences afterwards than was the case before. But in suggesting that this is an appropriate basis upon which we should be making our evaluations, the economist is, willy nilly, taking a controversial stand on an important issue in moral philosophy.

To this, the economist - reluctant philosopher that he is - might object, offering one of two objections. First, he might say that he is not in fact recommending anything. Rather, he is simply explicating what happens under certain assumptions, and discussing whether ideas meet certain criteria. It is up to other people - non-economists - to make what use of his work they may. They will only be guided by it in so far as they find its premises compelling. To all this, the appropriate response is: all the detailed work that economists are undertaking within such an approach only has a point if it is assumed to be closely related to our actual moral concerns. Yet there seems no strong reason to believe that Pareto improvement comes even close to capturing people's actual moral concerns. Unless there is such a connection, welfare economics becomes simply so much formal play - and it is not (or so the mathematicians would presumably assure us) of much intrinsic interest if considered on its merits as a purely formal exercise.

Second, the economist might suggest that the legitimacy of his approach in some way follows from the assumption of ethical non-cognitivism, or from the (equally false) idea that people are in fact motivated just on the basis of self-interest. However, if one looks at such attempts as have actually been made to derive economists' starting-points from their alleged foundations in individual self-interest, one discovers that this leads, rather, to massacres of the weak, slavery, and so on,[7] than to the economist's account within which, as it were, individuals' preferences are treated as ends in themselves.

Accordingly, it seems to me that the typical starting-point of the welfare economist stands in need of support by ethical argument. Rather than it being something that coheres with the amoral cynicism which economists so often seem to adopt as the mark of their profession, such assumptions, if taken seriously, would undermine rather than provide foundations for the starting-points of their analysis. This should be good news for those economists who have an interest in individual moral philosophy; for it would seem to me as if something of this sort is required to provide a rationale for welfare economists' customary approaches.

However, once we grant that moral ideas must be taken seriously, Hayek's approach becomes more attractive. For as individuals we may recognize the moral attractiveness of social arrangements that permit the flourishing of individuals' lives. We may make positive appraisals of societies of which we are not members, on such grounds, even if it is not the case that every individual prospers within them. We may intelligibly judge a society in which we are living and which has such characteristics to be a good society, even if we are ourselves one of those who are not successful within it.

One may also approach this issue from another direction. If one considers the characteristics of markets that Hayek has highlighted, their desirable characteristics would indeed seem to occur at an aggregate level. That is to say, it would seem to strain things if one had to argue that markets, as Hayek depicts them, must in fact be in the interest of everyone. Indeed, this is almost a commonplace for any approach which looks at issues of institutional choice. But in order to fit the desirability of markets within a rational-choice perspective, writers typically have recourse to ideas about a hypothetical social contract. In this, people are invited to assume a persona other than their actual one. This persona abstracts from their actual situation, life-history, talents and personality. The hope is that choices which are not to people's actual advantage may appear to be to their advantage if viewed from such a position. What is not clear is why people should be making their appraisals upon such a basis, rather than from the positions which they actually hold.[8]

In response, it might be argued that Hayek's claims about the desirable, collective characteristics of market based societies could be disaggregated in terms of the probability of each individual enjoying the benefits in question.[9] This suggestion is interesting. But it does not seem to me to work, for two reasons. First, it is not clear that the disaggregation could be accomplished in the way indicated such that everyone received the same probability. For we know more about ourselves - and some others - than would have to be the case for each of us to receive the same probability of, say, becoming rich or not being coerced in a society of the kind that Hayek favours. It is, accordingly, not clear that rationally self-interested people would be willing to co-operate on equal terms. Second, part of the force of Hayek's claims is that we may find them attractive even when we know we would not ourselves benefit. Hayek, it seems to me, is correct in his implicit repudiation of contractarianism[10] and in his insistence that market-based societies possess certain morally desirable characteristics. What he does not do - and what it seems to me would be needed for his view to be fully cogent - is to spell out just what he is doing when he is commending such institutions to people, even when participation in them may not be in their personal interest.

It could be argued that this is something that Hayek at least attempts. However, it seems to me that Hayek is less than wholehearted in developing such an argument. While his work is studded with appeals to moral notions which might seem to be playing this role, they occur in an unsystematic and, notably in his later writings, a somewhat confused form. (Thus it is often difficult to understand whether Hayek is commending to us moral ideas because they lead to the survival of large populations, or trying to explain why we, as members of such populations, happen to have inherited such ideas.) There is certainly no clear and systematic exposition of his views on these issues, still less by way of sustained argument for them. I suspect that the reason for this may be his own tendency towards ethical non-cognitivism, together with a certain reluctance to discuss ethical issues which seems to have been widespread among Austrians of his generation. All this, however, seems to me to be a handicap, when the assumption that there is a moral case for markets plays an important role in one's views. Hayek often seems reduced to making an implicit appeal to people whose preferences are something like his own; to arguing that those preferences may be realized in market-based societies, and to explaining that certain other preferences cannot be realized within such societies without adversely affecting their performance - and thus the realization of other, more pressing, concerns.

HAYEK'S ARGUMENTS FOR MARKETS

But in what terms can Hayek argue for market-based societies? Here, some interesting problems arise. First, what can be shown concerning market-based societies? Hayek's argument for markets is broadly consequentialist in its character. But this leads to certain problems. For in situations in which we are ignorant, and in which individuals are free as to how they will act and may have a wide variety of motives, it may be very difficult to say anything of substance about what we can expect from such societies at all. Yet a consequentialist argument is only as strong as what we can say about consequences. Further, Hayek has himself argued that in the social sciences we are typically dealing with complex phenomena, in respect of which we can at best make qualitative, pattern predictions.

On the face of it, Hayek would seem to have scored an impressive own goal: he would seem to be a consequentialist whose substantive views and ideas about the philosophy of the social sciences imply that one cannot make out a consequentialist case for his own ideals. The problems are, I think, heightened by the fact that the kinds of argument that Hayek offers are ones in which the advantages of market-based societies have also to be weighed against some of their admitted disadvantages. Various factors are here of importance. Within the kind of society that Hayek favours, much decision-making may be described as disaggregated, in the sense that decisions are made as consequences of the actions of particular individuals in their various different social situations, rather than through some process of collective decision-taking. But this has its various pros and cons.

First, if decision-taking is disaggregated in a market-based society, we may gain from the fact that socially dispersed knowledge may be utilized. But we may also lose from the fact that resources may be wasted in the duplication of capital expenditure by people who do not realize that others are making a bid for the same market, or from under-investment because people fear that others might make similar investments, and so do not themselves act at all.[11] More generally, individuals in such societies are constantly taking decisions which have wider social consequences, in settings where they cannot anticipate what these consequences will be.

Second, by choosing to live in such a society, one also chooses the kinds of pressures and incentives that will play a formative role in shaping one's preferences and thus, in some measure, the kind of person that one will be.

In my view, argument *is* possible concerning the pros and cons of different forms of social arrangement. To make some judgement about such matters, one needs to spell out what institutional choices would be involved in our proceeding in one way or another, and what the likely consequences might be of our making one rather than another such choice - for example, by exploring what kinds of knowledge and decision-making, and what kinds of incentives would operate in various such systems. Such an enterprise, sensitive to the kinds of factors a concern for which has distinguished Hayek's work, would seem to me to be called for if Hayek's consequentialist argument for markets is to be valid. Economic argument of this 'comparative institutional' kind, however, stands in need of supplementation by relevant empirical studies. It is all very well for rational-choice theorists to look at different forms of decision-making on an *a priori* basis. But Hayek's concerns - not least about cultural influences upon our values - should surely lead us also to the analysis of the empirical records of various forms of institutional organization. If, say, we are interested in assessing the merits of more purely market-based forms of social organization *vis-à-vis* corporatism or consociational democracy, or comparing voluntaristic systems of market and co-operative health provision with a universalist or a minimalist state system, we need surely (also) to look at what has happened when such systems have actually been tried out. The same, it seems to me, is true of the more positive parts of Hayek's programme; for example, his ideas about forms of economic organization as systems within which learning can take place. This - at least on the face of it - suggests an interesting programme for the empirical and theoretical investigation of organizational behaviour,[12] which would then feed back into matters of institutional choice. But as far as I know, no such work has actually been undertaken by economists in the 'Austrian' tradition.

The reference to institutional choice, however, leads me to a second issue. It concerns the criteria on the basis of which choices are made for different institutions. Hayek offers us an account of the development of market-based societies within which we are ourselves seen as the products of a process of social evolution. On Hayek's account, we are equipped with two - often conflicting - sets of preferences; one, attuned to a large-scale market-based society; the other to smaller, face-to-face societies. Whether or not one accepts Hayek's account of how we come to be equipped with these different concerns, he is surely correct that we may experience tensions between them of the kind that he highlights. What is not clear is how they are supposed to be resolved.

In some cases, it may not be too difficult. For it may be the case that we have preferences which, when acted upon, may generate unintended and highly undesirable consequences. Thus, for example, we may have 'communitarian' preferences. It might also be the case that the consequences of our acting upon these preferences - directly, or by way of the actions of others which our actions provoke - are things which we would not in fact wish to occur. Analysis of the kind offered by Hayek, and other economists, may clarify such things for us.

However, in some cases it would seem as if we face choices between things which may matter to *us* a lot, and the ethical features of markets that Hayek has stressed. We might, for example, find that we are faced with a practical tension between our concern for people with whom we feel a kinship, or for the cultural characteristics of a society that goes in some way to form our own self-identity, and the universalistic characteristics of a market-based society. We may appreciate that, say, acting politically to preserve things that we favour may damage the fabric of a market-based society, and that it may lead to the blighting of opportunities for others with whom we are not in face-to-face contact. But we may also judge that these are matters in which we are not much interested - at least in comparison with the other matters about which we are more concerned.[13]

All this, it seems to me, occurs as a practical problem for Hayek's own views. Consider, for example, the contrast to which I referred at the end of the first section between co-operative behaviour within a market and co-operation by way of an individual's attachment to the rules of a specific legal or moral system. In respect of the former kind of co-operation, it did not matter what substantive concerns an individual might have. Co-operation, say, is taking place when a pharmacist who is, in his spare time, a Special Constable, sells a quantity of chemicals to a homicidal maniac who plans (later) to use them to kill everyone in the area. Each pursues his own plans in that particular market transaction. But what of their co-operation in sustaining the legal order under which these transactions take place? It is not clear that such things can be sustained by people regardless of what their substantive concerns are. But at the same time, it is not clear what, in a society of the kind that Hayek depicts, will be responsible for individuals' participating in behaviour which leads to the sustaining of specific and substantive values.

A problem that is in some ways similar has been raised for Hayek by Irving Kristol.[14] Kristol argued that a market-based society, as Hayek presents it, lacks moral legitimacy. For what Hayek says about it (and what he says about the defects of older arguments, such as that markets reward hard work and diligence) is not such as to render it morally compelling to the individual citizen. Hayek, I think, is right in repudiating the idea that citizens should be lied to in order to gain their support for a free society. But this leaves him with the problem: just what is to be said to them?

One line of response – followed in recent times by Buchanan, Gauthier, Narveson, and in some respects Schmidtz[15] – is to suggest that the espousal of a market order is not moral but prudential. It in effect tries to offer to each individual a prudential rationale for choosing a market order and for broadly moral conduct within it. Such arguments are interesting. But at the same time, they seem to me to have three broad defects. First, as I suggested earlier, it is not clear that from them one can in fact develop an argument upon a strictly prudential basis that leads to a universal liberalism: that accords liberal rights to everybody. Second, once liberal rights have been established – such that one is not going to kill or enslave others but may cheat them if it pays to do so – the prudential argument for co-operation seems at its strongest with respect to iterated face-to-face transactions. The more distant one's connection with others and the less likely it is that one will be interacting with them again (or that they will recognize you if you do) and the more people with whom one is interacting, the stronger the rationale may seem to be to defect.[16] Yet it is just in such cases that there will be the biggest pull towards, say, giving preferences to those with whom one has some private tie, whether of family, community, culture or whatever over the more abstract norms of the market and of universal moral codes. Third, such arguments are conducted from a rational-choice perspective, which is a long way removed from the actual situations of individuals and their uncertainties and unclarities. It is also conducted using the ideal type, rational economic man. This has its advantages because of the generality of the argument which it offers. It has, however, its disadvantages too. For it may lead us to lose sight of the fact that the arguments for – and against – markets may be grounded in attachments to specific values, people's orientation towards which may differ from their orientation towards, say, different bundles of apples and oranges.

People's attachments to specific visions of the good may generate something closer to a lexicographical ordering than the more usual patterns of indifference curves that we would think of as being generated by maximisation between differing bundles of goods. Second, they may hold their preferences in a cognitivist manner. By this I mean two things: first, that the fact that they hold a preference may itself be dependent upon intersubjective, cognitive reinforcement that this is a preference that it is appropriate that they should hold; second, that the judgement as to what is appropriate may depend upon relatively fixed criteria, which reflect its relationship to some other goal.

A second response – by way of contrast with those grounded in rational choice – would be to explicate more clearly, and to argue for, the basis upon which the institutions of a market-based society are to be valued upon moral grounds rather than on the basis of self-interest. Indeed, from such a perspective, self-interested action would itself stand in need of moral legitimation. (I am not suggesting that it would be difficult to do this; merely emphasizing that, from such a perspective, it has to be done.) How such arguments might be developed is a topic on which I have ideas of my own, but they must await another occasion as their exploration would take us too far from Hayek's work.[17]

However, even if such arguments were explicated, and cogently, the person who advances them might still face a problem. It is a problem that also faces Hayek's own views concerning the moral case for markets, and might be called the test of disaggregation.

SOME PROBLEMS OF DISAGGREGATION

Hayek has stressed the significance of the fact that in markets decision-making is disaggregated.[18] He has further stressed the importance of markets as enabling us to make use of the knowledge that individuals possess in such circumstances. These points seem to me not only of importance in their own right, but to stand at the heart of his critique of the ideal of social justice. Hayek's argument on this issue seems to me to rest on the idea that there is a powerful moral case for our choosing an economic system based upon markets. However, this very choice in its turn has the consequence that we decide many things upon a disaggregated basis, and decision-making of this kind is incompatible with the pursuit of the ideal of social justice. For even if some ideal of social justice seemed compelling, morally, for us to try to realize, there seems good reason to believe that this is not something that we could do within a market-based society within which decision-taking that affects this ideal is disaggregated, for reasons that relate both to information and to incentives.[19]

I wish here to argue a related point: that in considering any kind of properties that it seems to us desirable that a social order should possess, we must bear in mind that they have to be sustained through the decisions of individuals in their various situations. I am not arguing that they must be sustained on the basis of self-interest: this seems to me an unacceptably narrow reading of human behaviour. At the same time, we must be realistic concerning how people will behave in the face of tensions between self-interest and moral concerns. Above all, we should accept that people can only be relied upon to behave in ways that make intelligible sense in the situations in which they are acting. It is all very well to allocate to each individual a particular task in some large project. But unless the task as it is faced in the situation in which it is being undertaken has some positive rationale, it seems to me hopeless to expect that it will be performed. Even when individuals may approve of the overall goal in the large, unless the component parts of the action make intelligible sense, and people have the appropriate motivation to perform them, there seems to me every reason to suppose that they will not undertake the tasks in question. To be sure, it may be possible for us to make changes to a person's situation in ways that may affect their motivation. But such changes must themselves operate through the intrumentality of other individuals' actions, and must, thus, make sense at every stage to each of those individuals, in their turn. Further, individuals may also take steps to avoid features of their situation which impose constraints upon them which they do not like, and the rationale for which they cannot appreciate.

Thus, a tax system could be viewed as a means through which resources needed to finance some vision of a moral ordering of society are to be raised. (We are here putting public-choice considerations and the little matter of coercion to one side.) But it also serves as a system of practical incentives, in the face of which people may take steps to minimize their tax liability. Further, tax inspectors will themselves only do what it makes sense for them to do in the situations in which they find themselves. All this suggests that some ideals concerning the distribution of goods in a society would not be attainable, even if they were broadly approved of by all citizens. For such distributional patterns would have to be sustained through the particular actions of individual citizens. The relationships between the overall issues of distribution and those particular actions are – to say the least – not transparent. The larger the system and the less transparent the connection between the larger vision and the specific actions that people are taking, the less these actions can sustain even a vision which all the people in question wish to uphold.

Some distributional ideals may be impossible to attain, just because different citizens have different possibilities for avoiding – in what will seem to them to be morally legitimate ways – the actions that they would have to take if such goals were to be realized.[20] To put the matter in simple terms, it is clearly possible for the rich to purchase advice as to how to order their affairs in relation to tax codes in a way that is not feasible for the rest of us. Similarly, the employee can be taxed on his salary in ways which cannot be applied to the taxation of the self-employed because of the role that is played in their activities by tax-deductible expenses. Similarly, it should come as no surprise that Julian Le Grand has discovered that the educated middle classes benefit more than do the poor and inarticulate from Britain's National Health Service.[21]

In making these points, I should stress again that my argument does not depend on the idea that individuals' behaviour must be self-interested. Rather, it rests on the idea that people will only behave in ways that are intelligible to them. This may involve their behaving in ways that run against their pecuniary self-interest. But it seems to me that if something is to outweigh their self-interest it must be both intelligible and powerful as it confronts their interests in the situation in which they are acting.

The point of my argument, however, is not simply to offer a gloss on Hayek's critique of the idea of social justice. Rather, I wish to suggest that Hayek's own aggregative moral case for the market is hit by these considerations in much the same way as is the ideal of social justice. If I am right, it may be of little use to make even a superb case for the moral desirability of markets and their associated institutions, unless that case could also be disaggregated so as to render it compelling at the level of individual action in the various situations of our day-to-day lives. Indeed, the very strength of markets themselves is that within them decisions that (arguably) have desirable large-scale social consequences can be taken on a completely disaggregated basis. The problem facing Hayek is to explain how the institutions of a market-based society can command support upon such a disaggregated basis.

CONCLUDING REMARKS

But how is this to be done? This is not an issue that I will try to address in the present chapter. However, I will offer two remarks about the kind of task that the theorist of classical liberalism seems to me to face.

The first is that he needs to keep firmly in his sights what is going on at the level of the behaviour of the individual. By this, however, I mean not individual behaviour as maximization, but the ways in which individuals more or less creatively make sense of their lives and the settings in which they live, on a day-to-day basis. For it is the ideas and patterns of conduct that they make use of to cope with such matters that he will have to call on to sustain the grander institutions of the market. Accordingly, the task facing the normative theorist of the free society is to offer us an account of how its institutions could be sustained through the conduct of citizens when they are engaged in such behaviour. I also suspect that this is the point at which we should leave aside the ideal type of rational economic man, for a richer view of human beings, which considers them as having sexes - and sex - and different kinds of relationships over time, and also as, in succession, being born, young, middle aged, old and dead. (If such a task were accomplished successfully, however, it would generate the further problem - which goes back at least to Montesquieu - of whether markets will in their turn produce the situations which will foster this conduct.)[22]

In writing in such terms, however, there is a danger that I may seem to be conjuring up a demon from the early history of classical liberalism: Mandeville's manipulative 'statesman' who structures our situations such that private interest will then sustain the public good. But such statesmen, in my view, do not exist. If they did, it is not clear that they would have a legitimate role within classical liberal social theory. For this, while it may be illuminated by theoretical discourse about society and its characteristics, must itself eventually work in terms of the actions of citizens, not of puppet-masters standing above and directing the activities of the rest of us. In short, while theory may offer us a God's eye view of our society and its problems, liberal social theory must move from this perspective to showing us how a liberal society can be sustained on the basis of ideas that are comprehended by ordinary citizens, and of actions that they will plausibly take to resolve the problems that they encounter in the various situations in which they find themselves.[23]

However, while I wish to repudiate Mandeville's statesman, I think that there is none the less something to the idea - and that he may be rendered harmless if he is privatized, and operates on the basis of consent.

One characteristic feature of classical liberal political theory in recent years, it seems to me, is that it has addressed us as if we are individuals who somehow have to create social order either by universal agreement or as the result of one-on-one transactions and their unintended consequences or through some form of social evolution. I do not see why we are restricted to such options. Rather, just as in other market settings we make choices between products that are the creations of entrepreneurs, so, it seems to me, it can be the case for our social institutions.

Accordingly, the question of how one renders compelling markets and the institutions upon which they rest on the basis of day-to-day human conduct looks to me as much a practical as a theoretical task. While the theorist typically considers himself someone who has little to say concerning people's day-to-day conduct, if my *theoretical* argument in this chapter is correct, this is the level to which he must address himself. The theorist who favours a market-based society has, in effect, the task of suggesting a code of behaviour that is intrinsically attractive, or which can be adopted without undue tensions at the level of people's day-to-day lives, but which as a by-product will serve to maintain the institutions of a market-based society. If the theorist thinks that he can solve these problems theoretically, there is no reason why he should not be willing to try them out practically, too. Accordingly, if my general line of argument in this chapter is correct, the theorist who favours markets might even *enter* them, and see whether people will indeed buy a code of conduct the pursuit of which will sustain the institutions that he thinks are of such importance for mankind as part, say, of the life of a *private* suburb or even a city, in which they might choose to live.[24]

NOTES

Earlier versions of this chapter were delivered at the Fairfax Austrian Economics Discussion Group, and at the American Economic Association, Washington DC, December 1990. I would like to thank participants in those meetings for criticism and suggestions.

1 Compare my 'From Hayek to Menger', in B. Caldwell (ed.) *Carl Menger and His Legacy in Economics*, Durham and London: Duke University Press, 1990, pp. 189–212.
2 Compare my 'The Austrian Connection', in W. Grassl and B. Smith (eds) *Austrian Economics: Historical and Philosophical Background*, London: Croom Helm, 1986.
3 Compare, on the themes of this paragraph, Hayek's Inaugural Address at the LSE, 'The Trend of Economic Thinking', *Economica*, 40, 1934: 121–37.
4 See, on this, my 'Subjectivism, Falsification and Positive Economics', in J. Wiseman (ed.) *Beyond Positive Economics*, London: Macmillan, 1983, pp. 65–86, and my 'Subjectivism, Explanation and the Austrian Tradition', forthcoming in B. Caldwell and S. Boehm (eds) *Austrian Economics: Tensions and New Directions*, Boston, Dordrecht and London: Kluwer, 1993, pp. 103–28.
5 This account oversimplifies the matter considerably. For a fuller discussion see my University of London PhD dissertation 'THE POLITICAL THOUGHT OF F.A. VON HAYEK', 1987.
6 Hayek's work in these respects constitutes an important restatement and development of themes in Adam Smith. Compare I. Hont and M. Ignatieff, 'Needs and Justice in The Wealth of Nations', in I. Hont and M. Ignatieff

(eds) *Wealth and Virtue*, Cambridge: Cambridge University Press, 1983, pp. 1–44.

7 Compare my 'The Scope and Status of Prudential Liberalism', *Review of Politics*, 54(2) Spring 1992: 211–30.

8 If there is a moral rationale as to why they should make such an appraisal, that is a different matter. My point is that such an appraisal seems to me to have no place within a rational choice approach.

9 This suggestion was put to me in discussion by Roy Cordato.

10 Although the reader might recall that Hayek has occasionally drawn a parallel between his views and Rawls' notion of a veil of ignorance. There is, however, a more important parallel between Hayek's approach and the non-contractarian approach of Hume and of Smith.

11 Argument along these lines was offered by some of those who were critical of markets, on informational grounds, during the 1930s.

12 For example, in his 'Economics and Knowledge', section 6, see his *Individualism and Economic Order*, Chicago: University of Chicago Press, 1948, pp. 44–5.

13 These are ideas which I am not commending but which I am suggesting might well represent people's actual responses to the kinds of situation that I have discussed in the text.

14 See Irving Kristol, (1978) 'When Virtue Loses her Loveliness', in his *Two Cheers for Capitalism*, New York: Basic Books, pp. 255–70.

15 Compare James Buchanan, *The Limits of Liberty*,Chicago: University of Chicago Press, 1975; David Gauthier, *Morals by Agreement*, New York: Oxford University Press, 1986; Jan Narveson, *The Libertarian Idea*, Philadelphia: Temple University Press, 1988, and David Schmidtz, *The Limits of Government*, Boulder, Colo.: Westview Press, 1991, and, for discussion, my 'The Scope and Status of Prudential Liberalism', *op. cit.*

16 Compare, however, on issues of reputation in non face-to-face situations, Daniel Klein, 'Promise-Keeping in the Great Society', *Economics and Politics* 4, July 1992: 117–36.

17 Compare, however, my 'Epistemological Limits of the State', *Political Studies*, XXXVIII, Oxford: Clarendon Press, 1990, pp. 116–25, and my 'From Dialogue Rights to Property Rights', *Critical Review* 4(1–2), 1990: 106–32.

18 I have discussed this issue at some length in an unpublished paper, 'Markets, Social Justice and Disaggregation'.

19 This is argued in more detail, with particular emphasis on issues raised by implementation theory, in Paul S. Edwards and J. Shearmur, 'Street-Level Jurisprudence', paper delivered at the American Political Science Association, Chicago, Ill., August 1992.

20 Compare R. Goodin and J. Le Grand, *Not Only the Poor*, London: Allen & Unwin, 1987.

21 Compare my 'Adam Smith and the Cultural Contradictions of Capitalism', in N. Elliott (ed.) *The Legacy of Adam Smith*, London: Adam Smith Institute, 1990.

22 It is in this connection that the emphasis placed by Donald Winch, in 'Adam Smith and the Liberal Tradition', in K. Haakonssen (ed.) *Traditions of Liberalism*, St Leonards, NSW: Centre for Independent Studies, 1988, pp. 83–104, on the role that Adam Smith gives to the statesman, while perhaps factually correct, is normatively pointless, unless it is

accompanied by an argument as to how people exercising such influence within a society like that depicted by Smith can be expected to play the functional role that is being allocated to them. This point is particularly pressing, given that Smith was so concerned in other cases (e.g. university teachers) not just to allocate a functional role, but also to suggest a system of incentives to ensure that they would indeed play it.

23 My suggestion is thus that one might treat these issues as comparable to those of physical infrastructure, on the private provision of which compare David Beito, 'The Formation of Urban Infrastructure Through Non-Government Planning', *Journal of Urban History* 16, May 1990: 263–303.

11

HAYEK'S CRITIQUE OF SOCIALISM

Willem Keizer

DIFFERENT VERSIONS OF HAYEK'S ROLE IN THE SOCIALIST CALCULATION DEBATE

The 'socialist calculation debate' between Austrian and socialist economists may rightly be called the greatest economic debate of the twentieth century. It is certainly the longest, now having lasted for seventy-two years. During this time it underwent several metamorphoses, the latest of which started only two years ago. Over the entire span of the debate the following phases or debates-within-the-debate can be distinguished:

1 L. von Mises versus Central European socialists, 1920–33.
2 F.A. Hayek versus Anglo-Saxon socialist economists, 1935–45.
3 Hayekians versus neoclassical economists, 1975–90.
4 Misesians versus Hayekians, 1990 to the present day.

The important role Hayek played in the debate is shown by his involvement in three of the sub-debates listed above. Corresponding to the three parties involved, there are three sequential versions of this 'Great Debate': the standard socialist/neoclassical version and the Hayekian and Misesian versions.

The standard version of the debate was established just after the Second World War and was accepted by the majority of economists until the 1980s. According to this version Mises had stated that in principle economic rationality was impossible under socialism. As there could be no market or market prices for the means of production, there could be no rational cost calculation and hence no rational allocation of producer goods and production of final goods. A rational socialist economy was theoretically impossible, as the central planners could not calculate. However, in 1908 the Italian economist E. Barone had already constructed a general-equilibrium model of a socialist economy and proved that it was determinate if the central planners possessed all the relevant information and satisfied the equilibrium conditions. In Hayek's 1935 survey of the debate he admitted that general-equilibrium models proved a rational socialist economy to be possible in principle, but that the computational difficulty of solving millions of equations simultaneously made it impossible in practice (Hayek 1935: 153). In the place of Mises 'theoretically impossible' Hayek proposed a weaker 'impractical' argument. The Polish socialist economist O. Lange claimed that Hayek had retreated to a weaker second line of defence, thereby admitting the theoretical possibility of rational socialism (Lange 1936–7: 63).

In 1936–7 Lange replied to this computation argument with his 'competitive solution' of market socialism. The decentralization of decision-making in this model obviated the need for solving millions of equations and so refuted Hayek's stand on the impracticality issue. With Lerner's 'The Economics of Control' (1944) and Bergson's survey of the debate in 1948 the majority of the economists thought the controversy settled. The consensus was that the socialists had won the debate: the general equilibrium models of Barone and others proved that rational calculation was theoretically possible in a centrally planned socialist economy; and Lange's market socialist solution showed that the computational problems of central planning could be overcome with the aid of markets and a trial-and-error market-clearing procedure. This 'standard' version of the socialist calculation debate is found in most accounts of it published between 1948 and 1980 (for a critical survey see Lavoie 1981: 43–5; 1985: 10–20).

In the middle of the 1970s there was a general revival of Austrian thought, especially in the United States; a sign of it being the granting of the Nobel Prize for Economics to Hayek in 1974. This led *inter alia* to a rediscovery of Hayek's arguments against socialism, as part of the struggle against neoclassical mainstream economics by a new generation of American neo-Austrians. Whereas in the past it had been Mises's contributions which were highlighted in any survey of the debate, these young 'Hayekians' now declared Hayek's arguments to be the more important and fruitful. This may be seen as a reaction against the neoclassical tendency to ridicule Mises and ignore the arguments of Hayek (Vaughn 1980: 537). The Austrian revival gave rise to the second or 'Hayekian' version of the debate, which incorporated the neo-Austrian theories of the market process and entrepreneurship of I. Kirzner.[1] It should be seen as a rational reconstruction of Hayek's argumentation in the debate. In many instances his arguments were more traditional and, where genuinely innovative, less clearly and elaborately articulated than their reconstruction by the Hayekians make them out to be (see also n. 8).

In recent years this 'Hayekian palace revolution' aroused the wrath of the adherents of Mises centred around the Mises Institute at Auburn University, Alabama. In a number of articles they have exposed the differences between Mises and Hayek on virtually all characteristics of the Austrian paradigm. In doing so they clarified Mises's own argumentation in the debate and showed where Hayek deviated from it, in their opinion distorting the 'true' Austrian critique of socialism (Rothbard 1991, 1992; Salerno 1990).

This chapter will be devoted to Hayek's critique of socialism, as distinct from that of Mises and the rational reconstruction of it by the Hayekians. Its purpose is to survey Hayek's arguments in the socialist calculation debate and to assess the importance of his contribution. This chapter will show that

1 Hayek's arguments in the debate differ greatly from those of Mises.
2 They do not constitute a 'retreat' from the latter's critique.
3 He cricitizes central planning on epistemological grounds.
4 His pro-market arguments are complementary to those of Mises in favour of private property rights.
5 They mark important advances in the development of Austrian thought.
6 Hayek's epistemological and political arguments in the socialist debate were instrumental in the development of his political philosophy.
7 The failure of socialism in Eastern Europe can be partly explained by his critique of socialist economics.

CHRONOLOGY OF HAYEK'S CONTRIBUTIONS

The socialist calculation debate started in 1920 with Mises's famous article 'Economic Calculation in the Socialist Commonwealth' (Hayek 1935: 87–130). Hayek only joined in the debate from 1935 onwards, when he edited a collection of continental articles entitled *Collectivist Economic Planning* for publication in England. This publication transposed the hitherto Central European calculation debate to the Anglo-Saxon economic forum.[2] As the editor Hayek contributed two articles, the introductory 'The Nature and History of the Problem' (Hayek 1935, I) and the concluding 'The Present State of the Debate' (Hayek 1935, II). Already in these first contributions he deviates from the Misesian arguments, especially as far as the question of 'impossible in *principle* or in *practice*?' is concerned. In 1937 he wrote a seminal article on the role of knowledge in economics, which arose directly out of his involvement in the debate (Hayek 1937).

In 1940 he returned to the debate with his reply 'The Competitive Solution' (Hayek 1940) to Lange's model of market socialism of 1936–7 and H.D. Dickinson's 'Economics of Socialism' of 1939. In his critique of these market socialist models he applied the new insights gained from his epistemological studies, as well as giving a detailed microeconomic analysis. He showed them to have numerous theoretical and institutional deficiencies and doubted whether they could be implemented in practice.

Finally, deeply disturbed by the rise of totalitarianism and by the war, he raised several political charges against socialism. These political and institutional arguments were elaborated in his major polemic against state planning and socialism, *The Road to Serfdom* of 1944. The 1945 article 'The Use of Knowledge in Society' elaborates his earlier epistemological arguments against socialist planning (Hayek 1945). At the end of his life he returned to the socialist debate with *The Fatal Conceit: The Errors of Socialism* (1989). In this synthesis of his thoughts on socialism over the past half-century he integrates his earlier critiques of socialism, 'scientism' and 'constructivist rationalism' with his epistemology and later theories on the benevolence of spontaneous institutions (especially the competitive market) and the growth of civilization through their selective evolution.

Hayek's original contributions to the debate therefore consist of two books and five articles. This is more than any other participant wrote on the subject, even when judged merely quantitatively. It may be said that he shaped the course of the socialist calculation debate to a large extent, both by the nature of his arguments and by the responses of his opponents. Had he, for instance, not brought forward the computation argument against the general-equilibrium models, the models of market socialism might not have been constructed and the controversy would have taken a different course.

HAYEK'S CRITICISMS OF SOCIALIST ECONOMICS

Hayek's critique of socialism comprises many more points of criticism than Mises's original challenge. The latter had mainly argued one point, that socialism could not calculate rationally without private property rights in the means of production. Hayek adds several further charges, which are given here as much as possible in his original wording. They are presented in more or less chronological order.

1 Socialism cannot establish a social welfare function valid for the whole of society.
2 It cannot formulate or solve the 'millions of equations' of a general-equilibrium model.

3 Central planning is incapable of using the specific knowledge of time and place dispersed over millions of individuals.
4 Socialism must of necessity be authoritarian and lead to political dictatorship.
5 The models of market socialism suffer from several deficiencies compared to competitive capitalism.

In the course of his involvement in the debate Hayek switched his major charges against socialism a few times, so that four phases can be identified. In 1935 he started with the first two criticisms, which are still fairly mainstream economics. After his 1937 article on the role of knowledge in economics he switched to the third point, his original and most influential contribution to the debate. During the war he raised a number of political charges against socialism and all attempts at national planning. These four phases depended in part on what he saw at that time as the nature of the economic problem confronting society, which economics as a science and socialism as an economic system should solve. At least four such denotations of the 'central economic problem' can be discerned over the period 1935–45:

1 How to allocate resources rationally over alternative uses (1935).
2 How to achieve co-ordination of the individual actions of millions of human beings (1937), and how to do so without state coercion (1944–5).
3 How to use the knowledge dispersed over millions of individuals optimally (1945).
4 How to secure rapid and complete adaption of the economy to changes in the circumstances of time and place (1945).

Each formulation of 'the' economic problem led to its own set of criticisms of socialism. This explains the variety of charges with their supporting arguments.

Criticism 1: The impossibility of a social welfare function

When he entered the debate in 1935 Hayek's main argument was that the socialist planning authority could not allocate the scarce resources over the infinite number of competing ends in a rational way, because it could not establish a consistent scale of priorities.[3] In *The Road to Serfdom* nine years later he supplied the theoretical basis for his conviction that there is no single scale of values (in terms of modern welfare theory: a non-cyclical social welfare function) valid for all individuals. Scales of values can only exist in the individual minds. Only individual scales of values exist, and they are different and often conflicting. Therefore each individual should be allowed to pursue his own preferences and not be dictated to by anyone else (Hayek 1944: 60).

It does not mean that 'social' ends do not exist, but that these are merely the coinciding ends of many individuals. Only in the case when there is voluntary agreement on ends may the state direct economic activities. State control is bound to suppress individual freedom when there is no such agreement (Hayek 1944: 60).

In 'The Competitive Solution' of 1940 he gives a political twist to this point. Under socialism, as under fascism, the distinction between politics and economics will be abolished. In a planned economy all economic questions become political questions, because planning requires that all citizens hold a common scale of values (Hayek 1940: 206–7). It therefore requires a great deal more social uniformity than normally exists in a society. If the individuals do not have a common welfare function, one will have to be imposed upon them by force and propaganda (Hayek 1940: 206). It takes a dictatorship to make national central planning possible, because that is the most efficient instrument for the enforcement of collective ideals (Hayek 1944: 70). However, when planners suppress the values of the individuals, they are likely to substitute their own in their stead (Hayek 1944: 65). He concludes that socialism is bound to become totalitarian. When considering its political implications, this point of the uniform scale of values turns into criticism 4 listed above, the authoritarian nature of socialism.

Criticism 2: The impossibility of solving general-equilibrium models

Early in 'The Present State of the Debate' Hayek says that in a society with consumer and worker sovereignty the central direction of all economic activity is a task that cannot be rationally solved. All that socialists try to show is that '"in principle" a solution is conceivable. Little or no claim is made that such a solution is *practicable*' (Hayek 1935, II: 148–9, emphasis added). Further on he refers to 'the practicality of these mathematical solutions' (ibid.: 155). Here he switches the issue to the 'practicality' argument, suggesting that even if the calculation problem under socialism can be solved in principle, it cannot be done in practice (with the implicit assumption that this is more important). On the basis of this statement Lange claimed that Hayek had deserted the Misesian critique of 'theoretically impossible' and had retreated to the weaker criticism of 'possible in theory, but not in pracice'.

Hayek mentions computational difficulties as the main reason for the impracticality of central planning, when discussing general-equilibrium models as a solution to the Austrian challenge:

> Now, it must be admitted that this is not an impossibility in the sense that it is logically contradictory. But the contention that a determination of prices by such a procedure being logically conceivable in any way invalidates the contention that it is not a possible solution . . . it is only necessary to attempt to visualize what the application of this method would imply in practice in order to rule it out as humanly impracticable and impossible.
> (ibid.: 152–3)

Referring to Barone's model, Hayek says that 'What is practically relevant here is not the formal structure of this system, but the nature and amount of concrete information required . . . and the magnitude of the task' (Hayek ibid.: 153). Hayek supports his computation argument by referring to enormous informational requirements of the centralist solution. As nearly all goods are unique in time, place and circumstances, nearly every item will have to be treated as a separate good. Central planning will have to deal with details of the most minute description. All these data will have to enter the calculations of the Central Planning Bureau (CPB), so that the statistical task would be enormous. It is physically impossible to solve the millions of equations of general-equilibrium models, which would then also have to be done continuously (ibid.: 156). The neoclassical socialists were correct in seeing Hayek's main argument against central planning in 1935 as being one of computational impossibility, as far as the centralist solution of general-equilibrium models was concerned.

In the Hayekian version of the debate the Hayekians downplay this computation argument in favour of the knowledge one. Lavoie regrets that Hayek 'muddied the waters' by introducing it at all (Lavoie: 1985, 92). They reinterpret it as not really meaning that the central planners cannot solve the great number of mathematical equations, but that they will lack the decentralized knowledge to formulate them (Lavoie 1985: 87–91; see also Keizer 1989: 71, 74–5). They thereby switch from Hayek's computation argument of 1935 to his post-1937 knowledge argument. The chronology of Hayek's contributions to the debate shows that in 1935 he indeed still saw the computational difficulties of general-equilibrium models as the main problem of socialist calculation. He published his ideas on the role of knowledge in economics only in 1937, that is *after* Lange had published his response to his 1935 computation argument. The Hayekians cannot accuse Lange *et al.* of replying to the wrong argument, as Hayek had not yet formulated the right one by the time they replied to his earlier charge.

Even so, the criticism of the impossibility of solving billions of equations simultaneously and continuously still stands today. The spectacular development of computer technology and the growth of modern planning theories have still not made the solution of general-equilibrium models possible, as Lange and other 'planometricians' had hoped (Lavoie 1985: 94–5).

Criticism 3: The inability to discover and use all dispersed knowledge

Already in 1935 Hayek introduces his major original contribution to the Austrian critique of socialism: the economic consequences of the dispersal of human knowledge. General-equilibrium models assume that all the knowledge required for solving them is both given and concentrated in the minds of the few members of the central planning board. Hayek rejects both informational assumptions. The idea that all the relevant knowledge is concentrated in the minds of a few experts in the CPB is absurd (Hayek 1935, II: 155). Second, much knowledge does not exist in a ready-made form, but consists of inarticulated knowledge, 'techniques of thought' in the minds of the decision-makers. However, in 1935 this argument is still underelaborated when compared to his detailed arguments on the impracticality of central planning. It gained greater importance with the seminal articles of 1937 and 1945, until it finally came to be his major charge against planning and socialism. This corroborates Kirzner's argument that the Austrians only gradually discovered and evolved their specific paradigm during the course of the calculation debate (Kirzner 1988: 2).

In 'Economics and Knowledge' Hayek distinguishes between two concepts of 'data': the objective facts and the subjective knowledge individuals have. The latter means the 'facts' present in the mind of the acting person, things known subjectively to him (Hayek 1937: 36). This leads to the concept of 'relevant knowledge', the knowledge relevant to a particular individual. The specific knowledge of time and place exists solely as dispersed bits of knowledge possessed by the individuals (Hayek 1945: 77). With respect to this 'unorganized' knowledge every individual has some advantage over all others because he possesses some unique information. As a result there is a 'division of knowledge' between the individuals, analogous to and as important as the division of labour. Mises had already spoken of it as 'the intellectual division of labour'. Now Hayek says that the real central problem of economics is how the spontaneous interaction of numerous individuals, each possessing only bits of subjective knowledge, brings about the co-ordination of their activities (Hayek 1937, 50–1).[4] Hayek's co-ordination problem is: how can the spontaneous actions of individuals bring about a distribution of resources as if made according to a single plan, although nobody has planned it?

It is inadmissable to assume that all the knowledge dispersed over millions of individuals would automatically be in the possession of a central planning authority, as general-equilibrium models do. To assume that this authority possesses the same information as all the decentralized subjects together is to be guilty of the fallacy of composition (Hayek 1940: 202). The reason why these models cannot solve the economic problem is that the 'data' from which they start are not and cannot be given to a single mind to work out the solution. The specific knowledge of time and place does not exist in a concentrated form, but solely as dispersed bits of incomplete and even contradictory knowledge in the possession of individuals (Hayek 1945: 77). The real problem is not so much that the central planner cannot *solve* the millions of equations of a general-equilibrium model, but that he lacks the knowledge to *formulate* them (Vaughn 1980: 545; Lavoie 1985: 87–91). In the Hayekian version of the debate the computational difficulties are subordinate to this informational problem.

The economic problem facing any society is not the neoclassical 'pure logic of choice' of how to allocate given resources over known ends, which is a trivial optimization problem and begs the Austrian question (Bernholz 1987: 149–50; Keizer 1989: 72–3). It is rather how to obtain the best use of resources known to all the members of a society, for ends whose relative importance they alone know. It is a problem of the use of knowledge which is not given to anyone in its totality (Hayek 1945: 78). Kirzner calls the problem created by the decentralized nature of subjective knowledge the 'Hayek knowledge problem'. It is a special case of the 'basic knowledge problem', which is every individual's (including the central planners') basic ignorance of all the facts (Kirzner 1984: 409).

In the context of the socialist controversy the question then is: who is to do the planning? There has to be planning, but is it to be done centrally by the state or by the millions of individuals? The choice is between central and decentralized planning (Hayek 1944: 35). The choice of the rational economic order boils down to the question which of the two allocation mechanisms will make better use of all existing knowledge (Hayek 1945: 79).

The unorganized knowledge of the specific circumstances of time and place cannot enter into statistics and cannot be communicated in statistical form to a central authority. Central planning cannot take them into account and must necessarily use less of the knowledge available in society (Hayek 1945: 83). The central planners cannot solve the 'Hayek knowledge problem' (Kirzner 1984: 413–14). Furthermore, the dispersed facts are continuously changing and these changes can never be fully known, collected and disseminated by any one centre. If the economic problem is that of rapid adaption to changes in the particular circumstances of time and place, then the decisions should be taken by the people possessing the relevant knowledge. Only decentralized decision-making ensures that the knowledge of time and place will be promptly used (Hayek 1945: 84).[5]

Instead of making central planning more necessary, as the proponents of planning maintain, the increasing complexity of the modern division of labour makes market competition the only efficient method for bringing about co-ordination.[6] The more complicated the economy is, the more dependent we are on the division of knowledge between individuals and the more inadequate central planning becomes. Thus the historical development from simple to complex or 'extended' societies works against, instead of for, central planning and socialism.

The separate efforts of the individuals are co-ordinated by the price mechanism, which transmits the relevant information between them (Hayek 1944: 49–50). Hayek sees the price system as an institution which evolved through history to solve the problem of using and co-ordinating dispersed knowledge. In the market the relevant information is communicated to all agents through the intermediary of prices. The price system is a means of communicating information, an 'epistemic machine' functioning with great economy. The individual needs to know very little in order to take the right action. The relevant information is relayed in an abbreviated form, and only to those concerned (Hayek 1945: 86). He calls the market mechanism a 'marvel' and believes it would have been acclaimed as one of the greatest triumphs of the human mind, had it been the result of deliberate human design. The fact that it is not makes people unaware of the guidance it gives their actions. The market extends the span of human utilization of resources beyond that achievable by any one mind, and yet does so without conscious control.

Here Hayek anticipates his later theories of spontaneously evolved institutions and of institutional evolution. Civlization advances by increasing the number of operations mankind performs without thinking about them. In modern capitalist society, which Hayek calls the 'extended order', man uses rules and institutions whose meaning he does not understand. This enables him to avail himself of knowledge which he does not possess individually. The competitive price mechanism discovers and communicates the specific information individuals need, both in order to achieve their own ends and to contribute to the achievement of those of others, of whose existence and purposes they are not even aware. The market is one of those institutions man learnt to use after he had stumbled onto it without understanding it (Hayek 1945: 88).

Criticism 4: Socialist planning leads to economic and political authoritarianism

Already in 'The Competitive Solution' (1940) Hayek raises some non-economic arguments against socialism, anticipating *The Road to Serfdom* of four years later. He asks himself how much personal and political freedom will be preserved under competitive socialism. Despite Lange and Dickinson's claims that consumer sovereignty will prevail in their models, Hayek lists many important instances where the central planners would make arbitrary decisions (Hayek 1940: 204). The first is the volume and direction of new investment; and through that, of a substantial part of the production of final goods as well. Second, there is the choice between private and collective goods. In view of the socialists' preference for communal consumption, this further reduces the area of individual choice and subjects it to authoritarian decision-making. Third, there is the choice between work and leisure, referring to the age-old socialist ideal of labour duty for all citizens. Furthermore, the state will use modern means of consumer manipulation to divert demand into 'socially-desirable' directions. Finally, foreign trade will be controlled as well, as free trade is inconsistent with the principles of collectivism. Hayek concludes that 'there will be precious little economic activity which will not be more or less immediately guided by arbitrary decisions' (Hayek 1940: 205).

He rejected Dobb's authoritarian proposal to make central planning easier by abolishing consumer and worker sovereignty. Such measures might simplify the computation task, but even if production was planned according to the planners' own preferences, they would still need rational scarcity prices and economic calculation. Absolishing consumer sovereignty neither obviates nor solves the calculation problem (Hayek 1935, II: 160). He also rejected the then current belief that socialist planning might well restrict the individuals' freedom of choice, but that this would be limited to the economic sphere of life only. Hayek rejects the erroneous belief that there are purely economic ends of life, which may be sacrificed for higher aims. The ultimate ends of human beings are never economic. There are only economic factors constraining the pursuit of other, non-economic, goals. If a dictator rules over the economic life of individuals, he also controls the means for realising their non-economic goals.

> Economic control is not merely control of a sector of human life which can be separated from the rest; it is the control of the means for all our ends . . . Economic planning would involve direction of almost the whole of our life . . . an authority

directing the whole economic system would be the most powerful monopolist conceivable.

(Hayek 1944: 92–3)

Already in his first contribution to the debate Hayek argued against partial planning for specific sectors of the economy. Isolated planning measures will not work and partial attempts to plan 'will necessitate further and further measures of control until all economic activity is brought under one central authority' (Hayek 1935, I: 21). He refers to 'self-frustrating tendencies of any isolated act of planning' (Hayek 1935, I: 23). The close interdependence between all economic phenomena makes it difficult to stop planning at any particular point. Once the working of the market is impeded beyond a certain degree, the planner will be forced to extend his controls until they become all-pervasive. Once the state sector exceeds a certain proportion of the whole economy, the effects of its actions dominate the whole system (Hayek 1944: 61).

Market competition is the only method by means of which human activities can be adjusted to each other without coercive or arbitrary intervention by authority. His plea for competition is therefore also political, because it dispenses with the need for conscious social control (Hayek 1944: 36). His knowledge argument provides him with a scientific basis for the case against dictatorship. Dictatorships have an inferior economic performance compared to democracies with a competitive market. The reason is that in a dictatorship decision-making is based on the knowledge of the dictator only. He cannot possess the knowledge the millions of individuals have and he will suppress their preferences anyway. His decisions must take less account of the specific circumstances known to them only and are therefore less optimal.

Criticism 5: Shortcomings of the market socialist model

Hayek starts his 1940 critique of the 'competitive' or 'market socialist' models by saying that the Austrian critique had thus far successfully refuted two proposals for a socialist economy:

1 The original socialist belief in a money- and priceless-economy (*Naturalwirtschaft*)
2 The hope that the equations of general-equilibrium models could be solved by a central planning authority.

The models of 'competitive socialism' of Lange and Dickinson are their reply to his computation argument against general-equilibrium models. He rejects Lange's statement that the Austrian critique is theoretically refuted by scientific proof that the principles of economic theory also apply to a socialist economy (as demonstrated by Barone). He resents Lange's insinuation that Mises and he had denied that such principles *ought* to apply - on the contrary, this had already been argued by Wieser in 1884. Their critique said that these principles *could* not be applied in a socialist economy. Lange in fact appropriates an argument of the Austrians and presents it as proof against them. The socialists cover up their own retreat by creating confusion about the issue at stake (Hayek 1940: 183).

Hayek criticizes the competitive models under three headings:

1 Do they still substitute a 'planned' system for the 'anarchy of the market', as all socialists intended?
2 Does the competitive solution solve the problem of rational calculation, that is, will it be efficient?
3 Are the competitive models applicable in practice?

He rejects the competitive models' claim to be called 'socialist'. They will disappoint all socialists who want to replace the 'anarchy' of the market by a deliberately planned system. What is left of the vaunted superiority of planning over the market, if the 'planned' economy must rely on market competition? Can one still speak of 'planning' and of 'socialism' in these models? Orthodox Marxists like P.M. Sweezy and M. Dobb also rejected them as not being socialist and they were anathema under the communist regimes in Eastern Europe.[7] In 1971 P.C. Roberts concluded that these models do not replace the market, as Marxist socialism demands they should, but vindicate it instead. They merely dress the market up in planning terminology. Instead of refuting Mises and Hayek, they actually admit the correctness of their critique (Roberts 1971: 566, 575).

Hayek rejects claims that the trial-and-error procedure will lead as rapidly to the same efficiency prices as does the competitive market. He ascribes this fallacy of the neoclassical socialists to their preoccupation with stationary-equilibrium theory. In the real world where continuous change is the rule, Hayek believes the bureaucratic CPB adjustment procedure to be far inferior to decentralized market adjustment in securing the most rapid and complete adaption to changing circumstances (Hayek 1940: 188).

He rejected a circumvention of the computation problem suggested by the socialists, that one should start with the prices of the old capitalist regime and by a method of trial and error gradually seek to establish the new values for the socialist system (Lange 1936: 86). Hayek believes the transition from capitalism to socialism will be so great that the elaborate system of capitalist price relations would not survive. Furthermore, separate price changes on individual markets will alter scarcity relationships on all the others, obviating their partial equilibrating possibilities. Central price-setting must take the form of the solution of a general-equilibrium model or else be abandoned (Hayek 1935, II: 157–8).

The competitive solution is inapplicable to non-homogenous goods, such as goods produced to individual order, buildings, ships, and so on. Here prices cannot be fixed so as to equate demand and supply. Either the trial-and-error procedure will be abandoned and the CPB sets their prices on an authoritative basis, or the 'central' setting becomes a pure formality (Hayek 1940: 188–9). There will be less differentiation between prices according to the differences in quality of the goods and the specific circumstances of time and place. The managers would have no inducement nor the possibility of making use of their knowledge of the special opportunities offered by the circumstances of time and place (ibid.: 192–3).

Lange and Dickenson stated that the prices set by the CPB are to be fixed for some time, and that the managers must treat them as constant. For how long are they to be fixed? Is it to be for a definite period in advance, or are they changed whenever the CPB thinks it advisable? Hayek concludes that price changes under market socialism will occur later than they would if prices were to be determined by decentralized market parties (Hayek ibid.: 192). In practice they would only be changed at lengthy intervals and many prices would differ substantially from those obtaining in a free market system. This means that the managers will make faulty decisions on the basis of obsolete and hence irrational prices. If such prices exercise a parametric funtion they will give the wrong signals to the managers. They would cause excess demands and supplies and lead to resource misallocation (ibid.: 193–4; Vaughn 1980: 546).

Another problem caused by changing prices periodically by decree is the anticipation of future price changes. Lange wants the managers to treat prices as constant when deciding on the quantities to be produced, but how must they behave when they know that the present prices are wrong and will be changed? Must they anticipate the expected price changes, or act as if they did not know? Furthermore, costs also depend on price expectations and future prices. Present costs do not only depend on present prices but also on whether these prices were correctly foreseen in the past. Therefore managerial decisions under the Langean rules depend partly on expectations. But the managers cannot be blamed for incorrectly anticipating the future, if that depends on the decisions of the central planning authorities (Hayek 1940; 198).

Hayek asks how the CPB will *ensure* that the managers produce at the point where price equals lowest marginal costs? Cost reductions under capitalism are brought about by price competition, but that is absent in Lange's market socialism. The neoclassical socialists treat cost curves as if they were objectively given facts. They are not aware that the cheapest method of production is not given, but a thing to be continuously *discovered* by the entrepreneur. It is not always the established man in charge of an existing plant who will discover what the best method is. How can the CPB apply its marginal cost rules if 'costs are not objective and given, but subjective and known only to the 'man on the spot' (Bradley 1981: 33). Competitive capitalism gives newcomers the opportunity to break into a market by undercutting the existing producers. This is no longer possible when prices are fixed by the CPB. The CPB must now be convinced theoretically that the newcomer should be given a chance to try and produce at lower than the existing costs. But he cannot experiment with undercutting the existing firms in practice (Hayek 1940: 196–7). Here Hayek introduces two important concepts into economic theory: the subjectivity of costs and the discovery of knowledge as an active process under competitive capitalism.[8]

Hayek briefly mentions the issue of bureaucracy in market socialism. All the calculations of the managers will have to be examined by the CPB, who must control not only what they did, but also what they might have done. This will lead to 'the worst forms of bureaucracy' (ibid.: 199). Lange indeed admitted that the greatest danger to (market) socialism is that of bureaucratization (Lange 1936–7: 109).

On the issue of managerial risk-taking under market socialism Hayek holds the opposite view to Mises and Dickinson. Whereas they believed propertyless managers would be excessively risk-prone, he thinks that they will be afraid of taking risks. The reason is that someone else in authority must decide afterwards whether they were justified in doing so (Hayek 1940; 199).

Modern Hayekians conclude that the market socialist models of Lange *et al.* were fundamentally misconceived. They were conceived as an answer to Hayek's static computation argument, rather than to the basic thrust of the Austrian challenge. They tried to solve a very different problem from the one Mises had originally posed, but which Hayek himself in 1935 had sidetracked onto the issue of computability (Lavoie 1985: 117). Neither socialist nor neoclassical economics understood the real meaning and importance of the Austrian critique until the Austrian revival of the 1980s.

DIFFERENCES BETWEEN THE CRITIQUES OF MISES AND HAYEK

The critiques of socialism by Mises and Hayek differ considerably, partly on account of the different times they wrote and opponents they faced and partly on account of the major theoretical discoveries each of them made. Mises countered the utopian proposals of marxist revolutionaries at the zenith of the socialist tide. His original critique was aimed at various proposals for

1 A moneyless socialist *Naturalwirtschaft*.
2 Marxist socialism without markets and scarcity prices.
3 All marxist proposals for the abolition of private property rights in the means of production.

In 1920 he had to fight several different socialist misconceptions simultaneously, with the result that he mixes his arguments against them. The author has argued that his critique can be interpreted in terms of modern property rights and principal–agent theory (Keizer 1993). Mises advocated dispersed private property rights in the means of production as the only way to establish genuine scarcity prices and as a means of solving the principal-agent problem in managerial firms. His critique is ultimately based upon private-property rights, no matter how often he mentions the necessity of money, markets and prices. It is private property rights in the means of production that give rise to genuine scarcity prices, which enable the individuals to calculate and act rationally. Mises defines socialism exclusively in terms of its property rights: as state ownership of the means of production. Central planning is merely a corollary of this. In his view it is state ownership of the means of production that causes the economic irrationality of socialism, not the concomitant allocation mechanism of central or any other kind of planning.

Hayek, on the other hand, sees state planning as the essence of socialism and directs his critique at the allocation mechanism. He defines socialism as a system of state planning, as opposed to Mises, who defined it as a system of state property. It is noticeable that property rights play no role in Hayek's argumentation and are not mentioned in his contributions to the debate in the period between 1935 and 1945. Only in his final work on socialism does 'several property' play a minor role. But it does so in the context of his *political* philosophy, as an element of the private domain of the individual and as the prerequisite for his freedom (Hayek 1989, Ch. 2). He does not discuss the economic functions of property rights under capitalism and socialism. In his contributions to the debate, Hayek argues solely in defence of the competitive market mechanism, as opposed to central or Langean CPB planning.

The critiques of the two Austrians can be reconciled by seeing them as complementary: Mises arguing the necessity of private property rights in the means of production and Hayek the superiority of the competitive market mechanism. Together they present the Austrian case for the institutions of capitalism, private property and market allocation, as against those of socialism, state ownership and central planning.

The differences between them can also be understood by referring to the opponents each of them faced. Whereas Mises confronted Central European Marxists with no knowledge of marginalist microeconomics, Hayek debated with Anglo-Saxon economists well versed in mainstream theory. Mises had to argue fundamental institutional matters with non-economists, whereas Hayek debated the functioning of alternative allocation mechanisms with neoclassical economists. This made his critique more comprehensible to mainstream economists than that of Mises, but also precluded him from analysing institutional issues like property rights and incentives.

As a result both authors differ in their treatment of motivational issues. The lack of effective managerial incentives under socialism plays a major role in Mises's critique. Hayek on the other hand hardly mentions the subject. This is due to his disregard of institutional matters, such as the incentive functions of property rights. This neglect he shares with his neoclassical opponents, who explicitly relegated motivational issues to the field of sociology. In none of his contributions does he discuss incentive mechanisms to motivate the socialist managers. Neither does he respond to the socialists' claim that the salaried managers of modern corporations will perform as well for the socialist state as they previously did for the capitalist shareholders. They believed that the efficiency of the salaried managers (and hence that of their firms) would persist under a socialist regime. The 'managerial revolution' poses a serious threat to the Austrian case against socialism (Reekie 1984: 136 ff.). It can be argued that Mises's property rights approach refutes this point (Keizer 1993). Hayek curiously does not discuss this matter at all. The reason must be that this problem refers to a concrete institutional matter, the incentive effects of property rights, on which subject Hayek is silent.

In recent years the American Misesians Rothbard and Salerno have accused the Hayekians of distorting the 'true' Austrian paradigm. Their charge comprises all aspects of the Austrian paradigm, such as its methodology, epistemology, purposefulness, the role of the entrepreneur, and so on. In this chapter only their quarrel over what constitutes the 'real' Austrian critique of socialism is relevant. The Hayekians Vaughn and Lavoie maintain that the core of the Austrian critique is the 'knowledge' argument of Hayek (supported by the 'alert actor' theory of Kirzner), whilst the Misesians stress the 'calculation' argument (Salerno 1990; Rothbard 1991, 1992).

During the Austrian revival of the 1980s Vaughn and Lavoie elaborated Hayek's arguments against neoclassical theory and the socialist models. They stress the role of the competitive market as an epistemic institution, discovering and disseminating knowledge to all participants by means of price signals. They also accentuate the uncertainty caused by the continuous change characterizing real-life economies, which will prevent the CPB from ever acquiring all the relevant information. To them Hayek's great discovery was the problem that dispersed knowledge poses in economics, as well as the concept of the competitive market as a spontaneously evolved institution for overcoming it. Therefore they elaborate Hayek's knowledge argument in their version of the Austrian critique of socialism (Vaughn 1980, 1990; Lavoie 1985).

The Misesians on the other hand say Mises's critique of socialism is that the socialist planner or manager cannot calculate rationally in the absence of private property and a market for the means of production. According to Mises they still could not calculate even if they *did* possess all the relevant information assumed absent by the Hayekians. The absence of markets for the means of production does not deny the CPB 'knowledge', but the possibility of economic *calculation*. They find the entire Hayekian emphasis on knowledge misconceived and accuse the Hayekians of fatally changing the entire focus of the Austrian critique (Rothbard 1990: 65; 1992: 19–20).

Despite these differences the Misesians and Hayekians agree that:

1 Economic rationality is theoretically and practically impossible under socialism: neither the general-equilibrium models of Barone *et al.*, nor the 'competitive socialist' models of Lange, Dickinson and Lerner refute the Austrian charge of economic irrationality.
2 Hayek's 1935 arguments were no admission that Mises's original challenge was wrong and they constituted no retreat from Mises's challenge.

They differ, however, on most other aspects of their critiques. It seems that the fourth phase of the 'socialist' debate will be between the neo-Austrians themselves, on the subject of what constitutes the 'true' Austrian paradigm and the 'real' Austrian critique of socialism.

THE INFLUENCE OF THE DEBATE ON HAYEK'S THOUGHT

The socialist calculation debate had a decisive influence on the development of Hayek's thought and on modern Austrian economics. It was through his involvement in the debate that Hayek came to realize the nature of the specifically 'Austrian' paradigm in economics and that he developed many of his ideas on economics, epistemology, methodology and political philosophy. Kirzner says that the debate functioned as a catalyst in the development of modern Austrian thought: it made the Austrians clarify and articulate their dissent from mainstream economics and develop their own paradigm (Kirzner 1988: 1). This applies especially to Hayek. It was in the course of his controversies with the neoclassical socialists Lange and Dickinson that he gradually realized how much his ideas differed not only from theirs, but actually from the neoclassical tradition they represented. Before the debate he still saw himself as a mainstream marginalist. It was only through the differences manifested in the socialist calculation debate that he and Mises became aware of the gulf separating them from the other marginalist schools.

To the Walrasian school the general equilibrium models of Barone, Bilimovich and others proved adequately that rational calculation under socialism was theoretically possible. To the Marshallians the market socialist model of Lange was a perfectly logical rebuttal of Hayek's computation criticism. If the Austrians rejected these proposed solutions to their critiques, they had to advance other than immanent reasons for doing so. Only by rejecting the paradigm on which these models were based could they successfully refute them as 'solutions' to their problems. In doing so they gradually developed their own conceptions of the Austrian paradigm. In their view the neoclassical paradigm applies the wrong methodology to solve the wrong problem. The methodology to be used is not that of the natural sciences, a practice Hayek criticized as 'scientism'. The economic problem is not the one defined by L. Robbins as the maximization of known ends with given means, what Hayek called 'the pure logic of choice'; nor is it the achievement of equilibrium in the context of a static environment. For Hayek the economic problem is the discovery and use of dispersed knowledge for purposes which the individuals themselves only know, in such a way as to achieve the co-ordination of all their individual plans. This occurs in a world of perpetual change, where uncertainty necessitates speculative behaviour based on the individual expectations of the future.

It is said that the years after 1936 were Hayek's 'years in the wilderness'. He is supposed to have turned away from economics and dedicated himself to the study of legal theory and political science after his business cycle theory had been eclipsed by that of Keynes. However, his undoubted withdrawal from pure economics after the early 1940s need not be seen in this disparaging light. It can equally well be said that his involvement in the socialist calculation debate shifted his focus of interest from purely economic to meta-economic issues. He found the root cause of 'constructivist rationalism' to lie in the spheres of methodology and political thought, rather than in that of economics. The fact that the late 1930s were years of high politicization, with the noontide of fascism and Stalinism, also played a role. Under these circumstances his resistance to what he saw as encroaching interventionism, central planning, étatism and totalitarianism may well have seemed more important to him than further additions to economic theory. For these reasons the debate on socialism played a major role in turning his theoretical attention away from pure economics towards methodology, legal theory and political philosophy.

It was soon after his publication of *Collectivist Economic Planning* in 1935 that he made his major epistemological discoveries about the nature and dispersal of knowledge. It can be argued that these discoveries were partly due to his participation in the socialist-calculation debate. It can also be shown that his socio-political philosophy follows from these epistemological premisses. Hayek constructed an integrated body of social, legal and political theory on the basis of his theory of knowledge. Some of these ideas were already discussed and in the context of this chapter we can only list his further socio-political contributions:

1. The price mechanism as epistemic institution disseminating knowledge.
2. The nature of competition as a discovery process.
3. The methodology of the social and the natural sciences.
4. The truth status of economic theories.
5. Different concepts of freedom and the nature of a free society.
6. Different concepts of justice.
7. The Rule of Law.
8. The usefulness of unconscious rule following.
9. Conscious design versus the spontaneous creation of institutions.
10. The socio-biological theory of institutional evolution.

These manifold contributions of Hayek in the fields of economics, methodology, sociology, legal and political philosophy and his own brand of institutional evolutionism may be seen as partly deriving from his involvement in the socialist calculation debate.

HAYEK'S CRITIQUE AND THE FAILURE OF SOCIALISM

With the collapse of the socialist economies in Eastern Europe after 1989 it seems that the Austrian critics of socialist economics were right after all. Theory as well as decades of practice proved socialism to be a fundamentally irrational economic system, as they had spent all their lives arguing. The question then arises whether the failure of socialism can be attributed to any of the reasons advanced by the

Austrians; and if so, whether those of Mises or of Hayek are the more relevant? It is doubtful if the socialist collapse can be wholly explained by either of the two Austrian critiques. Hayek and the Hayekians would attribute it to the central planners' lack of knowledge and its economic consequences, whereas the Misesians would ascribe it to their inability to calculate and act rationally. Both explanations seem too abstract and monocausal to explain the failure of existing socialism in all its concrete manifestations.

The most important single cause of the collapse seems to be the notorious inefficiency of the giant state enterprises with their perennial losses, which drained the socialist economies. This general inefficiency had various causes, amongst them calculatory and motivational ones fitting the Austrian critique. The notorious irrationality of the socialist price system can be explained by both the Misesian and the Hayekian theories. Mises has shown the fundamental irrationality of socialist prices in the absence of real markets for the means of production, leading to arbitrary and irrational decisions. Hayek showed that socialist prices would be obsolete and in disequilibrium for most of the time, not reflecting the real scarcities and giving wrong signals to the enterprise managers. The different criticisms of both authors explain the calculation problems of the socialist economies due to their irrational price systems. Both Austrians say that without rational prices there can be no rational economic calculation and allocation. As Mises graphically formulated it in 1920, the socialist economy would 'flounder in the ocean of possible and conceivable economic combinations, without the compass of economic calculation' (Mises in Hayek 1935: 110).

Another major factor contributing to the inefficiency of the socialist economies was the poor motivation of the state enterprise managers (and through them, the rest of the workforce). This is a purely Misesian reason for the failure of socialism. Poor motivation is evidence of a badly solved principal–agent problem, that the principal has ineffective control over his agents. The population (represented by its government and central planners) as the ultimate owners of the nationalized means of production is the 'principal' and the managers and workers are its 'agents'. Under the socialist property rights structure the population lacks effective control over the managers. This enabled them to pursue their own objectives (comprising *inter alia* managerial perquisites and 'leisure at work') at the expense of the income and wealth of the population. In these terms property rights theory explains the low productivity and profitability of socialist industry, contributing to the ultimate collapse of the economy (Keizer 1993). This explanation is more in line with Mises's critique than with the knowledge argument of Hayek.

Hayek's prime argument – the central planners' lack of the specific knowledge of time and place – is applicable to the central determination of the annual production plans for the state enterprises and collective farms. The Soviet planners tried to overcome the Hayek knowledge problem by acquiring decentralized information from the enterprise directors by means of 'counterplans'. These were annual plans the directors had to draw up themselves on the basis of their knowledge of local conditions and capabilities and send on to their superior authorities. The central and decentralized plans were then aligned (or 'balanced') at a middle level in the planning pyramid. This practice of 'planning from above and from below' was meant to yield optimal plans incorporating the specific knowledge of the decentralized agents. However, the badly solved principal–agent problem between the central planners and the enterprise managers thwarted this solution. The managers pursued their own objectives by striving for 'slack plans' with easy plan targets. To this effect they understated their production capacities and overstated their input requirements. The central planners anticipated on this behaviour by initially over-tightening their central plans. In this way the 'planning' under existing socialism turned into strategic tugs-of-war between the central planners on the one hand and the enterprise directors on the other over the 'tautness' of the plans. This was euphemistically called 'man-to-man planning', the outcome of which depended on the relative bargaining power of both parties. It had nothing to do with the objective capabilities of the enterprises. In this way the true specific knowledge of time and place was not incorporated in the Soviet enterprise plans, lowering the productivity of the economy.

This was even more the case with the collective farms, whose production plans were determined in Moscow regardless of local conditions and knowledge. The farms received mandatory plans for growing crops locally known to be totally unsuited to the conditions in the area. In many instances (e.g. the notorious 'virgin lands' campaign) the results were agricultural or ecological disasters. In both instances Hayek's knowledge criticism is relevant: central planning must dispense with decentralized knowledge and is therefore based on less and worse knowledge than the competitive market. In this sense Hayek's knowledge critique does explain a major part of the failure of existing socialism.

Hayek's contention that the socialist managers would be risk-averse is, however, proved wrong by empirical evidence from Eastern Europe. Under existing socialism their demand for investment capital was insatiable, as it was supplied free or at too low a rate of interest. As the state budget ultimately recompensed the state enterprises for losses (Kornai's 'soft budget restraint'), there was no limit to the 'investment hunger' of socialist managers, with the resultant waste of investment capital and the creation of 'investment cycles'. Mises's expectation that they would take excessive risks (and therefore demand too much capital) was more correct than Hayek's opposite view.

After the collapse of the communist dictatorships in Eastern Europe there is an increasing appreciation of Hayek's economic and socio-political arguments in favour of the free market, as well as interest in his legal and political philosophy, such as his plea for the Rule of Law and for spontaneous social institutions. Whereas in the West it may still be fashionable to decry *The Road to Serfdom* as a 'mere political pamphlet', it is widely read in newly democratized countries like Czechoslovakia and Hungary. It is quite possible that Hayek's greatest conributions to the social sciences do not lie in the field of economics but in that of legal and political philosophy. If, following Lange's gibe, a statue of Mises should be erected in the hall of the Central Planning Board of the socialist state, then one of Friedrich Hayek should be set up in the parliaments of the new democratic states in Eastern Europe.

NOTES

1 The major contributions to the Hayekian version are Lavoie (1981) and (1985) and Vaughn (1980) and (1990). The Mises version is revived in P. Murrell (1983), 'Did the Theory of Market Socialism Answer the Challenge of von Mises? A reinterpretation of the Socialist Controversy', *History of Political Economy* 15(1). For a survey of the literature of the Austrian revival on this subject, see Keizer (1989).

2 It did not start the debate on socialist economics in Great Britain though, as in the previous years there had already been a high-level controversy on the subject between M. Dobb, A.P. Lerner, H.D. Dickinson and others.

3 'This fact that one central authority has to solve the economic problem of distributing a limited amount of resources between a practically infinite number of competing purposes, that constitutes the problem of socialism' (Hayek 1935, I: 16–17).

4 Hayek formulates his 'co-ordination problem' as follows: 'that central question of all social sciences: how can the combination of fragments of knowledge existing in different minds bring about results which, if they were to be brought about deliberately, would require a knowledge on the part of the directing mind which no single person can possess?' (Hayek 1937: 54).

5 It will be noticed that Hayek mentions two different criteria for judging the efficiency of an economic system: that of using all knowledge and that of adapting to change. He deemed both of major importance and found them neglected by traditional theory.

6 'Compared with this method of solving the economic problem by means of decentralisation plus automatic coordination, the more obvious method of central direction is incredibly clumsy, primitive and limited in scope' (Hayek 1944: 50).

7 For orthodox Marxist critiques of the market socialist models, see P.M. Sweezy, *Socialism*, New York: McGraw Hill, 1949, and M. Dobb, *Welfare Economics and the Economics of Socialism*, Cambridge: Cambridge University Press, 1969.

8 Hayek (1978) worked out the idea of the discovery of knowledge more fully. However, both the 'subjectivity' and the 'discovery' points are hardly worked out by Hayek in his contributions to the debate. In their rational reconstruction of the 'Hayekian version' of the debate the Hayekians tend to read more into these statements than he actually wrote (see Vaughn 1980: 549–50; Lavoie 1985: 101, 164).

REFERENCES

Bergson, A.P. (1948) 'Socialist Economics', in H.S. Ellis (ed.) *A Survey of Contemporary Economics*, Philadelphia: Blakistan, pp. 412–48.

Bernholz, P. (1987) 'Information, Motivation and the Problem of Rational Economic Calculation in Socialism', in S. Pejovich, (ed.) *Socialism: Institutional, Philosophical and Economic Issues*, Dordrecht: Kluwer.

Bradley, R. (1981) 'Market Socialism: A Subjectivist Evaluation', *The Journal of Libertarian Studies* 5(1): 23–39.

Hayek, F.A. (1935, I) 'The Nature and History of the Problem', in F.A. Hayek (ed.) *Collectivist Economic Planning*, London: Routledge & Kegan Paul, 1935, pp. 1–40.

—— (1935, II) 'The Present State of the Debate', in F.A. Hayek (ed.) *Collectivist Economic Planning*, London: Routledge & Kegan Paul, 1935, pp. 201–43.

—— (1937) 'Economics and Knowledge', in F.A. Hayek *Individualism and Economic Order*, London: Routledge & Kegan Paul, 1949, pp. 33–56.

—— (1940) 'Socialist Calculation II: The Competitive "Solution"', in F.A. Hayek, *Individualism and Economic Order*, London: Routledge & Kegan Paul, 1949, pp. 81–208.

—— (1944) *The Road to Serfdom*, Chicago: University of Chicago Press.

—— (1945) 'The Use of Knowledge in Society', in F.A. Hayek, *Individualism and Economic Order*, London: Routledge & Kegan Paul, 1949, pp. 77–91.

—— (1978) 'Competition as a discovery procedure', in F.A. Hayek *New Studies in Philosophy, Politics, Economics and the History of Ideas*,Chicago: University of Chicago Press.

—— (1989) *The Fatal Conceit: The Errors of Socialism*, London: Routledge.

Keizer, W. (1989) 'Recent Reinterpretations of the Socialist Calculation Debate', in J. Krabbe, A. Nentjes and H. Visser (eds) *Austrian Economics: Roots and Ramifications Reconsidered*, Manchester: MCB University Press, 1989, pp. 63–83.

—— (1993) 'The Property Rights Basis of von Mises' Arguments against Socialism', in J.G. Backhaus (ed.) *Modern Applications of Austrian Thought* (forthcoming).

Kirzner, I.M. (1984) 'Economic Planning and the Knowledge Problem' *Cato Journal* 4(2): 407–18.

—— (1988) 'The Economic Calculation Debate: Lessons for Austrians', *The Review of Austrian Economics* 2: 1–18.

Lange, O. (1936–7) 'On the Economic Theory of Socialism', in B.E. Lippincott (ed.) *On the Economic Theory of Socialism*, New York: McGraw Hill, 1964.

Lavoie, D. (1981) 'A Critique of the Standard Account of the Socialist Calculation Debate', *Journal of Libertarian Studies* 5(1): 44–87.

—— (1985) *Rivalry and Central Planning*, Cambridge: Cambridge University Press.

Lerner, A.P. (1944) *The Economics of Control*, New York:Macmillan.

Murrell, P. (1983) 'Did the theory of market socialism answer the challenge of von Mises? A reinterpretation of the socialist controversy', History of Political Economy, 15(1): 92–105.

Reekie, W.D. (1984) *Markets, Entrepreneurs and Liberty*, Brighton: Harvester.

Roberts, P.C. (1971) 'Oskar Lange's Theory of Socialist Planning', *Journal of Political Economy*, 19(3) pp. 564–77.

Rothbard, M.N. (1991) 'The End of Socialism and the Calculation Debate Revisted', *Review of Austrian Economics* 5(2): 51–76.

—— (1992) 'The Present State of Austrian Economics', working paper of the Ludwig von Mises Institute, Auburn (AL): 1–44.

Salerno, J.T. (1990) 'Ludwig von Mises as Social Rationalist', in M.N. Rothbard (ed.) *Review of Austrian Economics* 4: 26–54.

Vaughn, K. (1980) 'Economic Calculation under Socialism: The Austrian Contribution', *Economic Inquiry* 18 (4): 535–54.

—— (1990) 'Introduction' to T.J.B. Hoff, *Economic Calculation in the Socialist Economy*, Indianapolis: Liberty Press (first published in 1949).

12

HAYEK'S SPONTANEOUS ORDER

The 'correct' versus the 'corrigible' society

Marina Bianchi

In the recent resurgence of institutional ideas, and in particular of the emergence and evolution of social norms and institutions, Hayek occupies a central position. Two themes are dominant in his research: (1) the role of knowledge, or the way knowledge is created and diffused in society and (2) the role of social evolution, or the way norms are produced and learnt through a gradual process of trial and error. Hayek's sustained insistence on these two features of the constitution of societal rules has helped give the recent institutional debate new directions.

In the first place, if knowledge exists only in dispersed and partial forms and nobody can step out of society and decide its overall order, then the way norms evolve takes the form of a spontaneous, unintended outcome.

In the second place, if this process of unplanned emergence of social rules can be represented as a process of learning, of acquiring and transmitting knowledge, then the process by which rules emerge is necessarily a process of change and discovery.

Finally, the individualism propagated by Hayek forces us to think about rule formation in terms of individual choice incentives rather than by assuming a general disposition to accept common rules.

If we translate some paradigmatic situations of social interaction and interdependency of decisions into a game-theoretic structure, as has become more and more common in the recent institutional literature, Hayek's analysis of social order offers a strong theoretical basis for a game theorist to model the way institutions form. Hayek's unintended-consequences argument, for example, captures the passage of time and the experimentation process that seems to intervene in repeated games; individualism underpins the use of dominant strategies in determining equilibrium solutions; the role of knowledge may become an important tool in the selection of equilibrium and, also, in the discovery of new equilibrium solutions.

We shall see, however, that while Hayek is more sensitive to the role of learning and error correction, a feature that cannot be (easily) structured in a game-theoretic form, game theory helps us to be more precise about the incentive structure that regulates rule creation.

The essay is organized as follows. I start by recollecting some of the main features Hayek attributes to the constitution of social rules. I then compare them to some of the results recently reached in institutionalist literature using, to facilitate the comparison, a game-theoretic approach. Mutual clarification results from this comparison. Finally, I use some of Hayek's suggestions to outline further possible developments in both approaches.

DESIGNED VERSUS SPONTANEOUS ORDER

In comparing different rules of social order Hayek draws a first fundamental distinction which remains the dominant theme of all his reflections. The distinction is between norms that result from conscious design and planned action and norms which, on the contrary, are a spontaneous creation, the gradual result and accumulated experience of many generations. The first set of rules belongs to the internal behaviour of organizations, the second describes the external interdependencies among organizations.[1]

The main source of error in describing how institutions emerge and work consists, for Hayek, in collapsing these two different explanations and features of social structures into one. Such collapsing occurs when we consider all rules of social interaction to be the result of a planning mind and when we assimilate all social rules to the rules of organizations.

In this uniform sort of explanation all beneficial institutions are ascribed to design; moreover, their social usefulness is actually deduced from the fact that they are planned: 'only such design has made or can make them useful for our purpose' (Hayek 1973:9). This muddling can be traced back to the Cartesian rationalistic approach and to its development in the contractarian theory of Rousseau (Hayek 1978:5–6). The idea is that 'man's reason alone should enable him to construct society anew' (Hayek 1973:10). This is an idea that has been dubbed more recently the 'artificer bias' kind of explanation (Ullmann-Margalit 1978): since social structures show orderly, patterned rules, they are (must be) planned – or, what amounts to the same thing, only because planned, are social structures orderly.

This view, which attributes the origin of all social institutions to invention or design, is sharply contrasted by Hayek to another, according to which the orderliness of society is largely due to a process labelled initially simply 'growth' and later 'evolution' (Hayek 1973:9). What Hayek has in mind here is the order that descends from a process of experimentation and trials, from a process of error correction which requires the efforts and accumulated 'hard-earned' experience of many generations (Hayek 1960: 60). This pre-Darwinian evolutionary view is, for Hayek, the great contribution of that tradition of thought initiated by Mandeville and Hume and continued by the Scottish moral philosophers of the eighteenth century, such as Adam Smith and Ferguson in the field of economics, and Edmund Burke in the field of political thought (Hayek 1948: 8–9; 1973: 22).

But what makes this view of evolutionary, spontaneous order a better analytical tool than the view of planned order? The answer is based on what Hayek describes as the use of knowledge in society, the way knowledge is acquired and transmitted through social interaction. This represents his main contribution to the problem.

THE CO-ORDINATING ROLE OF THE MARKET

In the complex order of modern society knowledge exists only in 'the dispersed bits of incomplete and frequently contradictory knowledge which all the separate individuals possess' (Hayek 1945:77). The problem of social order therefore becomes the problem of how to connect and match independent plans and individual expectations; how to utilize a knowledge that nobody possesses in its totality (ibid.: 78). To turn this problem over to a central authority would require not only that the authority collect all the information surrounding individual decisions, but also that it convey back to individuals the additional information necessary for their plans to be modified and mutually adjusted. But no central authority, be it a central planning board or a wise legislator, is up to the task; hence it is clear that the problem, thus regarded, has no solution. No single mind can ever reach the infinite micro-level precision that each particular decision process implies.

The solution must rely therefore on a mechanism that is able to utilize individual knowledge without any individual really needing to know the overall outcome, a system which, though based on the decentralized contribution of every one of its members, does not rely, for its existence, on any of them (Hayek 1946: 12). This mechanism, which embodies more knowledge than does any collective body of social planners, is for Hayek the mechanism of the spontaneous, self-generating order. It is through this system of undeliberate collecting and disseminating knowledge that the complex set of rules which connects us into societies slowly emerges.

Evolved codes of law, languages, family organizations, moral rules as well as rules of conduct, are the result of this process, which gradually and tentatively selected better-fit and socially more beneficial institutions (see, for example, Hayek 1978:253). The market with its system of property rights and legally enforceable rules, represents the best example of this evolved set of institutions.

The problem that the market has to solve is in fact how the particular knowledge embedded in every individual plan can be diffused and made general. How, for example, can the minimum cost of production be discovered; how can the desires and attitudes of unknown customers become known (Hayek 1946:100–1); which goods are scarce goods and just how scarce are they (Hayek 1978:181). These are all problems that measure the efficiency of the communication system of the market. The price system is the communication system here. Prices are the informational device which enables individuals to acquire the information necessary constantly to change and readjust their choices. 'Prices direct their attention to what is worth finding out about market offers for various things and services' (ibid.: 182). Prices detect potential and unused opportunities and transform them into effective ones (ibid.: 185, 188).

Simply by letting themselves be guided by these common indicators (Hayek 1978: 60), people have learnt to substitute abstract rules for 'the needs of known fellows' and for coercive, imposed ends (ibid.: 61). Through this system an entire new set of opportunities to be exploited has been opened up.[2]

Market prices, therefore, do not simply constitute a matching-of-expectations device. Beyond this, they signal where new opportunities are present, where as yet unexplored needs can be satisfied, and how completely unknown people can be reached. In this way they activate a process of discovery, a process unthinkable under face-to-face exchange relationships, much less when a multitude of unconnected individuals is forcibly ordered in their behaviour by central edict.[3]

This is a point which is worth stressing further.

COMMUNICATION FAILURES

In an article commenting on the role that in Hayek's analysis the price mechanism plays in solving the problem of dispersed knowledge, Kirzner compares the market price system to the lights regulating traffic (Kirzner 1985: 193ff.). Drivers approaching street intersections face a problem of communication and co-ordination among their mutual and interdependent decisions. Failures to co-ordinate, which may obviously result in costly delays and destructive collisions, reflect a problem of the dispersal of knowledge (ibid.:194). Each driver, though perfectly aware of his own intentions, simply does not know those of the other drivers. In the absence of a superior 'planning mind' (ibid.: 195), a system of traffic signals, by providing a communication mechanism which 'reveals' each (rule-following) driver's intentions, will solve the co-ordination problem. This is a move towards efficiency.

There is, however, Kirzner adds, another way in which we can say that the traffic signalling system achieves co-ordination efficiently. This second way is clearer when we start to ask how the system works in, say, trying to eliminate delays. If the system is programmed so as to register daily traffic frequency and to correct timing correspondingly, a timing co-ordination will be reached. But this co-ordinating activity now results in the system's ability to detect information from the uncoordinated activity of the drivers as the base for further improving timing. This signal system achieves co-ordination by 'including its property of improving itself by learning from the unfortunate results of its earlier imperfections' (ibid.: 196).

The same considerations apply to the case of competitive equilibrium prices. On the one hand, they provide the information necessary for co-ordination without anybody knowing the infinite details pertinent to exchange. They are an 'apparatus of registration which automatically records all the relevant effects of individual actions' (Hayek 1944: 49). On the other, as in the example of the initially only partially efficient traffic signal mechanism, co-ordination starts when prices fail to co-ordinate and when the resulting regrets (costs) induce improved forms of market decisions. Prices do not simply summarize an already discovered information set, they also provide the incentives for 'digging out' what has to be discovered (Kirzner 1985: 200, 204). It is this latter aspect of co-ordination that Hayek refers to, and Kirzner emphasizes, when he defines the market process as a process of *discovery* (see Hayek 1946 and 1968).

Kirzner is here making a very strong point. Dispersed knowledge is what determines co-ordination failures and what poses a communication challenge. This is solved not by assuming a fully co-ordinated signalling system, but by providing the system of incentive signals for the revision of initially uncoordinated decisions. In other words, communication cannot be reached without providing the appropriate incentives for the communication system to be discovered or at least further improved.

Though Kirzner does not address this point, it is clear that the same discovery procedure which characterizes the functioning of a co-ordination system can be called upon to explain the way rules of co-ordination have actually emerged. Not by chance, traffic signals are often used by game theorists as an example for explaining the emergence of co-ordination rules when players cannot communicate with each other. If a condition of repeated uncoordinated outcomes is the result of strategic interplay, we may expect that agents will learn to select the appropriate communication system necessary for co-ordination. Language and rules of social conduct, money and the price system, all may be viewed as belonging to this category - that is, as emerging as the unplanned, spontaneous result of a trial-and-error procedure under conditions of dispersed knowledge.

Before focusing on this point more closely, and by way of brief conclusion to this first part, I suggest the following interpretation of Hayek's conception of the role of social rules. The process of rules creation that for Hayek characterizes the social order of modern complex societies, can be represented as a generalization of the process just discussed. Rules of order are viewed by him mainly as a solution to a problem of co-ordination, as the gradual discovery of that system of general rules of communication that enables people to make the best use of their specific knowledge, without any recourse to 'conscious social control' (Hayek 1944: 36). From the sensory order to the rules of language, we constantly observe a progressive displacement of the concrete by the abstract. Abstract rules filter and make intelligible the general characteristics of the environment (Hayek 1952 and 1967). Correspondingly, with the development of those 'symbols which we call market prices' (Hayek 1978: 60), abstract signals take the place of specific imposed ends. Within this system people become able to co-ordinate while remaining free to adapt their resources and abilities to their own purposes. Conversely, legal institutions and coercion are required only in the degree necessary for the flow of information which prices spontaneously provide to run more smoothly and freely, for creating the conditions which will make competition work as effectively as possible. Planning should be used *for* competition and not *against* it (see, for example Hayek, 1944: 35 ff.).

But not all institutions are expressions of communication failures. Is Hayek's model of the emergence of co-ordination rules still usable in these other cases?

CO-ORDINATION FAILURES

In dealing with the emergence of social rules and institutions game theorists correctly distinguish between rules of co-operation and rules of co-ordination. The latter are the ones we have dealt with so far. If we represent some problem of interdependent decisions as a game of strategy, a situation which represents a problem of co-ordination can be described as a situation in which each of the players has to choose a course of action - a strategy - according to his expectations of the other players' choice of strategy and in which the success or failure of one translate into the success or failure of the others. In the example of cars approaching an intersection without a signalling system or a codified set of rules, it will be very difficult for each driver to outguess the multiplicity of strategic rules that other drivers might have chosen. In an exchange without a price signalling system it will be very difficult for the many buyers and sellers to discover their mutual intentions and desires. In both cases the inability to communicate case by case translates into an inability for all the parties to co-ordinate.

More formally, in a situation representing a traffic problem and involving only two (identical) players, 1 and 2, and two strategies, *R* and *L*, where *R* indicates that the driver approaching an intersection gives the precedence to the driver coming from the right, and *L* to the driver coming from the left, if $i = \{1 \ldots N\}$ is the set of players and 1, $2^{t}i$, we can can describe the following symmetric game:

$$G = [(1, 2)\ (s_1, s_2)\ (q_1, q_2)]$$

where the strategy set is:

$$s_1 = s_2 = [R, L]$$

and

$$q_1 = q_1(s_1, s_2),\ q_2 = q_2(s_2, s_1)$$

indicates the payoffs which result by playing one or the other strategy. For both players the preference ordering associated with the payoff function measured in some utility terms is:

$$RR = LL > LR = RL$$

For both players the best reply to the other player's strategy (their dominant strategy) is to play *R* when the other plays *R*, and *L* when the other plays *L* (the normal form representation of this game is given in the Appendix to this chapter as game number (1). As usual, the first number in the row represents player 1's payoff and the second 2's). Since the equilibrium solution of the game requires that each strategy in the pair chosen by the players is the best reply to the other and since both pairs *RR* and *LL* obey this condition, *G* has two equilibria. Games of co-ordination describe therefore the fact that the players desire to co-ordinate but, having a multiplicity of equilibrium options (these increase with the number of strategies involved), may fail to do so. This characteristic of this kind of game captures players' dispersed knowledge – that is, the fact that the players do not have any pre-knowledge of each other's strategy. Within the rules of the game no unique equilibrium will emerge unless we allow (also assuming the game is repeated over time) that the players have an ability to learn. As Hayek correctly suggested, they must have an ability to discover what has to be discovered. In this way we may expect that players will be able to introduce some rule of identification and selection of one of the equilibria and that some commonly accepted norms of co-ordination will slowly emerge.[4]

The increased order that is gained through these rules is clear. They help to overcome the dispersed knowledge problem through an abstract system of decoding and transmitting information, throughout the mass of noisy signals that accompany communication. Intelligibility is their main characteristic.[5]

There is, however, another set of rules which we may expect to emerge as a solution to a different class of problems - those related to failures to co-operate. Co-operation failures arise in those game situations in which the players, by pursuing their private interests (i.e. by playing their dominant strategy) obtain an equilibrium outcome that is worse than the outcome that they would have obtained had they played more co-operatively. These game situations are, as is widely understood, situations of a Prisoner's Dilemma (PD) type.

If the game representing this situation is the same two-player, two-strategies symmetric game as before, and the strategy set is, now, $s_1 = s_2 = [D, C]$, where D indicates the choice of a defect strategy by the players and C, the choice of the co-operative one, the preference ordering associated with the payoffs is, for player 1:

$$DC > CC > DD > CD$$

and for player 2:

$$CD > CC > DD > DC$$

(The normal form representation is in the Appendix, game number 2.) Since for both players the choice to defect is always the best reply to the other player's choice (no matter what he chooses between C and D), the strategy pair DD is the equilibrium outcome, despite the fact that this outcome is ranked lower in the preference ordering of both players.

The dilemma the players face therefore is that in trying to reach their best outcome (or in avoiding their worst outcome), they end up in a situation that could have been avoided had they both chosen the co-operative strategy. The equilibrium outcome corresponds to a situation in which both players fail to co-operate, even though mutual co-operation is in fact better than mutual defection. Before analysing how and if the players can escape this kind of situation, let us first see what kind of solutions are forbidden.

The first solution which comes to mind is: why should the players follow their dominant strategy if this is so ruinous for them? If we could assume that players behave a little bit less 'rationally' than the game prescribes, or follow less stubbornly what their dominant strategy suggests, then the co-operative outcome would appear.[6] If the players, for example, are more trustworthy, or more sympathetic to each other, then, once they exchange mutual promises of co-operation, we can expect that they will in fact co-operate.

Theories of social contract, which assume that the agreed upon social rule will be complied with, are assuming this sort of common sharing of trust among the players. Appealing though they might be, these solutions are not, however, a solution to the PD game. The reason is simple: if players share the common goal of co-operation then co-operation surely will prevail, but simply because the reasons for its original failure are taken away. This kind of solution simply represents an (unexplained) transformation of the original PD game into a situation in which the preference ordering is altered so as to allow for one strategic option only, *CC*. (For examples of games which are represented as, but are in fact not, PD games, see Binmore 1992b.) In other words, a social order now prevails though there is no need for a social order (co-operation now prevails but the original game has become superfluous).[7]

It is not difficult to recognize in this argument Hayek's criticism of the 'false' individualism inherent in such theories.[8] They assume that society as a whole can be made an object of choice, as if people's different goals and purposes could be subsumed under the common denominator of the social goal (see Hayek 1978: 20). Through a logical fallacy the problem of co-operation is not solved but simply assumed away.

But this line of argument shows also that co-operation problems cannot be reduced to communication problems. It is true that a problem of knowledge is implied in the discovery of the different needs and desires of the people adhering to a set of common rules, but even if this problem was overcome, still co-operation would not be possible. Hayek's paradigm of social order as the order that the market guarantees through a system of decentralized decisions and a generalized obedience to a set of highly symbolic rules, such as the price system, is of no help here. It is clear that the reason for co-operation failures does not depend uniquely on the existence of dispersed knowledge. A player's choice of defection is made irrespective of other player's choices. Therefore even perfect intelligibility of one's opponent's intentions and willingness to adhere to a co-operative rule does not change the original strategic choice to defect, because there still remains the incentive for the players not to follow the agreement. The origin of a failure to co-operate is due to the contrast of interests that arises from the gains associated with the possibility of outcompeting the rival. Unless the rules of the game are changed, and a new incentive structure is provided so that the reasons for contrast disappear, the mutual losses that accompany this symmetric competitive behaviour are the unique solution in PD situations.

REPEATING THE GAME

Things are different, however, if the game is repeated over time, either indefinitely or without the players knowing the end of the game (the same conclusions do not hold if the game has a known end because, as the game unravels backward, it confirms, at each stage, the one shot solution; for a more formal analysis, see Binmore 1992a: 354). With this different setting, game theorists define a new structure for the PD game which allows for different equilibrium solutions to appear. Contrary to one-shot games, the players here can discover and learn to enforce co-operative strategies that involve a system of rewards for the co-operators or of punishments for the transgressors. What is in fact shown by this new (super)game version of PD situations is that the co-operative outcome is now possible. It is possible, but not unique. The solution of an infinitely repeated game has a multiplicity of equilibria which include the *CC* outcome but also a host of different co-operative combinations (see Kreps 1990). Moreover, the *DD* outcome still remains an equilibrium solution. The problem of co-operation thus becomes that of what kind of cooperative rules can be selected among this variety of strategic equilibrium options, while excluding the defect strategy.

The repetition of the game may therefore be very useful in order to represent an endogenous, spontaneous outcome which includes the possibility of learning and adaptation towards some form of co-operation, but the way players learn to select the unique co-operation outcome has proved much more difficult to demonstrate. Nor can we expect to find the answer to this problem in the game-theoretic approach. Within this approach, we are able to show how and when a particular co-operative strategy is an equilibrium, but we cannot show how this particular strategy has been discovered, learnt and selected. In other words, game theory does not, and cannot, offer any modelling of the learning process of the players, nor therefore of the particular selecting procedure that players may adopt to choose among different equilibrium options. Game theory suffices to describe the conditions under which mutual expectations are matched, but not the process. Out-of-equilibrium moves are what they are, 'irrational', dominated strategies and not possible steps of a learning process where error-making and error-correcting are as informative as the final solution. Hayek's and Kirzner's idea that non-coordinated behaviour informs how co-ordination proceeds is lost here.[9]

Things being this way: Is the Hayekian discovery procedure, the idea that the orderly outcome goes together with the process that brings about the outcome, of any help here?

Before answering I shall discuss briefly how the conclusions we have just reached by analysing the case of co-operation failures can be confronted with Hayek's framework of spontaneous order.

CONFLICTING INTERESTS

While discussing the basis of true individualism as opposed to the false individualism of the rationalistic tradition, Hayek refers to the notion of private interest as the basic unit of social interaction. By private interest Hayek means the specific knowledge embedded in the individually freely chosen ends (Hayek 1948: 14).

Analysing PD situations, we have seen, however, that private interests and the search for individual gain, when generalized, may become the source of mutually harmful results. In this kind of situation private knowledge and interests cannot be generalized, cannot become a social rule, without generating mutual losses. There seem to be situations therefore where individual interests are not the basic unit of orderly interaction but reason for conflict (everybody wants to be the only defector).

We have seen, moreover, that the repetition of the game and the accumulation of losses deriving from these contrasting interests do not necessarily, or automatically, guarantee their convergence towards the co-operative outcome. In addition, even when such an agreement to co-operate should spontaneously arise, still some rule enforcing the agreement against violators has to be discovered. If we exclude the possibility of simply postulating an external agency which provides the enforcement structure, we must explain how an enforcement rule could emerge spontaneously in the degree necessary for co-operation to prevail.[10] Two additional examples of games of conflict will clarify the point.

In the so-called game of Chicken (game number 3 in the Appendix), the players, as in the PD game, gain from defection when the other is co-operating, but each of them would be better off by collaborating than by defecting when the other is defecting. For example, in a bargaining situation seller and buyer gain by firmly defending their previously established price, but it is better for them to concede rather than remaining firm and failing to agree. With the same *G* structure as the PD game, the preference ordering now is:

for player 1: *DC* > *CC* > *CD* > *DD*

for player 2: *CD* > *CC*> *DC* > *DD*

which implies two equilibria in pure strategies, *CD* and *DC*, and one in mixed strategies (the strategy mix which results by playing *D* and *C* randomly). It seems here that by repeating the game it would be easier to select one of the multiple equilibrium options. However, here too a shared agreement has to be believed to become effective and requires some enforcement rule to be stable (for a similar situation of two 'inequality' equilibria - plus one in mixed strategies - see the Battle of the Sexes game, number 4 in the Appendix).

In the Stag Hunt game (number 5 in the Appendix), the players are trying to catch a deer, an activity that requires the collaboration of both. If they succeed they reach their highest outcome. The possibility of co-operation failures here derives from the fact that by defecting - by shooting at a hare, which can be done without the collaboration of the other, and which scares any deer - the players obtain a safer outcome than by cooperating: by trying to shoot a deer when the other is shooting at the hare, a player obtains nothing. The preference ordering is therefore:

for player 1: *CC* > *DC* > *DD* > *CD*

for player 2: *CC* > *CD*> *DD* > *DC*

which implies two equilibria in pure strategies *CC* and *DD*, where the second risk dominates the first (Harsanyi and Selten 1988; for more on this point, see Binmore 1992a). Here too therefore without trust and enforcement rules the co-operative outcome does not necessarily prevail.

As all these examples make clear, and despite the various attempts to abbreviate the path, the steps towards rules of social order are complicated and difficult to discover and to explain when contrasting interests are involved. The paradox here is in fact that private interests cannot be generalized without losses, but what can be generalized (moral codes) does not obey private motivations.

Hayek is clearly aware of the difficulties connected to the presence of contrasting interests in society (see, for example, Hayek 1944: 38; 1946: 18–19).[11] Still, he never analyses their specific nature or explains how they are reconciled.[12] He surely insists on the spontaneity of the process of composition, but, by not showing how, specifically, this self-generating system works, he conveys the impression that he attributes to the grown order the compositive power that others attribute to the made order. Moreover, by referring almost exclusively to the co-ordinating role of the market as the example of social order, he seems to represent all institutions as the result of communication problems. This interpretation scheme, we have already seen, does not apply here. For, without an evolved and continuously adjusting system of enforcement rules, conflictual interests prevail.[13] In fact, Hayek justifies a role for political and deliberate intervention in all those cases which involve the presence of externalities such as the provision of public goods, the use of air, the right to patent inventions. He defines them as competition failures, thus suggesting that the information and transactions costs involved in these situations - for example, the costs of gathering information for signing and enforcing contracts, the costs of identifying trading partners - frustrate the co-ordinating role of the market. But the analysis of PD games shows that these situations involve much more than information problems.[14]

I shall now turn more specifically to the role of competitive markets: how they work when strategic interaction of the type discussed in PD games is involved. In analysing this problem I will also try to answer the question left unanswered earlier of how Hayek's idea of the market's discovery procedure can be utilized.

STRATEGIC COMPETITION

Though the role of competitive markets is, as Hayek and Kirzner emphasize, that of providing a system for the emergence of the information necessary to co-ordinate all the dispersed activities involved in the exchange, this is not its only role. Nor are the strategic considerations only of the sort connected to the predictability of each other's intentions and desires. The second role, and the second meaning as well, of competition is that of providing an incentives framework for outcompeting one's rival. The strategic considerations now involve finding always new ways of, and new opportunities for, competitive gains. These competitive gains do not necessarily derive from socially 'good' actions, such as the introduction of a cheaper technology, but may also involve more 'vicious' activities such as stealing, cheating, concealing information, defrauding. Mandeville's idea of competition as the place for individual vices to become social, is a less-purified version of Hayek's idea of private interests as private knowledge, but more in touch with this strategic aspect of competition.

PD situations describe, admittedly in a very simplified manner, how the search for competitive gains may result in a mutually harmful outcome. Engaging in price-cutting activities, or stealing from the common pool of irrigating water, or of clean air, or of pasture grass, are all activities that, as we have seen, cannot become social without generating mutual losses. But these same problem situations may become the occasion for a discovery process to start. These are situations which, it has been said (Ullmann-Margalit 1977), call for norms, for the generation of a new set of rules which change the game in favour of co-operation. These are situations which, we may add, call for learning, for the discovery of new ways of dealing with the problem. The way the problem is structured suggests where to look for the solution. What the literature on co-operation rules has in fact emphasized is the incentive structure, the system of reward and punishment, the critical mass of adherents, which may sustain less self-interested, less competitive, forms of behaviour.[15] Competition, in this second sense, is smothered by this process. But this is not the only way. What competitive markets show is that the way competition works is in finding always new forms, new sources of competitive gains, in substituting individual advantages which have revealed themselves to be (mutually) harmful with less harmful ones. For example, a ruinous price war is replaced by quality confrontation, by better customer services, by investments in reputation, knowledge, organization. The literature on firm behaviour offers a variety of examples of these investments in 'invisible' assets, assets that not only offer different sources of competitive gains, but also a flexibility of adjustment from one source to another (see, for example, Chandler 1990; Itami 1987). Price competition is not the only form of competition (this shows once more how reductive Hayek's view is). These examples show also a new, stronger meaning of the discovery procedure that goes beyond simply transmitting information and economizing knowledge. Competition is not only the place for arbitrage gains, for 'stepping in' and grasping first an opportunity (see Hayek 1948: 83), but also searching for, and the means of rewarding, new forms of gain. Mandeville has a powerful expression which applies to this form of competitive behaviour: in the market process players learn to play the passion against itself. Vices are not replaced by virtues; they remain vices, only they become more sociable in their effects. Nothing guarantees that this form of socialization proceeds steadily and irreversibly (see Bianchi 1992). But the learning procedure that is implied in the process will provide the flexibility for adjustments and corrections. The meaning of 'order' changes; it is not a state of affairs, but a process; not a correct state, but a corrigible one.

CONCLUSIONS: SOCIAL ORDER AS AN ABILITY TO LEARN

Hayek's analysis of social order can be formulated as follows. Among the multiple ways by which society can be organized and kept together, one has proved to be more efficient than others. This is represented by that spontaneous and unintended set of rules which characterizes a free competitive market and the corresponding system of enforcing laws. The reason the system has proved to be good is that it enables people to learn, to check and correct their errors and to discover new solutions. It provides the institutional setting for alternative and different solutions to be experimented with, tested and modified. Nothing guarantees, however, that the best, or socially more efficient, solution will prevail as if through a steady process of growth. Hayek's insistence on the communication aspect of social rules and on that impersonal and efficient system of spreading information represented by market prices, may suggest this conclusion. However, we have seen that the presence of problems of co-ordination makes the existence of a social order as a static set of co-ordination rules much more difficult to be sustained. On the one hand, a complex system of moral codes, rules of fairness, as well as an articulated system of punishments for the violators, has to be continuously discovered and adjusted. On the other hand, the search for competitive gains must always find new channels. In this different setting the market game, Hayek's game of catallaxy, not only teaches the players how to transform the enemy into friend (Hayek 1978: 60), it also provides the incentive structure to discover and reward more social ways of 'defection'. In this process of constant changes and adjustments we do not see the amended, compositive society but the amendable one. Not the social order, but an order that, through learning, can be made more social.

NOTES

1. The distinction is between two concepts of order: *taxis*, the exogenous, made order, the artificial construction typical of organizations, and *cosmos*, the grown, self-generating, endogenous order, an order that is of 'nobody's deliberate making' (Hayek 1973: 37).
2. In this system of abstract relations, individual man can be directed by the private knowledge of his own purposes, and not by the knowledge of other people's needs, which is outside the range of his perceptions (Hayek 1978: 268; 1946: 15). He can be guided by his free choice and intentions and not by command and coercion.
3. That this process is very far from the traditional concept of perfectly competitive equilibrium where the data are known in advance and the process is deprived of all its discovery potential, is repeatedly made clear by Hayek (see, for example, 1937, 1945 and 1946).
4. 'Focal points', or conventions, have been called those rules which work as general attractors for selecting equilibria (see Schelling 1960; Sugden 1986). (Consider Adam Smith's 'natural' prices of production, for example. Sugden's idea of convention, or rule-based behaviour as a *solution* to these games is not, however, strictly correct (Sugden 1991). With the appearance – and acceptance – of a convention, a co-ordination game is not solved but simply changed into a new game of co-ordination

with focal point. For a convention to appear we have therefore to assume some meta-rule, such as players' ability to learn or to introduce new moves (patterns, routines, symbols). Within the rules of the game no unique solution will ever spontaneously, or endogenously, appear. This same criticism will reappear later in the text when I discuss so-called 'solutions' to the Prisoner's Dilemma game.

5 See Hayek (1978: 34): 'We are only beginning to understand on how subtle a communication system the functioning of an advanced industrial society is based – a communication system which we call the market and which turns out to be a more efficient mechanism for digesting dispersed information than any that man has deliberately designed'.

6 See, for example, Aumann (1988) for the infinitely small amount of irrationality that is required for the Pareto superior outcome to appear. The problem with this solution, as will be clear in the text, is of course that it introduces a solution by simply assuming away the conditions which prevented that solution obtaining in the first place.

7 A more subtle version of this solution rests on the following argument: since both players are rational and both know they are rational, both know that *CC* is better than *DD*, therefore *CC* is chosen: by transforming two players into one the alternative *DC*, *CD* disappears. See Campbell and Sowden (1985) and Binmore (1992b), the first for a description of this kind of solution, the second for a discussion of its fallacy.

8 By true individualism, by contrast, Hayek means the principle that social phenomena can be understood only 'through our understanding of individual actions directed towards other people and guided by their expected behavior' (Hayek 1946: 6). In other words, there is no presupposition of the existence, and the knowledge, of a common goal that can be mastered by a single designing mind (ibid.: 8–9). That this sort of individualism is not in contrast with, but actually facilitates, a theory of institutional change is well argued by Agassi (1975).

9 As is lost, too, in the equilibrium concepts of perfectly competitive markets, which focus exclusively on the co-ordinating role of already adjusted prices (see Kirzner 1985: 201).

10 Recent attempts at using repeated PD problems to analyse contractarian agreements through coalition formation and the spontaneous emergence of a dominant protecting agency (such as the minimal state depicted by Nozick), show how difficult it is to meet all the conditions for such an emergence (see, for example, Okada and Kliemt 1991). In particular, the formation of a protective agency is not self-enforcing unless its coercive powers extend also over non-adherents. But this clearly violates the contractarian premises of purely voluntary, agreed-upon rules (ibid.: 182). A similar line of argument, which stresses, however, the problem connected with the creation of credible constraints over the power of the agency itself, can be found in Witt (1992).

11 These contrasting interests should not be confused with the disappointments and regrets that inevitably occur in the process of expectations adjustment, or with income inequalities which, for Hayek, are incurable in a free society where nobody knows what just distribution means (see the chapter 'The Atavism of Social Justice' in Hayek 1978). Nor are they the same as the overlapping rules of social order that are present, and often clash, in our societies (Hayek 1988: 19).

12 It should be stressed once more that this kind of PD conflict is not a conflict between group interests and private interests - even if it is often portrayed in this way. To assume the existence of a group interest amounts to assuming already a disposition to recognize and accept a common goal, an assumption that violates individualism. Though Hayek is perfectly aware of the impossibility of assuming the existence of group interests, he sometimes refers to group selection as the way through which beneficial institutions emerge (see Hayek 1973: 18; 1967). For a discussion of this important point see Vanberg (1986) and Hodgson (1991).

13 I entirely agree with Vanberg and Buchanan (1988), who maintain a similar idea: that spontaneous order explanations - from Hume to Menger to Hayek - share a tendency to subsume all rule-emergence problems under co-ordination problems. There is an exception, however, that of Mandeville, who not only stressed the enforcement problem connected with defecting behaviour, but showed also the beneficial effects of this kind of behaviour (see Bianchi 1993).

14 An example of Prisoner's Dilemma situations reduced to problems of co-ordination is in Breeden and Toumanoff (1985).

15 For example, the very complex incentive structure that is required in solving PD problems in the absence of any sanctioning mechanism, is analysed by Weissig and Ostrom (1991) for the specific case of the common use of an irrigation system. One of the most interesting results of their research is that, contrary to intuition, no equilibrium is found without any defecting strategy. If there is zero defection, nobody has to monitor; if there is zero monitoring, positive incentives to defect re-emerge.

BIBLIOGRAPHY

Agassi, J. (1975) 'Institutional Individualism', *British Journal of Sociology* 26: 144-55.

Aumann, R.J. (1988) 'Preliminary Notes on Irrationality in Game Theory', IMSSS Summer Seminar in Economic Theory, Stanford.

Bianchi, M. (1992) 'Evoloutionary Metaphors and the Justification of Economic Efficiency', *Finnish Economic Papers* (forthcoming).

—— (1993) 'How to Learn Sociality: True and False Solutions to Mandeville's Problem', *History of Political Economy*, 25(2): 209-40.

Binmore, K. (1992a) *Fun and Games*, Lexington: D.C. Heath.

—— (1992b) 'Playing Fair', book manuscript.

Breeden, C.H. and Toumanoff, P.G. (1985) 'Transaction Costs and Economic Institutions', in Leube and Zlabinger (1985), 161-77.

Campbell, R. and Sowden, L. (eds) (1985) *Paradoxes of Rationality and Cooperation: Prisoner's Dilemma and Newcomb's Problem*, Vancouver: University of Columbia Press.

Chandler, A.D., Jr (1990) *Scale and Scope: The Dynamics of Industrial Capitalism*, Cambridge Mass.: Belknap Press.

Harsanyi, J. and Selten, R. (1988) *A General Theory of Equilibrium Selection in Games*, Cambridge, Mass.: MIT Press.

Hayek, F.A. (1937) 'Economics and Knowledge', *Economica*, 4: 33-54, repr. in Hayek 1948, pp. 33-56.

—— (1944) *The Road to Serfdom*, Chicago: University of Chicago Press.
—— (1945) 'The Use of Knowledge in Society', *American Economic Review* 4: 519–30, repr. in Hayek 1948, pp. 77–91.
—— (1946) 'The Meaning of Competition', in Hayek 1948, pp. 92–106.
—— (1948) *Individualism and Economic Order*, Chicago: University of Chicago Press.
—— (1952) *The Sensory Order*, Chicago: University of Chicago Press.
—— (1960) *The Constitution of Liberty*, Chicago: University of Chicago Press.
—— (1968) 'Competition as a Discovery Procedure', in Hayek 1978, pp. 179–90.
—— (1967) *Studies in Philosophy, Politics and Economics*, Chicago: University of Chicago Press.
—— (1973) *Law, Legislation and Liberty*, Chicago: University of Chicago Press, vol. 1.
—— (1978) *New Studies in Philosophy, Politics, Economics and the History of Ideas*, Chicago: University of Chicago Press.
—— (1988) *The Fatal Conceit: The Errors of Socialism*, London: Routledge.
Hodgson, G.M. (1991) 'Hayek's Theory of Cultural Evolution: An Evaluation in the Light of Vanberg Critique', *Economics and Philosophy* 1: 67–82.
Itami, H. (1987) *Mobilizing Invisible Assets*, Cambridge, Mass.: Harvard University Press.
Kirzner, I.M. (1985) 'Prices, the Communication of Knowledge, and the Discovery Process', in Leube and Zlabinger 1985, pp. 193–206.
Kreps, D.M. (1990) *A Course in Microeconomic Theory*, Princeton, NJ: Princeton University Press.
Leube, K.R. and Zlabinger, A.H. (eds) (1985) *The Political Economy of Freedom: Essays in Honor of F.A. Hayek*, Munich, Vienna: Philosophia Verlag.
Mandeville, B. (1924 [1714]) *The Fable of the Bees, or Private Vices, Publick Benefits*, ed. F.B. Kaye, 2 vols, Oxford: Clarendon Press; facsimile edn, Indianapolis: Liberty Classics, 1988.
Okada, A. and Kliemt, H. (1991) 'Anarchy and Agreement: A Game Theoretic Analysis of Some Aspects of Contractarianism', in Selten 1991, pp. 164–87.
Schelling, T.C. (1960) *The Strategy of Conflict*, Cambridge, Mass.: Harvard University Press.
Selten, R. (ed.) (1991) *Game Equilibrium Models II: Methods, Morals and Markets*, Berlin: Springer-Verlag.
Sugden, R. (1986) *The Economics of Rights, Co-operation and Welfare*, New York: Blackwell.
—— (1991) 'Convention, Creativity and Conflict', in Y. Varoufakis and D. Young (eds) *Conflict in Economics*, New York: Harvester Wheatsheaf, pp. 68–90.
Ullmann-Margalit, E. (1977) *The Emergence of Norms*, Oxford: Clarendon Press.
—— (1978) 'Invisible-Hand Explanations', *Syntese* 39: 263–291.
Vanberg, V. (1986) 'Spontaneous Market Order and Social Rules', *Economics and Philosophy* 2: 75–100.
Vanberg, V. and Buchanan, J.M. (1988) 'Rational Choice and Moral Order', *Analyse & Kritik* 10: 138–60.

Weissig, F. and Ostrom, E (1991) 'Irrigation Institutions and the Games Irrigators Play: Rule Enforcement without Guards', in Selten 1991, pp. 188–262.

Witt, U. (1992) 'The Emergence of a Protective Agency and the Constitutional Dilemma', *Constitutional Political Economy* 3(2): 255–66.

APPENDIX

(1) **Traffic game**

1 \ 2	*R*	*L*
R	2, 2	0, 0
L	0, 0	2, 2

RR = *LL* > *LR* = *RL*

(2) **Prisoner's dilemma**

1 \ 2	*C*	*D*
C	2, 2	0, 3
D	3, 0	1, 1

CD > *CC* > *DD* > *CD*

(3) **Chicken game**

1 \ 2	*C*	*D*
C	2, 2	1, 3
D	3, 1	0, 0

DC > *CC* > *CD* > *DD*

(4) **Battle of the sexes**

1 \ 2	*C*	*D*
C	0, 0	1, 2
D	2, 1	0, 0

DC > *CD* > *CC* = *DD*

(5) **Stag-hunt game**

1 \ 2	*C*	*D*
C	3, 3	0, 2
D	2, 0	1, 1

CC > *DC* > *DD* > *CD*

Part III

LAW AND SOCIAL ORDER

13

HAYEK ON THE RULE OF LAW

Inez Kotterman-van de Vosse

NO DEPENDENCE ON VIRTUES OR VICES

Before I turn to Hayek's conception of the rule of law, I would like to bring to your notice a fable written by Machiavelli. It is the story of Belfagor, a devil who got married. Machiavelli asks us to believe the following:

> It is recorded in the old chronicles of Florentine history how a most holy man, well known among his contemporaries, prayed with religious zeal and saw that, among the many miserable souls who died without God's grace and went to Hell, all (or most of them) complained that it was only their wives who were to blame for their desperate fate and all the misery that was brought upon them. Minos and Rhadamanthos, together with all the other judges of Hell, were quite bewildered. They simply couldn't believe that these accusations against the fairer sex were true, but the complaints mounted up day by day. The problem was duly reported to Pluto, whereupon it was decided that there should be a thorough investigation by all the princes of Hell. They were to leave no stone unturned to discover whether these men had spoken the truth. Having called them all together, Pluto spoke to the council: 'My dearly beloved friends! Since by heavenly decree and irrevocable destiny I hold this kingdom, I cannot be bound by any judgement whatever, be it earthly or heavenly; nevertheless, because *it is a sign of great wisdom when they who have supreme power allow themselves to be ruled by law* and take due note of other people's opinions, I have decided to seek your advice on handling a case that could bring shame on our empire . . .
>
> (Machiavelli 1927: 133–4)[1]

Though not directly relevant to my issue, I will not withhold some juicy details. To cut a long story short: after ample discussion it was agreed upon that the archdevil Belfagor, a former archangel who had fallen from Heaven, should be sent to earth, in the guise of a handsome man and provided with a large fortune. He was to take a wife and live with her for ten years. And so it came to pass. The devil chose a bride and let himself be bullied by the beautiful but arrogant and prodigal Onesta. According to Belfagor, she had even more pride than Lucifer. How at long last, with a sigh of relief, he returned to Hell, preferring its eternal fires to the tortures of married life, does not, as I said, really concern my subject. How Pluto appeared to preserve the rule of fair procedure by applying the principle of hearing both sides, though the prevailing prejudice against the weaker sex made the outcome a foregone conclusion, is typical of that period in our history but not exactly relevant either. My point is that Machiavelli, who wrote this fable sometime in the early sixteenth century, made Pluto pronounce one of the most fundamental characteristics of the rule of law.

It was not really a new idea, since, to some extent, we can trace it back to ancient Greek and Roman political history, but I still think it remarkable that Machiavelli produced this explicit formulation three centuries before the relation between sovereign and state became topical in Western Europe. Pluto has stated a principle that comprises the very core of Hayek's legal philosophy: neither the ruler, nor the government, not even the democratic majority - so no human beings with all their virtues and vices - but ***abstract and general rules, fixed and made publicly known beforehand***, should be in supreme command. Since the law-giver is ignorant of the particular situations or persons to which his rules will apply and because the judges, in considering the cases brought before them, must draw conclusions from these known general rules, we can claim that we are ruled by laws and not by men (Hayek 1976b: 153).

EVOLUTION AND CONSTRUCTION

Rules, for that matter, in Hayek's view are not just a technical achievement of the law-maker. He profoundly rejects what he calls the 'naïve rationalism' or 'rationalist constructivism' of thinkers like Francis Bacon, Thomas Hobbes and especially René Descartes. Hayek rebuts their contention that all the useful human institutions were intentionally created in the past and ought to be invented likewise in the future, in clear awareness of their desirable effects. Such a 'hubristic' and 'constructivist' rationalism is fundamentally contrary to the conception of the growth of social formations he shares with evolutionists like David Hume, Adam Smith and Adam Ferguson. These thinkers elaborate their insight that many institutions of civilization are not the product of deliberate human design but the unintended outcome of countless human activities. He also draws our attention to the fact that the lawyer who regards himself as no more than the executive of a democratic decision will frequently have to work out consequences, unquestionably implied by it, but actually neither foreseen nor wanted by those who made it. Yet the mere fact that certain consequences do follow from a decision is often taken as proof of their intentionality. To Hayek it is no accident that Cartesian rationalists, prone to extol the powers of human reason, completely disregard the forces of historical evolution. His own epistemological view on the limitations of the human intellect is incompatible with their proposition 'that man in the full knowledge of what he was doing should deliberately create such a civilization and social order as the process of his reason enabled him to design' (Hayek 1980a: 85).[2]

Hayek perceives in this kind of reasoning the evil source of all modern socialism, planning and totalitarianism. He, on the other hand, is convinced that most of the rules governing the social life of a community emerge 'spontaneously' and generally tend to be selected according to their capacity for promoting human survival. These rules fight their way to acceptance through a gradual process in which the experience of successive generations helps to give them their present shape (Hayek 1976b: 157), for 'no single human intelligence is capable of inventing the most appropriate abstract rules because those rules which have evolved in the process of growth of society embody the experience of many more trials and errors than any individual mind could acquire' (Hayek 1980a: 88).

Hayek tells us that in primitive human society unarticulated rules of conduct manifested themselves only in their being obeyed. When in the course of evolution individual minds became more complex, the need to express these rules in communicable form made itself felt. Without the observance of some common rules the formation of a general kind of order would have been impossible. This holds particularly for the rules of law (Hayek 1964: 7–8). The fact that many essential rules are the product of social evolution does not mean, however, that they do not need critical scrutiny, but it does place a burden of proof on those who wish to reform them (Hayek 1988: 20). If we want to improve upon a rule by deliberate legislation, we must try to understand what its general function is to be, what purpose it must serve (Hayek 1976b: 157).

THE LEGAL EMBODIMENT OF FREEDOM

Thus the constitution of a people is to a large extent determined by these grown rules. Their evolutionary character accounts for the fact that Hayek assigns so much authority to them and, as a consequence, to the rule of law. The latter he regards as one of the greatest achievements of the liberal age, not only as a safeguard but as the legal embodiment of freedom (Hayek 1971: 61). In 'Planning and the Rule of Law' he definitely links this ideal to a free community, stating:

> Nothing distinguishes more clearly conditions in a free country from those in a country under arbitrary government than the observance in the former of the great principles known as the Rule of Law. Stripped of all technicalities this means that government in all its actions is bound by rules fixed and announced beforehand – rules which make it possible to foresee with fair certainty how the authority will use its coercive powers in given circumstances, and to plan one's individual affairs on the basis of this knowledge.
>
> (Hayek 1971: 54)

From this statement one could easily, but erroneously, gain the impression that the 'technicalities' of which Hayek stripped his definition are of minor importance. That would be a great mistake, for an analysis of the passages where he discusses the subject inevitably leads to the conclusion that these technicalities are in fact a whole range of formal as well as substantive requirements to be fulfilled. Hayek warns us: to believe that the rule of law will be preserved so long as all actions of the state are duly authorized by legislation, is completely to misconceive its meaning. As *The Road to Serfdom* was written during the Second World War, his illustration of this statement was obvious:

> It may well be that Hitler has obtained his unlimited powers in a strictly constitutional manner and that whatever he does is therefore legal in the juridical sense. But who would suggest for that reason that the Rule of Law still prevails in Germany?
>
> (Hayek 1971: 61)

This is the penetrating question Hayek puts before us. It is also his main reason for rejecting a purely formal interpretation of the rule of law. He regrets the process by which existing liberal societies gradually replaced the 'normative' thinking of liberal law by a conception of law directed at a 'concrete order formation' and, as a result, were progressively transformed into totalitarian states. He is convinced that this historical development is due to the fact that their representative assemblies had entered into a confusion of functions. Not only had they been charged with the task of laying down rules of individual conduct but also with that of laying down rules and giving orders concerning the organization and conduct of government. As a consequence, the term 'law' came to imply any rule of organization or even any particular command approved by the constitutionally appointed legislature.

> Such a conception of the rule of law which merely demands that a command be legitimately issued and not that it be a rule of justice equally applicable to all (what the Germans call the merely *formelle Rechtsstaat*), of course no longer provides any protection of individual freedom.
>
> (Hayek 1980c: 169–70)

The Road to Serfdom contains a powerful and cogent plea for the principle of the rule of law as Hayek conceives it, but the first systematic and comprehensive treatment of his conception is actually found in *The Constitution of Liberty* (Chs 14–16), which next to *The Road to Serfdom*, is his most popular work. I am not sure whether he had this elaboration already in mind when he created *The Road to Serfdom*, but I assume that it may well be the outcome of an evolutionary and rational thought process. During that process the implications of his proposition that 'legal in the juridical sense' does not inherently imply conformity to the rule of law, must have crystallized into a more and more definite shape. Before outlining these implications, I will touch on the broad distinction that is made between two basically different ways of approaching the meaning – and thus also the value – of the rule of law.

The preliminary question concerns the nature of a *Rechtsstaat* (I leave the German term untranslated, as Hayek often does, because it has no precise equivalent in English). The question is whether every state is a *Rechtsstaat*, provided that a juridical norm underlies it, but irrespective of its political character. Should the answer be positive, then it would be irrelevant whether it is a democratic or an undemocratic state. Such a formal approach is the way of adherents to the 'pure theory of law' as expounded by the legal positivist Hans Kelsen in his famous work *Reine Rechtslehre*. Others, like Hayek, argue that the fundamental norm itself should comply with certain requirements as to the organization of the state and the relation of the state to its members. In the liberal *Rechtsstaat* these demands imply that normative restrictions be imposed on the coercive authority of the government and on the manner in which it may actually exercise its powers. First and foremost it is the civil rights that should thus be protected: the basic rights of individual liberty. The government ensures order and security and interferes as little as possible with the private affairs of the people.

LEGALITY IS NOT DECISIVE

Now, what does Hayek regard as defining properties or integral parts of the rule of law? His conception of this political ideal presupposes complete legality. This, however, is a necessary but not yet a sufficient condition. The example of Hitler's legal authority gives us food for thought on this matter. The wish to prevent bad rulers from wielding such pernicious power and spreading their poisonous ideas is exactly why Hayek's rule requires that laws conform to certain principles. In fact, it imposes limitations on all legislation, and as such it cannot be a law in the same sense as the laws emanating from the legislature. Hayek explicitly states that it is not a rule *of* the law, but a rule *concerning* the law. It bears upon what the law ought to be. He characterizes it as a meta-legal doctrine or a political ideal. He realizes, however, that it will not be effective unless the legislator feels bound by it and in a democracy this implies that 'it will not prevail unless it forms part of the moral tradition of the community, a common ideal shared and unquestioningly accepted by the majority' (Hayek 1976b: 205–6).

In *The Constitution of Liberty* Hayek analyses the similarities and differences between liberalism and democracy. Just like the rule of law, liberalism is a doctrine about the contents of the law, whereas democracy is a doctrine on the method of determining what will be the law. Liberalism, like democracy, regards it as desirable that only what the majority accepts should in fact become law, but it does not believe that the observance of the majority rule does of necessity render *good* law. That is to say, liberalism accepts, for lack of a better one, this system as the best manner of coming to a decision, but not as an authority on the moral value of that decision (Hayek 1976b: 103–4). It considers the majority rule as a means and certainly not as an end. 'Democracy is essentially a means, a utilitarian device for safeguarding internal peace and individual freedom. As such it is by no means infallible or certain' (Hayek 1971: 52). For the doctrinaire democrat, however, the fact that the majority wants something is sufficient ground for regarding it as good: the will of the majority determines not only what is *law*, but what is *good law*. Such a doctrinarian, Hayek says, acknowledges only one limit to government, and that is current majority opinion (Hayek 1976b: 103).

One of the main reasons why Hayek fundamentally disagrees with doctrinaire democrats on the absolute authority of the majority rule stems from his conviction that there are certain principles – he calls them basic principles or long-term principles (Hayek 1976b: 106–7) – that must not be neglected or, even worse, be abolished by a temporary majority. These principles comprehend the values that underlie our legal system. If we want the principle of the rule of law to work within a community, if we want a group to agree on articulated rules of just conduct, its members must hold common values and opinions that to a certain extent coincide. It may well be that persons differing in their general values occasionally come to terms about the pursuit of some concrete goals and that they combine forces to achieve them, but such efforts will never suffice for forming a permanent order (Hayek 1982: 95). The overall order that we call society cannot come into being or continue to exist unless its (prospective) members submit to abstract rules that conform to the more general principles of a constitution. It is due to our restricted intellectual capacities that we are prone to sacrifice long-term advantages to direct needs, but a certain degree of rationality or consistency in making particular decisions can only be obtained by observing general principles, irrespective of such needs. It is a matter of prudence as well as of justice, for 'as we want to prevent the judge from infringing the law for some particular reason, so we also want to prevent the legislature from infringing certain general principles for the sake of temporary and immediate aims' (Hayek 1976b: 179).

A logical consequence of Hayek's views on the evolution of rules is that laws, in principle, should not aim at the realization of concrete schemes or projects, but should have an abstract and general character. They should not serve any specific purpose, but form a framework providing the means for pursuing a large number of different ends. Law is a condition for the successful pursuit of most purposes, and Hayek believes that of all multi-purpose instruments it is probably the one after language which supports the greatest variety of human ends (Hayek 1982: 113).

A general purpose that played and still plays an important part in the evolution and laying down of abstract and general rules concerns the safeguard of the individual from coercion by others and especially from arbitrary interference by the state. The paradox here is that the only means whereby the state can prevent the coercion of one individual by another is the very threat of coercion. How this threat can be deprived of its harmful and objectionable character is also discussed at some length in *The Constitution of Liberty* (Ch. 10).

EQUALITY BEFORE THE LAW

These two basic insights – the necessity of preserving fundamental norms as a guiding principle for all legislation, and the prerequisite of rules having a general and abstract character – underlie Hayek's conception of the rule of law. Closely related to his demand for rules having an abstract and general character is his insistence upon equality before the law. He rejects arbitrariness, but a law laid down irrespective of concrete cases and in ignorance of how it will affect certain known people, is not arbitrary. Its generality, its equal application to everybody in similar circumstances, is for Hayek one of the major aspects of its abstractness. Now, it is evident that treating different people equally may easily lead to inequality in their material positions. The opposite course of action – trying to place them in equal positions – would require different treatment of different people, which is, of course, incompatible with equality before the law. However praiseworthy may be the desire of making people more alike in their conditions of life, Hayek urges that the discriminatory coercion involved cannot be tolerated if we wish to preserve a free society. Its enforcement would imply the impression upon society of a deliberately chosen pattern of distribution, which can find no favour in his eyes, whether it be an order of equality or of inequality (Hayek 1976b: 87).

The demand for equality, however, does not mean that rules may never apply to distinct classes of people. Because people possess different properties, this will be inevitable. There may be rules that can apply only to women or to handicapped people or to persons above a certain age. In most of such cases it would not even be necessary to mention the category in question. Only a woman, for example, can be raped (says Hayek) or made pregnant. But such distinctions are not arbitrary. They will not make one group dependent on the will of others. So long as the majority of the group involved and a majority among the outsiders equally recognize the rule as just, we may presume that it is to the benefit of all parties. If, however, only the insiders of the group favour the rule, we have a clear case of privilege; whereas, in the opposite case, there is discrimination. 'What is privilege to some is, of course, always discrimination to the rest' (Hayek 1976b: 153–4). From the demand of equality before the law Hayek draws the conclusion that everybody is entitled to an equal share in making the law. I have already mentioned the restraints on this competence, to the effect that long-term principles be observed.

AN INDIVIDUAL SPHERE OF PRIVACY

Another main characteristic is that of individual liberty. Every individual has a right to secure for himself some sphere of privacy. He must be able to count on certain facts not being deliberately shaped, or rather not being manipulated by other people. He must also be sure that the authority will use its powers in a predictable way. Therefore, it is of paramount importance that in wielding its coercive powers the state is bound by the rules of a permanent legal framework. This enables individuals to plan their behaviour with a fair amount of certainty as to its consequences (Hayek 1976b: 222). In this framework of rules the rights of the individual play a crucial part. However, the recognition of an individual sphere of privacy must not itself become an instrument of coercion. That is why these general rules must stipulate the conditions under which objects or circumstances become part of such a protected sphere. The legitimacy of one's expectations, the rights of the individual, are the result of the recognition of such a sphere of privacy (Hayek 1976b: 139). It includes all action that is not explicitly restricted by a general law (Hayek 1976b: 216). The most important implication of this point of view lies in the field of criminal law. It is called the *nullum crimen, nulla poena sine lege* principle, which prescribes that nobody be punished unless he should break a general rule (Hayek 1976b: 206). It is also the law that determines the penalty, which depends on the nature of the crime.

In order to safeguard the individual's liberty, the rules must apply to those who lay them down as well as to those who apply them, that is both the government and the governed. Moreover, nobody should have the power to grant exceptions. Rules are not likely to conflict with liberal principles if they are meant to be lasting and if they are not used to favour or harm particular individuals. Of course, it is inevitable that sometimes the short-term effects on certain people are clearly known, but Hayek assumes that the desirability of these concrete effects is not the guiding consideration for the legislator. Anyway, it ought not to be so! However, as the immediate and predictable consequences become of more importance than the long-run effects, we approach a dangerous borderline. This is where the distinction, however clear in principle, becomes blurred in practice (Hayek 1971: 60–1).

Another feature of Hayek's approach has, just like the former instances, to do with the contrast between legislation and policy. It is his insistence that not only should the authority's executive power be based on a general rule, but also that its actions be subject to review by an impartial and independent body. This body should have the power to decide whether the government agency involved was justified in acting as it did, but also if *what* it did was required by the law (Hayek 1976b: 14; 1971: 61). So this postulation sets legal limits to the discretionary powers of the executive and demands that all actions deriving from these powers be liable to judicial review. What Hayek regards as a crucial issue concerns this limitation of governmental powers as a whole: the scope of administration should not overlap the free dominion of the individual. If somebody experiences such an infringement of his sphere of privacy, if he finds a governmental agency trespassing over the borderline, he should have the right to appeal to an impartial court (Hayek 1976b: 212–14; 1971: 54).

EMERGENCY POWERS

You may have gained the impression that, in Hayek's opinion, individual rights must never be infringed upon. This is not the case. To be sure, the normal running of society is based on them and any departure from them requires special justification, but even the most fundamental principles of a free society may have to be temporarily abandoned in extraordinary circumstances. Hayek acknowledges this necessity, but only when it is a question of preserving liberty in the long run. There exists widespread agreement on the need for emergency powers of government in situations of war, natural catastrophes or other disasters. Fundamental rights may have to be curtailed in cases of clear and present danger due to acts of God or the King's enemies. 'Like an animal in flight from mortal danger society may in such situations have to suspend temporarily even vital functions on which in the long run its existence depends if it is to escape destruction' (Hayek 1982–3: 124). However, in order to conform to the rule of law Hayek claims that three conditions must be fulfilled: first, it is imperative that such actions be confined to exceptional cases defined by rule, so that their justification does not rest on the arbitrary decision of any authority; second, that the individuals affected should not be harmed by the disappointment of their legitimate expectations but be fully indemnified for any damage they suffer as a result of such action (Hayek 1976b: 217); and third, that the exceptional powers will not be retained once the emergency ceases to exist (Hayek 1982–3: 124).

The right to compensation for damages is essential in Hayek's view of the *Rechtsstaat*, but I think Eugene Miller made a point when he criticized it as follows: 'It is clear how this principle might work in some cases, such as the expropriation of property, but not in a case where individuals are required to sacrifice their lives for the common good, as in wartime' (Miller 197: 191). So far I agree with him.

GROWN RULES MAY REQUIRE CORRECTION

I think, however, that Miller is not fair in stating, as he did, that 'Hayek intends a radical subordination of reason to law in areas where practical reason or prudence was traditionally assigned a place of supremacy'. I disagree with his claim that Hayek has no need of a prudent legislator 'since a system of law, properly speaking, is conceived as the product of an unconscious process and not of rational design' (Miller 1979: 191). Of course, in Hayek's view of the development of rules the spontaneous character of their evolution plays the most important part (I have touched on that already): like most of our social institutions, rules are 'the result of human action but not the execution of human design' - a famous and frequently used expression that Hayek borrows from Adam Ferguson, and which Ferguson for his part credits to De Retz (Ferguson 1991: 122) - but this does not imply a denial by Hayek that these rules still stand in need of being discovered, formulated and, if need be, corrected. He explicitly stipulates this in several places (Hayek 1976b; 148–9, 210; 1982-1: 88–9; 1988: 20). Neither do I believe that Miller is correct in saying that Hayek does not require prudence in applying or interpreting the law. I have not found Hayek stating that 'the law points more or less automatically to its specific applications', nor that 'prudence is not needed to determine policy in the absence of law, since government does not have a broad power to act for the common good where the laws are silent' (Miller 1979: 191).

To be sure, Hayek's theory of knowledge stresses the point that the intellectual capacities of the individual man could not consciously achieve the complex structures resulting from the anonymous processes of social and economic interaction in society: interaction that is mainly determined by people diligently pursuing their own ends. What Hayek does advocate - referring to Adam Smith - is the necessity of a system under which bad men can do least harm. That means

> a social system which does not depend for its functioning on our finding good men for running it, or on all men becoming better than they now are, but which makes use of men in all their given variety and complexity, sometimes good and sometimes bad, sometimes intelligent and more often stupid.
>
> (Hayek 1976a: 11–12)

It is true that Hayek does not think highly of man's individual capacities and virtues in this field; but of course, if there is a choice, Hayek, like anyone endowed with common sense, will prefer wise and good men to do the job rather than bad or stupid ones.

THE RULE OF GOOD LAW

Other critics of Hayek's conception of the rule of law are the adherents of the formal approach. Joseph Raz, for instance, praises Hayek's stripped' definition as conveyed in *The Road to Serfdom* as 'one of the clearest and most powerful formulations of the ideal of the rule of law'. He heartily disagrees, however, with some of the conclusions Hayek draws from his own definition. Raz accuses Hayek of confusing the rule of law with the rule of good law, and of overestimating its importance, which, according to Raz, are the two main fallacies in the contemporary treatment of the rule of law doctrine (Raz 1986: 210).

> If the rule of law is the rule of the good law, then to explain its nature is to propound a complete social philosophy. But if so the term lacks any useful function. We have no need to be converted to the rule of law just in order to discover that to believe in it is to believe that good should triumph. The rule of law is a political ideal which a legal system may lack or may possess to a greater or lesser degree. . . . It . . . is just one of the virtues which a legal system may possess and by which it is to be judged. It is not to be confused with democracy, justice, equality (before the law or otherwise), human rights of any kind or respect for persons or for the dignity of man.
>
> (ibid.: 11)

On this negative qualification Raz founds his claim that

> a non-democratic legal system, based on the denial of human rights, on extensive poverty, on racial segregation, sexual inequalities, and religious persecution may, in principle, conform to the requirements of the rule of law better than any of the legal systems of the more enlightened Western democracies.
>
> (ibid.: 211)

To put our minds at rest he adds that this does not mean that such a system will be better than the ones of the Western democracies. On the contrary, 'it will be an immeasurably worse legal system, but it will excel in one respect: in its conformity to the rule of law'. Though Raz is well aware of the fact that his proposition will alarm many, he claims that 'it presents a coherent view of one important virtue which legal systems should possess' and that 'it is not original' because he is 'following in the footsteps of Hayek and of many others who understood "the rule of law" in similar ways' (ibid.).

I think that Raz's reproaching Hayek for overestimating the importance of the rule of law is unjust, and that Raz himself is guilty of committing a fallacy here. First, he projects his own barren formal interpretation of the rule of law into Hayek's theory and then he blames Hayek for giving it an overriding importance and drawing the wrong conclusions from it. But Hayek himself would be the first to acknowledge that the rule of law as conceived by Raz can only be of minor significance. By stripping the principle of every substantive criterion Raz turns it into a trivial conception which, in my opinion, has nothing to do with a political ideal. His 'following in the footsteps of Hayek' can only concern Hayek's 'stripped definition' as conveyed in *The Road to Serfdom*, a definition which does not do justice to the position he worked out in *The Constitution of Liberty*. We saw that certain elements which, according to Raz, should not be confused with the rule of law, play a crucial part in Hayek's description. Of course, it is all a matter of definitions, but a purely formal notion of the rule of law will hardly contribute anything to the justice of a regime. In this respect - as in many others (not all) - I am a faithful adherent of Hayek, whose elaboration of the subject serves that very purpose.

During his career as an insatiable and many-sided investigator, a career that lasted almost seventy years, he has shared with us the countless fruits of his intellectual curiosity. He has shown himself a man of absolute honesty and truth, always making a point of mentioning and paying deference to the sources of his knowledge. His view on the evolution of rules and the supremacy of the rule of law reflects the essence of his legal and political philosophy, a philosophy based on his notions about man, mind and society, which, in their turn, are the result of protracted and intensive multi-disciplinary study. Hayek has not lived to see his ninety-third birthday, but I consider it an honour that the initiators of the commemorative symposium on this special day have enabled me to pay tribute to a great scholar.

NOTES

This lecture was delivered at the commemorative symposium in honour of Friedrich August von Hayek, 8 May 1992, at the University of Maastricht.

1 My translation and italics, I.K.
2 For a brief outline of Hayek's view on two traditions of rationalism, see P.B. Cliteur, 'Why Hayek is a Conservative', *Archiv für Rechts-und Sozialphilosophie*, 1990, 76(4): 467f.

REFERENCES

Ferguson, A. (1991) *An Essay on the History of Civil Society*, New Brunswick, NJ: Transaction (first published in 1767).

Hayek, F.A. (1955) 'Freedom and the Rule of Law', *The Political Ideal of the Rule of Law, Cairo: National Bank of Egypt.*

—— *(1964) 'Kinds of Order in Society', New Individualist Review* 3(2), Indianapolis Winter 1964: 3-12.

—— (1971) *The Road to Serfdom*, London: Routledge & Kegan Paul (first published in 1944).

—— (1976a) *Individualism and Economic Order*, London: Routledge & Kegan Paul (first published in 1949).

—— (1976b) *The Constitution of Liberty*, London: Routledge & Kegan Paul (first published in 1960).

—— (1980a) 'Kinds of Rationalism', *Studies in Philosophy, Politics and Economics*, Chicago: University of Chicago Press (first published in 1967).

—— (1980b) 'The Legal and Political Philosophy of David Hume', *Studies in Philosophy, Politics and Economics*, Chicago: University of Chicago Press (first published in 1967).

—— (1980c) 'The Principles of a Liberal Social Order', *Studies in Philosophy, Politics and Economics*, Chicago: University of Chicago Press (first published in 1967).

—— (1982) *Law, Legislation and Liberty*, London: Routledge & Kegan Paul.

—— (1988)*The Fatal Conceit: The Errors of Socialism*, The Collected Works of Friedrich August Hayek, vol. I, edited by W.W. Bartley, III, Routledge, London.

Machiavelli, N. (1927) 'Belfagor Arcidiavolo', *La Mandragola, La Clizia, Belfagor, Classici del Ridere*, terza edizione, A.F. Formiggini editore in Roma.

Miller, E.F. (1979) 'Prudence and the Rule of Law', *The American Journal of Jurisprudence*, 4: 181–206.

Raz, J. (1986) 'The Rule of Law and its Virtue', *The Authority of Law, Essays on Law and Morality*, Oxford: Clarendon Press (first published in 1979).

14

HAYEK AND NATURAL LAW

The Humean connection

Frank van Dun

Can Hayek's ideas be helpful in giving new force to the philosophy of natural law? The ruling positivist conception of law is in a state of crisis and some reformulation of natural law theory may well provide a way out of the present conundrums. Because there are a number of points of contact between Hayek and the natural law tradition, and it is beyond dispute that he was acutely aware of the confusions in modern legal thought, I shall look at some aspects of Hayek's notion of the social order and of Hume's legal philosophy, which has been Hayek's main source of inspiration in developing his own brand of liberalism. The final section addresses the question of the consistency of Hayek's conception of the liberal social order.

NATURAL LAW AND POSITIVISM

In the history of legal and political thought the idea of natural law is that laws derive their validity from their relation to reality or nature. Regardless of the many metaphysical and theological guises under which this idea has been presented, the core of natural law thinking is the conviction that laws serve a purpose and can be judged according to their fitness with respect to this purpose. The purpose of law, according to one interpretation of the old adage *ubi societas ibi ius*, is to make social life possible: where there is no law (*ius*) there is no society. Because a functioning society is at once a precondition for the successful achievement of whatever ends human beings may be pursuing, and a fragile thing, society and therefore law is understood as something that ought to be. The point of using the word 'precondition' is of course to stress that social order is not a means to human ends. It is rather the only framework within which the ideas of means, ends and of valuing are intelligible. As I read Hayek this core of natural law thinking is present in his works. Legal positivism, which also comes in many varieties, has consistently denied that the reason for the validity of laws is to be found in nature. The validity of laws derives instead from the authority of those who make, apply and/or enforce them.

In many accounts the opposition between the two schools of thought is reduced to the question whether law is a part of morality. However, this approach diverts attention from the core of natural law. For it is the link to nature, not some moral content, which underlies the ambition of natural law thinking to provide a critical perspective on jurisprudence and law-making.

There is no logical or other need for a natural law theorist to deny the existence of positive laws which are valid only because they are properly enacted by the proper authorities. Nor is the natural law theorist compelled to deny legal validity to a contract merely because it contains clauses of an immoral character. Natural law theory rejects the positivist doctrine on the sources of law, which makes legislation the primary and supreme source or arbiter of all law. Moreover, natural laws are said to be more fundamental than mere enactments. Outside the context of natural law, legislation is nothing but an expression of sheer political power, of might, not of right.

Hayek's distinction between law and legislation is familiar to natural law theorists. For Hayek, as for them, most law, indeed the most important law, could not be legislated law. They also, of course, accept Hayek's claim that law is something to be discovered, not made. They have no need to deny the existence of custom as a source of law. But, again, they would insist that custom can be a source of law only within the context of natural law. Custom cannot be the ultimate source for the same reason legislation cannot be. Outside the context of natural law, custom is as much a question of might as is legislation. Nevertheless, a custom can be unjust or immoral and still be a source of law, if it keeps to its proper role. It may be immoral to cut off a thief's hand, but a customary or legislated rule imposing this punishment would still be a law if it served the purposes of natural law, however imperfectly. Natural law thus sets the boundary within which human enactments and practices can be said to have a law-like character, or to participate in the enterprise of law.

One of the unfortunate consequences of reducing the opposition between natural law and legal positivism to the question of whether law is necessarily a part of morality concerns the meaning of validity. Legal positivists have generally defined the validity of rules or norms in terms of their effectiveness, that is, the degree to which they actually determine the behaviour of those to whom they are addressed. Thus the commands of an effective or powerful political regime are said to be valid, and therefore to be part of the law, for no other reason than that they are in fact obeyed. Hence comes the positivists' claim that they deal only with the law as it is or exists, not with the law as someone might feel it ought to be. Law as law exists only if it is effective. The position taken by the positivists suggests that natural law theory is merely concerned with law as it ought to be, and that therefore natural law has no legal validity because it is not as such effective. Relegated to a realm of pure oughtness, natural law is transformed into a woolly concoction of idealist speculation, completely divorced from the facts, and hence declared to be no matter of scientific concern.

Against this positivist view, one should stress that the aim of natural law theory is not to dispense with the creative inputs of lawyers and judges or even legislators, but to spell out the principles which these practical men ought to apply in order to justify their claim to be 'practitioners of the law'. Far from seeking the principles of law in a realm of pure oughtness, natural law theorists turned to nature, the realm of necessary effectiveness. Law which is not in accordance with nature is not effective at all. What the positivists regard as effectiveness is merely a mark of the existence of political power of man over man. But the effectiveness of such power does not by itself explain why it should be considered a source of law, much less the only source of law. Unless the ends of power are the ends of law (i.e. the preservation of social life) effective power is not the same thing as effective law.

If we now turn to Hayek, with a view to finding out whether his theories share the central concern of natural law with respect to linking the concept of law to an effective reality, we can begin with what are arguably his most striking contributions to the critique of contemporary society: his conception of social order and its implications for assessing the claims of socialists and interventionists. My point is that, for Hayek, the reality of the social order and its fragility explain the necessary failures of socialist experiments and the destructive tendencies of interventionist policies.

HAYEK'S NOTION OF SOCIAL ORDER

One of the enduring themes in Hayek's thought is that much of what we usually refer to as social phenomena is the consequence or 'result of human action, but not of human design'. Quoting Ortega y Gasset, Hayek maintained that order is not something imposed on society from without, but 'an equilibrium set up from within'.[1] Social order is not something artificial, in the way in which a clock is an artificial thing, but neither is it something natural, in the way in which a tree or a cloud is a natural thing.

Such a view of human society can be dialectically opposed either (1) to the view that society is a fully artificial thing or (2) to the view that society is a strictly natural thing, not the product of some design, but not a consequence of human action either. Hayek has fought on both fronts, against the 'constructivists' as well as against the 'holists' and 'organicists'. Against the former he argued that human society cannot be, and could not have been, designed. Against the organicists and holists he argued that individual human beings are not and could not be the passive parts or cells making up a large natural organism. They have an entrepreneuerial capacity to initiate change, not because they are somehow outside their social and cultural context, but because their actions are necessarily underdetermined by that context. The two arguments share a common ground in Hayek's views on the complexity of the social order and of the human mind.[2] These are complex orders not just in the sense of having many parts and many relations, but primarily in the sense of being unsimulatable. There can be no predictive model of the social order which is not as complex as the social order itself. As a result, the consequences of an action cannot be predicted very far into the future or outside the immediate neighbourhood of the place where it originated: unforeseen and unintended consequences abound. On the other hand, the social order has within it human beings who are similarly complex: tracing the consequences of a social influence on an individual runs into similar limitations. At best we may be able to recognize and predict patterns, but there is no basis for assuming that the patterns themselves are causally active.

Hayek argued that socialist or collectivist central planning was a mistake, not because mistakes were made in implementing the grand designs, but because the very idea of collectivist central planning betrays a fundamental misunderstanding of the nature of social reality. Socialism is a mistake because it does not respect the objective limits to what is possible. It is, in a word, a denial of natural law, and as such bound to fail.[3] Socialist theories were based on the idea that central planning would vastly improve upon the efficiency of the market with the fully informed *ex ante* co-ordination of the command economy. This could only be a fantasy, because the market uses much more knowledge or information than could possibly be made available to a central planner. If the market uses this knowledge less efficiently than one might hope, it is still true that the only way to remedy the deficiency is to exploit more of the opportunities the market order offers.

The centralization of dispersed knowledge in one centre is hopeless if, as Hayek maintained, a significant part of the knowledge actually used is of a type that cannot be collected and communicated without great or absolute loss of informational content. Thus, on account of the Hayekian knowledge problem, the central planner is an impossibility, and every attempt to have one must necessarily run out of steam far below the standard set by the market. It was in this context that Hayek began to stress the importance of the particular localized knowledge of particular objects and relations at a particular time and place, which is useful only if acted on immediately by those who possess it, and the knowledge embedded in skills and personal experiences, which cannot be separated from the person who has it. 'Tacit knowledge' became for him a very wide category indeed. It encompassed also the knowledge embedded in social practices, rules of conduct, institutions, which we follow without ever fully understanding them, because they are the outcomes of historical processes the details of which, being tied up with the subjective experiences, actions and choices of innumerable men and women in innumerable generations, are vitally important yet forever lost.

The Hayekian knowledge problem has made it clear that the economic system is far more complex than most people had realized. But it is not clear why an advocate of collectivist planning should regard it as a decisive refutation of the socialist ideal. However, there is an alternative argument against socialism, developed by Ludwig von Mises, which Hayek may have presupposed but did not stress.

It was Mises who started the debate on the 'impossibility' of socialism.[4] Mises made it clear that the command economy, whether of socialist inspiration or not, by displacing the market, deprived itself of a vital compass. All action is speculative, directed towards an unknown future that can only be anticipated on the basis of an understanding of how changes may affect present conditions. In a market economy people can speculate about future prices and on the basis of these calculate and compare the expected costs and revenues of various courses of action. When they embark on the one or the other of these courses of action they can then monitor their performance by comparing the prognosticated prices with the actual prices as they become known as well as with new assessments of future prices. This enables them to make adjustments to their plans on the basis of a continual evaluation. Market prices are essential for economic calculation and recalculation, and therefore for avoiding waste.

Thus, for Mises, even if the knowledge problem could be overcome, central planning could not exist except in the form of blind commands imposed without any calculational rationality and without any possibility for detecting errors. A socialist society will end up consuming its capital in wasteful efforts to implement plans that are simply irrelevant from an economic point of view.

There is a striking difference between Hayek and Mises here. Mises did not make much of the knowledge problem, not because he failed to recognize it, but because it is essentially the same in a market economy as in a socialist economy. With respect to making present arrangements for future outcomes people in a market economy have individually no more knowledge (in the Hayekian sense) than the socialist planner. They may and usually do have some information about 'present [i.e. recent] prices'. However, the observed prices are simply raw, uninterpreted data, excusing no one from speculatively assessing their significance. For Mises, then, the decisive argument against central planning is that it could not calculate even if perfect knowledge is assumed; whereas the argument for the market order is that regardless of the imperfections of knowledge it is capable of calculation. Hayek on the other hand seems to have lost interest in the calculation problem, perhaps because he became more and more interested in explaining social order in terms of the dark, unreasoned, under-the-surface tectonic movements of customs, traditions and institutions.

The main point of this discussion is to emphasize that for Hayek, as for Mises, the evaluation of socialism does not really depend on one's ideology or ultimate values, but on one's grasp of the reality of social order. Socialism is condemned because it is not in accordance with the nature of the thing it purports to be concerned about.

Both Hayek and Mises attempted to extend their criticism of socialist doctrines to interventionist ideas. If replacing the market economy with the centrally planned command economy is a mistake, then intervening in the market by way of coercive policies is also a mistake. Stated in this way the argument is a non-sequitur. But it can be backed up with a slippery-slope argument to the effect that interventions in the market economy tend to call forth further interventions, strengthen the role of the state, and eventually lead to full socialism. This strategy was in fact an important element in Hayek's and Mises's attacks on interventionism. Hayek used it to explain why we were on 'the road to serfdom',[5] and Mises warned that 'middle-of-the-road policy leads to socialism'.[6]

The gravitational pull which causes the movement down the slope is explained first by the argument that interventions will produce unforeseen and unintended consequences which will often turn out to be the opposite of the stated aims of the intervention. The typical example is a price ceiling motivated by the desire to allow more people to buy the commodity. But if this maximum price increases the demand for the good (the intended consequence), it may also induce producers to cut back on production or to switch to other lines of business (the unintended consequence): shortages will develop, and one may expect calls for rationing the commodity, or for subsidizing production, that is, for further interventions.

Another element in the explanation of the movement down the slope is that intervention creates new formations of groups with vested interests in maintaining or expanding the interventionist apparatus of the state. For the members of such groups (politicians, bureaucrats and recipients of subsidies) power, influence, social standing and wealth are direct results of the interventionist policies. Not only will such groups defend their advantages, other people will be tempted to make interventionism work for their own benefit as well.

The main institutional aspect of the slippery-slope argument is indeed that interventionism opens up an additional way for reaching one's goals. Political action, which aims at having the state provide goods or benefits at the expense of the taxpaying and/or of the law-abiding community (as in the case of regulations, restrictions of economic freedom), becomes available as an alternative to provision of the goods through the market. It is now rational for any individual, organization or group to ask whether it should invest in political or in economic means. Interventionism thus weakens reliance on market processes. Democratic pressures as well as the self-interest of politicians and bureaucrats may greatly increase the availability of opportunities and avenues of political action, thereby decreasing the opportunity costs of such action relative to action through the market.

To the extent that the critique of socialism is a critique of the idea of an economic organization that professes to dispense with the market, it does not matter that none of the arguments mentioned here demonstrates that what lies at the bottom of the slope is socialism. For the slippery-slope argument surely purports to say that interventionism tends towards the destruction of the market order.

Hayek's views on social evolution are particularly strong supports of the slippery-slope argument. If social institutions are the product of an evolutionary process, if they are embedded in a wide-ranging set of customs, traditions, modes of thought, and if they are mutually dependent in that not one of them is not an adaptation to other institutions in its environment, it should not be expected that a set of institutions, once destroyed or seriously impaired, can easily be restored. The market order is the result of a long process of learning, but not a result that can be divorced from the process that gave rise to it. It is a spontaneous social order, and as such cannot be imposed 'from without', only 'set up from within'. The evolutionary aspect of Hayek's thought does not support an optimistic attitude with respect to the (re)emergence of a market order in a setting where most of the customary and traditional sources from which it must draw its strength have dried up.

Compared to Hayek, Mises comes across as a rationalist. He insisted on the importance of ideology. 'Society' he wrote in *Human Action*, 'is a product of human action. Human action is directed by ideologies. Thus society and any concrete order of social affairs are an outcome of ideologies'. Mises did not mean to say that societies are rationally designed.[7] For him, reason (i.e. understanding) was a necessary condition for maintaining a complex social order. Not denying that a social order may come into existence as an unintended outcome of an innumerable set of interactions, he nevertheless rejected the Hayekian approach which eventually made customs, traditions, and so on, virtually the ultimate referents of social analysis. Without an articulate theory of social order any marginal deviation from established custom would be as likely to be allowed as any other. The weight and direction of custom would shift in imperceptible ways, and social disorder would be as spontaneous as social order, if people act according to a false ideology, or are incapable of recognizing false doctrines of social causation. For Mises, then, social order and its progressive development require that people grasp or understand why certain types of actions are to be forbidden and others to be allowed. Consequently Mises had a much more positive view of formal constitutions and explicit conventions. Hayek had a tendency to approve of these only if they express a knowledge embedded in customs and traditions. For Mises the question was whether they express an understanding of how individual actions produce social effects.[8]

Whether the slippery-slope argument itself is sound or not, it should be obvious that it too relies on the primacy of real forces. What is wrong with interventionism is that it does not have an adequate idea of how the social order links causes and effects into recurring patterns. That is why interventionism tends to undermine social institutions even if that is not its intention. It too is a violation of the natural laws of social order.

THE HUMEAN CONNECTION

If Hayek has a contribution to make to natural law, the most obvious place to look for it is Hume's theory of natural law, which Hayek has openly and repeatedly praised as the first true philosophy of his own brand of liberalism.[9] Of course, such an undertaking must avoid the Scylla of seeing Hayek as a Kantian as well as the Charibdis of seeing Hume as a utilitarian, since in either case we shall miss the link to the central concern of natural law theory. Nevertheless, I do not think the voyage is doomed to fail from the start.

'The sense of justice', Hume wrote, 'cannot be derived from nature, but arises artificially, tho' necessarily from education and human conventions.'[10] This concept of something that is at once artificial and necessary is basic to Hume's theory of natural law. Once it is understood, there can be no objection to calling what it denotes 'natural':

> Mankind is an inventive species; and where an invention is obvious and absolutely necessary, it may as properly be said to be natural as any thing that proceeds immediately from original principles, without the intervention of thought and reflection. Tho' the rules of justice be artificial, they are not arbitrary. Nor is the expression improper to call them Laws of Nature; if by natural we understand what is common to any species, or even if we confine it to mean what is inseparable from the species.[11]

Human survival would not be possible without the invention of rules of justice, which are the result of thought and reflection, judgement and understanding, that is, of what Hume called the natural remedies, 'for what is irregular and incommodious in the affections'.[12] But thought or reason could never have grasped the laws of justice as such if it had not been for the long experience with the effects of adhering to, and departing from, them.

The basic rules of justice, in Hume's account of natural law, are 'the stability of possessions, the transference of possession by consent, and the performance of promises'. It is because men appreciate its vital importance for the maintenance of society and therefore of their own well-being and subsistence, that they come to see justice as something that ought to be, even if irregular and incommodious affections prevent it from being assured. Stability of possessions is the first natural law of society, and therefore of justice and property. Property is 'nothing but those goods, whose constant possession is establish'd by the laws of society; that is by the laws of justice'. A person's property is some relation to external objects, but the relation is 'not natural, but moral, and founded on justice'. Property, then, is an artificial yet necessary and non-arbitrary relation; it is a natural right in the same sense in which the laws of justice or of society are natural.

The natural laws of society should be distinguished from natural laws of human behaviour, or of human action – that is, the laws which govern man's pursuit of his interests. Obviously human action is capable both of strengthening and of impairing the conditions for social life. Therefore the laws of society are compatible with, but not implied by, the laws of human action. That is, basically, why Hume felt it necessary to insist on the artificial character of the rules of justice, while at the same time affirming their necessity. The necessity is natural, however, if we consider that man and human society are coeval. Language, reason, understanding, judgement are attributes of social man, and that is the only sort of man there really is.

Self-interest cannot be a sufficient motive for the performance of just acts. If nothing else, death may shield us from the consequences of our own actions. Our own injustice may have its rewards in this life, and impose its costs only on those who come after us. Thus mortality allows us to ignore justice, reap the rewards, escape the inevitable costs and raise our children in the belief that our conduct instantiates the preconditions for their welfare and happiness. That is why blind custom or the rule of precedent is not necessarily a store of wisdom, but possibly the accumulation of folly.

The problem, then, is that while 'society' cannot escape the 'punishment' for unjust acts, it is different for the individuals responsible for them. Society cannot escape the punishment because it is a real order, a pervasive network of causal relationships. Some people will have to pay, and to pay dearly, because the effects of injustice in the end reduce themselves to the destruction of the social order. Injustice, therefore, is objectively bad in its consequences, and naturally esteemed to be wrong. We cannot sympathize with what is objectively bad, and we cannot approve of it when there is no personal interest which in our own estimation outweighs its badness for others. But the only interest we can have in something for which we have no other personal interest is that of sympathy. Hume's argument is that sympathy is a natural sentiment, which if it were not naturally present in the soul could not be produced by 'any combination or convention'. Sympathy explains why we feel we ought to respect the laws of justice.

It is therefore a mistake to claim that Hume gave a utilitarian account of morality and law. His is a consequentialist argument, but only because it relies heavily on the notion that causes produce effects. Actions may produce social order, but they may also destroy it; they can be good as well as bad. Because man is a social being, endowed with a capacity for sympathy, he cannot escape rating actions according to the contribution they make to the good or to the bad. But there is no calculus and no maximizing of any sort of utility. There could not be, because there is no calculating subject choosing morality or law. We naturally approve of what tends to be beneficial to society, not because we want to benefit society, but because we recognize in what is beneficial to society the solution to a problem we all have to deal with. If we are led astray in our sympathies, the reason must be that we have a false conception of what social order really is.

For the reasons set out above, one cannot induce an individual to conform to the natural laws of justice only by appealing to his self-interest. We can convince him of their rightness, by an appeal to his sympathy, but only if he has a clear understanding of the causal relations which make justice what it is, the fountainhead of all human welfare and happiness. But such conviction cannot be expected to carry much weight in practice, however conclusive it may be for the person in a speculative or philosophical mood. The continued existence of social order requires institutions which provide ways to make the individual effectively accountable for even the remoter consequences of his actions. It requires institutions which make him self-interestedly concerned to behave in accordance with the natural laws of justice.

Property and freedom of contract may be natural rights (in the sense referred to earlier), but respect for them is not automatically secured. Here we enter into the province of positive or man-made law (whether customary or judge-made or legislated law). Property law and contract law as well as liability rules are rooted in the natural laws of justice, but they do not define the conditions of social order, they are only methods for securing their observance. Their conventional component is therefore much more prominent. There can be no *a priori* determination of the form they should take, because their concern is to secure the principles of social order under the particular circumstances of time and place - hence the variety of national legal rules. Nevertheless, as they are means to secure the natural laws of justice, and partake in the morality of justice only because they are means to that end, they can claim no validity in and by themselves. This is so because they are and can be effective only to the extent they determine (i.e. apply) the natural laws of justice. To think of them as effective in any other sense - for example, because they are effectively enforced by the authorities or adhered to by the masses - is to regard them as no more than the particular actions of particular men seeking particular ends: it is to disregard their law-like character.

Hayek has wholeheartedly accepted the Humean philosophy of law, and extended it with his own insights on the co-ordination problem and on what became known as the Hayekian knowledge problem. The laws of justice are accepted as necessary conditions for solving the problem of co-ordinating the actions of many people in an environment characterized by radical ignorance. For the rules of justice can be translated into the basic institutions of the market order, which Hayek has consistently defended as the only type of social order in which that problem can be solved. As long as man is a social being and as such unable to stand outside society, all we can know is a number of patterns or laws of society, which do not express knowledge of the thing itself in all its complexity, but an abstract understanding of what makes it tick. The application of these articulated rules must necessarily be underdetermined at the conscious level and therefore proceed on the basis of tacit knowledge the full articulation of which will forever elude us.

If, as Hayek has argued, it is a mistake to assume that we have or can have knowledge about society we cannot in fact have, it is equally mistaken to assume that any combination of abstract rules of justice can be made to work. To assume that the transference of possessions by universal consent is a 'better' rule of justice may not be to assume knowledge we cannot in fact have, but is none the less a denial of the reality of the social order. Also, to guarantee the stability of possessions regardless of property relations – for example, by enforcing an arrangement under which the income earned by an individual is regarded as the property of some other individual – is to forget that the rules of justice are necessarily what they are given the historical processes and the realities of the factors that produced them, especially human nature and scarcity.

It is thus a mistake to regard the Hayekian conception of the rules of justice as merely procedural. They are procedural in that they do not prescribe specific outcomes or end-states, but it is not their procedural character, nor even their being concerned with possessions, consent and promise, that accounts for their justice. They have to be seen in connection with entitlements. For these too evolved over time in response to practical problems. I doubt that either Hume or Hayek would have cared to speculate about the evolution of a system of entitlements that was radically at odds with Locke's theories of self-ownership and labour. In fact, while Locke, like Hobbes and Rousseau, presented his thoughts on property in the context of a social contract theory, his picture of the state of nature, unlike their accounts of it, was merely a description of a society governed by the customs and traditions of social life with which he was familiar – including the rules of justice, but leaving out the formal apparatus of government. He described the prevailing sentiments about the justice of entitlements other than legal entitlements deriving from the exercise of political authority or conquest. From a Hayekian perspective this Lockean approach is an eminently sensible and commonsensical way to proceed when one endeavours to criticize one aspect of a culture, in this case the development of a practice of absolutist rule. How else can one consider its consistency with the rest of the culture, which is, according to Hayek, the only possible way to practice the art of social criticism?

One difficulty in understanding Hayek is the problem of reconciling his ideas of immanent criticism of aspects of a culture within a process of cultural evolution and of our radical ignorance of what is going on, on the one hand, with his advocacy of the market order, liberty and liberalism as a superior social and political philosophy, on the other. Part of the problem is that talk about traditions tends to evoke images of traditional societies which are usually not known for their highly developed division of labour or extensive markets, but rather for their hierarchical, or in some cases egalitarian, social structures. If such societies are considered, one could easily find that there is absolutely no basis in tradition or cultural history for advocating say a market economy or liberty. But Hayek's (and Hume's) frame of reference was the great society, the extended order, where the problem of co-ordination exceeds the capacities for explicit direct social control either by a cohesive hierarchy or by mutual observation. While he obviously did not believe that nothing can destroy the great society, he did believe that there is no way back - either we learn to live comfortably with it or we had better be prepared to die miserably without it. Once it has emerged, regardless of how it did so, the critical task is to improve it within the limits of what is practically and epistemologically possible and on the basis of the laws that make it what it is.

NEUTRALITY

The main characteristic of the great society is that whatever unity it possesses can no longer be traced back to common ends. Its problem of co-ordination is precisely that it is not one of arranging means towards the attainment of a single goal. The great society is the home of people who are not only strangers to one another, but who are also exponents of different cultures and traditions, who have widely divergent moral and religious beliefs, personal backgrounds and ambitions. How can they live and work together with a minimum of conflict? For Hayek, the problem of co-ordination must be solved without disregard for the many divergent aims people have. The rules of justice of a great society can take no account of the particular ends people pursue, but only of the manner in which they do so.

The implication of this view is that law and morality should be separated. For law, being related to the real conditions of the existence of the social order, is now called upon not merely to express tradition, but to co-ordinate the actions and outputs of people about whose cultural background almost nothing is known. In other words, the great society requires the evolution of a specifically legal tradition. This is what happened with fits and starts in the history of Western civilization. But Hayek was not happy with the more recent developments of the legal tradition in the West. Rather than adapting itself to the requirements of the social order of a great society, it adapted itself to the requirements of a hierarchical structure, the state, with the result that it now seems that legislation is the primary source of law, rather than an incidental aspect of law.

The preceding discussion of Hayek's reasoning on the co-ordination problem suggests the hypothesis that the separation of law and morality is a conclusion of applying natural law thinking to the problems of a great society. For it was on the basis of the real constraints on what is possible that he came to see the neutrality of law with respect to particular ends as an implication of its justice.

I believe the hypothesis can be used to defuse a common criticism of Hayek's thesis about the requirement of neutrality and the distinction between law and morality, and therefore of his liberalism. One recent exponent is Jeffrey Friedman, who has boldly declared that 'liberal neutrality is a myth'.[13] 'The reason', he says, 'is that . . . to adhere to the value of neutrality is patently to take a moral position: it is to say that it is better for the law to allow people to do what is "morally wrong" than to force them to do what is morally right.' However, from the perspective of natural law, the question, whether it is better for the law to do this or that, hardly makes sense. The more appropriate question is whether natural law allows people to force other people to do what the first think or claim is morally right. The answer to this question is not a matter of choice or of consequentialist evaluation, but of appreciating the nature of things. With respect to liberty, the natural law answer is not that liberty produces consequences which one may or may not value higher than the consequences of interfering with liberty. The answer is, rather, that liberty or justice is the precondition of complex social order without which no economic, moral or political values could exist. In any particular case one's verdict on the merits of interfering with someone's liberty as against the merits of non-interference may be in favour of the former, but even if this were true in all cases, the argument for liberty or justice would still stand. For it does not depend on a utilitarian calculus (i.e. on perceptions, expectations and the valuation of consequences), but on the conditions for the existence of the social order itself.[14] It is, then, not necessarily the case that 'to adhere to the value of neutrality is patently to take a moral position'. Moral choice presupposes the conditions of social existence; it is not about those conditions. The liberal contention is, in Hume's words, that the

> question . . . concerning the wickedness or goodness of human nature, enters not in the least into that other question concerning the origin of society. . . . For whether the passion of self-interest be esteemed vicious or virtuous, 'tis all a case; since itself alone restrains it: So that if it be virtuous men become social by their virtue; if vicious, their vice has the same effect.[15]

Friedman also finds that neutrality is paradoxical 'when we prize liberty as an intrinsic good rather than as a means to good consequences'.[16] He notes that freedom 'is properly the description of an agent before he or she chooses a value .... Seen in this way, morality is fundamentally at odds with freedom: freedom is the multiplication of options, morality is the narrowing of them by the selection of one over the others'.[17] But this argument begs the question: it presupposes the reduction of politics and law to morality. Let us accept the definition that moral freedom is the absence of moral obligations towards oneself or others ('I am not free tonight: I have to prepare for my exams/my parents are coming over'); it does not follow that there is such a thing as moral freedom, or that a person in society is at any time without moral obligations. In any case, this is hardly what we mean by political freedom. One is free, in the politically relevant sense, to the extent one's rights are respected. Far from being at odds with morality, such political freedom is a precondition of moral action. Yet Friedman boldly asserts that 'libertarian liberalism implicitly denies the legitimacy of any other values, since what it values is not values but the pre-moral condition of freedom to select among them'.[18] But to value the pre-moral condition of political freedom is not the same thing as to value moral freedom, that is, the condition of being under no moral obligations. That I resent being coerced does not mean I resent taking care of my children.

Friedman goes on to state that 'attempts to enforce a given standard of appropriate behavior are seen in libertarian societies as mere efforts to "impose one person's values on another"'.[19] But there is, to begin with, a distinction between 'a mere effort to impose one's values on another' (without which it is difficult to see how there could be cultural transmission and communication of values) and 'enforcing a given standard of appropriate behavior' (which presumably means coercively preventing people from acting on their own values). There is no need for a liberal to say that coercively imposing one's values on another is wrong *because* it is a form of imposing one's values.

Friedman also repeats the old canard that the argument for the separation of law and morality requires the assumption that individual choice is 'a mere exercise of what economists like to call "individual tastes"'.[20] Natural law theory, and Hayek's Humean theory as well, regard persons as real things with a complexity that can never be completely mastered, not even by themselves. There is an objective quality to the person which allows him to act on the basis, not of whim or mere taste or preference, but of his (limited) understanding of himself. True, such choices are still relative to himself, but they are not merely subjective or whimsical.

This will not satisfy Friedman. So intent is he on finding paradox upon paradox, that he now claims that liberalism is really a form of determinism:

> Libertarianism rests implicitly on an endogenous determinism, which just as effectively as the exogenous variety stops one (let alone others) from criticizing oneself, i.e. from accounting for one's tastes in order to consider the possibility of changing them, rather than merely expressing them.[21]

Again this goes far too fast. To begin with, whether there is such a natural self is a question of fact. But if there is one (and I cannot see how there could not be one),[22] why should this be taken to mean that there is no room for criticizing what one does or wants? Friedman undercuts his own claim, that 'anyone with a modicum of self-awareness understands that there is no spontaneous "there" in there', by immediately qualifying it out of existence with the remark 'that one's actions are in large measure susceptible to rational control'.[23] Consistency would have required him to say 'fully susceptible'. On the Hayekian view, of course, there is a spontaneous 'there' in there, which is why we can never have more than a measure of rational control over our actions, but also why we can contextually criticize our actions and choices as being consistent with what we are.

What is the reason for Friedman's claim that liberalism reduces the self to 'given (and as such uncriticizable) wants'? Apparently none other than his belief that to oppose interference in the market is to defend whatever people want on the ground that it is freely chosen.[24] But, again, to oppose coercive interference in the market is not to defend or even condone whatever outcomes the market produces. It is not to free the individual of moral responsibility, but to insist on it. For the rules of the market at least tend to ensure that people bear the consequences of their own actions; but they do not rule out non-coercive attempts to improve the morals of other people. For Friedman this is not enough: the failure of liberalism is that it does not allow coercive paternalism. He adds, that *we* – but who does he have in mind? – should practice such paternalism whenever it will not 'backfire'.[25] This is to sweep aside all warnings about the limitations of our knowledge, which Hume had in mind when he said that 'Tis impossible to separate the good from the ill'. Reading Hayek from a natural law perspective, I can only conclude that there is no substance to the charge that liberalism is inconsistent because of its claims of moral neutrality.

NOTES

This paper was prepared for a symposium on Hayek organized by Jack Birner held at the University of Limburg, 8 May 1992.

1 F.A. von Hayek, *The Constitution of Liberty*, London; Routledge & Kegan Paul, 1976, motto for Chapter 10.

2 Hayek's first thoughts on complex orders were concerned with the mind, although these were not published until 1952, in *The Sensory Order*, Chicago: University of Chicago Press.

3 Hayek's comments on socialism can be followed from his early contributions to the debate on collectivist economic planning in the 1930s to his last book, *The Fatal Conceit*, London: Routledge, 1988, where he declares that 'socialist aims and programmes are factually impossible' and even 'logically impossible' (p. 7).

4 Ludwig von Mises, 'Economic Calculation in the Socialist Commonwealth', in F.A. von Hayek (ed.) *Collectivist Economic Planning*, London: Routledge & Kegan Paul, 1935, pp. 89–130. Originally published in German in the *Archiv für Sozialwissenschaften*, 1920.

5 The title of his famous polemical tract of 1944.

6 The title of one of Mises's many papers on interventionism.

7 'The individual does not plan and execute actions intended to construct society. His conduct and the corresponding conduct of others generate social bodies': *Human Action*, Chicago: Regnery, 1966, p. 188.

8 But it should be remembered that Hayek (notably in the first volume of *Law, Legislation and Liberty*, Chicago: University of Chicago Press, 1973) repeatedly backed away from the position that customs and traditions are unopposable and sacrosanct, although his views on our 'inevitable ignorance' often seem to imply it.

9 F.A. von Hayek, 'The Legal and Political Philosophy of David Hume', in *Studies in Philosophy, Politics, and Economics*, Chicago: University of Chicago Press, 1967. The link has been obscured by and even depreciated on account of Hayek's attempts to state his social and political philosophy in Kantian terms. See, for example, John Gray, *Hayek on Liberty*, Oxford: Blackwell, 1984, and Chandran Kukathas, *Hayek and Modern Liberalism*, Oxford: Clarendon Press, 1989. To what extent the Kantian influences should be discounted or given a prominent place in an interpretation of Hayek is a question I cannot deal with (See the contribution by Nico Roos, Ch. 15 of this volume.) However, it seems to be beyond dispute that Hayek has always tried to present Kant as being in all important respects in accord with Hume.

10 David Hume, *A Treatise of Human Nature*, ed. L.A. Selby-Bigge, Oxford: Oxford University press III, 2, 1.

11 Ibid.

12 Ibid., III, 2, 2.

13 Jeffrey Friedman, 'Accounting for Political Preferences: Cultural Theory versus Cultural History', *Critical Review* 5(3), 1991: 327.

14 'However single acts of injustice may be contrary, either to public or private interest, 'tis certain, that the whole plan or scheme is highly conducive, or indeed absolutely requisite, both to the support of

society, and the well-being of every individual. 'Tis impossible to separate the good from the ill' (Hume, *Treatise*, III, 2, 2).

15 Hume, *Treatise*, III, 2, 2.
16 Friedman, 'Accounting for Political Preferences', p. 327.
17 Ibid., p. 328.
18 Ibid.
19 Ibid., p. 327.
20 Ibid.
21 Ibid., p. 329–30.
22 Cf. Frank van Dun *Het Fundamenteel rechtsbeginsel*, Antwerpen: Kluwer-Rechtswetenschappen, 1982.
23 Friedman, 'Accounting for Political preferences', p. 330 (emphasis added).
24 Ibid.
25 Ibid., p. 329. I admit that in a free society an act of coercive paternalism may sometimes be found to be excusable, even if condemned as a matter of principle. But this no more calls into question the coherence of the idea of neutrality (separation of law and morality) than does the fact that in some cases an act of premeditated murder may be found to be excusable.

15

HAYEK'S KANTIAN HERITAGE AND NATURAL LAW

Nikolas H. M. Roos

In his *Hayek on Liberty* John Gray comes to the conclusion that 'the result of the moral emptiness of Hayek's theory of cultural evolution for political philosophy is that his system lacks definite normative standards for the critical assessment of political practice'. He then raises the question, 'How then might this effect be remedied?' and answers, 'Not, to be sure, by recourse to any doctrine of natural rights. . . . Theories of natural law, are . . . indefensible in modern terms. They presuppose a teleology of nature' (Gray 1986: 142). It will be argued here that Gray's opinion is mistaken. He says that 'doctrines of natural law are at home only in the contexts in which they emerged historically – in Aristotle's mystical biology and in Locke's theism' (ibid.: 143). Gray thus ignores Kant's theory of morality and (natural) law. Kant's theory of natural law does not presuppose a teleology of nature, even though he assumed a belief in God as a regulative idea of moral and historical philosophy. That Gray ignored Kant, is surprising in view of his characterization of Hayek's thinking as 'informed by a distinctively Kantian approach' (ibid.: 4). Moreover, Hayek himself has recognized the closeness between Kant's and his own philosophy of law (Hayek 1982, vol. 2; 166).[1] Contrary to Gray again, it will also be argued that Hayek's view of natural law theory should be taken into consideration by those liberals who think that Hayek's views on law, state and politics are more or less what they stand for, but who are not convinced that Hayek's theoretical framework is consistent and strong enough.

An alternative theory, which I believe to be both consistent and sufficiently strong, 'law as second-order morality', will be presented in this chapter, be it very briefly. The name reflects the epistemological approach to law which Kant initiated. Some of the value of the Kantian approach was revived in Popper's critical rationalism, but Popper and his followers limited that value by an empiricist-evolutionistic interpretation of the cognitive process and by ignoring to a large extent the pragmatic presuppositions of science and epistemology. Hayek himself recognized a deep similarity between his own and Popper's theory as well as between Popper's falsificationism and Kant's (as well as his own) theory of law. However, it never made him think more thoroughly about their relationship.[2] In fact, the same defect as just mentioned in relation to Popper, empiricism and evolutionism, is what will be criticized presently in Hayek's theory of law.

The order of the exposition will be as follows. In the first section I will argue that Hayek's idea that natural law is objectionable because of its *a priori*-speculative character is unconvincing, if natural law can also have an epistemological foundation. Modern epistemology cannot be classified simply on the basis of the *a prior– a posteriori* distinction. In the second section a number of reasons will be considered which suggest why Hayek's theoretical framework for the explanation of the development of law and society is inconsistent and too weak. The third section will raise the question of whether the historical role of rational natural law theory in the development of a liberal society, almost ignored by Hayek, is just coincidental. It will be argued that this is not the case. Furthermore, Hayek's ideas on law (natural and customary), legislation and liberty will be criticized on both theoretical and empirical grounds, leading us to the conclusion that the empiricist-evolutionist surface hides a naïve belief in the necessary connection between moral, cultural and social-economic progress. In the fourth section it will be shown that Hayek's (belated) recognition of his closeness to Kant is not well founded.[3] Hayek rather followed Hume, although I do not want to suggest that he followed him very closely.[4] In the same section the Kantian philosophy of law will be critically reviewed. In the fifth section a brief sketch will be presented of a derivation of the essence of Hayek's political theory of legitimate tasks of the state on the basis of 'law as second-order morality'. In the sixth and last section the idea of natural law as an epistemology of law will be explained further.

THE EPISTEMOLOGICAL STATUS OF EPISTEMOLOGY

According to Hayek, the notion of 'natural law' as referring to customary or judge-made law in contrast to deliberately created or positive law was perverted in the sixteenth and seventeenth centuries by the rise of constructivist rationalism into 'the assumption that law could be logically derived from *a priori* premises' (Hayek 1982, vol. I: 21). Hayek ascribes this perversion to the 'Cartesian relapse into anthropomorphic thinking'. However,

> it came increasingly to be seen that the formation of regular patterns in human relations that were not the conscious aim of human actions raised a problem which required the development of systematic social theory', a need which was 'met by the Scottish moral philosophers . . . after a new start was made by Bernard Mandeville and David Hume, the spiritual fathers of 'the evolutionary approach'
>
> (Hayek 1982, vol. I: 22)

It is commonly accepted that Kant's philosophy was an attempt to save rationalism from Hume's empiricist criticism of rationalism. Kant credited Hume for having awakened him out of a rationalist 'dogmatic slumber', but he believed to have found a way out of Hume's criticism via his famous 'Copernican turn' to epistemology. As Kant defended a theory of natural law, Hayek's belated recognition of Kant's theory of law as very close to his own makes one wonder why he rejected natural law theory so firmly.

Apart from the question concerning the adequacy of Hayek's account of the development of rational natural law theory, the question is why *a priori* premises should be necessarily anthropomorphic in nature. With Hayek, the term anthropomorphic means, in this connection at least, the assumption that society functions or could function according to a rational design (Hayek 1982 vol. I: 27). The critical meaning of this qualification is unclear. Hayek's account of the role of the common law judge underlines that his task is to develop law according to its principles, as rationally reconstructable from earlier case law. Furthermore, he admits that case law can at times be so disfunctional or messy that it calls for a reconstruction through legislation. The history of English law, on which Hayek largely draws, contains many examples of such reconstructions.[5] There is evidently no black-white dichotomy between more or less unconscious development and design of legal rules. However, many natural law theorists, including Kant, had the ambition only to clarify the deeper nature and principles of law which they saw partly realized already in practice. Most of them aimed at logical reconstruction, not at a totally new design.

All normative social theories contain an anthropology, from which they derive moral and social principles without, however, necessarily giving an anthropomorphic account of the functioning of society in the sense that society is or could be the product of conscious design by human beings. Whether or not a social theory has such a naïve view would seem to depend on the content of its premises and not on their *a priori* or *a posteriori* character. Moreover, the *a priori* – *a posteriori* dilemma is false. When Karl Popper, for instance, connects his falsificationist epistemology with a theory of politics in the open society as collective decision-making by trial and error (Popper 1945), he may be accused of constructivist-rationalist and anthropomorphic tendencies (Gray 1986; 110–15); but it would be silly to argue that Popper was wrong because he developed his theory from *a priori* reasons. Popper's epistemology is clearly also not *a posteriori* in the way that empirical science is. His epistemology is based on 'rational reconstruction', a subject we will go deeper into in the fourth section.

The accusation of apriorism is believed to be fatal because, as John Gray tells us, 'the project of giving liberal society a foundation in natural law is closed to any philosophy which accepts the terms of contemporary scientific empiricism' (Gray 1986: 143). That leaves open the question of why one should accept these terms when matters of practical reason are at stake. Law, in the empiricist approach, is a social phenomenon like any other and the only critical test of law from this perspective may be functionality or, if treated in legal terms, coherence within a legal system as a whole. Within that approach 'the very idea of an ethical theory that attains a point of Archimedean leverage on moral practice is incoherent – a rationalist illusion spawned by a false picture of reasoning itself' (ibid.). Hayek certainly ascribed an important or even exaggerated role to the influence of ideas on society (Barry 1982: 90). However, notwithstanding Hayek's criticism of the economic and the socio-biological approach to social evolution, in which he points to the constitutive nature of social ideas as irreducible to simple biological or economic interests (Gray 1986: 47), he does not believe that ideas can determine the course of evolution on the basis of their own merits, but only in relationship to their evolutionary utility. Unfortunately, Hayek's ideas on how utility manifests its selective potential, are very vague and unconvincing (ibid.: 141).

It would certainly be naïve to believe that ideas can prevail because of their theoretical merits alone. They need the leverage of the interests of important social groups. At the same time, they may be constitutive in *creating* the groups that carry these ideas or give them a sense of identity and social and historical mission. In that sense they may have a crucial influence on the course of history. On the other hand, it is just speculation that evolutionary 'fitness' of ideas has anything to do with the fact that they help certain social groups to prevail over others. I suspect that the idea that this is the case represents a nineteenth century empiricist version of enlightened belief in progress. Not only is Hayek's criticism of idealist explanations of history unconvincing, but his evolutionary approach to social development in general and to law in particular cannot stand closer theoretical and empirical scrutiny.

HAYEK'S EVOLUTIONARY APPROACH TO LAW AND SOCIETY

Hayek's theory of social evolution is one of the most thoroughly criticized elements of his theory (Gray 1986: 135–8). David Ramsay Steele has argued that Hayek's emphasis on group selection is not in agreement with the views of modern biological evolution theory. Group benefits are generally much slower in establishing themselves or competing against individual benefits in nature and, *a fortiori*, in society, where the process of evolutionary competition is not limited by genetic constraints. Hayek's view on cultural evolution, says Ramsay Steele, is inconsistent with his individualist methodology; its holistic approach goes along with a providentialist view of evolution, which makes the functionalistic error of concluding from survival to an evolutionary function (Ramsay Steele 1987: 171–95).

Another incisive criticism has been given by Viktor Vanberg, who argues that if Hayek's theory of social evolution is correct, his criticism of society must be incorrect (Vanberg 1985). Hayek's criticism of present-day state policies is based on the incoherence of their principles, an incoherence which leads to negative effects in practice. Since Hayek is discussing a structural feature of modern states, he would have to explain how it can be that this incoherence can persist, its huge non-beneficial effects notwithstanding.

Hayek's explanation for the problem of persistence is, in fact, very idealistic. He does not claim that such 'incoherently principled' societies can endure because the poorer part of the population finds it profitable to rob the richer part or because these societies have proven to be superior in the competition between states. Such a claim would either refute his group theory of social evolution or restrict his critical theory to a world without states as competing organizations. Instead, Hayek claims that people who support modern state policies are *misled* as they do not understand the positive value of ignorance. They believe that the painful correction by the invisible hand of errors of judgement which are made in a free market can be cut short by the state, which is supposed to be able to avoid such errors of co-ordination in advance. However, if mistaken beliefs can structurally determine the course of social evolution, his own belief in social evolution as an explanatory factor seems to be mistaken.

In fact, when Hayek applies the evolutionary explanation in his account of the development of law, it cannot stand the scrutiny of modern anthropology of law. Like anthropology in general (Sampson 1964), the anthropology of law (Roberts 1979, Ch. 11) has almost completely rejected evolutionism except for some well-established findings concerning the relationship between cultural development and institutional complexity (Schwartz and Miller 1964; Wimberley 1973). But these findings invite a social-system perspective. In that perspective the non-liberal role of the modern state cannot easily be explained as just dysfunctional noise. No doubt, an amazing amount of money and energy is wasted in state activities. But in this respect the state does not differ very much from other large organizations. Moreover, as long as it serves learning processes, waste as such is not objectionable from an evolutionary perspective. The development of legal restraints on budgetary and monetary policies as well as the incorporation of effectiveness studies as a monitoring device in almost any costly piece of new state policies illustrate that modern welfare states have gone through quite a learning process concerning the limits of state interference during the last twenty years.

From a liberal perspective, a theory of social evolution is a discomforting device. Not only is there no necessary theoretical connection between freedom, spontaneous social order and social evolution (Rothbard 1980), there is also no convincing empirical evidence that countries which follow the liberal model more closely are superior in terms of social integration and cultural and economic performance to countries like Germany and Japan, which succeed in combining formal or informal corporatism with a high degree of economic competitiveness. But even if such only partially liberal societies were superior from an evolutionary point of view, a liberal might still prefer a liberal society as being more just. In that case Hayek's theory would be of no avail to him. Norman Barry has tried to save Hayek from this predicament by arguing that liberty maximizes experimentation in the growth and acquisition of knowledge (Barry 1982: 68–9). Barry's argument takes Hayek's false dilemma of central planning versus liberty for granted, but in practice the two can live together quite happily by avoiding extremes. Barry and Hayek suggest that social evolution can only be hindered when political structures ignore and hinder free social-economic development. However, too much liberty may lead to a lack of structure and co-ordination in solving problems of transaction costs, positive and negative externalities or risks of long-term investments. Moreover, a part of the possible (in principle) blessings of a free market cannot be realized because of international political and military rivalry, which can make a lack of state support suicidal. This is especially the case in the high-tech area, which demands investments of a size that private firms are not willing to risk without public support. Liberalism is faced with a Prisoner's Dilemma here as long as there is no really free market or a reliable peace-keeping system on a world scale. To claim, as Barry does, that the 'benefits may not be immediately observable but in the long run the advantages of the system [of liberty] are obvious' (Barry 1982: 69), is to replace observation and social system theory by a dogma. The belief in the evolutionary superiority of a liberal society has its origin in Enlightenment-illusions about the inner connection and value of freedom, scientific and social-economic progress. By now, in the time of 'risk society' (Beck 1992), we are more in need of a liberal theory of justice which helps us to control the many negative aspects of 'progress' to some extent.[6]

LAW, LEGISLATION AND LIBERTY

We will now take a closer look at Hayek's theory of law and its development and see how its defects are related to the criticized evolutionist foundation of liberty.

Hayek seems to neglect almost completely the impact which rational natural law theory had upon the idea of the rule of law and (negative) fundamental rights (d'Entrèves 1981: 57), to which Hayek assigns an essential role in the liberal society that he advocates. Hayek mentions Locke in connection with the history of the idea of the rule of law (Hayek 1976: 167). However, he misses the essential point here, which is that Locke connected the idea of fundamental natural rights with the older idea of checks and balances in politics as an institutional guarantee that laws will be made in conformity with fundamental rights and will be applied generally and equally. In his discussion of the development of the idea of the rule of law Hayek concentrates almost exclusively on England. Locke had much less impact on England, however, than on the American and French constitutions, the first two liberal ones in the world. In England, in fact, the idea of the rule of law was just a continuation of the ancient and medieval principle that lawmaker and citizens are equally bound by the law and that liberties once acquired may not be abrogated without the consent of the people. The idea of human rights is rather foreign to the English mind even today.[7]

One may reject this observation as irrelevant, as it is not unusual and quite understandable within an evolutionary perspective like Hayek's that mistaken theories give birth to institutions whose vital importance is not or insufficiently understood by these theories. Certainly, there was no necessary relationship between liberalism and (rational) natural law theory as it 'flourished under the benign rule of the absolute princes' (d'Entrèves 1981: 60).

The distinctive character of rational natural law theory, in comparison to earlier forms of natural law theory, was the combination of rationalism and individualism. Its central problem was to explain and legitimize the emergence and existence of social order starting from an individualist methodological position. This methodological basis has no necessary connection with liberalism, as Hobbes's *Leviathan* illustrates. It has a weaker kind of connection to it, however, in an attribution of the burden of proof. It is not the individual who has to legitimize his position and rights against the state. On the contrary, a limitation of individual rights as being in the best interest of the individual has to be proven. This being the case, it is not to be expected that, as Hayek says, the rationalist-individualist approach necessarily leads to a blueprint theory of state and society in the sense of a centrally planned society, nor is there historical evidence for this.

What Hayek has to say about justice is based on a conceptual analysis of that notion through which he relates it to the characteristics of legal rules (as *nomos*) as being abstract and negative. The 'abstractness' of legal rules refers to their not aiming at particular end-states, but being concerned with the right forms of social interaction, through which 'domains of individual freedom' (Hayek 1982, vol. 1: 34) are protected. By implication, such rules apply to an indefinite number of cases. The negative nature of just rules is somewhat harder to understand. Hayek credits Kant for the insight that 'though we have no positive criteria of justice, we do have negative criteria which show us what is unjust' (Hayek 1982, vol. 2: 42). In the next section we will argue why this opinion is incorrect. Kant's criterion is that a rule should be consistently compatible with individual autonomy. For Kant it is not enough that a rule is general and abstract. Kant would not agree with Hayek that all just rules are in fact just prohibitions to interfere with the domain of freedom of someone else.

Hayek acknowledges that there are positive duties also, but he calls them 'duties incurred by one's own actions'. That exception may explain tort law, but not contractual obligation in cases where not fulfilling a contractual obligation makes the creditor no worse off than before the contract. The legal enforcibility of contractual duty is in fact a sanction on the positive use of personal freedom. It constitutes a socialization of personal freedom across the boundaries of individual domains. The obligational character of contractual promise as such cannot be explained by its utility or lower transaction costs alone, because it is questionable whether a rule which makes a mere promise contractually binding is more efficient.

Hayek also allows rules as prohibitions for duties which result from circumstances beyond the control of an individual (e.g. the duty to save a drowning person if it can be done without too much risk to oneself). He does not explain why such duties are acceptable and felt to be 'just'. For Kant the explanation from the respect owed to others as persons is straightforward. Again from the point of view of social evolution and utility, it is not evident why such duties should exist, as evolutionary selection might be better served if they did not.

Admitting this second exception to laws as prohibitions is not as innocent as it may seem, because it raises the question concerning the limits of such obligations. Hayek does not explain why other duties to assist people in less acute but apparent need of help might not be included into the notion of justice, as Christians and social democrats demand. He remarks that 'it may be that in the future there will be further developments in this direction; but they will probably be limited because of the great difficulty of specifying by a general rule on whom such a duty rests' (Hayek 1982, vol. 2: 36). Hayek ignores that this limitation is irrelevant for those who will happily collectivize unspecifiable duties via taxes. For a Kantian delimitation of such duties is not difficult in principle: only extreme duress will affect personal autonomy as such.

Hayek's theory of liberal justice, based as it is on utility as determined by social evolution, also fails to explain why there is no general duty not to harm anybody without good reason. The point is that a liberal theory of justice should not only justify harming others because it is generally useful (e.g. no longer doing business with John, whose goods have become too expensive), but even doing harm for totally personal reasons such as, 'I do not like John's face any longer'. Again, for Kant this explanation is no problem, as he limited law to the bare necessities of a viable social order. To him, as we will see in the next section, there are moral reasons why law should not pretend to be a device to make people decent or try to protect them from all indecently inflicted harm.

This criticism of Hayek's theory of liberal justice shows that such a theory cannot be based on considerations of social utility alone. Moreover, the notions of justice and individual freedom must be connected on a deeper level so as to explain both the limits of individual freedom and the limits of state power. Hayek's theory of the limits of governmental power does not fulfil that requirement, as it is based on a theory of collective goods largely unrelated to a theory of justice (Hayek 1982, Ch. 14).[8] Furthermore, Hayek's theory of collective goods is vulnerable to the more recent criticism of that theory (De Jasay 1989).[9] Even if a certain 'good' *could* only be produced collectively, that does not imply that it *should* be produced. Conversely, it is not prima facie absurd to think that some goods which may be produced privately, should be produced collectively, for example, support of poor physically handicapped people, because it concerns a task which a legitimate legal order should fulfil in order to prevent free-riding on other people's greater altruism in the face of distress.

Hayek's view on social evolution is correlated with his middle course between natural law and legal positivism. Much of what he has to say about 'embodied' knowledge in law and society can be traced back to the Historical School of law with its doctrine of the unconscious *Volksgeist* as the source of legal customary law. However, he represents the ultra-romantic and conservative wing of that school. Even Savigny had taken into account that customary law was gradually being rationalized by legal science and that this rationalization would lead to a positivization of customary law in the form of codifications once legal science would have developed itself sufficiently. Although it is true, of course, that the way in which law develops in codified systems differs from common law systems, the belief that codifications represent 'taxis' law rather than 'nomic' law cannot stand empirical scrutiny, even though it is true that in enlightened absolutism there is a historical connection between natural law theory and the codification movement. In fact, Hayek does not say that codifications represent 'blueprint' law - he has not much to say about modern codifications at all - but it may be inferred from his criticism of legal positivism, which he identifies, incorrectly (Barry 1982: 95), with a command-theory of law. Although Hayek does not reject all legislation in the field of 'nomic' law, as we have seen, he clearly sees it as a form of piecemeal corrective engineering only. Anyhow, given the fact that part of the 'nomic' law will have its source in legislation, he leaves us in the dark about the jurisprudential relationship between customary law and legislation.

Hayek's belief that only common law systems can operate in a jurisprudentially responsible way is most questionable. According to him, judges should try to develop law by striving for coherence and consistency. However, if we compare English and continental law on the basis of that criterion, it would seem that codified law offers the judge much support. Comparative studies show that Max Weber's thesis that English law is more irrational from an internal point of view, was (Sugarman 1991) and is (Rinkes and Samuel 1992) essentially correct. It is also correct to say, however, that the English common law is in general spirit closer to liberalism than German and French law (Roos 1992). This shows that the degree of jurisprudential consistency and coherence is relatively independent of the political nature of a legal system. Hayek just assumes that what may be best from an external point of view is also best from an internal legal point of view, an assumption which is sociologically mistaken as he might have known from Max Weber (Roos 1984). Under Hayek's empiricist surface a naïve Enlightenment belief in reason lies hidden which assumes that legal, cultural and social-economic progress is one and the same process.

NATURAL LAW THEORY AS EPISTEMOLOGY OF LAW

We have seen that Hayek's theory of the nature and development of law is empirically untenable. We will go deeper into Kant's theory of natural justice now, as it appeared to offer more promising perspectives.

Although, as John Gray has stated (Gray 1986: 134), the first important element of Hayek's social theory is an 'epistemological turn' - the conception of social institutions as embodied knowledge - the idea never seems to have occurred to him that natural law may be viewed and developed as a critical-analytical theory of knowledge of law. This is surprising, because Hayek, after having credited Kant for the recognition of the negative character of our insight into criteria of justice, comes very close to recognizing this. He remarks that

> there exists a close parallel between this treatment of rules of justice as prohibitions and as subject to a negative test and the modern development in the philosophy of science, especially by Karl Popper, which treats the laws of nature as prohibitions and regards as their test the failure of persistent efforts of falsification, a test which, in the last resort, also proves to be a test of internal consistency of the whole system.
>
> (Hayek 1982, vol. 2: 43)

It will be argued that relating Kant's natural law theory as based on a negative test with epistemology, is a fruitful idea. But before developing that idea further, the self-admitted close relationship between Hayek and Kant will be discussed.

Hayek first points to the negativity of the universalizability test in Kant's theory of law and then criticizes the positivity of the very same test in Kant's theory of morality (Hayek 1982, vol. 2: 167, n. 24). In this implicit way he admits that for Kant there is no difference between the test of validity for moral and for legal rules, although the latter have to meet two extra demands according to Kant, as we will see. Kant's test for both moral and legal rules is much stronger than Hayek's. For Kant it is not enough that a rule is abstract. It must also protect and promote the value of individual autonomy. In fact, Hayek tries to back up his position by suggesting that Kant had correctly taken Hume's idea on the rule of law, but was wrong in turning it into a deductive principle for his theory of morality. This suggestion ignores the fact that Kant could not accept Hume's empirical and therefore relativist view on law and morality, because morality presupposes, in Kant's view, the idea of freedom or autonomy, which he had taken from Rousseau.

Next to the categorical imperative Kant has two other criteria for legal rules. These criteria guarantee what Kant calls the 'externality' of law in contrast to the internal nature of that part of morality which may not be enforced with legal means:

1 It should take people's behaviour, not their motives as such as object of evaluation.
2 Only those rules which are necessary to protect property and public order should be legalized, as the function of law is to prevent society from falling back into a war of all against all.

The first criterion is based on the idea that law should not aim at enforcing morality for morality's sake, as it would corrupt proper moral behaviour as motivated by the respect for morality alone. To force people to be virtuous, as Rousseau had advocated, is a pragmatic paradox according to Kant.[10]. The second criterion is clearly inspired by the Hobbesian Prisoner's Dilemma. It is complementary to the first criterion. To maintain social order, people's motives do not matter, but only what they do. But even when they do things which are morally objectionable, such behaviour should not be sanctioned legally as long as it does not endanger the social order. Someone's lack of politeness may be morally reproachable, but it is not socially dangerous, as polite people will avoid such people. It is a form of behaviour which is likely to call forth its own informal sanctions. But even if it would not, because rudeness has become rather common in a certain society, it will not help to punish such behaviour in a legal way, because it would raise the suspicion against any correct behaviour that it is motivated by fear of punishment rather than by spontaneous moral respect.

Kant's derivation of the necessity of a state is taken from Locke. The state is there to protect the natural right to (individual) property. Kant does not explain very well, however, how natural rights to property can be justified. He could not simply answer in the way of the ancient and medieval philosophers, who saw property as a necessary condition for a virtuous life. Not that he would deny this, but this simple justification raises questions concerning the proper amount of property needed for a virtuous life and whether that amount does not justify redistribution from the rich to the poor. Kant was opposed to such 'social justice' – and is praised for that by Hayek (1988, vol. 2: 62) – because people's needs differ subjectively and because redistribution will invite laziness and free-ridership. He also did not embrace Locke's labour theory of value, as he rightly saw the problems of that theory with respect to the justification of capital-rents. Instead, Kant based the right to property on (lawful) seizure. As a consequence Kant had no proper theory of law and the economy, because he regarded law as part of the moral world and the economy as part of the natural world. Law elevates, as it were, a natural fact, seizure, to the moral realm. Kant lapsed back behind Smith and even Locke in grasping the moral nature of property and contract.

All the other misunderstandings aside, Hayek's distinction between Kant and *a priori* natural law theorists is correct in so far as Kant's approach is epistemological ('transcendental') in nature. It starts from certain simple facts, such as the fact that there is a natural science, that we make moral judgements and that we have property and states, and asks how rational judgements concerning these facts and their interrelationships are possible. Kant introduced the 'transcendental' method on the basis of the idea that we cannot know reality as such, but only with the help of the concepts we use. These concepts must be analysed and systematized reconstructively. But despite his interactionist conception of the relationship between subject and object, Kant maintained the idea of an *a priori* metaphysical difference between nature as the realm of causal necessity and spirit as the realm of reason and freedom. Thus Kant fell back into a Cartesian dualism. As a consequence of this dualism Kant never succeeded in explaining the inner relationship between theoretical and practical reason. Although he admitted that theoretical reason is ultimately practical (Kant 1928: 169), he never explained theoretical reason as part of practical reason or *vice versa*. Kant was just concerned with the limitation of theoretical reason in its - unallowed - application to practical reason in order to vindicate a proper domain for rational ethics against Hume. He did not, however, consider theoretical reason's practical function, its practical foundations and its pragmatic presuppositions philosophically interesting questions.[11]

Kant gave no proper answer to the vexing question 'Why be moral?', but only to the question 'How does moral acting make sense rationally?'. Kant's answer is that morality makes sense only if man's capacity of rational self-determination ('freedom') is presupposed. The epistemological 'trick' of Kant's moral philosophy is to turn this presupposition, a necessary condition of morality, into a sufficient condition in the form of the famous 'categorical imperative'. According to Kant, an act is morally correct if the rule on which it is based is consistent with rational self-determination. Inconsistency exists if a rule can be reduced to the principle 'Do what you think is advantageous for you'. But this is a non-principle, as people would act thus even if they had no moral freedom. But why be moral at all? Kant gave no direct answer. In the abstract, he admits, it is a matter of indifference whether there are, for instance, promises or not. However, if someone made a promise and did not regard himself to be bound by that promise, that person would implicitly assume that making an exception for oneself is compatible with the conventional understanding of what it means to make a promise. That would lead to a dissolution of moral speech and frustrate the possibility of rationality in moral matters, because moral words would not make sense any longer.[12] The question 'Why be moral?' can thus be reduced to 'Why be rational?', a question which Kant did not answer, because he took it for granted that no human being can survive without using moral language. To be explicit and reduce morality as a technique of survival was impossible in the case of Kant, as it would have reduced morality to a natural motive and would have conflicted with Kant's strict division between the natural and the moral realm. However, if one does not follow Kant in his metaphysics, 'survival' is not a bad motive for being morally rational and respecting the law. After all, Kant himself regarded law as that part of morality which has to be enforced 'externally' in order to prevent a war of all against all.

Why is it rational to assume that rationality will help to solve disputable matters? The only reason, as far as theoretical matters are concerned, is the success of rational methods and discussion, a success which is explained by theories of scientific discovery and development. As far as practical matters are concerned, good experiences may be motives to be rational, but these experiences cannot explain the internal rationality of morality. A theoretical explanation may not be contingent on varying empirical circumstances. An interest to be rational in practical matters must be specified and it must be shown how such rationality can be consistently put into practice.

As to the first point, it is evident that an endless variety of conflicting moralities are possible on a dogmatic basis. One cannot argue against someone who holds a certain belief that he or she is irrational, because this already presupposes an answer to the question 'Why be rational?'. The question is unanswerable on theoretical grounds because it is a meta-theoretical question. However, it is evident that no peaceful interaction will be possible if people cling fanatically to their beliefs. Thus there is a rational motive for a rational morality. It is the avoidance of a war of all against all.

The essential question for those who prefer peace over a war of conflicting moralities is how rational debate is possible between people holding conflicting moral convictions. There are two possibilities. One is that there is no common basis for rational discussion, but that the desire for peace is such that one agrees on some formal rule, for example, democratic majority voting. This Buchananian line of thinking is not rational in a theoretical sense because it exposes one to the contingencies of the democratic game. One may include insurances against such contingencies in the form of fundamental rights and other constitutional devices limiting legislative powers or even constitutionalize Rawls's difference principle. But both Buchanan's and Rawls's political philosophy entail the possibility of a substantial confiscation of individual properties and conflict essentially with the assumption which one recognizes implicitly as soon as one enters rational debate: the recognition of the independence of rational embodied beings.[13] Opting for rationality, one implicitly assumes that those to whom one addresses oneself are autonomous embodied rational beings like oneself. The bodily aspect is necessarily included as no individual identification would even be possible without embodiment. Without identification accountability for communicative and other acts would be impossible. A rational person must be regarded as the natural owner of his body in so far as he is supposed to keep it from interfering with his faculty of reason.

The final step towards a theory of natural law has now been taken. Rational moral discourse starts from the assumption of the mastership of each individual over himself. Being a master over himself, however, nobody should be hindered from doing anything he likes, unless he would interfere with the equal liberty of others.[14] Interference may be acceptable if its aim is to prevent or repair illegally inflicted damage or to protect the social order that makes the application of natural law feasible. Consequently, one has to develop the justification and limits of state activity from the limits of a spontaneous order based on the principle that each individual is his own master. In other words, advocates of the state will have to shoulder the burden of proof of showing that the very protection of that natural right justifies certain limitations to it by a public authority, or that a certain legal rule does not impair anybody's natural rights. This burden is specific in the sense that arguments have to be given for each specific area of state intervention, delimiting its powers precisely enough to give the rule of law material content.

Although the burden of proof rests upon the argumentation in favour of the state, the whole enterprise would become pointless if the language of individual rights could not be formalized in a consistent and complete system. Frank van Dun has shown that this is possible (Dun 1993). The next question then is whether a truly liberal anarchistic modern society is possible. I do not think it is.[15]

LAW AS SECOND-ORDER MORALITY

The phrase 'law as second-order morality' is chosen to express three related aspects of morality. First, it expresses the idea that a secularized morality can no longer be based on any supposedly objective nature of man, as the pre-modern natural law theorists believed. Instead it must be based on epistemological reflection, an insight which broke through forcefully with Kant. Second, the name expresses that the traditional relationship between morality and law has been turned upside down. Law is at the bottom, morality is above it, as it were. There are no moral rules above the law, except those which are freely or at least implicitly recognized by people, although this recognition may have legal consequences again by raising legally relevant expectations, for example, in the form of conventional rules of trade.[16] Third, the name refers to the fact that law does not represent pure morality, but one which is mixed with considerations of a physical, biological and social kind which justify a limited amount of state interference.

The derivation of the legitimate powers of a state that now follows is very sketchy. The aim is first of all to show how the derivation is done by founding all state activity on the need to protect natural rights or promote social interests without violating any natural rights. Second, I want to show that these tasks are more or less the same as those which Hayek recognized as legitimate, although he had no true limiting device.

First of all, it is a trivial fact of life that even decent people are not angels and will prefer to survive, if necessary by illegal acts. There is no point in holding people legally responsible for such acts, as they are beyond the control of a normal person. This may justify the imposition of a social-security system, a public-health system and some amount of compulsory education as well as rules which prevent the normal use of rights when vital interests of others are at stake. An example of the latter is a right to trespass if one's own territory is completely enclosed. In the same way one can justify a publicly accessible road system.

Second, an effective system of legal protection operating according to the rule of law is unlikely to be established on the basis of private agreement only. Furthermore, conflicts about rights are usually not costless. The old maxim *lites finiri oportet* also has a financial and economic rationale; the preference to live by the law may not be frustrated by endless debate about the choice of judges or by endless appeal which only wealthy people can afford. A legal system must also provide for criminal law, as living from crime may become a profitable affair because the chance of being caught is usually low even if there is an organized form of crime control. As much as one needs criminal law, one will need a military organization to prevent organized large-scale physical aggression.

Third, there is the problem of transaction costs in relation to conventional rules. Conventional rules are rules which serve no other purpose than to make other people's behaviour predictable without there being other cost-benefit questions involved in the choice between the rules. An example is the rule to drive on the left-hand or the right-hand side of streets.

Fourth, there is plainly a need for rules against the abuse of rights. This is the case in situations where the interest of the right-holder at stake is negligible or has its origin in no other desire than to frustrate others, for example (to use a famous example from Dutch legal history), the erection of a watertower with no other purpose than to spoil the view of a neighbour. Conversely, rights may be granted which are to the advantage of both right-holders and duty-holders, without forcing the right-holder to use them. An example is patent law. Without patent law, inventions would be kept secret or would not be made because of the risk of a loss of investments. It saves an enormous amount of cost and insecurity if an invention can be legally protected for a certain period. That is no disadvantage for the right-holder, because he is still free not to apply for a patent and keep his invention secret. Nor is it a disadvantage for the duty-holders, because they can profit from an invention which might otherwise not be available and they may also use the published knowledge concerning the invention to improve upon it.

Fifth, rules which aim at the prevention of predictable and costly conflicts of rights may be justified. This is the case, for instance, with zoning rules or rules which make certain formalities obligatory to make sure that legal matters are well planned and recorded.

Finally, one needs a tax system through which the public order is maintained in such a way that there is a fair relationship between the tax paid and the profits that each individual derives from that tax. Of course, the relationship can only be approximate because of the collective nature of the public order.

The areas for legitimate state action just identified are about the same as those mentioned by Hayek. Hayek, however, had no legal criterion for distinguishing legitimate from non-legitimate public goods. Against De Jasay's criticism of the public-goods argument it can be maintained that all legitimate collective goods might be provided through private means, with the possible exception of the legal system itself. However, the approach followed here is a normative one: not only is it 'unjust' if the collective goods mentioned are not provided by public means if private means provide them in insufficient quantities, it is also unjust that freeridership is allowed for goods which are truly in the general interest.

NATURAL LAW AS EPISTEMOLOGY OF LAW AND LIBERAL POLITICAL IDEOLOGY

As compared to Kant, Hayek and Popper were not radical enough in their epistemological approach. All their criticism of positivism notwithstanding, they did not follow Pierce's anti-metaphysical pragmatic reinterpretation of Kant's approach (Apel 1976). As a consequence, their critical rationalism is a predominantly empiricist one. Both tried to objectify human thinking, including epistemology, within the framework of a theory of evolution. Such an attempt to jump over one's own cognitive shadow, although prompted by a demand for radical consistency, implies a paradoxical negation of man's capacity to create his own irreducible social-cultural world. It is a paradoxical negation because it implies an historization of the very theory of evolution on the basis of which one pretends to make metahistorical statements; if, however, epistemology were to be excepted from a theory of social evolution, the validity of the latter would become question-begging.

In the case of Hayek paradox turns into irony. It is ironic that Hayek did not notice the historical relativity of his own theory, although his evolutionary approach should have made him sensitive to it. Although liberalism may be the only consistent political philosophy from a purely theoretical or epistemological point of view, social and political systems can also be built more or less coherently on the basis of all kinds of dogmas or half-way plausible empirical social theories, without necessarily becoming unpracticable. From an evolutionary or pragmatic point of view, the Western purely theoretical approach, of which liberalism is the political expression, can be seen as a strategy of survival in a secularized world. From that same point of view, however, the belief that this strategy will appear to be the best qualifies as a piece of rationalist speculation. Admitting that the speculation may be wrong is important for liberalism, because it helps to dissociate it from its traditional idolatry of technical and economic progress. However, it also makes liberalism vulnerable, because it makes it imaginable that someone might deliberately give up liberalism if alternative ideologies, though less rational from an internal perspective, would appear to be empirically superior in promoting peaceful social interaction and helping the world to survive. This may be an uneasy, schizophrenic position, but not necessarily one that is 'irrational'. One cannot exclude dogmatically that Hayek may have been more right than he would have liked to be. It may be that, due to the outdated but genetically firmly established gregarious instincts of man, one cannot organize a society according to blueprint rationality, not even if that blueprint has a liberal signature. However, the burden of proof in that matter rests on the anti-liberals, not on the advocates of liberalism.

NOTES

1 Referring to M.J. Gregor's *Laws of Freedom* (1964), Hayek says, 'I owe it to this excellent book that I became aware *how* closely my conclusions agree with Kant's philosophy of law, which, apart from occasional references, I had not seriously examined since my student days' (Hayek, 1982: 166, note 24).

2 Kant's natural law theory as such was never discussed by Hayek, although he borrows important categories from him, giving them a different interpretation. Thus in *Law, Legislation and Liberty* he refers to Kant for the 'purposeless' character of legal rules (Hayek, 1982, vol. 1: 113), to 'universalizability' (ibid., vol. 2: 28) and its negative character (ibid., vol. 2: 43).

3 It is noteworthy that Kant himself believed in a progressive evolution guided by Divine Providence in the direction of an ever-increasing realization of moral and lawful behaviour.

4 See the contribution in this volume by Frank von Dun (Ch. 14), who suggests that Hayek could have done better by following Hume more closely and by not taking for granted that Hume's views are incompatible with natural law theory.

5 Hayek ignores the fact that so many reparations of English law during the nineteenth century were actually taken from that terrible blueprint rationalist Jeremy Bentham, the great enemy of the common law tradition.

6 Let me just mention as a spectacular example of injustice in the name of technical progress the limitation of tort responsibility for nuclear accidents. Had it not been limited, most of the present-day nuclear power plants would have been uninsurable.

7 The English view on fundamental rights is well expressed in Burke's 'Reflections on the Revolution in France' (1808): the liberties of an Englishman do not exist in abstract principles, but in the common law tradition.

8 Corresponding to this lack of relationship Hayek qualifies public law simply as 'rules of organization', as if what the state organization does and how it should do that, should not be the fundamental question. As Hayek realized that his categorization of law left an empty space at least for criminal law, he simply announced that he would follow the English tradition and place criminal law under the heading of private law (Hayek 1982, vol. 1: 132). This was an innocent manoeuvre as he had nothing much to offer by way of a theory of the principles of criminal law anyway. That criminal law has the function of maintaining 'rules of just conduct' (ibid., vol. 2: 34) is literally all he had to say on the subject.

9 De Jasay argues that no good is properly collective, as it is always possible in principle that an entrepreneur tries to organize groups with sufficient proper interest to pay for a collective good, the costs of the organization included. If such an entrepreneur is unsuccessful, this simply means that there is not enough interest to provide a certain good. I find

De Jasay's exposition not totally convincing as he assumes that people will honestly report what they are willing to pay and do not speculate that their own dishonesty has a negligible effect on the outcome. What is more important, however, is that De Jasay pays no attention to questions of justice concerning collective goods. Assuming one provides a convincing theory of public rights, it would be unfair to let some people free-ride on the civic mindedness of others to pay for the realization of these rights.

10 The well-known criticism of Kant's characterization of law as affecting behaviour from the outside only, that law looks at motives of behaviour, is based on a misinterpretation. Kant just meant that law should not punish people for having immoral motives as such, as long as their outward behaviour is correct. That Kant was not totally consistent in his separation of law and morality follows from his well-known dictum that, if the apocalypse would take place tomorrow, we should hang the last murderers today.

11 As to its practical function it would have been consistent within a Kantian perspective to regard theoretical reason as an attempt to increase the technical control over nature as a precondition of moral freedom making more practical sense. As to its practical foundations the concept of theorizing as acting could have led to the fruitful idea that fundamental categories of science, like time, space and causality, are related to fundamental motorial, sensual and perceptual properties of the human body and brain related. Finally, the analysis of pragmatic presuppositions might have led to an earlier discovery of (theoretical) speech as speech *act*.

12 The rigour which Kant gave to the categorical imperative comes from the attempt to establish a strict analogy with physical laws. In fact, Kant had a concept of the moral universe as a balance of moral forces derived from the mechanistic model of nature as a balance of physical forces. As a consequence, Kant would strictly deny, for example, that it would ever be justified to lie for a good purpose. Physical laws are valid without exception and they do not conflict with each other.

13 Buchanan reduces the individual to a rational calculator, whereas Rawls abstracts from whatever distinguishes one person from the next.

14 This does not imply that a person can alienate his body as he can alienate any other piece of property, because such alienation would amount to a pragmatic paradox: the acting person, by acting, would declare himself to exist no longer as a person. There is only one way one can do so, and that is by committing suicide.

15 I should add that Frank van Dun and I differ sharply in opinion here.

16 An important part of those freely accepted rules, however, cannot be legalized, because they presuppose spontaneity (rules of politeness, for instance). Usually they are sufficiently protected via informal sanctions. Informal sanctions may be sufficient also in the case of rules where spontaneity is not essential. If not, legalization will be necessary if its benefits are high enough in comparison to doing nothing or to insurance.

REFERENCES

Apel, K.-O. (1976) 'Von Kant zu Pierce', *Transformation der Philosophie*, Frankfurt, vol. 2, pp. 157-77.

Barry, N.P. (1982) *Hayek's Social and Economic Philosophy*, London: Macmillan.

Beck, U. (1992) *Risk Society*, London: Sage.

Burke, E. (1808) 'Reflections on the Revolution in France', in *The Works*, London: Bell.

Dun, F. van (1993) *A Formal Theory of Rights*, forthcoming.

De Jasay, A. (1989) *Social Contract, Free Ride*, Oxford: Clarendon Press.

d'Entrèves, A.P. (1981) *Natural Law*, London: Hutchinson University Library.

Gray, J. (1986) *Hayek on Liberty*, Oxford: Basil Blackwell.

Gregor, M.J. (1964) *Laws of Freedom*, London.

Hayek, F.A. (1976) *The Constitution of Liberty*, London and Chicago: Routledge & Kegan Paul.

—— (1982) *Law, Legislation and Liberty*, 3 vols, London: Routledge & Kegan Paul.

Kant, I. (1928) *Kritik der praktischen Vernunft*, Leipzig: Felix Meiner Verlag.

Popper, K.R. (1945) *The Open Society and Its Enemies*, London: Routledge & Kegan Paul.

Ramsay Steele, D. (1987) 'Hayek's Theory of Cultural Group Selection', *The Journal of Libertarian Studies* 8(2): 171-95.

Rinkes, J.G.J. and Samuel, G.H. (1992) *Contractual and Non-Contractual Obligations in English Law*, Nijmegen: Ars Aequi Libri.

Roberts, S. (1979) *Order and Dispute*, London: Martin Robertson.

Roos, N.H.M. (1984) 'Anti-formale Tendenzen im modernen Recht', in S. Breuer and H. Treiber (eds) *Zur Rechtssoziologie Max Webers: Interpretation, Kritik, Weiterentwicklung*, Opladen, pp. 223-68.

—— (1992) 'Dinosaur-complex versus Legal Pluralism', in B. de Witte and C. Forder (eds) *The Common Law of Europe and the Future of Legal Education*, Deventer, pp. 639-60.

Rothbard, M.N. (1980) 'Hayek and the Concept of Coercion', *Ordo* 31, Stuttgart and New York, pp. 171-93.

Sampson, R.V. (1964) 'Evolution', in J. Gould and W. Kolb (eds) *A Dictionary of the Social Sciences*, London: The Free Press of Glencoe.

Schwartz, R.D. and Miller, J. (1964) 'Legal Evolution and Societal Complexity', *American Journal of Sociology* 20: 159-69.

Sugarman, D. (1991) 'A Hatred of Disorder: Legal Science, Liberalism and Imperialism', in P. Fitzpatrick (ed.), *Dangerous Supplements: Resistance and Renewal in Jurisprudence*, Durham: Duke University Press, pp. 34-67.

Vanberg, V. (1985) 'Cultural Evolution vs. Rationalism in Hayek's Thought', *Cato Policy Report* 7(1).

Wimberley, H. (1973) 'Legal Evolution: One Further Step', *American Journal of Sociology* 79: 78-86.

Part IV

MIND, KNOWLEDGE AND SCIENCE

16

THE PLACE OF HAYEK'S THEORY OF MIND AND PERCEPTION IN THE HISTORY OF PHILOSOPHY AND PSYCHOLOGY

Robert P. de Vries

Hayek's *The Sensory Order* is an intriguing book. The essence of the book was contained in a paper he had written in 1921. Thereafter Hayek became busy in economics and only in the late 1940s, when public interest in his economic theories faded away, did he find the time to finish it. It was published in 1952, more than thirty years after he first conceived it. It essentially comprises Hayek's criticism of the psychology of perception and the philosophy of mind from before 1918, both of which were dominated by the ideas of Ernst Mach. In 1952 Hayek added to his former criticism of Mach new objections to behaviourism and Gestalt theory.

The most important chapters are the first, the second and the last. In the first chapter Hayek states the mind-body problem and related epistemological problems of perception in a way which remains unsurpassed. In the second chapter he presents his solution to these problems. He describes his model of the human mind and the mechanisms of perception in very general (functionalistic) terms. In the last chapter he summarizes the philosophical consequences of his model. In the chapters in between he guesses, on the basis of existing physiological literature from the 1920s, 1930s and 1940s, how the human mind and human perception are physiologically realized. This part has, of course, been superseded by modern neurophysiology. But in 1952 Hayek's physiological speculations were amazingly modern for someone who was not a professional neuropsychologist or psychophysiologist. Hayek was an outsider. Therefore he did not know D.O. Hebb's *Organization of Behaviour* (1949) until the final version of his own book was practically finished. Hebb's vision was in so many respects similar to his own that Hayek doubted for a while whether he should publish it. However, Hebb was more concerned with physiological details and less with general principles, which were Hayek's main interest. Hayek thought Hebb did not formulate the general principles as clearly as might have been possible. Nor did he state the philosophical consequences of his theory. So in the end Hayek published his *The Sensory Order* as a kind of complementary volume to Hebb's *Organization of Behaviour*.

Hayek's theory of mind and perception deserves a separate monograph. His ideas on this subject are still relevant to the philosophy of the natural, the human and the social sciences. Many questions still remain to be answered about the internal connections and coherence of his ideas on economics, evolution, human mind, knowledge, science and general methodology. There are many connections and some contradictions between the proposed theories in *The Sensory Order*, *The Counter-revolution of Science* (1952) and the articles collected in his two volumes of essays *Studies in Philosophy, Politics and Economics* (1967) and *New Studies in Philosophy, Politics, Economics and the History of Ideas* (1978). Butos (1989) made some preliminary remarks on the impact of Hayek's theory of mind on his economic theories. Walter Weimer (1979, 1982) started to study the consequences of Hayek's economic and psychological theories on the general theory of knowledge and on the systems theory of complex phenomena. Other important topics are the differences and similarities between the ideas of Hayek and his friend and fellow liberal Popper. For people interested in Austrian economics and especially in Hayek's ideas on economics, psychology and philosophy, a big task lies ahead. In this chapter I will make a start with some preparatory questions. What was the beginning of it all? What was the place of Hayek's theory of mind and perception within the philosophical tradition?

HAYEK, A STUBBORN TRESPASSER

Hayek was never one to respect division lines between disciplines. Although he was awarded the Nobel Prize for Economics, he was not an average professional. His life was dedicated to the big issues of philosophy and politics: the essence of freedom and a free society and the role of knowledge in a free society. These are interdisciplinary themes. Nothing is more pure economics than his *The Pure Theory of Capital* (1941) and most of his other publications in the 1930s, but during nearly all his scientific career (maybe 'scientific life' is a better term in his case) he moved between the domains of social science, philosophy of science, mind and social sciences, methodology, law and even psychology and biology. In this respect, Hayek is a true heir to David Hume, Adam Smith and the other Scottish Enlightenment philosophers he admired so much. In this sense he was old-fashioned, not giving in to the siren song of narrow specialization.

When Hayek as a young man returned from the First World War, he was interested in the social issues which were the consequences of that war. He had a family background in biology, but became interested in the social and philosophical discussions of his time. In contrast to his later friend and brother in arms in the intellectual fight for freedom and democracy Karl Popper, Hayek was right from the beginning an opponent of Marxism.

When in 1918 Hayek began his studies at the University of Vienna, Ernst Mach had died only two years earlier. His psychological and physical theories and his philosophical ideas were still a living force in Viennese scientific and intellectual circles. For young people seriously interested in the social and ethical problems of their time and dissatisfied with current orthodoxy, inexact and metaphysical as it was, Mach's scientific world-view was a very appealing intellectual instrument of criticism. No wonder Marxist philosophers with their pretence of possessing the one and only scientific world-view saw the philosophy of Mach and his followers as a big competitor. Lenin's criticism of the ideas of Mach and the Machians, in *Materialism and Empirio-criticism* (1908), was a hotly discussed topic when Hayek arrived at the university. Austrian Marxists like Friedrich Adler defended Mach and tried to reconcile his ideas with Marxist contentions. As a student Hayek was against using Mach's ideas to back up socialism. One of the lasting themes in Hayek's work originated in this period: the fatal errors and consequences of socialist thinking (whether of the social-democratic or the communist variant).

Hayek read Mach's *Populär-wissenschaftliche Vorlesungen* (1895), *Die Mechanik in ihrer Entwichlung historisch-kritisch dargestellt* (1893), *Erkenntris und Irrtum* (1915) and especially *Die Analyse der Empfindungen* (1896). The last work was the reason why, although he officially studied law from 1918 till 1921 and although he completed his study successfully with a degree in law, he dedicated most of these three years to economics and psychology, dividing his time equally between both. He took up law because professors in that discipline were available at the time, whereas the University of Vienna had, according to Hayek, no professorships in psychology at that particular moment. It was more due to the necessities of life than to intellectual preference that he became an economist after he obtained his degree. As he mentions himself, he had to earn a living and to confine his extracurricular activities to one of those subjects (Hayek 1982). In his own words:

> I chose economics, perhaps wrongly; the fascination of physiological psychology never quite left me, though for the next 25 years – struggling to get on as an economist (and rapidly forgetting

> my law) – I could devote no time to following the development of psychology.
>
> (ibid.: 288)

The 'perhaps wrongly' is a funny side-remark for one who was a Nobel Laureate in economics. But perhaps this is not so strange for the man who said in his Nobel Lecture that it was wrong there existed a Nobel Prize for Economics at all, as it creates the false impression that economics is comparable to the natural sciences in its explanatory and predictive power. However, Hayek's reading of Mach was not without consequences. It left him with a preliminary draft of *The Sensory Order*, which he then put on the shelf for more than twenty-five years. But it also gave him two other lasting themes: knowledge and the problems and limits to the applicability of the methods of natural science to the social sciences. On those topics Mach was Hayek's starting-point, but he developed his own ideas by criticizing Mach's philosophy of mind and perception.

THE HISTORICAL ORIGINS OF THE MIND–BODY PROBLEM AND THE PHILOSOPHICAL PROBLEMS OF THE THEORY OF PERCEPTION

The scientific revolution split our everyday world (our *Lebenswelt*). Great scientists such as Galileo Galilei and René Descartes succeeded in isolating a new domain: the world of physics. In this world everything is reduced to mathematical relations between mathematically defined entities. Form, size and movement are the fundamental dimensions of reality. They are the objects of mathematical disciplines such as geometry and kinematics. They are the basic concepts of the new science of physics.

The book of nature is written in the language of mathematics, says Galileo. In *The Assayer* he writes, 'But I cannot believe that there exists in external bodies anything other than their size, shape or motion, which could excite in us our tastes, sounds and odours'. After that he proposes a rather cruel (thought) experiment: 'And indeed I should judge that if ears, tongues and noses be taken away, the number, shape and motion of bodies would remain, but not their tastes, sounds and odours' (Galilei 1623: 26–30). In other passages he says the same about colours. Furthermore, he suggests that the names for different colours, sounds, tastes and odours do not refer to real properties of the outside world. He compares those properties with pain and titillations, which do not refer to an outside world either, but are the consequences of the workings of physical processes from the outside world on our senses or of the autonomous working of our senses. From his writings we know that Galileo fully realized that this meant a revolution in thinking and from time to time he expresses his admiration for people like Aristarchus and Copernicus, who were so courageous as to disregard the testimony of the senses. He uses very strong terms like 'who violated their senses'.

But there remained of course a problem, which Galileo left to Descartes to formulate. The world of physics is not the only world. There is another world, the world of our (qualitative) experiences. A world of colours, sounds, tastes and odours. The world in which the sun moves and in which we live on a stable earth. It is true this world is occasioned by the senses and the brain. But they are not themselves inhabitants of this world. The brain and the senses are citizens of the physical world of size, form and movement. They do not have a dual nationality. So there exist two worlds with different inhabitants: the objective world of physical objects with primary qualities like form, size and movement, and the subjective world of the human mind, experiences of secondary qualities such as colour, odour, and so on. The physical world of form, size and movement has of course a counterpart in the subjective world. To objective form, size and movement correspond perceived form, perceived size and perceived movement. Even more than Descartes, Leibniz emphasized this fact.

Ever since Descartes, philosophy and psychology have been haunted by questions such as: What is the nature of these two worlds? Which is the fundamental one? Is it possible to explain the second world in terms of the first or *vice versa*? If there are two irreducible worlds, how do they interact? How do we know the physical world if the world of qualitative experiences is the only one we are directly acquainted with? This mixture of epistemological and ontological questions is known in Western philosophy as the mind-body problem.

The answer of the seventeenth-century philosopher-scientists was interactionistic dualism. According to Descartes the universe was divided in two interacting domains. The physical domain was indirectly known to us via the mental domain. Of course there were some problems with this interaction. But interaction was one of those primordial facts about the universe which could not be explained. Every theory has to stop somewhere. At the end of the day there always remains an unexplained, irreducible residue. Newton added 'force' as another quality to Descartes' and Galileo's primary qualities, and although his theory differed in many other aspects, he was an interactionistic dualist, too.

Interactionist dualism was the position of the majority of scientists until the second half of the nineteenth century, when Mayer and Helmholtz formulated their versions of the law of conservation of energy. This law is not compatible with mind–brain interactionism unless the human mind is a purely physical system. But then of course the problem completely disappears, for in that case mind–brain interaction is just physical interaction.

ERNST MACH'S 'ANALYSIS OF SENSATIONS'

After Helmholtz, interactionism was not very plausible. Neither was materialism, because mind and conscious experiences did not play any role in contemporary physical and physiological theories. Most serious scientists were not materialists. Materialism was a philosophy for laymen and ideologues (de Vries 1980). The official scientific viewpoint was agnosticism, elegantly formulated by the famous physiologist Dubois-Reymond: 'Ignoramus, ignorabimus' (We don't know and we won't know).

The physicist and philosopher Mach was dissatisfied with the situation of the existence of two domains, a physical domain and a realm of the mind, between which no interaction was conceivable. This situation in itself is unsatisfactory enough. What makes matters even worse is that as a consequence of the strict division between mind and nature, the existence of our perception and our knowledge of nature is a mystery. Knowledge and perception of an object without interaction with that object are unintelligible.

Mach was the first in a long line of famous revolutionaries against dualism. He thought the contemporary dominant interpretation of physics was responsible for the existing philosophical aporias. That interpretation was still essentially Cartesian: physics reveals a world of physical entities which hide behind a veil of appearances, which are themselves of a mental nature. His radical reinterpretation of physics solves both the epistemological and the mind–body problem. To this end he reversed the Galilean world-view. He rejected the existence of a physical reality behind our subjective experiences. As a consequence of this rejection the aim of science cannot be to discover this reality behind the subjective appearances and to explain those experiences with the help of theories about physical reality. Mach thought that people who believe in this reality behind the appearances are still in a primitive stage of thought, one which has been of practical value in everyday life. In science we must clear our thought of these metaphysical speculations. The only 'things' we know are sensations (sense-data): colours, sounds, temperatures, pressures, odours, time and space sensations. According to Mach, ideas, feelings, moods and volitions are also sensations (although he is not always clear on this issue). The physical world and the things in it are nothing but complexes of these sensations. In Mach's own words: 'Bodies do not produce sensations, but complexes of sensations make up bodies' (Mach, 1896).

A table is nothing more than our perception of that table, a complex of sensations like colours, forms, odours and tactile sensations. Every 'material', 'physical' object can, in the end, be reduced to sense-data. In the ocean of sensations some complexes of sensations stand out more prominently than others. They are more fixed and permanent. They cohere more strongly internally than externally with other sensations or complexes of sensations. That is the reason why we give them names. They are things. So things are complexes of sensations which cohere more strongly internally than with other sensations. 'Cohere strongly' means that the sensations in the complex occur frequently together. The aim of science is to analyse and reclassify those things so that the frequent 'togetherness' of these sensations can be transformed in an invariant 'togetherness'. The aim of science is to find functional relations between elementary sensations and to describe them. It tries to do so as economically as possible, with the smallest possible number of elementary sensations and functional relations. For Mach this means the end of the mind–body problem.

In the same way Mach deconstructs the human mind, human consciousness and the human ego. They, too, are nothing but complexes of sensations which cohere strongly. Mach's position is called neutral monism. 'Monism' because sensations or sense-data are the only elements the existence of which is presupposed by the Machians. There is no fundamental difference between mind and body. 'Neutral' because those sensations, or sense-data, are not sense-data in the usual sense. They are the fundamental elements of the universe and they are neither physical nor mental. In Mach's view sensations are neutral elements. That means there are no fundamentally different domains of reality. Reality consists of ontologically homogeneous elements. So the mind–body problem ceases to exist.

Some problems still remain. If the aim of science is to find functional relations between (neutral) elements, the question arises: Why do we have dualistic intuitions and why are there different sciences like physics and psychology? Mach gives the following answer. The universe consists of a totality of (sensory) elements which falls apart in three subsets, which we will designate by the letters *A*, *B*, *C* . . . *K*, *L*, *M* . . . *a*, *b*, *c* . . . . The complexes of elements *A*, *B*, *C* . . . refer to what we are used to calling physical objects. They show strong internal regularities. This subset of complexes is the subject of physics. The complex of elements *K*, *L*, *M* . . . is a subset of the so-called physical objects. It is our body which is the subject of physiology. The complex of memory images, experiences of our will, and so on, we will designate by *a*, *b*, *c* . . . . It is our mental life and it also hangs strongly together. *K*, *L*, *M* . . . *a*, *b*, *c* . . . is often called our ego because it, too, hangs strongly together. It is the subject of psychology.

It is possible to organize these subsets in relatively autonomous sciences because the elements show more coherence within the subsets than between the subsets. Mach explains this fact in his *The Analysis of Sensations* by his version of Darwin's theory of evolution (Mach 1902).

HAYEK'S 'SENSORY ORDER'

Hayek's *The Sensory Order* takes its starting-point in Mach's universe of sensations, which Hayek calls the sensory order. But unlike Mach he makes a distinction between a phenomenal and a physical order. He uses the same criterion Mach uses to distinguish the objects of physical science from those of psychology: physics studies (sensory) elements in relation to each other; psychology studies those elements in relation to us. Like Mach, Hayek has abandoned a substance view of physical and psychological entities, but in contrast to Mach, who had a sense-data ontology, he (supposedly under the influence of developments in the sciences of his day) sees the world as consisting of functionally related events. So his is an event ontology. This is the first difference with Mach's position.

From this criterion and his event ontology Hayek concludes that the contrast between the phenomenal order and the physical order is based on the differences of events in their effects upon each other and the differences in their effects on us. However, Hayek does not accept Mach's neutral monism:

> In order to be able to give a satisfactory account of the regularities existing in the physical world the physical sciences have been forced to define the objects of which this world exists increasingly in terms of the observed relations between those objects, and at the same time more and more to disregard the way in which these objects appear.
>
> (Hayek 1952a: 2–3)

In order to find functional relations between optical and accoustical sensory elements science has to postulate invisible events. Nothing is more characteristic of this situation, according to Hayek, than that we, nowadays, find it necessary to speak of visible light and audible sound if we want to refer to the objects of sense perception.

The description of the functional relations of the input and output of a coffee machine can illustrate this point and show the necessity of postulating invisible events or states. Suppose you have a coffee machine in your neighbourhood. Coffee costs 10 pence. You always get coffee when you put 10 pence into the machine. Sometimes you get coffee if you put 5 pence into the machine, and sometimes you do not. Table 10.1 represents this situation.

Table 10.1 Black-box functional description

Input (I)	*Output (O)*	*Functional description*
5	N(o) C(offee)	$NC = F(5)$
5	C(offee)	$C = F(5)$
10	C(offee)	$C = F(10)$

It is impossible to describe the output *O* as one unambiguous function of input *I* ($O = F(I)$). So here we are not able to realize Mach's aim of science. We cannot bring the observable input and output in a functional relationship. To realize an unambiguous functional description, we have to postulate two unobservable (internal) states S_0 and S_1 Then it is possible to give a complete functional description of the coffee machine (Table 10.2).

Table 10.2 Complete functional description

Input	*Internal state*	*Output*	*Functional description*
5:	S_0	*NC*	$NC = F(5,S_0)$
5:	S_1	*C*	$C = F(5,S_1)$
10	S_0	*C*	$C = F(10,S_0)$
10	S_1	*C*	$C = F(10,S_1)$

This is an unambiguous mathematical function. However, the description is not complete. We still have to formulate the state equations *G*: $S_1 = G_1(S_0,5)$, $S_1 = G_1(S_1,10)$, $S_0 = G_0(S_1,5)$ and $S_0 = G_0(S_0,10)$. Together they form two unambiguous state functions $S_1 = G_1(S,I)$, $S_0 = G_0(S,I)$. It is not difficult to interpret the internal states and the events the equations describe. The machine is in state S_0 when it is empty. It is in state S_1 when 5 pence have been put into it already. The correct interpretation of the input–output function and the state function follows automatically from the interpretation of S_0 and S_1.

The description of the functional relations of the (sensory) elements that the universe consists of is the aim of science according to Mach. But if scientists want to attain that goal, they have to go beyond the phenomenal world and postulate elements, events, states and processes which have no sensory character. This is accepted by Hayek. It is the second difference between Hayek and Mach. But once you have accepted unobservables, the step to extend the aim of science from description to explanation is not a giant step. Hayek accepts this aim, too. This is his third important deviation from Mach's philosophy.

There is a fourth aspect in which Hayek's view differs from Mach's. Mach saw sensory elements as ultimately given. They were the fundamental data science had to look for. Formulated in an un-Machian vocabulary: 'They were more true than the objective, physical elements of nature'. Hayek reverses this perspective. Science, especially physics, forces us to reclassify the phenomenal world. Mach accepted this fact. It is even probable that Hayek borrowed his opinion from Mach's *The Analysis of Sensations*. But Mach was not aware of the radical consequences of this view for his philosophy as a whole. The human mind is an active classificatory system. New input forces the human mind to change itself and as a consequence reclassify phenomenal reality. Hayek even believes that the reclassifying response of the human mind can cause the emergence of new kinds of sensations and feelings. We reclassify our phenomenal world for the same reason that we postulate unobservables.

An example from linguistics illustrates this point. (Hayek himself sometimes gives other examples from linguistics in *The Sensory Order*). Suppose someone who never had any formal education in grammar but who is very inquisitive starts to think about the linear order of words in sentences. This person observes the following regularities:

John has called his sister.
Peter can buy a bicycle.
People won't die.

Has John called his sister?
Can Peter buy a bicycle?
Won't people die?

What does our naïve linguist do? He formulates the following 'law': statements can be changed into questions by reversing the first and second words. His observed universe consists of statements, questions, and first, second (etc.) words.

But now some new linguistic phenomena arise in his world which refute his hypothetical 'law':

The big house is cheap
People without lungs will die.

Is the big house cheap?
Will people without lungs die?

If his 'law' were true, the questions would have the following syntactic form: 'Big the house is cheap?' and 'Without people lungs will die?' So the 'law' he formulated cannot be true.

A professional linguist can teach our brave scientist to reclassify this linguistic universe, or if he is a very gifted researcher he can learn to do so by himself. First, second (etc.) words are not the fundamental elements of this grammatical world; but other constituents such as subjects, objects, predicates and finite verbs are. After reclassifying his language experiences, our researcher can replace his former law by a new one: statements can be transformed into questions by reversing the subject and the finite verb of a sentence. This last example illustrates Hayek's fourth deviation from Mach's theories.

Historians and philosophers who study Hayek's work have suggested an early influence of Mach. But these were no more than suggestions. Hayek acknowledges *The Analysis of Sensations* as the starting-point of *The Sensory Order*. But *The Sensory Order* is condensely written and Hayek never gives his criticism of Mach in any detail. His positive theory is of course an implicit rejection of Mach's ontology and theory of perception. In this chapter I have tried to describe the historical background of Mach's and Hayek's philosophical problem situation and to give an explicit and more detailed explanation of his four major points of criticism of Mach's *The Analysis of Sensations*. This is in my opinion a necessary preparation for a thorough study of his views on mind, knowledge and perception. None of Hayek's positive views were discussed. That is something for another occasion.

BIBLIOGRAPHY

Blackmore, John T. (1972) *Ernst Mach: His Work, Life, and Influence*, Berkeley: University of California Press.

Butos, William N. (1989) 'Rational expectations and Hayek's theoretical psychology', paper for the EEAC, Baltimore.

Galilei, Galileo (1623) *The Assayer*, excerpts translated by A.C. Danto, in A.C. Danto and S. Morgenbesser (eds) (1960) *Philosophy of Science*, New York.

Hayek, Friedrich A. (1941) *The Pure Theory of Capital*, London: Routledge & Kegan Paul.

—— (1952a) *The Sensory Order*, London: Routledge & Kegan Paul.

—— (1952b) *The Counter-Revolution of Science*, Glencoe (Ill.): The Free Press.

—— (1967) *Studies in Philosophy, Politics and Economics*, Chicago: University of Chicago Press.

—— (1979) *New Studies in Philosophy, Politics, Economics and the History of Ideas*, London: Routledge & Kegan Paul.

—— (1982) 'The Sensory Order after 25 years', in Walter B. Weimer and David S. Palermo (eds) *Cognition and the Symbolic Processes*, 2, Hillsdale (NY): Erlbaum.

Hebb, Donald O. (1949) *The Organization of Behaviour*, London: Wiley.

Lenin, Vladimir I. (1908) *Materialism and Empirio-criticism*, in *Collected Works*, 13, London: Lawrence and Wishart, 1938.

Mach, Ernst (1883) *Die Mechanik in ihrer Entwichlung historisch-kritisch dargestellt*, Leipzig: Brockhaus. Translated as *The Science of Mechanics*, Chicago: Open Court, 1893.

Mach, Ernst (1895) *Populär-wissenschaftliche Vorlesungen*, Leipzig: Barth. Translated as *Popular Scientific Lectures*, Chicago: Open Court, 1896.

Mach, Ernst (1896) *Die Analyse der Empfindungen*, Jena: Fischer. Translated as *The Analysis of Sensations*, Chicago: Open Court, 1902.

Mach, Ernst (1905) *Erkenntnist und Irrtum*, Leipzig: Barth.

de Vries, Robert P. (1980) 'Ignoramus, ignoramibus – het geest-lichaam probleem tussen ideologie en objectiviteit', *Kennis en Methode* 4, Meppel: Boom.

Weimer, Walter (1979) *Notes on the Methodology of Scientific Research*, Hillsdale (NY): Erlbaum.

17

IN PURSUIT OF RATIONALITY

A Note on Hayek's *The Counter-Revolution of Science*

Karl Milford

I have indeed been led to the conviction that not only some of the scientific but also the most important political (or 'ideological') differences of our time rest ultimately on certain basic philosophical differences between two schools of thought, of which one can be shown to be mistaken. They are both commonly referred to as rationalism, but I shall have to distinguish between them as the evolutionary (or, as Sir Karl Popper calls it, 'critical') rationalism on the one hand, and the erroneous constructivist (Popper's 'naive') rationalism on the other.

(Hayek 1973: 5)

I

There is no doubt that Hayek's book *The Counter-Revolution of Science: Studies on the Abuse of Reason* (1979) is one of the most important classics in the social science literature. For in this book Hayek shows the disastrous political consequences of the epistemological position of relativism. Relativists hold that we have to reject the ideal of objective and absolute truth,[1] and they attempt to replace it by psychological and sociological investigations into a person's belief that something is true, or into the scientists' decisions of accepting a theory as true (Popper 1966, vol. 2: 199–244). Some relativists even hold that scientific theories can be incomparable in principle – incommensurable – and that the preference for one of two competing theories is arbitrary: it has to be explained sociologically or psychologically, rather than as part of a process of attempting to approach the truth. Many relativists would say that scientific progress in the sense of coming nearer to the truth is no more than a myth.

The disastrous political consequence that emerges from this epistemological relativism is, as Hayek emphasizes, a political and moral relativism, which is especially dangerous because it is often confused with pluralism and with tolerance. It does not lead to an open and tolerant society: on the contrary, as Hayek argues, it causes society to drift along the road to totalitarianism and dictatorship – the road to serfdom (Hayek 1944). The rejection of the ideal of objective and absolute truth leads to a political relativism with terrible dangers for freedom, democracy and science. Hayek writes:

> If truth is no longer discovered by observation, reasoning and argument, but by uncovering hidden causes which unknown to the thinker have determined his conclusions, if whether a statement is true or false is no longer decided by logical argument and empirical tests, but by examining the social position of the person who has made it, when in consequence it becomes the membership of a class or race which secures or prevents the achievement of truth, and when in the end it is claimed that the sure instinct of a particular class or a people is always right, reason has been finally driven out.
>
> (Hayek 1979: 159)

In order to investigate the close relation between dubious epistemological positions – relativistic positions – and their disastrous political and moral consequences Hayek undertakes historical as well as epistemological and methodological studies in his book *The Counter-Revolution of Science*. In particular he argues that relativistic positions are unsuccessful attempts to solve a number of epistemological and methodological problems of the social sciences. These problems and their solutions exert, according to Hayek, a decisive influence on our life. They may well determine whether we are (or will be) living in a free, liberal and democratic society, or in a totalitarian police state. But although the problems Hayek discusses are most complex, he makes it quite plain that many of them are rooted in one fundamental problem. This problem is a demarcation problem, the problem of distinguishing the social sciences from ideologies or from other areas of enquiry such as the natural sciences, mathematics and logic, morality and ethics, philosophy and metaphysics. In particular Hayek wants to clarify the epistemological status of the social sciences, that is, whether they are empirical sciences or sciences whose epistemological status is *sui generis* or whether they share the status of logic or metaphysics.

II

The investigation of the close relation of scientific (i.e. economic) and methodological problems that features so prominently in Hayek's works is certainly a dominant characteristic of the whole approach of the Austrian School of Economics, of which he was one of the most important and original representatives. The explanation for this particular Austrian approach lies in the problem situation in which its founder, Carl Menger, happened to find himself in the early 1870s. Basically this problem situation consisted of two major elements of which one concerned the unresolved problems of value and price theory in economics and the other the methodological problems of the structure of a satisfactory theoretical explanation in economics and that of demarcating economics from other disciplines. Menger's preoccupation with these two elements is reflected in the publication of two books, the *Principles*, published in 1871, and the *Investigations*, published in 1883.[2] While Menger, in the first book, primarily deals with unresolved problems of economic theory and in particular tries to develop a unified price theory on the basis of a theory of subjective evaluations linked to methodological individualism, he devoted his second book to the exclusive consideration of methodological problems. Both books develop a most fruitful research programme for economics and for the philosophy of the social sciences in general and became the heart of the specific Austrian tradition, which studies economic problems in close connection with philosophical ones. But apart from reflecting the two major elements of Menger's problem situation, the two books also show something else with respect to that problem situation. They show that Menger's problem situation was determined by the particular course the development of German economics took in the first third of the nineteenth century. This development is characterized by the attempt to explain the determination of prices on the basis of a theory of subjective evaluation, but also by the gradual replacement of methodological individualism, which originally was linked to that theory, by inductivist and collectivist methods.

The aforementioned link of subjective value theory and methodological individualism, which today is so familiar to us, was developed as early as 1807 by the German author G. Hufeland (Hufeland 1807). Hufeland, although a strong admirer of A. Smith, was well aware of the deficiencies and failures of Smith's value and price theory (Hufeland 1807, Introduction: 15).[3] Criticizing Smith's explanation of value and prices, he nevertheless follows his basic methodological ideas with respect to the task of the social sciences, and holds that this task consists in the explanation of social institutions as unintended consequences of intended actions (ibid.: 26). Hufeland combined this methodological idea with a subjective value theory and was well aware of the revolutionary importance of this link (ibid.: 18). Apart from his intention to develop a better price theory, Hufeland believed that only the link of subjective value theory and methodological individualism provides the possibility of satisfactory explanations of the origin, development and functioning of social institutions. In particular he considered this link to be the only satisfactory alternative to the rationalistic-contract theoretical explanations of social institutions (ibid.: 25).

It is interesting to note that in the course of the further development of German economics Hufeland's specific link disappears. The further development of German economics is characterized by elaborating economic theory and, for that matter, price theory on the basis of a theory of subjective evaluations (Streissler 1990: 31–68). The idea of explaining economic behaviour on the basis of a theory of subjective evaluations is retained by the German economists; but the idea of methodological individualism and Hufeland's insight into the importance of this link with a theory of subjective evaluations is neglected. The most important German economist who explicitly rejects methodological individualism is Roscher, the founding father of the German Historical School of economics (Roscher 1886).

It seems that the reasons for this development lay partly in the internal difficulties that remained with these proto-neoclassical economic theories. Some of them, however, seem to lie in unresolved methodological problems concerning the structure of social science explanations and the epistemological status of economic theories. Roscher, although basically following the subjective approach as developed by Rau (1826) and Hermann (1832), was dissatisfied by the attempt to explain human actions and their outcomes on the basis of an exclusive goal-orientated optimizing behaviour (Roscher 1886: 22). Confusing the concepts of methodological individualism and egoism he emphasized the falsity of the hypothesis that individuals in general behave egoistically. But Roscher not only believed that an economic theory animated by such an empirically false hypothesis was necessarily wrong and useless, but also concluded that theories that were based on this hypothesis were unable to provide conclusive explanations of the factors that integrate atomistically dispersed individuals and make them form a society. According to Roscher, theories based on the assumption of egoistic behaviour can only explain the disintegration of society, but not the factors that hold society together. In his view, however, this disintegration of society is checked by social institutions, whose origin, development and functioning cannot therefore be explained on this basis. Roscher emphasized that since individuals act within a social framework, satisfactory explanations of human actions first need to explain the emergence and development of this framework and only then can turn to explaining such phenomena as the determination of prices.

In view of this situation Roscher developed a research programme for the social sciences which became the heart of the German Historical

School of economics. This research programme holds that the social sciences are nothing but theoretical history and that their task is accordingly to uncover the laws of the historical development of social institutions, nations, economic systems and other collective entities by inductive methods. Roscher elaborated these inductive methods, as well as the idea that they demarcate empirical science from other disciplines in his first major publication, a book on the life, work and times of the historian Thukydides, which appeared in 1842 (Roscher 1842). Basically Roscher's other works are realizations of this research programme (Roscher 1843, 1854, 1868, 1874, 1885, 1886, 1893). With respect to the emergence of the typical characteristics of the Austrian tradition, and of Menger's problem situation, however, two important points have to be made here. First, in economics Roscher was not able to develop a coherent and unified price theory on the basis of a subjective value theory, so that these problems still awaited their resolution. Second, with respect to methodology the problem of the structure of satisfactory explanations in the social sciences and inductivism subsequently became a major issue of discussion in the next several years.[4]

About thirty years after the publication of Roscher's *Thukydides* (1842) Menger revived Hufeland's link of subjective value theory and methodological individualism and tried to develop a unified price theory on this basis. With respect to their development of subjective value theory, Menger regarded the German economists' work as most fruitful; but he also believed that it was their collectivist and inductivist methods that were to blame for their not developing a coherent and satisfactory price theory (Menger 1871: Vorrede vii, x). Menger therefore particularly emphasized the link of methodological individualism and subjective value theory, which in his view opened the possibility of resolving many fundamental problems and internal difficulties of economic theory. Roscher and other authors, however, did not grasp Menger's intention of emphasizing the importance of this link, as their reactions to the *Principles* show (Roscher 1874: 1040). Disappointed by these reactions, Menger wrote the *Investigations*, in which he dealt a disastrous blow to the research programme of the Historical School. In this analysis he showed the falsity of the Historical School's methodological ideas with respect to the structure of explanations in the social sciences and its failure to cope with the logical problem of inductive inference (i.e. the problem of induction) and thereby to solve the problem of demarcating the social sciences *qua* theoretical and empirical disciplines (Milford 1990: 215–39). In this book Menger succeeded fairly well in giving an account of the structure of scientific explanations, but he, too, failed to solve the problem of induction, although his suggested solution surpassed the naïve inductivism of the Historical School and did not neglect the logical impossibility of inductive inference as the German authors had done.

III

It is interesting to note that Menger's followers who explicitly dealt with these problems, for example Böhm-Bawerk (1924), Wieser (1924), Mises (1949, 1962), Schumpeter (1908) and Hayek (1967a: 3–22; 1967b: 22–43), did not come to one shared view with respect to the epistemological status of the social sciences, or, in other words, to a solution of the demarcation problem, although they did agree on the nature of a satisfactory explanation in the social sciences. Menger, for instance, distinguished between two epistemological positions – that is, strict empiricism or strict positivism and apriorism – and tried to establish the latter by introducing a principle of induction (Milford 1990). In contrast to Menger, Böhm-Bawerk held that the theoretical social sciences are empirical sciences because experience may require their theories to be discarded. He concluded that social theories therefore cannot claim full but only partial certainty. Wieser and Mises believed that social theories are not only genetically or psychologically *a priori*, but also *a priori* valid. Schumpeter considered social theories, especially economics, as systems of implicit definitions. In contrast to these representatives of the Austrian School, Hayek developed an epistemological position which one may label 'hypothecism', a form of critical rationalism. According to Hayek the social sciences are empirical sciences whose theories are falsifiable but not verifiable and therefore always hypothetical.

Hayek's epistemological and philosophical investigations are not carried out for their own sake but to contribute to a solution of the scientific problems from which they originate. In contrast to the widely-held belief that scientific problems originate in philosophical problems, Hayek's work shows that philosophical and metaphysical problems originate in scientific problems which still await resolution. This can already be seen in his early economic work, for instance in the opening chapters of his *Monetary Theory and the Trade Cycle*, first published in German in 1929 (Hayek 1933). There, Hayek explains that the failure of business cycle theory is partly due to the inductivism and methodological collectivism that is applied in order to explain business cycle phenomena. In other words, Hayek holds that the failure of business cycle theory is partly due to wrong conceptions of what constitutes a satisfactory theoretical explanation in the social sciences and in particular in economics. Unresolved problems of economic theory lead Hayek to consider methodological and epistemological problems, and we find him arguing against the inductivist methodology according to which economists ought to infer the laws of the trade cycle from a vast amount of observations. In contrast to these methodological views he emphasizes that theories must always come before the observations they explain, since they tell us what to look for, and that satisfactory explanations in economics are of the methodological individualistic kind. Another early example of how unresolved scientific problems in economics led him to consider methodological and epistemological questions is his famous article 'Economics and Knowledge' (Hayek 1937). In this article Hayek investigates internal difficulties of economic theory - especially those of formal general equilibrium theory - and he is led by these considerations to philosophical questions such as the explanatory power of economic theories and their epistemological status. In this article, which later became one of the intellectual roots of present-day information economics, Hayek argues that the empirical content of economic theories depends on hypotheses concerning the different knowledge individuals have and the way they acquire it. Otherwise, according to Hayek, formal equilibrium analysis in economics would simply amount to a set of definitions which tell us nothing about the real world.

In *The Counter-Revolution of Science*, Hayek performs historical and methodological investigations which clearly are Austrian in character and spirit in the sense that they show a great similarity in scope and method to those that were performed by Menger. In the first part of the book he develops his own epistemological and methodological position (i.e. hypothecism) on the basis of an immanent criticism of positions which he labels 'scientism'. Parts II and III of the book are historical investigations with respect to the origin and development of the historicist, collectivist and inductivist positions in the social sciences. Although Hayek intended to cover the development of these positions in France, Germany, Britain and the United States, he, unlike Menger, who for historical reasons focused on the German development, investigated primarily the French origins of this development and dealt only briefly with that in Germany.

According to Hayek the origin of the historicist, collectivist and inductivist positions is rooted to a large extent in the attempt to transfer the methods of the natural sciences uncritically to the social sciences in order to make them more scientific. This uncritical attempt he calls scientism since its followers are concerned 'with the slavish imitation of the method and language of Science' (Hayek 1979: 24). Hayek therefore starts his analysis with an account of those methods which the followers of scientism believe to be the methods of the natural sciences. However, he makes it quite plain that he does not want to discuss the question of whether these views are correct. He emphasizes that his

> comments on the methods of the natural sciences . . . do not necessarily claim to be a true account of what scientists in fact do, but an account of the views on the nature of scientific method which were dominant in recent times.
>
> (Hayek 1979: 23)

Although Hayek does not state that what he refers to as the 'dominant views of science' hold that the method of the natural sciences is induction, this clearly follows from the account he gives of scientism, as well as from other sources where he explicitly refers to induction when describing scientism (Hayek 1969: 915–17). In his view the followers of scientism believe that the methods of the natural sciences are characterized by concepts such as repeated observation, generalization and absolutely certain or highly probable knowledge, which are characteristic features of inductive methods. However, he does not want to criticize inductive methods as such. He rather attempts to show that even if such methods existed, they could not be applied fruitfully within the social sciences. He asserts that the different forms of scientistic explanations of social events or processes – that is, objectivism, collectivism and historicism – all fail because they do not take into account that the opinions and evaluations of individuals as well as their different knowledge in fact trigger the social sphere. Since, in Hayek's view, the origin and the existence of social institutions can only be satisfactorily explained by individualistic explanations, scientism necessarily collapses because it cannot achieve satisfactory explanations of social events or processes, that is, it cannot achieve the aims which it set out to achieve.

On the basis of this immanent criticism, Hayek, not unlike Menger, develops his own epistemological position. This position shows great similariies to that developed by Popper, and Hayek presumably was influenced by Popper's position to a large extent. However, in *The Counter-Revolution of Science* he explains this position only very briefly and he developed it to a greater extent in a number of articles which appeared later (Hayek 1949b; 1967a: 3–22; 1967b: 22–43). Like Menger, Hayek develops his position from considerations concerning the different structures of theoretical explanations in the natural and social sciences. He distinguishes between 'explanations in detail' and 'explanations in principle' and explains that the former are designed to explain single events and processes, while the latter explain typical kinds of events and processes (Hayek 1967a: 6, 7). By the term 'explanation in detail' Hayek refers to the logical structure of a singular explanation and in particular to the detailed specification of the initial conditions that are needed for such explanations. But he also emphasizes that the possibility to provide singular explanations depends to a large extent on the specific epistemic situation of a discipline. For this reason he believes that many disciplines cannot provide singular explanations and find their task in developing models which explain typical events and processes and to this end use typical initial conditions and animating laws (Hayek 1949b: 67–75; 1967b: 24; Popper 1985: 357–65).

According to Hayek the natural sciences are primarily interested in providing singular explanations, because they investigate isolated and closed systems which may be natural (the solar system) or artificial (experiments) (Hayek 1967a: 8). In his view the natural sciences find themselves in an epistemic situation which permits a rather precise specification of initial conditions and the discovery of testable general relationships between a few variables. For this reason the natural sciences are interested above all in finding strictly universal statements or laws and not so much in the construction of models, although they regard them as a most useful analytical device. But the prediction of a solar eclipse does not necessarily require the construction of a (mechanical) model of the solar system if the initial conditions and natural laws are adequately specified.

However, Hayek believes that in contrast to the natural sciences the social sciences find themselves in a very different epistemic situation, which precludes the formulation of satisfactory singular explanations. The social sciences therefore typically provide models in order to explain typical events or processes. But in Hayek's view there is a major difference between the models of the natural sciences and those of the social sciences (Hayek 1967a: 5–10; 1967b: 35). Whereas models of the natural sciences are animated by animating laws whose epistemological status is that of empirical and strictly universal hypotheses, the models of the social sciences are animated by the so-called rationality principle, which does not have this epistemological status. According to Hayek this principle follows from the methodology itself, which in his view is the only method that provides satisfactory theoretical explanations of human actions in the social sciences, that is methodological individualism.

Hayek is at pains to explain that this principle is not an empirical and strictly universal hypothesis, as is, for instance, a psychological law. In his view the reason for this misunderstanding can be clarified if we

> try to restate the correct argument in simple language. If we put it concisely by saying that people are and ought to be guided in their actions by their interests and desires, this will at once be misunderstood or distorted into the false contention that they

> are or ought to be exclusively guided by their personal needs or selfish interests, while what we mean is that they ought to be allowed to strive for whatever they think desirable.
>
> (Hayek 1949a: 15)

He emphasizes that, instead of being a psychological law that, like the laws of physics, animates models, this idea is rather a consequence of the individualistic methodology. If satisfactory explanations in the theoretical social sciences are individualistic explanations, the models that depict typical situations in which individuals decide according to their preferences and their aims simply have to be animated by the principle that individuals try to achieve their aims.

Hayek's view with respect to the role of animating laws in models and in particular to that of the rationality principle and its epistemological status might give rise to the opinion that the models of the social sciences have no empirical content apart from that which is contained in the typical initial conditions. But such a view certainly would contradict Hayek's epistemological position of hypothecism. Hayek therefore tries to show that the rationality principle, although a methodological principle that animates the models of the social sciences, does not imply that the models of the social sciences have no empirical content. In order to show this he shifts the attention away from the model depicting the typical situation in which typical individuals happen to find themselves and focuses on the combination of such models. In his view the descriptions of typical situations that are animated by the rationality principle are only stepping stones to achieving the real aim of the theoretical social sciences, which consists in explaining the spontaneous order, the social structures that emerge as the unintended results of the intended actions of individuals. He explains that by assembling models of typical situations into larger ones – the compositive method as Menger had called this procedure – the social sciences achieve strictly universal hypotheses about the emergence and formation of certain specific patterns of interaction (Hayek 1937; 1949b: 68; 1967b: 24). In his view these hypotheses are falsifiable, since they forbid the formation and occurrence of certain other patterns of interaction. As Hayek puts it:

> our knowledge of the principle by which these phenomena are produced will rarely if ever enable us to predict the precise result of any concrete situation. While we can explain the principle on which certain phenomena are produced and can from this knowledge exclude the possibility of certain results, for example, of certain events occurring together, our knowledge will in a sense be only negative; that is, it will merely enable

> us to preclude certain results but not enable us to narrow the range of possibilities sufficiently so that only one remains.
>
> (Hayek 1979: 74)

Thus in Hayek's view the theories of the social sciences are falsifiable, since they exclude possibilities and therefore have potential falsifiers. For 'the prediction that a pattern of a certain kind will appear in defined circumstances is a falsifiable (and therefore empirical) statement' (Hayek 1967b: 28):

> The theory as such, as is true of all theories, describes merely a range of possibilities. In doing this it excludes other conceivable courses of events and thus can be falsified. Its empirical content consists in what it forbids.
>
> (ibid.: 32)

Although there hardly can be any doubt that Hayek already in his early publications favoured an empirical and deductivist position, some passages of *The Counter-Revolution of Science* seem to confirm the opposite. Indeed, some passages even seem to support aprioristic as well as pseudo-statement positions,[5] which of course contrast strongly with his hypothecist position. At one time he considers for instance the example of an archaeologist who tries to determine whether a certain stone is a gadget, an artefact made by man, or simply a product of nature which by chance happens to take the shape of an artefact. With respect to a solution of this kind of problem Hayek believes that

> There is no way of deciding this but by trying to understand the working of the mind of prehistoric man, of attempting to understand how he would have made such an implement. If we are not more aware that this is what we actually do in such cases and that we necessarily rely on our own knowledge of the working of a human mind, this is so mainly because of the impossibility of conceiving of an observer who does not possess a human mind and interprets what he sees in terms of the working of his own mind.
>
> (Hayek 1979: 46)

In another passage he says that

> The position of man, midway between natural and social phenomena – of the one of which he is an effect and of the other a cause – brings it about that the essential basic facts which we need for the explanation are part of common experience, part of the stuff of our thinking. In the social sciences it is the elements of the complex phenomena which are known to us beyond the

possibility of dispute. In the natural sciences they can be at best surmised.

(ibid.: 66, n. 3)

While these two passages in *The Counter-Revolution of Science* could support apriorism, there are others which rather seem to support a pseudo-statement position. For instance, following Stebbing and Russell, Hayek points out that the only appropriate language of science is mathematics, 'that is, the discipline developed to describe complexes of relationships between elements which have no attributes except these relations' (ibid.: 33). In Hayek's view the descriptions of such complexes of relationships are schemata or rules which serve as a kind of '"key", which enables us to translate them into statements about perceptible phenomena' (ibid.: 34). With reference to linguistic research and script analysis of dead languages he then indicates the way by which we may translate rules or schemata into statements about perceptible phenomena. According to Hayek:

> One might compare the relation of modern physical theory to the world of our senses to that between the different ways in which one might 'know' a dead language existing only in inscriptions in peculiar characters. The combinations of different characters of which these inscriptions are composed and which are the only form in which the language occurs correspond to the different combinations of sense qualities. As we come to know the language we gradually learn that the different combinations of these characters may mean the same thing and that in different contexts the same group of characters may mean different things. As we learn to recognize these new entities we penetrate into a new world where the units are different from the letters and obey in their relations definite laws not recognizable in the sequence of the individual letters. We can describe the laws of these new units, the laws of grammar, and all that can be expressed by combining the words according to these laws, without ever referring to the individual letters or the principle on which they are combined to make up the signs for whole words. It would be possible, for example, to know all about the grammar of Chinese or Greek and the meaning of all the words in these languages without knowing Chinese or Greek characters (or the sounds of the Chinese or Greek words). Yet if Chinese or Greek occurred only written in their respective characters, all this knowledge would be of as little use as knowledge of the laws of nature in terms of abstract entities or constructs without knowledge of the

> rules by which these can be translated into statements about phenomena perceptible by our senses.
>
> (ibid.: 34–5)

In the German edition of *The Counter-Revolution of Science* this passage is followed by a footnote where Hayek quotes from Russell's *Introduction to Mathematical Philosophy*. In doing so, Hayek reinforces the idea that scientific theories are schemata or rules:

> Given some statement in a language of which we know the grammar and syntax, but not the vocabulary, what are the possible meanings of such a statement, and what are the meanings of the unknown words that would make it true?
>
> (Hayek 1959: 29, n. 14a)[6]

These passages indeed seem to be very strange and certainly are irreconcilable with a hypothecist position. Nevertheless, it is quite clear that Hayek rejects the consequences of the positions which are supported by the quoted passages. Hayek favours neither an aprioristic position nor a pseudo-statement position, because he neither believes in any kind of evident truth which is decided on the grounds of some strong psychological experience as does, for instance, Mises, nor does he want to give up the idea of objective truth, which is rejected by the pseudo-statement positions, because he is aware that such a rejection leads to relativism. Above all, Hayek emphasizes the role of experience as an instrument of criticism not only in his later writings, such as in his articles 'The Theory of Complex Phenomena' (1967b) or in his 'Degrees of Explanation' (1967a), but he had already done so in his early writings such as *The Monetary Theory of the Trade Cycle* (1933). Given that in *The Counter-Revolution of Science* Hayek tries to develop the principles of a hypothecist position and strictly adheres to the ideas of objective truth and empiricism, these passages, although rather strange, should not obscure Hayek's general intentions.

IV

In section II of this chapter it was indicated that induction played a considerable role in the discussion of the epistemological status of the social sciences because induction was considered to be the only method that demarcates empirical from non-empirical science. It was believed that a solution of the problem of induction would also solve the problem of demarcation and so clarify the epistemological status of the social sciences. It is therefore not surprising that the epistemological positions held in the social sciences conform to different solutions of the problem of induction and also display systematic relationships to each other. This system also shows that the nature of Hayek's epistemological position is totally different from that of other representatives of the Austrian School. Apart from Hayek, who developed a deductivist position, the Austrians developed inductivist positions which for internal reasons are all invalid. In a way Hayek's deductivist position brings to an end the epistemological discussion within the Austrian camp that started with Menger and his attacks on the German Historical School.

In order to show the deductivist nature of Hayek's epistemological position and the inductivist nature of the different positions put forward by the rest of the Austrians one only needs a few premises from which the epistemological positions can be inferred as consequences. At first four premises are needed, which for reasons which will become clear later, are called special premises. Basically these premises describe the situation that emerges from the problem of induction. They are: (a) 'Full decidability': the truth values of genuine statements of science must be fully decidable; that is, it must be possible in principle to prove either their truth or their falsity. (b) 'Empiricism': the truth values of empirical statements are decided by experience exclusively; the 'principle of empiricism'. (c) 'Strict universality': the laws and theories science proposes are strictly universal and empirical; 'the principle of theoretism'. (d) 'Logical objection': it is logically impossible to verify empirical statements which are strictly universal.

Premise (a) defines the truth values that can be assigned to genuine scientific statements; premises (b) and (c) define 'empirical science' and follow from considerations concerning the structure of theoretical explanations and the task of science (Popper 1959: 59); (d) constitutes the problem of induction by raising a contradiction between (b) and (c). From this it follows that an acceptable solution of the problem of induction (and that of demarcation) must resolve the contradiction between (b) and (c). But obvoiusly there are two approaches to solving this problem: either one seeks a positive solution to this problem in the sense that one stays within an inductive framework; or one seeks a negative solution and rejects the inductive framework altogether and tries to resolve (b) and (c) within a deductivist one. Because of these possibilities two general premises have to be added to the special ones, one describing inductivism and the other the general approach of deductivism. We now have the following situation:

Inductivist framework: premises

General: Genuine statements of science are inferred from singular statements describing observations or personal experiences (introspection).

Special:

(a) 'Full decidability': the truth values of genuine statements of science must be fully decidable; that is, it must be possible in principle to prove either their truth or their falsity.
(b) 'Empiricism': the truth values of empirical statements are decided by experience exclusively; the 'principle of empiricism'.
(c) 'Strict universality': the laws and theories science proposes are strictly universal and empirical; 'the principle of theoretism'.
(d) 'Logical objection': it is logically impossible to verify empirical statements which are strictly universal.

Deductivist framework: premises

General: Induction does not exist in the logic of knowledge. Genuine statements of science are not inferred from singular statements.

Special:

(a) 'Full decidability': the truth values of genuine statements of science must be fully decidable; that is, it must be possible in principle to prove either their truth or their falsity.
(b) 'Empiricism': the truth values of empirical statements are decided by experience exclusively; the 'principle of empiricism'.
(c) 'Strict universality': the laws and theories science proposes are strictly universal and empirical; 'the principle of theoretism'.
(d) 'Logical objection': it is logically impossible to verify empirical statements which are strictly universal.

From the special premises and the general premise of inductivism we obtain the inductivist positions as consequences by denying one premise at a time:

Inductivist positions

1 'Naïve inductivism': it is possible to resolve the conflict between (b) and (c) if (d) is rejected. Strictly universal statements (laws) are verifiable.

2 'Strict positivism': it is impossible to resolve the conflict between (b) and (c); however, (c) can be rejected. The universal statements of science are not strictly but only numerically general; they are a kind of record, a summary of singular observational statements.

3 'Apriorism': it is impossible to resolve the conflict between (b) and (c); however, (b) can be rejected. Strictly universal statements are not decided by experience exclusively.

4 'Probability positions': it is possible to resolve the conflict between (b), (c) and (d) if (a) is rejected. Between truth and falsity there are truth values of degrees of probability. The truth of strictly universal statements cannot be proven; they are not fully but only partially certain (i.e. 'probable'); only their probabilities can be decided.

5 'Pseudo-statement positions': it is impossible to resolve the conflict between (b), (c) and (d); but it is not necessary to resolve it if (a) is rejected. Strictly universal statements are not genuine statements of science but are pragmatic entities and the conflict between (b), (c) and (d) is irrelevant to success.

The deductivist positions are obtained from the special premises and the general premise of deductivism and by denying one premise at a time:

Deductivist positions

1 'Conventionalism': it is impossible to resolve the conflict between (b), (c) and (d); (c) has to be rejected. Strictly universal statements are arbitrary definitions (analytical statements).

2 'Intuitive universalism': it is not possible to resolve the conflict between (b), (c) and (d). (d) shows that the method of induction cannot yield genuine scientific knowledge that is certain knowledge. (c) needs to be rejected: genuine laws of science are not strictly universal and empirical laws which describe the co-existence and the succession of phenomena, but laws that govern essences. These laws are discovered by intuition.

3 'Hypothecism' (critical rationalism): it is possible to resolve the conflict between (b), (c) and (d) if (a) is rejected. Strictly universal statements are falsifiable conjectures – that is, partially but not fully decidable.

Naïve inductivism was held by Roscher; Menger developed a form of strict positivism (the empirical realistic orientation of theoretical research) and an aprioristic position (the exact orientation of theoretical research); Wieser and Mises also developed forms of apriorism; Böhm-Bawerk indicated a form of the probability position; and Schumpeter developed a form of pseudo-statement position. Only Hayek propounded a deductivist solution which is based on Popper's critical rationalism, the first philosopher who developed such a solution of the induction and demarcation problem. However, although Hayek indicated a position which shows that the theoretical social sciences are empirical sciences, he never developed the methodological rules that are needed in order to support his hypothecist position. Thus there remain many methodological problems that await resolution.

NOTES

My cordial thanks go to Sir Karl Popper, E. Streissler, D. Miller and M. Spak. All errors of course remain mine.

1 On the idea of objective truth, cf. Popper 1972: 319–40; on relativism Popper 1966, vol. 2: 369–96.
2 For an English translation of Menger (1871), cf. Menger (1981); and for an English translation of Menger (1883), cf. Menger (1985).
3 Page references refer to the Introduction of Hufeland's book and are mine because Hufeland's Introduction has no page numbers.
4 Cf., for instance, Knies (1930).
5 Cf. section IV of this chapter.
6 The quotation in the text is taken directly from Russell (1956: 55). Hayek's quote is a German translation.

REFERENCES

Böhm-Bawerk, E. (1924) 'Zur allgemeinen Theorie und zur Methodenlehre', in F.X. Weiss (ed.) *Gesammelte Schriften von E. von Böhm-Bawerk* vol. 2, Wien: Hölder-Pichler-Tempksy.

Hayek, F.A. (1933) *Monetary Theory and the Trade Cycle*, London: Cape.

—— (1937) 'Economics and Knowledge', *Economica*, N.S. 4(13): 33–54.

—— (1944) *The Road to Serfdom*, London: Routledge & Kegan Paul.

—— (1949a) 'Individualism: True and False', in F.A. Hayek, *Individualism and Economic Order*, London: Routledge & Kegan Paul.

—— (1949b) 'The Facts of the Social Sciences', in F.A. Hayek, *Individualism and Economic Order*, London: Routledge & Kegan Paul.

—— (1959) *Missbrauch und Verfall der Vernunft*, Frankfurt am Main: Knapp.

—— (1967a) 'Degrees of Explanation', in F.A. Hayek, *Studies in Philosophy, Politics and Economics*, London: Routledge & Kegan Paul.

—— (1967b) 'The Theory of Complex Phenomena', in F.A. Hayek, *Studies in Philosophy, Politics and Economics*, London: Routledge & Kegan Paul.

—— (1969) 'Szientismus', in D.L. Sills (ed.) *Wörterbuch der Soziologie*, 2nd edn, Stuttgart: Enke.

—— (1973) *Law, Legislation and Liberty: A New Statement of the Liberal Principles of Justice and Political Economy*, vol. 1, London: Routledge & Kegan Paul.

—— (1979) *The Counter-Revolution of Science: Studies on the Abuse of Reason*, Indianapolis: Liberty Press.

Hermann, F.B.W. (1832) *Staatswirthschaftliche Untersuchungen*, München: Weber.

Hufeland, G.(1807) *Neue Grundlegung der Staatswirthschaftskunst*, Giessen und Wetzler: Müller.

Menger, C. (1871) *Grundsätze der Volkswirthschaftslehre*, Wien: Braumüller.
—— (1883) *Untersuchungen über die Methode der Socialwissenschaften und der Politischen Oekonomie, insbesondere*, Leipzig: Duncker & Humblot.
—— (1981) *Principles of Economics*, trans. J.D. Dingwall and B.F. Hoselitz, New York: New York University Press.
—— (1985) *Investigations into the Method of the Social Sciences with Special Reference to Economics*, ed. L. Schneider, trans. F.J. Nock, New York: New York University Press.
Milford, K. (1990) 'Menger's Methodology', in B. Caldwell (ed.) *Carl Menger and His Legacy in Economics*, *History of Political Economy*, annual supplement to vol. 22, Durham and London: Duke University Press.
Mises, L. (1949) *Human Action*, London: Hodge.
—— (1962) *The Ultimate Foundation of Economic Science*, New York: van Nostrand.
Popper, K.R. (1966) *The Open Society and Its Enemies*, 5th edn, London: Routledge & Kegan Paul, vol. 2.
—— (1959) *The Logic of Scientific Discovery*, London: Hutchinson.
—— (1972) *Objective Knowledge*, Oxford: Clarendon Press.
—— (1985) 'The Rationality Principle', in D. Miller (ed.) *Popper Selections*, Princeton, NJ: Princeton University Press.
Rau, K.H. (1826) *Grundsätze der Volkswirthschaftslehre*, Heidelberg: Winter.
Roscher, W. (1842) *Leben, Werk und Zeitalter des Thukydides*, Göttingen: Vandenhoeck und Ruprecht.
—— (1843) *Grundriss zu Vorlesungen über Staatswirthschaft. Nach geschichtlicher Methode*, Göttingen: Dieterich.
—— (1854) *System der Volkswirthschaft. Die Grundlagen der Nationalökonomie*, Stuttgart: Cotta, vol. I.
—— (1868) *Ansichten der Volkswirthschaftslehre aus dem geschichtlichen Standpunkte*, Leipzig: Winter.
—— (1874) *Geschichte der National-Oekonomik in Deutschland*, München: Oldenbourg.
—— (1885) *Kolonien, Kolonialpolitik und Auswanderung*, Leipzig: Winter.
—— (1886) *System der Volkswirthschaft. Die Grundlagen der Nationalökonomie*, 18th edn, Stuttgart: Cotta, vol. 1.
—— (1893) *Politik: Geschichtliche Naturlehre der Monarchie, Aristokratie und Demokratie*, Stuttgart: Cotta.
Russell, B. (1956) *Introduction to Mathematical Philosophy*, London: Allen & Unwin.
Schumpeter, A. (1908) *Wesen und Hauptinhalt der theoretischen Nationalökonomie*, Berlin: Duncker & Humblot.
Streissler, E. (1990) 'The Influence of German Economics on the Work of Menger and Marshall', in B. Caldwell (ed.) *Carl Menger and His Legacy in Economics*, *History of Political Economy*, annual supplement to vol. 22, Durham and London: Duke University Press.
Wieser, F. (1924) *Theorie de gesellschaftlichen Wirtschaft*, Tübingen: J.C.B. Mohr (Paul Siebeck).

Part V

IDEAS OF THE PAST

18

HAYEK AS AN INTELLECTUAL HISTORIAN

D.P. O'Brien

The basic problem encountered by anyone trying to write about Hayek as an intellectual historian is this. His actual 'history of ideas' output is quite modest, while his total output is huge (even allowing for double counting) and the corpus as a whole contains much that is relevant for Hayek's treatment of the history of ideas. Moreover, Hayek's work extends well beyond economics; he was at least as much a philosopher with a good knowledge of economics (although the only system of which he was 'master' was the Menger–Wieser–Mises line) as an economist who wrote on philosophical subjects. All of his huge output is from the same mould as the intellectual-history material, in citing similar sources and stressing similar themes. This is not intended as a criticism; Hayek was neither propagandist nor polemicist. But it does make it necessary to try to take a view of his whole output.

Studying Hayek as an intellectual historian is in fact quite a good way of holding up a mirror to Hayek – a signal of the elements in economics, law and politics which he considered to be important. Indeed, in teaching the history of economic thought he told the students what he had learnt from other writers, not what those writers themselves would have regarded as their most important contributions (1978: 52).[1] Thus, in his view the decisive contributions of Hume and Smith lay in demonstrating the emergence of the rule of law and of spontaneous order (1978: 124–5).

Of course, all intellectual history is written within a particular intellectual framework. But the intellectual historian has an overriding duty to ask continuously whether the account of the history of the subject given would appear coherent to the unconverted. Most Marxist, and indeed much Keynesian, history of ideas fails this test. In a few instances the same is true of Hayek, as we shall see.

For Hayek, it was necessary that the historian should have commitment. His heroes in this context – de Tocqueville, Burke and above all Acton for whom his admiration was intense – showed the way (Hayek 1949: 4, 23; 1960; 1992: 209–18, 232–3, 247). The historian must have a moral standpoint (1992: 201–15). Relativism was not enough. The future historian who displayed a relativist attitude towards Hitler would end up by glorifying him (1992: 208). For Hayek – an agnostic in religious matters – the moral standard was freedom, a position he held passionately while the overwhelming majority of his academic colleagues adopted an attitude of judicious agnosticism and relativism towards the horrors of the Stalinist and other Marxist regimes. He believed that history teaching which failed to stress freedom could do, and indeed had done, great harm; in Germany it had been responsible for the spread of anti-liberal sentiments (1992: 243).

HAYEK AND THE HISTORY OF IDEAS

Hayek's original training, based on Menger, Wieser and Böhm-Bawerk, was distinctly narrow.[2] But he set about remedying this narrowness with great vigour. Apart from his association with Mises, which was undoubtedly decisive in the development of his macroeconomics, he made (with help from Schumpeter, who wrote him letters of introduction) a trip to the United States in the early 1920s to study American economics (1992: 19–41). He participated actively in the intellectual life of Vienna, and there are some signs in his work of an interest in the history of mathematics and natural science (1941, I: 9–10, 17). Throughout his life he seems to have read endlessly.[3] He was a book collector (1934a: 396, 419; 1992: 167) – indeed, he was a major collector of economic literature – and, if my own experience is anything to go by, he was very generous with his books.[4] It is thus not surprising that his great *Law, Legislation and Liberty* (1973–9) should reveal staggering erudition.[5] Indeed, about 25 per cent of the text was devoted to footnotes covering a huge range of literature from several centuries.[6] Whatever his standing as a political philosopher, there can be little doubt about his standing as a scholar (Hicks 1940; Clapham 1940; Fetter 1940; Machlup 1976: 25, 42, and 1979: 280), least of all as a scholar in the history of economics, though one whose range extended much further than that.

His erudition enabled him to be widely read in a number of different languages. It is true that he did not read Swedish (1933c: 115n); it is not clear whether in fact he could read Dutch (1991: 344) and his Greek citations, despite evident classical knowledge, are mainly from Loeb (parallel text) editions (1960: 419; 1978: 92, 122, 225–6; 1988: 38–47). But apart from an encyclopaedic knowledge of literature in German and English, he also read Italian (1978: 71) and displayed a detailed knowledge of the Latin texts of the later Schoolmen (1978: 5, 28, 123, 253–5; 1992: 43–4). He took a pleasure in nice linguistic points; *Geisteswissenschaft* was, he pointed out, introduced into German by the translator of J.S. Mill, so there was not a lot of point in borrowing it in English (1942–4, I: 277n). He read extensively in French, and displayed a remarkable knowledge of French intellectual history and of the history of the Enlightenment (1941).

To some extent this multilingual background causes problems for the reader. The great series of articles on 'Science and Scientism' (1941, 1942–4) read as if they are beautifully translated from the German, and the text is very dense.[7] Of course, some of Hayek's work did appear first in German (1978: 3, 31n7); but the problem seems to lie with texts which originally appeared in English. However, it is a problem which is much less significant in Hayek's later output – from about 1946 onwards – and indeed his later cool, elegant, incisive prose contrasts very favourably with much of the critical material written about him contained in the volumes edited by Wood and Woods (1991).

Hayek attached enormous importance to the history of ideas. He viewed the development of ideas as part of that seamless evolutionary development which was at the heart of his view of the world. The influence of ideas – whether disastrous as in 'scientism' and French positivism, or benign as in the doctrine of unintended consequences from Mandeville, Smith and Hume to Menger – was enormous. Individuals, seized of particular ideas, could do enormous harm; there was nothing 'historically inevitable' about what Bismarck had done to Germany, paving the way for the rise of Hitler (1992: 201–15, 223–36). It was necessary to understand the motivating ideas involved in particular events. Hayek agreed with Keynes's view, expressed in the famous quotation about 'Madmen in authority' (1949: 108; 1967: 182, 347; Keynes 1936: 383–4) and he was very much aware of the importance of historical myths, especially myths about the Industrial Revolution, the history of which had been largely written by socialists in his view (1954; 1991: 56–72). (Whether Thorold Rogers, Ashley or Archdeacon Cunningham could be described as socialists is of course very doubtful; but there are plenty of other individuals to support Hayek's general contention).

Although Hayek ranged far and wide in dealing with intellectual history, he was certainly a significant writer on the history of economics, of which he described himself as a student (1992: 19). He lectured for more than four decades on the history of economic thought 'and enjoyed so doing' (1978; 52n, 267). Indeed, the history of economic thought could be regarded as integral with Austrian economics (1968b: 25–6), as in the first volume of Böhm-Bawerk's *Capital* (1884–9). Menger himself lectured on the subject. Austrian scholarship thus helped to alleviate the narrowness of Hayek's original training. When Hayek himself turned to monetary theory, he approached it through the history of monetary thought (1984: 3; 1991: 127n), an exercise which in itself seems to have contributed significantly to the broadening of his knowledge. He developed a remarkable knowledge of French and Italian monetary literature (1991: 155–76); while Jacob Viner had a perhaps more profound knowledge of the English language literature (though even here Hayek's grasp (1991; 127–54, 177–244; 295–344) is certainly not negligible), Hayek's work ranged over the literature of four languages with assurance. Even within the English literature he showed remarkable knowledge; amongst his achievements here was the demonstration that the doctrine of forced saving originally owed something to Bentham. Others published earlier, but Bentham's work circulated in manuscript. From this source Hayek traced the development of the idea through to Walras and Wicksell (1932b; 1935: 18–24). The concept ultimately became a key part of the monetary theory of Mises (1935: 25), from which Hayek's own monetary theory was derived.

Ironically, it was only the monetary history part of the work which survived; the larger project of a book on money had to be abandoned because of the rise of the Nazis (1984: 3, 113n).

HAYEK'S INTELLECTUAL INSPIRATIONS

With the exception of David Hume, the three authors to whom Hayek refers most are Adam Smith, Adam Ferguson and Edmund Burke (1949: 4, 7; 1960; 1973–9; 1978: 264; 1988: 3, 34–5, 145; 1991: 106). It is on the work of these authors that Hayek grounded his ideas of spontaneous order, selective evolution, and the fundamental importance of unintended consequences of individual human actions taken on the basis of limited knowledge. Indeed, his treatment of Adam Smith is an interpretation so strongly in these terms that the more narrow aspects of Smith's analysis with which readers of the *Wealth of Nations* are familiar are obscured (1942–4, III: 28; 1978: 124–5; 1988: 34–5). It is perhaps because of this that Hayek confessed that, despite recognizing Smith's greatness, he found the history of economic thought lectures on Smith the hardest to give (1978: 267). But Smith, undoubtedly aware of the work of Mandeville (Hayek 1978: 252), not only provided the intellectual basis for a critique of socialism, but also (in his *History of Astronomy*) for a critique of the simple-minded application of natural science ideas to complex economic phenomena (Hayek 1942–4, I: 267). In attacking the 'man of system' Smith was, Hayek believed, attacking that 'constructivism' which was at the basis of socialism and social planning (1978: 269; 1988: 86). Even Smith's discussion of division of labour is interpreted as an example of the operation of unintended consequences (1978: 268).

Hayek also makes reference to Montesquieu and to Kant. Needless to say, Kant's separation of science and morals, his emphasis on the idea that morality consists in treating persons as ends and not as means, his insistence that rules of just conduct were independent of wider social goals, and his view that the state should provide general law, designed to protect individual freedoms, rather than detailed legislative interference, all appealed to Hayek. Yet, to this reader at least, it is doubtful how much Hayek derived ideas, as distinct from support, from the works of Kant. His overwhelming admiration was for David Hume, and Hume is much the most important single source for Hayek's general position. Hume was 'perhaps the greatest of all modern students of mind and society' (1978: 264).

It was Hume who had, through his critical rationalism, replaced constructivism with an explanation of the evolutionary nature of social and economic institutions where that evolution was governed by utility. It was Hume who, before Smith, had explained the end-independent nature of rules of just conduct. It was Hume who had explained the role of law, the importance of general laws rather than government by interests, and the emergence of spontaneous order within the framework provided by law. It was Hume who had explained how the market made it possible for individuals to perform services for others of whom they had no knowledge, through unintended consequences of their actions (Hayek 1949: 4; 1960; 1967: 106–21; 1973–9; 1978: 71–2, 77n, 124, 264; 1988: 13, 32–3, 86, 145; 1991: 101–18).

Hume is thus very important for Hayek. Indeed, a glance at the citations in his *Constitution of Liberty*, one of his major statements, demonstrates this. At times, perhaps, he claimed too much for Hume; it really is not correct to say that Hume anticipated most of classical international trade theory (1991: 153). But he was scrupulous in bringing out the strong possibility that Hume was familiar with Cantillon's *Essai* before its publication and thus owed it a debt (1935: 9; 1991: 151, 287–8).

Amongst the Austrians, it is undoubtedly true that Mises had a significant influence on Hayek. Hayek admired Mises very greatly, and was associated with him in his private seminar in Vienna. It was Mises who secured for Hayek his first job. Before coming in contact with Mises Hayek had been, by his own account, a Fabian-type socialist, but after reading Mises's *Gemeinwirtschaft*, published in 1922, he abandoned socialism (1942–4, I: 281n; 1992: 4, 53, 131). He was particularly impressed by Mises's insistence that things such as a commodity, an economic good or even money could not be defined in physical terms but only in terms of views that people held about them. A thoroughgoing subjectivist approach to economics was required. Needless to say, this ruled out physical planning. Mises's book on money (Mises 1912) was also an important influence on Hayek; indeed, it was the entire source for Hayek's monetary theory since it was through this book that the influence of Wicksell reached Hayek.

But the evolutionism on which Hayek laid such stress does not come from Mises.[8] It comes from what was undoubtedly the most fundamental Austrian influence on Hayek – Menger himself. Though Menger's influence on economics generally was limited and to a considerable extent indirect, the *Grundsätze* was effective in transmitting its main message (Hayek 1978: 274–81; 1988: 97). But it is not this book which exercised the key influence upon Hayek.

The key work was Menger's 1883 *Untersuchungen*. Again and again in Hayek's interpretation of other writers, it is the evolutionary themes, the treatment of law and the emphasis upon unintended consequences in that book which Hayek picks up in the earlier writers (1942–4, III: 27–30; 1960; 1973–9, II: 184–5; 1978: 3–22, 249–66; 1988; 1992: 28, 50, 77–8n; Menger 1883: 139–59, 223–34). In his attack on 'scientism', in his attacks upon constructs such as 'the nation' and 'society', and in his opposition to constructivism, it is the individualism of this book and the emphasis upon the evolution of law, language, the state, money and markets which Hayek starts from. It is undoubtedly the most important influence on his *Constitution of Liberty* (1960: v). The earlier writers treating these themes, especially Mandeville, are seen as leading to the definitive statement in Menger. It is this book which explains the importance which Hayek attached to the work of Mandeville and of Hume, and the particular interpretation which he gave to it and to that of Adam Smith. It is thus of considerable importance in understanding Hayek as an historian of ideas. But the emphasis upon evolution, in particular, requires some further examination.

EVOLUTION

Despite the fact that the influence of Menger's 1883 book is the key unifying factor in Hayek's treatment of the history of ideas, and indeed of much else – it is the unifying thread of his *Individualism and Economic Order* (1949) – there is a slight puzzle. For despite the narrowly Austrian nature of Hayek's training, this particular aspect of Menger's work does not seem to have impressed him at first. Hayek's early work in the history of economic thought, dealing with money, is not within the evolutionary mould. Both the history of John Law's schemes, and of the monetary antics of the revolutionary maniacs in the 1790s, provided plenty of material in support of Hayek's thesis about evolution in money and the dangers of 'constructivism' in monetary matters, that is, of the dangers of revolutionary monetary schemes irrespective of accumulated experience. That he made little play with this point suggests that in the late 1920s (1991: 155–76) he had not made evolutionism a key factor either in his thought or in his approach to the history of ideas. Its importance really dates from the late 1930s and his attacks upon 'scientism'.

Later on he was also to stress that the evolution of social forms embodies knowledge (1978: 3–22, 59, 71; 1988: 21) and that values are transmitted by the cultural environment (1978: 67–8). These values are socially beneficial. Individuals, acting within the constraints of these social values, created benefits which were beyond their design. The system which had evolved was designed to compensate for the extremely limited knowledge of each individual. Indeed, Hayek went so far as to argue that cultural evolution led to intelligent behaviour – to the surprise no doubt of those who think in left/right stereotypes, Hayek was firmly in the 'nurture' corner in the debate between 'nurture' and 'nature' (1978: 290–4).

The competitive selection of cultural institutions was linked directly to the key idea of unintended consequences of individual actions under partial information (1978: 11, 73; 1988: 71; 1991: 26; 1992: 2; Menger 1883: 146). Social forms evolved so that pursuit of individual goals could produce social good. None of our ancestors could have known that protection of property and contracts would lead to division of labour, specialization and the operation of markets. But the way in which unintended consequences produced an order, an order which was not designed, was, Hayek held, the key question in economics from the time of Hume and Smith onwards (1942–4, I: 284, 288; III: 27–30, 37; 1949: 15, 77–89; 1973–9, I: xviii–xix; 1978: 73).

This evolutionary approach was not, as it had indeed not been with Menger, confined to purely economic phenomena. Religion was also an evolutionary form (1988: 135–40). It was a spontaneous and unplanned development, embodying much of the necessary evolutionary cultural wisdom. A moral code was an evolutionary phenomenon, though this did not preclude the questioning of any single moral value within a given framework (1960: 397–411; 1978: 18–19, 84, 298–9; 1988: 52; Menger 1883: 8, 139–59). The same was true of institutions; we had to try to understand them, and there was always the possibility of improvement. But wholesale restructuring of society would simply destroy civilization (1988: 6; 1992: 259–60). Our civilization depended on the human co-operation and order associated with the market – or with 'capitalism', a word which, as Hayek pointed out, Sombart (not Marx) had introduced and which he associated with the Nazis (1988: 111). The evolved forms, produced without an overall purpose (1978: 77n), embodied the painful learning processes of society and were capable of incorporating that multiplicity of objectives which was necessary for freedom (1949: 19). It is important to stress in this context that the full range of these objectives could never be known in advance. Indeed, the market could not be judged by a hierarchy of known ends (1978: 90–2).

Needless to say, a number of earlier writers were criticized by Hayek for their failure to appreciate this viewpoint. Bentham, as a constructivist (1978–9, II: 45, 155) was contrasted with Hume the non-interventionist. Rousseau was roundly criticized for his substitution of the idea of a popular will for a general *opinion* embodying social learning (1978: 99; 1988: 13). He had, in Hayek's view, 'made what had been called the savage the virtual hero of progressive intellectuals' (1988: 49) because of his rejection of accumulated wisdom.

But it was Hobbes who received the sharpest criticism. It was Hobbes with his social-contract myth who was responsible for propagating 'naive design theories of human institutions' (1978: 256–7; 1988: 13). The idea of unlimited powers of government intervention, even under democracy, derived from sources like this. The argument that supreme authority must be unlimited was

> a misunderstanding deriving from the totalitarian-positivist conceptions of Francis Bacon and Thomas Hobbes, or the constructionism of Cartesian Rationalism, which fortunately in the Anglo-Saxon world was at least for a long time held back by the deeper understanding of Sir Edward Coke, Matthew Hale, John Locke and the Old Whigs.
>
> (1978: 158)

Hayek's introduction of the common lawyers here is important. Since this impinges upon his treatment of the history of ideas, it is necessary to say a little about his legal philosophy.

LAW

Hayek's general evolutionary framework gave him a particular interest in legal and constitutional theory and led him to stress the importance of *general* law (1978: 134), as distinct from interventionist government of the kind intensely vulnerable to pressure-group politics. He contrasted freedom under the law with the use of legislative machinery to interfere with freedom (1949: 18). It was general law as stressed, he argued, by Locke, Hume, Smith and Kant which was both the safeguard of individual freedom and the framework within which beneficial evolutionary development could take place.

There is no doubt that this position derives initially from Menger's 1883 book. But, as always, Hayek sought to place it within its context in the history of ideas. He was a great admirer of the Anglo-Saxon system of case law and in particular of the great common lawyers (1991: 77, 102–3; 1992: 257–8; Menger 1883: 9, 11, 223–34). The state undoubtedly has a role to play as a part of the framework for economic activity (1949: 22–3); but the role of general law (as distinct from particular state action) as espoused, Hayek believed, by the constitutional theorists whom he admired, was paramount. Thus it was to the British tradition, rather than to that of Continental liberalism which Hayek looked (1949: 28–9, 110; 1978: 119–20; 1992: 216, 244). He believed that evolutionary concepts predominant in British legal philosophy had protected ancient liberties which had been largely destroyed on the Continent. Indeed, French liberalism had remarkable totalitarian propensities. It had been corrupted by 'aggressive rationalism' and scientism 'which presumed that science was competent to tell us not only what is but also what ought to be' (1992: 244). This tradition, which had infected J.S. Mill, was contrary to the true (British) tradition of liberalism.

It is possible to see difficulties in this position. In citing 'the classical theorists of representative government', especially John Locke, in support of the idea that democratic government's law-making should be confined to general law-making (not specific interference, the latter making government vulnerable to pressure groups), Hayek neglected the fact that even very limited government could be (and at the time of these theorists was) subject to pressure groups – the phenomenon known as mercantilism. Indeed, under the (limited though non-democratic) Cromwellians, detailed regulations concerning personal life were laid down. There is a case for arguing that Hayek's view here was part romantic and part rhetorical. But it would be quite untrue to argue, on this basis, that there is no substance whatever in Hayek's position and in his treatment of these constitutional issues and their theorists.

Hayek believed, as we have seen, that Continental liberalism had become corrupted. Let us examine some of the sources of that corruption.

HISTORISM, CONSTRUCTIVISM AND SCIENTISM

History and historism

Hayek attacked the idea that it was possible to develop some kind of scientific history, an attempt which he called 'historism'. Such an approach involved two difficulties. First, it involved aggregating social phenomena in a way which had no real meaning – Hayek referred to the 'astounding assertion' (1941, III: 307) that in dealing with social phenomena the whole is better known than the sum of the parts. Second, it involved attempting to find laws governing the development of society when viewed in this holistic way. This historism was contrasted with genuine history (1941, III: 307–12; 1942–4, II: 50–63). Real historians attempt to understand real unique historical episodes whereas historism 'attempts to treat historical situations as species of a genus' (1941, III: 311–12). Historism was a product of a misconceived attempt to apply what were believed to be the methods of natural science to history. In fact, as Popper later convinced Hayek, natural scientists did not proceed in this way (1967: 8); but the belief that observation could lead to the formulation of historical 'laws' was certainly present in the literature, stretching from Comte to Marx, which Hayek criticized. The latter variant, for extrinsic rather than intrinsic reasons, was particularly important. 'Though merely one among many characteristic nineteenth-century products of this kind, Marxism more than any of the others has become the vehicle through which this result of scientism has gained so wide an influence' (1942–4, II: 59).

Such an approach, involving 'objectivism' (in opposition to the subjectivism of social science in general and Austrian economics in particular), collectivism (in opposition to individualism) and historism (in opposition to theory) led in turn to constructivism (1942–4, II: 34).

CONSTRUCTIVISM AND SCIENTISM

The consequence of historism and scientism was a failure to grasp that individual action produces socially coherent unplanned systems. Devotees of such an approach could not understand the evolution of social and economic systems. This led to their belief that if institutions were not designed they could not be satisfactory. From this they proceeded, by a non-sequitur, to the belief that we could simply refashion institutions in any way we desired (1942–4, III: 29–30; 1978: 3–22; Menger 1883: 8–9). As Hayek observed, 'This belief that processes which are consciously directed are necessarily superior to any spontaneous process is an unfounded superstition' (1942–4, III: 30).

Constructivism was in fundamental opposition to the individualism, subjectivism and evolutionism which Hayek had derived from Menger (Hayek 1941; 1942–4). Thus the origins of socialism lay in constructivism (1978: 15). From his detailed study of the work of Saint Simon and Comte, Hayek was able to conclude that the origins of both positivism and socialism were 'definitely reactionary and authoritarian' (1941, I: 31). These writers planned a complete reconstruction of society placing control in the hands of intellectuals. There was to be a dictatorship of the 'scientific' (1941, II: 122–4; 1941, III: 315).

In fact the constructivists suffered from scientific delusions. With a grand sweep, and a very impressive knowledge of the literature of the Enlightenment, Hayek traced – convincingly – the scientific pretensions not merely of those who wished to ape physics but of those who wished to plan society 'scientifically'.[9] These people engaged in 'slavish imitation of the method and language of Science' (1941, I: 16; 1942–4, I: 169).

Most of those who are guilty of this were themselves either undistinguished in science or not scientists at all (1942–4, I: 268; 1991: 77). Bacon was one prime example (Hayek 1991: 75–8); the dilettante picker of scientists' brains, Saint Simon, was another. None the less, Hayek believed that the origins of this view within French intellectual tradition lay with somebody whose mathematical credentials, at least, were not open to question – Descartes (Hayek 1949: 8; 1978: 5, 158, 255; 1988: 48).

But the truth was that natural scientific methods did not transfer to the vastly more complicated world of social science (1942–4, I: 267). Science attempted to look behind man's perceptions to ultimate realities; but social science had to deal with people's beliefs because it was upon these that action was based (1942–4, I: 271–81, 286). Most of the objects of human or social action were not objective facts which could be defined in physical terms. Moreover, there was no coherent and consistent body of the knowledge on which people based their actions. 'It only exists in the dispersed, incomplete and inconsistent form in which it appears in many individual minds and this dispersion and imperfection of all knowledge is one of the basic facts from which the social sciences have to start' (1942–4, I: 280). The essence of social sciences is subjectivism and methodological individualism, and introspection had a significant part to play in their constructs. Indeed, economists, unlike natural scientists, knew about individual elements, and the task of economics was to explain how these individual elements interacted to produce markets and allocation. Scientism, therefore, in attempting to transfer the procedures and priorities of natural science to social science was simply unscientific (1942–4, I: 269). Indeed, natural-science training did not enable one to *discern* order in social phenomena, so the scientists wished to *impose* it (1942–4, III: 38–9). Natural-science training also led to an extremely primitive attitude towards such complex matters as optimization – the engineering concept of optimization involved no more than a single maximand, namely technical efficiency (1942–4, III: 35–6).

Borrowing from the work of Mises and others, Hayek accepted that science had had to struggle to overcome many difficulties placed in its way by established philosophical positions. The struggle, once successful, had led through a so-called 'law of inertia' to an overshooting of the original objective with science claiming expertise in areas for which it was not suitable (1942–4, I: 270, 278). But this was only part of the explanation. Intellectuals in general displayed an infatuation with socialism, safe in the luxury of never having had to live under a regime which attempted the comprehensive planning of society (1967: 178–94; 1988: 85). Indeed, Hayek was able to illustrate his argument with some particularly silly statements by Albert Einstein about 'production for use' (1988: 58–9), and it is clear that he took a (somewhat sardonic) interest in the writings of scientists and, more particularly, of scientific popularizers, on matters of economics (1988: 55–60). To understand his attitude towards them it is necessary to explore a little further his attitude towards economic methodology.

SCIENCE AND ECONOMICS

Hayek had a strong interest in the philosophy of science and seems to have developed a close personal and intellectual relationship with Karl Popper (Hayek 1967: viii; 1991: 6, 9, 42n; Popper in Streissler 1969: 190). But, although Popper convinced him that natural scientists proceeded from theory to observation, Hayek remained convinced that natural-science methods did not transfer to economics. For the theory which economics developed was not suitable, for the most part, for testing with facts. As already noted, facts in economics were not physical attributes but mental perceptions (1949: 61–2). In fact, economic theory offered very few testable predictions (1942–4, I: 290; 1978: 278). Hayek had no doubt about the importance of systematic testing in *natural* science (1942–4, I: 272); but, although one author has seen signs of a definite change in Hayek's position from 1937 onwards (Hutchison 1981: 210–24), there seems to be little doubt that he remained highly sceptical about both measurement and testing in economics. Indeed, this was to remain a fundamental part of his opposition to Keynesian macroeconomics (1983: 46). It is true that in his 1937 article 'Economics and Knowledge' there are passages referring to 'verification', and a reference in a footnote to 'falsification' (1937a; 33). But what Hayek was talking about here was the nineteenth-century concept of 'verification' – testing whether the assumptions necessary for a theory were met. Elsewhere one can find plenty of references *after* 1937 dismissing the importance of prediction (1942–4, I: 290; II: 42, 49–50; 1949: 73; 1978: 180; 1992: 148).[10]

The emphasis upon subjectivism can be linked to Hayek's interest in psychology, which dated from his student days (1952; 1978: 38–9;

Klein in Hayek 1992: 4). It naturally led him to assign a key role to introspection (1942, I: 285–6, 289–90; II: 44–7, 61; 1949: 63; 1978: 277). This was crucial in separating social science from natural science.

> The physicist who wishes to understand the problems of the social sciences with the help of an analogy from his own field would have to imagine a world in which he knew by direct observation the inside of the atoms and had neither the possibility of making experiments with lumps of matter nor opportunity to observe more than the interactions of a comparatively few atoms during a limited period. From his knowledge of the different kinds of atoms he could build up models of all the various ways in which they could combine into larger units and make these models more and more closely reproduce all the features of the few instances in which he was able to observe more complex phenomena.
>
> (1942–4, I: 289–90)

Of course, introspection involves serious methodological difficulties since we can never be sure that our own introspection represents a uniform reaction, a question never really faced by apriorists from Cairnes to Mises. But, for our purposes here, the point is that this viewpoint gave Hayek a clearly defined perspective on intellectual history. He did not allow possible difficulties with introspection to affect his belief in its importance when dealing with the history of ideas. It is therefore hardly surprising that Hayek found the 'social physics' approach of French intellectualism, and especially of Comte, deeply distasteful.

SAINT SIMON AND COMTE

In his series of articles 'The Counter-Revolution of Science' (1941), Hayek developed a detailed and scholarly critique of the work of Saint Simon and of Comte. In the context of its time, this scholarly and ultimately devastating investigation, published in an institution whose staff contained not only Lasky but a great many who felt socialism was 'rational' if not, indeed, chic, must have been deeply unpopular. The pityless glare of Hayek's spotlight on the bizarre intellectual origins of totalitarianism – for this is indeed what was under discussion – is salutary indeed, not least because of the respectful support enjoyed by Marxist regimes from intellectuals in Western universities who talked glibly of 'the Soviet experiment' and other euphemisms. It is true that Hayek was able to draw upon a background of scholarly German literature for these articles and for the articles 'Scientism and the Study of Society' (1942–4); but for the English-speaking world

Hayek provided a significant exposition, while his focus on all the disparate elements was an important contribution to the study of the origins of collectivist and totalitarian ideas. Hayek's extraordinary learning enabled him to demonstrate the quite remarkable extent of the influence of Saint Simon (1941, III: 281–2, 292), which, as he pointed out, was much greater than normally realized because many who had borrowed his ideas attempted to distance themselves from the ridicule which the originator of those ideas had drawn upon himself by his antics in later years. Hayek showed that the influence spread through Belgium, Italy, Sweden, Russia, Spain and even South America as well as to the obvious countries, Britain and Germany. He was particularly effective in demonstrating the link to Hegelianism and, both directly and indirectly, to Marx (1941, II: 129, 131, 139, 145; III: 287, 289–92; 1942–4, II: 45). Indeed, those familiar only with Marx's borrowings from Hegelianism and from classical economics can find Hayek demonstrating how deeply unoriginal Marx was in other respects when account is taken of the French literature. It was from Saint Simon that the idea of only two classes, and these engaged in a class struggle, was borrowed, as was the idea that scientific politics has to discover the necessary laws of political development. Engels also drew from this source, and Proudhon was largely Saint Simonian in his socialist doctrines (1941, III: 289–92). Indeed, in some respects the French literature was well in advance of Marx and Engels, Hayek believed; for it broached the matter of the organization of a planned society and the problems of socialist calculation (1941, II: 145).

In all this Hayek showed a quite extraordinarily detailed knowledge of the original Saint Simonian literature (1941, II: 141) and indeed – though here he relied on work by others – of the character of Saint Simon (1941, I: 19–30) – part spiv, part self-deluding fraud, part 'visionary megalomaniac' (1941, I: 29). Saint Simon's chief asset seems to have been an ability to attract followers, some of whom were intellectually his superiors (1941, II: 119). His descent into the construction of a new religion, with a new theology, has strong elements of farce (1941, II: 133, 147, 149; III: 281). It resulted ultimately in the setting-up of a community which was acidly described by Hayek as half monastery, half Nazi *Führerschule* (1941, II: 149). But some of his other delusions, especially the idea that production as a whole could be planned (1941, II: 125–6), proved highly influential.

So also did the idea that liberty in society would impede planning and it must therefore be abolished – not merely economic liberty but even freedom of conscience (1941, II: 127, 130, 137). As Hayek showed – and the modern echoes are recognizable enough – the demands of the Saint Simonians for liberty were, as they acknowledged with 'an amazing frankness, rarely equalled by later socialists', purely to enable them to seize power (1941, II: 148).

The most able follower attracted by Saint Simon was Comte. His influence, too, was extremely widespread even though he was a 'singularly unattractive figure' who attracted few disciples in his lifetime (1941, III: 298, 318; 1978: 14). It was because the great figure of John Stuart Mill was attracted to him - though not permanently - that Comte was able to exercise an enormous, though indirect, influence.

Unlike Saint Simon, Comte did have a genuine scientific background. But his writings on economics and society are hardly coherent, and Hayek in his treatment showed exemplary patience in attempting to construct a coherent account from the published sources. But the account is not without entertainment; and Hayek reveals that Comte, in the course of abusing economics, of which he knew virtually nothing, originated the phrase 'in the long run we are all dead' associated with another flamboyant figure in intellectual history (1941, III: 314).

But the critique is serious and substantial. It revolves around three main issues. The first was Comtean 'holism', which, he argued, led to the paradox that we could only study man by rejecting every man and viewing society as a whole (1941, III: 299, 307; 1942–4, II: 41–6; 1988: 108). Hayek regarded it as an 'astounding assertion' (1941, III: 307) that in dealing with social phenomena the whole was better known than the sum of the parts. It led to the indefensible position that we could treat wholes like 'society' or 'the economy' or 'capitalism' as definitely given objects about which we could discover laws by observing their behaviour. We thus had the paradox of positivists postulating 'metaphysical entities' (1942–4, II: 45). Of course, this made it possible to talk in terms of conflicts between vague collectives - the class struggle and so on.

Second, Comte essayed to construct a 'social physics'. Sociology was to be social physics and Comte was determined to find laws governing the development of society as definite as gravity (1941, III: 303, 309; 1942–4, II: 39). Yet, as Hayek pointed out, on the crucial matter (in this context) of what constituted an 'observed fact' Comte was studiously vague (1941, III: 300–1).

The third basis for Hayek's criticism of Comte was the neat paradox that Comte believed that the human mind, which by its weakness had resulted in a society apparently in need of fundamental change, had the unique power to decide on a better plan of society. Even though one individual must act with extremely limited knowledge, within a small sphere, it was apparently possible for a human mind to comprehend the whole of society and to plan accordingly

(1941, III: 306, 310; 1942–4, III: 31, 33). But a major part of Hayek's output was taken up with a critique of socialism, and this deserves separate consideration.

SOCIALISM

There is some dispute about whether Hayek and Mises considered socialism impossible or merely inefficient. This is not surprising because Hayek was not entirely consistent about this matter (compare 1949: 90; and 1992: 127, 140), and in any case there is a fine line between impossibility and hopeless inefficiency leading to ultimate breakdown (as ultimately proved to be the case). But the threads of Hayek's criticism stem from his intellectual sources and thus throw some light upon his approach to intellectual history.

Hayek's original position seems to have been grounded upon the Austrian form of general equilibrium, stressing the sheer complexity of an economic society made up of a myriad of different individuals (1984: 159–62). Later on, as McCloughry has pointed out (in Hayek 1984: viii), Hayek changed his emphasis to one laying stress on the problem of knowledge (1937a; 1949: 91; Klein in Hayek 1992: 2).[11] This problem was serious enough in goods markets; but once factor markets were taken into account it became apparent that the idea of planning was incoherent, since, without a developed market system to register preferences for factor uses, there was simply no way of assigning values to factors (1949: 90, 123, 143, 167–8; 1978: 300). Without a developed factor market 'cost' simply had no meaning. Thus in his treatment of the body of ideas encompassed within the labels 'scientism', 'historism' and 'constructivism', Hayek was able to point to a central fallacy of the engineering approach deriving from Saint Simon, Comte and their associates – the engineer failed to appreciate that it was only a competitive society which provided him with the costs and prices which entered into his calculations. Thus an attempt to engineer *society* would lack such data. But from Saint Simon to Marx and Lenin the fallacy of the idea of running society as a single factory had seduced intellectuals (1942–4, III: 34–7).

From this vantage point Hayek was able to advance not merely a critique of such historical episodes as Bismarckian socialism, which, he maintained, had been the direct precursor of National Socialism (1988: 114; 1992: 223–36, esp. 228–9), but also to provide, as early as 1936, a prophetic critique of the 1960s vogue of 'indicative planning' (1984: 176–7).

A myth used to exist – surely the position is no longer tenable (Vaughn 1980) – that Mises, Hayek and Robbins were somehow 'defeated' in the socialist calculation debate by Lange and Taylor employing Lausanne general equilibrium. In fact, Hayek's extraordinarily fair-minded evaluation of the socialist calculation debate (1949: 148–80) made it perfectly clear that all these writers had done was to recognize that the formal (marginalist) principles of economic theory had to apply to a socialist economy – but they had, because of the knowledge problem, totally failed to demonstrate *how* this could be done without markets. But in any case, the perfect competition at the heart of the Lausanne model was completely irrelevant to any real economic system (1949: 92–106) – choice was not only an essential component of welfare (1984: 173–4) but also vital to successful and beneficial economic evolution.

MACROECONOMICS

Hayek's macroeconomic model

Hayek approached historical macroeconomic literature from an Austrian standpoint. Since Hayek's own macroeconomics has been the subject of extensive critical comment, it is necessary to identify the key elements in order to see what provided the basis for his evaluation of other writers.

The essential model is that derived from Mises. It is a variant of Wicksell's model in which a quantity theory approach is replaced by one in which the prices and output of consumer goods and those of producer goods are distinguished and given a key role. Hayek was thus opposed to the degree of aggregation involved in both Keynesian macroeconomics and in a purely quantity theory approach. The basic argument was that monetary expansion, through lowering the lending rate below the marginal rate of profit, altered the relative prices of consumption and investment goods, and in turn distorted factor markets. I have explained the basic model involved elsewhere (O'Brien 1988: 108–10) and there is no space to go into greater detail here. What it is necessary to emphasize, however, is that the 'period of production' is not only not essential to this macroeconomic model but it is absent from much of Hayek's macroeconomic writings and his attempts to grapple with the problem eventually brought these writings to a halt (1933c; 1939: 135–56; 1984: 5–32, 55–70, 71–117; Machlup 1976: 30). What is essential, however, is the idea that monetary disequilibrium results in an output of consumption goods and producer goods in proportions which are different from those reflected by consumer preferences for consumption goods and savings (1984: 71–117, 142).[12] To avoid such disequilibrium it is not enough, however, to aim for a stable price level; for with secularly rising productivity, a stable price level would require a secularly increasing money supply, which in turn would require the lending rate to be below the marginal rate of profit. This was a common idea amongst Austrian economists from the late 1920s, although it was a point originally put forward by the Swedish economist Davidson in controversy with Wicksell (1933c: 113–15; 1984: 122–4, 129).

The absolute worth of such a model need not detain us here. It certainly has a great deal to offer in considering the inflationary world since 1945; and Hayek's employment of it during the 1930s depression was wrong-headed, as he came reluctantly to recognize, because of an absolutely fundamental mistake on a matter of *fact* – a failure to recognize the catastrophic decline in the United States money supply (1984: 118–35 esp. 130). What is of concern for our present purposes is that it provided the intellectual basis for Hayek's writings on the history of monetary economics.

Cantillon

Although it was Higgs who did the pioneering work on Cantillon, and who deserves every credit for a great scholarly achievement, Hayek did much to establish the importance of Cantillon (1991: 245–94). Not surprisingly, the feature of Cantillon's analysis which he found most worthy of note was that Cantillon had pointed out the defects in the traditional quantity theory, as expounded by Locke, and had explained the importance of the path followed by an increase in the money supply and the effect on *relative* prices (1935: 1, 8; 1978: 216). But Hayek deserves great credit for bringing out what he called the 'subterranean influence' of Cantillon's book. He established that Smith was familiar with it, and demonstrated its influence upon the Physiocratic literature. His account of the recognition of Cantillon by different authors in several languages over the centuries showed a huge knowledge, although he was indebted, as he acknowledged, to Cannan. His account of Cantillon, although apparently written as early as 1931, is still an excellent reference, and his picture of Mirabeau's attempts to plagiarize Cantillon, and the success of others in so doing, is fascinating. In particular, he shows the way in which Postlethwayt incorporated, without acknowledgement, substantial chunks of the *Essai* in his own work (1991: 177n, 245), and despite his great admiration for David Hume, he insisted on the likelihood that Hume had also had access to the essay before writing his own *Essays*.

Classical monetary economics

Hayek's knowledge of English classical monetary writing was formidable by the late 1920s (1991: 177–244). Although there was a long

German-language tradition of interest in this literature, and although Mises was widely read in it, the latter's own *Money* does not provide the sort of systematic history of ideas treatment which Hayek wrote, although this was not published until late in life.

His judgement of the balance of the issues involved was, despite his particular standpoint, good. In particular, he clearly perceived Ricardo's singular lack of originality on matters of monetary economics as well as his over-simplification (1935: 14; 1991: 200–6, 321; Fetter 1940). He was particularly aware of Ricardo's debt to Thornton, though offering a generous view of Ricardo's lack of acknowledgement of him. Of course, as Hayek pointed out, Ricardo was hardly alone in this; Thornton's work was borrowed by Lord King, J.L. Foster and the Bullion Report as well. On the other side, he gave some recognition to Joplin at a very early date (1935: 15–16; 1991: 219–20, 319) even though he certainly did not appreciate Joplin's full significance and mistakenly believed that Joplin had borrowed ideas from Thornton which were in fact not only his own but pointed in a direction different from that of Thornton. He provided a beautiful little sketch of the work of George Warde Norman (Hayek 1933b), at that time a figure little known even in England, and recognized the value of Cairnes's work on international monetary transmission (1935: 10).

But it is his work on Thornton which is perhaps his major claim to fame as a monetary historian (1935: 11–14, 17; 1991: 295–344). Launched upon the task of producing an edition of Thornton's *Paper Credit* (Thornton 1802), Hayek drew upon extensive manuscript sources, as well as on historical material relating to the Clapham Sect, to provide not only a rounded picture of the banker and economist who was also a religious activist, but an account of his place as a monetary writer which is still of considerable interest today. He had earlier emphasized the importance of Thornton, whose monetary theory indeed had much in common with that of Mises and Hayek, in his *Prices and Production* and he was able, as a result of his detailed knowledge of classical monetary economics, to show the way in which Thornton's influence extended to Tooke, Horsley Palmer, Senior and (though watered down) J.S. Mill.

Given Hayek's own macroeconomic approach, it was hardly surprising that he should be both sympathetic and illuminating on the subject of Thornton. It is equally unsurprising that, if not always unilluminating, his attitude to Keynes, both personally and intellectually, was distinctly unsympathetic.

Keynes

Apart from his celebrated controversy with Keynes, following his adverse review of the *Treatise* (1931b; 1931c; Keynes 1931), Hayek wrote about Keynes on a number of occasions. Virtually none of these contributions is innocent of some dig at Keynes (1960: 447; 1967: 344–8; 1978: 283–9; 1983), even where he pays tribute to his intellectual powers. Moreover, Hayek distrusted Keynes's leanings in favour of significant state influence on the economy – as a German speaker he was aware of the preface to the German edition of the *General Theory* (Hayek 1967: 346), unlike many in this country.

The controversy between Keynes and Hayek was certainly restrained compared with the celebrated *Methodenstreit* between Menger and Schmoller (Hayek 1934a: 407). None the less, Hayek deplored both Keynes's lack of scholarship and, quite emphatically, what he considered to be Keynes's lack of knowledge of economics. His view was that Keynes really knew no economics outside Cambridge economics (1967: 345). On this topic he was noticeably more frank in an article written for the *Oriental Economist* (1978: 283–9) than in one written for the London *Economist* (1983). In particular, Keynes's knowledge of international trade theory and of capital theory was inadequate, Hayek believed, and in the monetary field he knew little of the classical monetary literature (even Thornton), while his inability to read German sufficiently well to understand the argument meant that he was unaware of important contributions by Wicksell and Mises (Hayek 1978: 218, 230–1). As Hayek put it, perhaps rather sardonically, 'The world might have been saved much if Lord Keynes's German had been a little better' (1992: 131).

While Hayek's standpoint is obvious enough, this is not entirely unfair. Certainly it would be difficult to deny that Keynes's Wicksellian *Treatise* would have benefited from a better knowledge (and acknowledgement) of Wicksell.

Hayek, familiar with the literature on under-consumption (1931a), regarded Keynes's *General Theory* as a 'tract for the times' (1978: 284). He believed, partly as a result of personal conversations with Keynes, with whom he seems, like Robbins, to have developed amicable personal relations during the war, that on seeing the inflationary effects produced by his disciples Keynes would have produced another tract for the times, had he lived. While he viewed what he regarded as Keynes's monetary nationalism with distinct disfavour, especially during the 1930s (1937b: 2; 1984: 118–35), he did not believe that Keynes himself could be blamed personally for the inflation associated with 'Keynesian' policies (1978: 23, 191–231, 286–7) even though he did draw a parallel between Keynes and John Law (ibid: 229).

But he was concerned that the dominance of macroeconomics after Keynes had brought about a significant decline in microeconomics - by which, of course, he meant Austrian microeconomics. Moreover, writing in the 1980s, he believed that the defeat of Keynesian economics had left economists bewildered because, during the era of Keynesian dominance, economists had 'forgotten much that had been fairly well understood before the "Keynesian revolution"' (1983: 45).

Hayek's parallel between Keynes and John Law has just enough truth in it to make it interesting. This is not an accidcent. Hayek had a detailed knowledge not only of John Law but also of monetary history in France.

John Law

An interest in the work of John Law was well established in the Austrian School. Menger had already recognized Law, whom he credited with founding a correct theory of the origin of money. In an essay on French paper money, written in the late 1920s, although not published until his old age, Hayek himself exhibited a detailed knowledge of Law's work and correctly identified the fundamental weakness in Law's macroeconomics - the proposition that a demand-determined money supply could do no harm (1991: 155-76). His account of Law is restrained and scholarly - remarkably so since he clearly had a detailed knowledge of Law's schemes and their discreditable collapse.

Law is one of a number of minor figures treated sympathetically and illuminatingly by Hayek. The cases of Cairnes and Norman have also been noted. But there were a number of other writers concerning whom he exhibited particular sympathy and expertise.

SYMPATHIES AND EXPERTISE

The minor cases

Hayek devoted his considerable scholarly resources to such figures as Bastiat (Hayek 1991: 347-50) (whom he treated with generosity,[13] noting that writer's intellectual vitality, though concentrating on the matter of unintended consequences and taking the opportunity to have a dig at Keynesian protectionism), and Dupuit (ibid.: 350-2), to whom he paid tribute as a pioneer of marginal utility analysis and an important influence on Walras. He produced a scholarly treatment of Macleod and his monetary theory (1933a), even though he was evidently irritated by Macleod's subjective originality and a certain feeling (possibly in his mind a Keynesian parallel) that Macleod, unappreciative of his own ignorance of his predecessors, had expected more recognition than he deserved. He wrote an eminently fair-minded obituary of Wesley Mitchell (Hayek 1948) even though his account of his trip to the United States as a young man (1992: 19–41) showed him to be unimpressed with Mitchell's work. He showed interest in John Rae (Hayek 1943a), exhibiting meticulous scholarship in matters of detail and being obviously drawn to Rae both by the connection with J.S. Mill and by Rae's pioneering work on capital theory. He wrote illuminatingly about the history of the LSE (1946), and his excellent narrative contains a fair and generous account of the activities of Sidney Webb, for whom, it is evident, Hayek had considerable regard despite their fundamental differences (the same could not be said, perhaps understandably, of Beatrice Webb) (1967: 341–4).

Mandeville

His treatment of Mandeville deserves special mention (Hayek 1978: 249–66). For Hayek regarded Mandeville as a very important writer. This was not primarily as an economist (despite his discussion of division of labour) or even (a reflection of Hayek's interest) as a psychologist. Rather Mandeville's importance lay in his pioneering statement of the doctrine of unintended consequences leading, so Hayek believed, to Hume and to Menger's 1883 book. Indeed, Mandeville had, as Menger was to do later, regarded language itself as an evolutionary phenomenon.

Mandeville's thesis – that what are private vices are often public benefits – had caused considerable outrage in his lifetime; but in Hayek's view it had become increasingly evident that it was simply a special case of the more general principle of unintended consequences. The complex order of society resulting from men's actions was very different from what they had intended, and individuals, in pursuing their own ends, whether selfish or altruistic, produced useful results for others which they could not anticipate. Indeed, the whole order of society resulted from the unintended consequences of individuals striving for their own ends, their strivings being channelled by the evolved rules of behaviour (1949: 4, 9; 1978: 252–3, 258–9; 1988: 13, 146).

The next step was for Mandeville to ask how it was that institutions grew up which achieved this result. His answer was the growth of law through an evolutionary process characterized by trial and error (1973–9, III: 153–4; 1978: 260; 1988: 86; 1991: 79–98). But Mandeville went far beyond the area of law to show that this evolutionary process applied to morality, convention, language and money. It was this which was passed to Hume, Smith, Ferguson, Burke and ultimately to Menger.

J.S. Mill

Like Lionel Robbins, Hayek showed not only interest in, but considerable affection for, John Stuart Mill (Hayek 1945; 1951). It was Hayek who did the pioneering work in organizing J.S. Mill's correspondence, which was finally edited by F.E. Mineka (1963). He greatly enjoyed the scholarly detective work involved, although he was less keen on the editorial work. Indeed, he believed that he had had the pleasure (in assembling much of the correspondence) while Mineka had had to do the hard work (Hayek in Mineka 1963: xxiv)

His reluctance to get involved in detailed editorial work stems from his publication (1951) of the correspondence of J.S. Mill and Harriet Taylor. The sympathy and care of his work on this correspondence is remarkable - even in dealing with the highly rationalist and constructivist Mrs Taylor, who, although dedicated to the emancipation of women, somehow neglected to have her daughter educated. Despite his instinctive sympathy for Mill himself, he was not at all blind to the weaknesses of character and personal judgement which the relationship made clear. But after his work on their correspondence, he came to the conclusion that the choice lay between doing editorial work and doing other work. Editorial work was simply too exhausting and time-consuming, and so he chose the latter.[14]

His work on J.S. Mill showed meticulous scholarship in matters of detail as well as considerable knowledge of nineteenth-century intellectual history far beyond the bounds of economics. He appreciated Mill's intellectual importance; but on the whole it seems fair to conclude that he did not appreciate the full extent of Mill's originality (Hayek in Mineka 1963: xvi; 1978: 270; Stigler 1955). He was also aware that Mill had ignored important developments during his lifetime (1978: 271; 1988: 148). But his attitude towards Mill's flirtations with socialism, and the Continental brand of liberalism, was judicious and temperate, though necessarily coloured by his own attitude towards socialism and constructivism (1949: 28–9, 110, 270n; 1988: 149); and he did not overplay the fact of Mill's ultimate realization that in endorsing (and, given his position, thus spreading the influence of) the work of Comte, he had been in the service of a totalitarian cause (1941, II: 132). Occasionally, Hayek's interpretations of Mill are idiosyncratic; thus the famous fourth proposition on capital (demand for commodities is not demand for labour) Hayek managed to interpret in terms of Mises–Hayek trade cycle theory (1984: 142, 157 n.6). But for the most part his interpretations of Mill are illuminating and scholarly.

The Austrian School

Hayek's writings as historian of the Austrian School (1934a; 1934b; 1944; 1968a; 1968b; 1968c; 1992: 19–41, 108–25, 160–5) are naturally of particular interest. His essays on Wieser (1968c; 1992: 108–25) are one of the most informative sources on the second generation of Austrians – much more so than Schumpeter's *History* (1954) in many ways. It is Hayek's humility and respect for individuality – which comes through in his writing on the history of ideas as much as in his methodological individualism – which contrasts so strongly with Schumpeter's bombast, even though Schumpeter was a great scholar and knew the older Austrians at first hand. Indeed, Menger is illuminating about Schumpeter himself (Hayek 1967: 339–41; 1992: 160–5) as well as about minor figures such as Schams, Strigl (Hayek 1944) and Mach. He also wrote informatively about Philippovich (Hayek 1934b) and explained Mises's failure to obtain an academic appointment – it was possible to obtain an academic appointment in Vienna if you were Jewish but only if you were of left-wing sympathies, since these were required to obtain the endorsement of the Jewish community there (1992: 128n).

Hayek was also able to write illuminatingly about Gossen, whose priority over the Austrians he acknowledged. As early as 1927 he wrote an introduction to the third edition of Gossen's *Entwicklung* with a complete bibliography of all the earlier writings on Gossen (1991: 352–71; 1992: 42–60). It was true that Menger did not know of Gossen's work before he wrote his *Grundsätze*; but this did not alter the objective fact of priority (1978: 273).

On Wieser – whose economics represented, in his opinion, a separate branch of Austrian economics (1968c; 1992: 122) – Hayek was also illuminating. As Hayek makes clear, it was Wieser who introduced marginal utility, imputation and indeed much of the apparatus associated with Austrian economics. There is no doubt that in some respects Hayek was over-generous to Wieser (notably in crediting Wieser with introducing marginal-utility analysis into monetary economics, followed 'somewhat later in the Anglo Saxon countries' (1992: 118–19)). But his appraisal is still interesting.

Perhaps because he had derived so much from Menger's 1883 book, it is his appraisals of Menger which hold particular interest (1934a; 1968b). Moreover, the first was published at a time when it was still possible to feel, at least at the LSE, that Austrian economics was the dominant school (1934a: 408–9). The key contributions which he stressed in his introduction to Menger's *Grundsätze* were the discussions of needs and of means of satisfying them, the distinction between goods of first and higher order, and complementarity (1934a: 399,

414; 1978: 275–6). This showed the importance which the Austrian School attached to 'the technical structure of production' (1934a: 399), by which, of course, he meant something very different from that understood by Marshall. He also believed that Menger had given a prominent role to time in his analysis, in contrast to Walras.

In Hayek's view, what made the *Grundsätze* effective was its 'persistent slow approach to its main object' (1978: 274–5) with a steady build-up of the subjective basis of the analysis, extending it to factor pricing. Important also was Menger's 'atomistic' method and his reliance upon introspection.

Indeed, Hayek sometimes wrote as if the extension of subjectivism, Austrian subjectivism, was co-terminal with advances in economics (1942–4; I: 280–3; 1988: 97; 1992: 55). According to Hayek, 'it is probably no exaggeration to say that every important advance in economic theory during the last hundred years was a further step in the consistent application of subjectivism' (1942–4, I: 281).

Even if one accepts such a view, for the purposes of argument, there is no doubt that Hayek was prone to overstate the importance of the Austrians within this process of advance. But in any case the approach is not really tenable. When Hayek attempts to illustrate his general thesis with a discussion of rent the problems become clear (1942–4, I: 282–3). For his account of the theory of rent is only just recognizable to anyone familiar with it and with the history of the concept, and his attempt to identify subjective factors in the theory of rent is notably unsuccessful.

Perhaps the biggest single puzzle concerning Hayek's discussion of the Austrian School relates to his treatment of Menger's 1883 *Untersuchungen*. For it is clear that this book was by far the most important one in providing Hayek with his standpoint on intellectual history; yet, as already noted, in dealing with Menger as a writer he emphasizes it relatively lightly (1968a: 460; 1968b: 125–6).

Although Hayek is fascinating on Austrian economists, he has relatively lttle to say about those in Germany. There are exceptions, notably Röpke and Eucken (1992: 195–9). But he seems to have felt a very marked distaste for much of intellectual life in Germany, well before 1933 (1922: 188), and there is little to be learnt about the German economists from his works.

ANTAGONISMS AND QUESTIONABLE JUDGEMENTS

As indicated above, some of Hayek's judgements in the matter of intellectual history are somewhat idiosyncratic. For the sake of completeness there are a few others which should also be mentioned. They include a curious contention that Aristotle, and the traditions stemming from him, were entirely innocent of the idea of evolution (1988: 143).[15] At the other end of the historical scale Beveridge, in a phrase no doubt reflecting a particular episode at the LSE, is dismissed as having 'understood no economics whatever' (1978: 230; Robbins 1971: 158). In between we find the remarkably over-generous interpretation of Petty, who 'deserves to be considered a forerunner of later business cycle theorists' (1991: 136–7), the contention that the labour theory of value caused the breakdown of classical economics (1949: 136) (a view easily derived from the emphasis on Austrian subjectivism but somewhat over-simple to put it mildly) and the surprising misconception that 'oligopoly' was invented by the Austrian financier Karl Schlesinger (Hayek 1992: 25) (Schumpeter certainly knew better than this; (Hayek 1954: 208)).

The two most serious criticisms to be made, however, relate to Marshall and to Ricardo. On the one hand there is absolutely no doubt that Hayek – perhaps because of an antipathy towards everything Cambridge – seriously underrated Marshall. It is certainly interesting that Marshall seems to have been more deeply read in Menger's work than his *Principles* would indicate – Hayek reported that Marshall's personal copy of the *Grundsätze* in the Marshall Library contained detailed marginal commentary (1968b: 124; 1978: 279). But to view Marshall, as Hayek seems to do, as merely one of the 'Anglo-Saxons' riding on the coat tails of not merely the first but the second generation Austrians, is hardly adequate.

His attitude to Ricardo (Hayek 1950) was distinctly temperate. Indeed, it is a welcome change to anyone not enamoured of the excesses of the Ricardo industry in the recent past, for he believed Ricardo's main contribution to be comparative cost. But in dealing with Ricardo there is a problem. It is the celebrated 'Ricardo Effect' (1939: 3–71; 1949: 220–54).

This effect, which would have been better called the 'Mises Effect' simply involves an increase in the use of less-capital-intensive methods of production as a result of a fall in real wages. As a proposition it is not particularly surprising to anyone familiar with the standard literature on investment decisions, although Hayek employed considerable ingenuity in some of his presentations (1978: 165–78). But it is not in Ricardo.[16] The two passages which Hayek cited – one from the chapter on value, dealing with the effect of a rise in wages in altering relative values of commodities produced with differing capital–labour ratios, even without factor substitution, and the other from the chapter on machinery (where Ricardo, following Barton, satisfied himself that mechanization could cause unemployment) – do not correspond in any serious sense to the point which Hayek was trying to make (Ricardo 1817: 38–43, 386–97). The question arises as to why Hayek did this. Was it excessive humility, or was it a rhetorical device? There seems to be no clear answer to this. My own suspicion is that it was, at least unconsciously, a desire to highlight what he considered to be a lack in Cambridge of knowledge of the established economic literature.

CONCLUSION

There is no doubt that Hayek was a very considerable scholar. Indeed, there are times when it seems that his own essential message is obscured by his scholarship. In a sense Hayek as an intellectual historian was his own worst enemy. The beautifully crafted but sometimes almost impenetrable prose, the lengths to which the scholarship drew him, the substitution of patient repetition (shades of Menger) for rhetoric and polemic – all these led to a situation in which his work to a significant extent remained unread. Anyone who has, as I have, ploughed through the 'Counter-Revolution of Science' and 'Scientism and the Study of Society' articles will recognize what I am saying – but not many, and certainly not many economists, have done so. The contrast with Robbins's lucid, polemical, beautifully written and at times impatient *Essay on the Nature and Significance of Economic Science* which *has* been widely read by economists, is clear. An episode involving Leontief is indeed a grotesque illustration of this. After Hayek (in 1976, following a lifetime of writing about the fallacies of economic planning, which were laid bare for even the most obdurate to see as the Soviet Empire collapsed) had criticized *inter alia* Leontief over the advocacy of planning, the latter replied that he knew of no published evidence that Hayek had any right to criticize him. That Hayek wrote that he despaired of rational debate with these people is understandable enough; but the form in which he delivered his message was in part the cause.

Hayek's scholarly care to acknowledge his predecessors has proved a significant disadvantage to him. For not only has it denied him the ability to make what Hicks, in reviewing Keynes's *General Theory*, regarded as Jevons-like claims to originality (Hicks 1936); it has also caused him to adhere to concepts like Böhm-Bawerk's 'period of production', which his macroeconomic theory did not need (and which neither its Wicksellian and Misesean origins nor its later Robbinsian formulation contained) and which Hayek himself later abandoned.

Of course, in a sense those who are prepared to plough through Hayek's work will find that, from a scholarly point of view, he commands the high moral ground; for much of the work critical of Hayek certainly does not adhere to comparable scholarly standards. Moreover, his patience and tenacity were remarkable. Indeed, so patient was he, especially with some of the works in the area of legal philosophy, that he might be regarded as having been patient to a fault. This was certainly Schumpeter's view when he reviewed *The Road to Serfdom* (Hayek 1967: 184n; 1973–9, I: 161n). But, as Hayek explained, his patience stemmed from a belief that many of those whose work he thought to be most deeply mistaken were fundamentally well-intentioned:

> It is necessary to realise that the sources of many of the most harmful agents in this world are often not evil men but high-minded idealists, and that in particular the foundations of totalitarian barbarism have been laid by honourable and well-meaning scholars who never recognise the offspring they produce.
>
> (1973–9, I: 70)

Hayek himself was a major scholar; and it is sad to reflect that he has rarely enjoyed this open-minded tolerance himself.

NOTES

1 Unless stated otherwise, text references are to works by Hayek.
2 This becomes very clear on reading the early essays reprinted in Hayek 1984, especially pp. 33–54.
3 Indeed, at the Adam Smith celebrations in Glasgow in 1976 he carried a holdall full of books.
4 When I began work on J.R. McCulloch he wrote to me, in response to a letter of mine asking for source material which the *Economist* published, offering to lend me his copy of H.G. Reid's sketch of McCulloch's life. The book was extremely rare and he had no personal knowledge of me at all.
5 Thus in 1973–9, I, p. 154 n. 48, he even noted a variation in different published versions of Hegel, a philosopher whom, as 'the fountain head of most modern irrationalism and totalitarianism' (ibid.: 32), Hayek did not venerate.
6 Thus in 1973–9, II, pp. 159–60 n.5 runs from Paley (1785) to Kelsen (1960) and contains quotations in English, French, German and Italian. Yet this was never a parade: Hayek paid his readers the compliment of assuming that they were as well read, and as linguistically versatile, as he was.
7 Consider the following sentence: 'Consistently pursued historism necessarily leads to the view that the human mind is itself variable and that not only are most or all manifestations of the human mind unintelligible to us apart from their historical setting, but that from our knowledge of how the whole situations succeed each other we can learn to recognise the laws according to which the human mind changes, and that it is the knowledge of these laws which alone puts us in a position to understand any particular manifestation of the human mind' (1942–4, II: 60).
8 See, however, Mises (1969: 42–3).

9 He slipped on one small point: see Stonier (1943) and Hayek (1943b).

10 'All that the theory of the social sciences attempts is to provide a technique of reasoning which assists us in connecting individual facts but which, like logic or mathematics, is not about facts. It can, therefore, . . . never be verified or falsified by reference to facts' (1949: 73).

11 'Any approach, such as that of much of mathematical economics with its simultaneous equations, which in effect starts from the assumption that people's *knowledge* corresponds with the objective *facts* of the situation, systematically leaves out what is our main task to explain.' (1949: 91)

12 Hayek made this clear in his *Profits, Interest and Investment:* 'The starting point for a fully developed theory of this kind would be (a) the intentions of all the consumers with respect to the way in which they wish to distribute at all the relevant dates all their resources (not merely their "income") between current consumption and provision for further consumption, and (b) the separate and independent decisions of the entrepreneurs with respect to the amounts of consumers' goods which they plan to provide at these various dates. Correspondence between these two groups of decisions would be characteristic of the kind of equilibrium which we now usually describe as a state where savings are equal to investments and with which the idea of an equilibrium rate of interest is connected. A rate of interest below that equilibrium rate would then induce entrepreneurs to devote a smaller share of the available resources to production for current consumption than the share of the income earned by these resources actually spent on consumption.' (1939: 153–4). Hayek then glosses this with reference to an 'investment period', but is is clearly not central to the argument.

13 See, however, Dorn (1981).

14 It is apparent from Hayek (1943b) that he had contemplated a complete edition of J.S. Mill's correspondence.

15 Sabine stresses the evolutionary nature of human society in Aristotle (Sabine 1951: 113–14, 228–9). Hayek's view of Artistotle seems to have come from Ernst Mayr (Hayek 1988: 148–9).

16 This is a separate question from the analytical validity of the 'Effect', on which see Moss and Vaughn (1986).

BIBLIOGRAPHY

Böhm-Bawerk, E.v. (1884–9) *Kapital und Kapitalzins*, 2 vols., Innsbruck: Wagner.

Cantillon, R. (*c.* 1730) *Essai sur la Nature du Commerce en Général*, trans. H. Higgs, repr. New York: Kelley, 1964.

Clapham, J.H. (1941) Review of F.A. Hayek (ed.) *An Enquiry into the Nature and Effects of the Paper Credit of Great Britain*, by Henry Thornton, *Economica*, NS 8 (May): 210–11.

Dorn, J.A. (1981) 'Law and Liberty: A Comparison of Hayek and Bastiat', *Journal of Libertarian Studies* 5 (Fall): 375–97, repr. in Wood and Woods 1991), vol. 3, pp. 306–30.

Fetter, F.W. (1940) Review of F.A. Hayek (ed.) *An Enquiry into the Nature and Effects of the Paper Credit of Great Britain*, by Henry Thornton, *Journal of Political Economy* 48(5): 766–7.

Garrison, R.W. and Kirzner, I.M. (1987) 'Hayek, Friedrich August von', in

J. Eatwell *et al.*, *The New Palgrave*, vol. 2, pp. 609–14, London: Macmillan.
Hayek, F.A. (1931a) 'The "Paradox" of Saving', *Economica* 11 (May): 125–69.
—— (1931b) 'Reflections on the Pure Theory of Money of Mr. J.M. Keynes', *Economica* 11 (Aug.): 270–95.
—— (1931c) 'A Rejoinder to Mr. Keynes', *Economica* 11 (Nov.): 398–403.
—— (1932a) 'Gossen, Hermann Heinrich', in E.R.A. Seligman (ed.) *Encyclopaedia of the Social Sciences*, New York: Macmillan, vol. 7, p. 3.
—— (1932b) 'A Note on the Development of the Doctrine of "Forced Saving"', *Quarterly Journal of Economics* 47 (Nov.): 123–33.
—— (1933a) 'Macleod, Henry Dunning (1821–1902)', in E.R.A. Seligman (ed.) *Encyclopaedia of the Social Sciences*, New York: Macmillan , vol. 10, p. 30.
—— (1933b) 'Norman, George Warde (1793–1882)', in E.R.A. Seligman (ed.) *Encyclopaedia of the Social Sciences*, New York: Macmillan , vol. 11, p. 397.
—— (1933c) *Monetary Theory and the Trade Cycle*, trans. N. Kaldor and H. Croome, London: Jonathan Cape.
—— (1934a) 'Carl Menger', *Economica*, NS 1 (Nov.): 393–420; also reprinted as the Introduction to the LSE reprint of Menger's *Grundsätze der Volkswirtschaftslehre*.
—— (1934b) 'Philippovich von Philippsberg, Eugen', in E.R.A. Seligman (ed.) *Encyclopaedia of the Social Sciences*, New York: Macmillan, vol. 12, p. 116.
—— (1935) *Prices and Production*, 2nd edn, London: Routledge & Kegan Paul.
—— (1937a) 'Economics and Knowledge', *Economica*, NS 4 (Feb.): 33–54.
—— (1937b) *Monetary Nationalism and International Stability*, London: Longman.
—— (1939) *Profits, Interest and Investment*, London: Routledge & Kegan Paul.
—— (1941) 'The Counter-Revolution of Science', Part I, *Economica*, NS 8 (Feb.): 9–36; Part II, *Economica*, (May): 119–50; Part III, *Economica* (Aug.): 281–320.
—— (1942–44) 'Scientism and the Study of Society', Part I, *Economica*, NS 9 (Aug. 1942): 267–91; Part II, *Economica*, NS 10 (Feb. 1943): 34–63; Part III, *Economica*, NS 11 (Feb. 1944): 27–39.
—— (1943a) 'John Rae and John Stuart Mill: A Correspondence', *Economica* NS 10 (Aug.): 253–5.
—— (1943b) 'Miscellaneous Notes', *Economica*, NS 10 (May): 188–9.
—— (1944) 'Richard von Strigl', *Economic Journal* 54 (June-Sept.): 284–6.
—— (1945) 'Notes on N.W. Senior's *Political Economy* by John Stuart Mill', *Economica*, NS 12 (Aug.): 134–9.
—— (1946) 'The London School of Economics 1895–1945', *Economica*, NS 13 (Feb.): 1–31.
—— (1948) 'Wesley Clair Mitchell, 1874–1948', *Journal of the Royal Statistical Society* 111(3): 254–5.
—— (1949) *Individualism and Economic Order*, London: Routledge & Kegan Paul.
—— (1950) 'Ricardo, David', in *Chambers Encyclopaedia*, new edition, London: George Newnes, vol. 11, pp. 680–1.
—— (1951) *John Stuart Mill and Harriet Taylor: Their Correspondence and Subsequent Marriage* , London: Routledge & Kegan Paul.

—— (1952) *The Sensory Order: An Inquiry into the Foundations of Theoretical Psychology*, London: Routledge & Kegan Paul.

—— (1954) *Capitalism and the Historians,* London: Routledge & Kegan Paul.

—— (1960) *The Constitution of Liberty*, London: Routledge & Kegan Paul.

—— (1967) *Studies in Philosophy, Politics and Economics*, London: Routledge & Kegan Paul.

—— 68a) 'The Austrian School', in D.L. Sills (ed.) *International Encyclopaedia of the Social Sciences*, New York: Macmillan and Free Press, vol. 4, pp. 458–62.

—— (1968b) 'Menger, Carl', in D.L. Sills (ed.) *International Encyclopaedia of the Social Sciences*, New York: Macmillan and Free Press, vol. 10, pp. 124–7.

—— (1968c) 'Wieser, Friedrich von', in D.L. Sills (ed.) *International Encyclopaedia of the Social Sciences*, New York: Macmillan and Free Press, vol. 16, pp. 549 50.

—— (1973–9) *Law, Legislation and Liberty*: vol. 1, *Rules and Order* (1973); vol. 2, *The Mirage of Social Justice* (1976); vol. 3, *The Political Order of a Free People* (1979); one-volume edition, London: Routledge & Kegan Paul.

—— (1978) *New Studies in Philosophy, Politics, Economics and the History of Ideas*, London: Routledge & Kegan Paul.

—— (1979) 'Foreword', pp. xix-xxiv in L. von Mises *Socialism*, repr. Indianapolis: Liberty Classics.

—— (1983) 'The Austrian Critique', *Economist*, 11 June, pp. 45–8.

—— (1984) *Money, Capital and Fluctuations: Early Essays*, ed. R. McCloughry, London: Routledge & Kegan Paul.

—— (1988) *The Fatal Conceit: The Errors of Socialism. The Collected Works of F.A. Hayek*, vol. 1, ed. W.W. Bartley III, London: Routledge.

—— (1991) *The Trend of Economic Thinking: Essays on Political Economists and Economic History. The Collected Works of F.A. Hayek*, ed. W.W. Bartley III and S. Kresge, London: Routledge, vol. 3.

—— (1992) *The Fortunes of Liberalism: Essays on Austrian Economics and the Idea of Freedom. The Collected Works of F.A. Hayek*, ed. P.G. Klein, London: Routledge, vol. 4.

Hicks, J.R. (1936) 'Mr Keynes' Theory of Employment', *Economic Journal* 46 (June): 238–53.

—— (1940) Review of F.A. Hayek (ed.) *An Enquiry into the Nature and Effects of the Paper Credit of Great Britain* by Henry Thornton, *Economic History Review* 10(2): 182.

—— (1967) *Critical Essays in Monetary Theory*, reprinted Oxford: Clarendon, 1979.

Hutchison, T.W. (1981) *The Politics and Philosophy of Economics: Marxians, Keynesians and Austrians*, Oxford: Blackwell.

Keynes, J.M. (1930) *A Treatise on Money*, 2 vols, reprinted London: Macmillan, for the Royal Economic Society, 1971.

—— (1931) 'The Pure Theory of Money: A Reply to Dr. Hayek', *Economica* 11 (Nov.): 387–97.

—— (1936) *The General Theory of Employment, Interest and Money*, reprinted London: Macmillan, for the Royal Economic Society, 1973.

Machlup, F. (ed.) (1976) *Essays on Hayek*, New York: New York University Press.

—— (1979) 'Hayek, Friedrich A. von', in D.L. Sills (ed.) *International Encyclopaedia of the Social Sciences*, New York: Free Press, vol. 18, pp. 274–82.

Menger, C. (1871) *Grundsätze der Volkswirtschaftslehre*, Wien: Braumüller; reprinted London: LSE, 1934.

—— (1883) *Untersuchung über die Methode der Socialwissenschaften und der Politischen Oekonomie insbesondere*, trans. F.J. Nock, ed. L. Schneider as *Problems of Economics and Sociology*, Urbana: University of Illinois Press, 1963.

Mineka, F. (ed.) (1963) *The Earlier Letters of John Stuart Mill*, Toronto: University of Toronto Press.

Mises, L. von (1912) *The Theory of Money and Credit*, 2nd edn 1924, trans. H.E. Batson, London: Jonathan Cape, 1953.

—— (1922) *Gemeinwirtschaft*, trans. as *Socialism*, by J. Kahane, reprinted Indianapolis: Liberty Classics, 1979.

—— (1969) *The Historical Setting of the Austrian School of Economics*, New Rochelle, New York: Arlington House.

Moss, L. and Vaughn, K. (1986) 'Hayek's Ricardo Effect: A Second Look', *History of Political Economy* 18 (Winter): 545–65; reprinted in Wood and Woods (1991), vol. 4, pp. 156–76.

O'Brien, D.P. (1988) *Lionel Robbins*, London: Macmillan.

Ricardo, D. (1817) *On the Principles of Political Economy and Taxation*; reprinted as vol. 1 of *The Works and Correspondence of David Ricardo*, ed. P. Sraffa, Cambridge: Cambridge University Press, 1951.

Robbins, L.C. (1932) *An Essay on the Nature and Significance of Economic Science*, 2nd edn, London: Macmillan, 1935.

—— (1934) *The Great Depression*, London: Macmillan.

—— (1971) *Autobiography of an Economist*, London: Macmillan.

Sabine, G.H. (1951) *A History of Political Theory*, 3rd edn, London: Harrap.

Schumpeter, J.A. (1954) *A History of Economic Analysis*, London: Allen & Unwin.

Stigler, G.J. (1955) 'The Nature and Role of Originality in Scientific Progress'; reprinted in *Essays in the History of Economics*, Chicago: University of Chicago Press, 1965, pp. 1–15.

Stonier, A.W. (1943) 'Miscellaneous Notes', *Economica*, NS 10 (May): 188.

Streissler, E. (ed.) (1969) *Roads to Freedom: Essays in Honour of Friedrich A. von Hayek*, London: Routledge & Kegan Paul.

Thornton, H. (1802) *An Enquiry into the Nature and Effects of the Paper Credit of Great Britain*, ed. F.A. Hayek, London: Allen & Unwin, 1939.

Vaughn, K.I. (1980) 'Economic Calculation under Socialism: The Austrian Contribution', *Economic Inquiry* 18 (Oct.): 535–54; reprinted in Wood and Woods (1991), vol. 3, pp. 206–26.

Wood, J.C. and Woods, R.N. (eds) (1991) *Friedrich A. Hayek: Critical Assessments*, 4 vols, London: Routledge.

NAME INDEX

NAME INDEX

SUBJECT INDEX